The Longest Struggle

THE LONGEST STRUGGLE

ANIMAL ADVOCACY
FROM PYTHAGORAS TO PETA

———◆———

NORM PHELPS

Lantern Books · New York

A Division of Booklight Inc.

2007
Lantern Books
One Union Square West, Suite 201
New York, NY 10003

All quotations from the Bible are from the *New American Standard Bible* (*NASB*), copyright 1995, the Lockman Foundation. Used by permission.

Printed in the United States of America.

Library of Congress Cataloging-in-Publication Data

Phelps, Norm.
  The longest struggle : animal advocacy from Pythagoras to PETA / Norm Phelps.
    p. cm.
  Includes bibliographical references.
  ISBN-13: 978-1-59056-106-5 (alk. paper)
  ISBN-10: 1-59056-106-6 (alk. paper)
  1. Animal rights--History. 2. Animal rights movement--History. 3. Animal welfare--History. 4. Human-animal relationships--History. I. Title.
  HV4705.P44 2007
  179'.3--dc22
                                    2006101668

Let no views of profit, no compliance with custom, and no fear of the ridicule of the world, ever tempt thee to the least act of cruelty or injustice to any creature whatsoever. But let this be your invariable rule, everywhere, and at all times, to do unto others as, in their condition, you would be done unto.

—HUMPHREY PRIMATT (1776)

TO THE UNKNOWN ANIMAL ACTIVIST

Representing the millions of animal advocates and caregivers around the world who labor in anonymity, whose names will never appear in any history book or chronicle of heroes, although every one of them belongs there. They do not seek recognition, and certainly not money—often they donate themselves into perpetual poverty. They seek only to relieve the suffering of the weakest, the most defenseless of those who live at the mercy of our merciless societies. They are the pride and hope of the human race.

Table of Contents

Acknowledgments

I want to thank Gene Baur, George Cave, Karen Davis, Freya Dinshah, Linda Doherty, Bruce Friedrich, John Goodwin, Kathy Snow Guillermo, Alex Hershaft, Steve Hindi, Sharon Lawson, Ingrid Newkirk, Merry Orling, Wayne Pacelle, Heidi Prescott, Paul Shapiro, Kim Stallwood, Rick Swain, and Freeman Wicklund, all of whom were extremely generous in providing information based on their first-hand knowledge.

I owe a special debt of gratitude to Bruce Friedrich, Michael Markarian, Andrew Page, Heidi Prescott, Patti Rogers, and Paul Shapiro, who took time out of their crowded schedules to read the manuscript and provide the benefit of their knowledge, experience, and insight.

Needless to say, responsibility for the final text, including the views expressed (unless they are attributed to someone else) and any errors or misstatements, rests entirely with me. In addition, I want to make it clear that the opinions expressed are my own and not those of any organization that I am affiliated with now or have been affiliated with in the past.

Martin Rowe's faith in this project and his editorial guidance, delivered with his characteristically gentle honesty—a quality all the more to be appreciated for being so rare—were instrumental in shaping the manuscript. I thank him. I also want to thank Lantern Books' Sarah Gallogly, Kara Davis, Erin MacLean, and Elizabeth Baber for the perceptiveness and expertise that contributed so greatly to the finished book.

Without the insights, encouragement, and support of my wife,

Patti Rogers, this book either would not exist at all, or would be less than it is. Patti is my teacher, guide, comforter, and partner. She fills my life with her wisdom, her patience, and her love and compassion for all sentient beings. I am indeed blessed.

Norm Phelps
Funkstown, Maryland

Tearing Off the Cloak of Invisibility

O ver a half-century ago, Ralph Ellison exposed the essence of racism in one of the most celebrated passages in American literature:

> I am an invisible man.... I am invisible, understand, because people simply refuse to see me.... When they approach me they see only my surroundings, themselves, or figments of their imaginations—indeed anything and everything except me. Nor is my invisibility exactly a matter of a biochemical accident to my epidérmis. That invisibility to which I refer occurs because of a peculiar disposition of the eyes of those with whom I come in contact. A matter of the construction of their *inner* eyes, those eyes with which they look through their physical eyes upon reality.[1]

Today, we see animals no better than whites saw blacks in 1952. We see their roles in our society: food, clothing, entertainment, research subjects. We see our appetites and fears projected onto them. And we see the comforting web of lies that we weave to justify their oppression—animals are stupid, they don't really suffer the way we do, they exist to serve us—the same web that whites once wove around people of color and men wove around women. But we do not see the animals as they are: sensitive, intelligent, living beings who suffer and die at our hands with no hope of relief.

The "peculiar disposition" of which Ellison wrote was not limited to personal encounters. It extended also to history. Until a generation ago, our understanding of the past was Euro- and androcentric. Our histories reflected the parochial perspective and defended the selfish interests of whites and males. We saw the past with a selective vision that showed only what flattered the pride and justified the appetites of the ruling race and gender. Women and people of color remained invisible to scholars and the public alike.

Today, our understanding of the past is anthropocentric. Our histories reflect the parochial perspective and defend the selfish interests of human beings while ignoring animals, whom we oppress more relentlessly and more brutally even than men have oppressed women and whites have oppressed people of color. We suffer from historical tunnel vision that shows us only what flatters our pride as the "crown of creation" or the "apex of evolution" and justifies the appetites for the sake of which we enslave and slaughter billions of our fellow sentient beings every year.

In the colonialized world and on the American frontier, when indigenous peoples came into contact with Europeans, it was frequently the occasion for a European atrocity—but in our histories, these crimes were either ignored or described as unprovoked attacks by savages against benevolent and civilizing Europeans. It took books like Dee Brown's *Bury My Heart at Wounded Knee* and Vine Deloria's *Custer Died for your Sins* to show that there was another, more truthful way to look at the European conquest of North America.

In much the same way, our crimes against animals are mentioned in our histories only rarely, and then it is to define them in terms of their benefits to humans. Browse through a library, and look at the index to any history book. How many citations do you find next to "animals," "vegetarianism," or "slaughterhouses"? With a depressing regularity, the answer will be, None. Can you imagine glancing through the index to a history of twentieth-century Europe and finding no references to "Jews," "anti-Semitism," or "concentration camps"? Or a history of America that contained no references to "slaves," "segregation," or "civil rights"? Our histories have now—at long last—begun to show us the lives and sufferings of human beings of all races, religions, and social classes and both genders, but history continues to shroud animals in a lethal cloak of invisibility.

One little-noticed effect of the animal rights movement is that in the past quarter-century, some scholars who are not animal advocates have begun to treat the history and sociology of human–animal relationships as a fit subject for academic study. In his 2005 book *Hunters, Herders, and Hamburgers*, for example, Columbia University historian Richard Bulliet argues that throughout history our relationship to animals has been an important factor in determining our morals and mores. But despite superficial appearances to the contrary, this body of work actually preserves the cloak of invisibility that protects animal exploitation by being anthropocentric (concerned about the impact of the relationship on humans while ignoring its impact on animals) and studiously amoral (failing to recognize that our treatment of animals is fundamentally a moral issue independent of its sociological context).

The need remains for the creation of a body of historical and sociological writing that abandons anthropocentrism by reflecting the interests and acknowledging the worth of all sentient beings. Just as a previous generation had to rid our histories of bias against women and people of color—and expose the wrongs that were being done to them—the generation coming of age today will have to create histories that acknowledge the worth of nonhuman animals and expose the wrongs that have been done to them since the advent of civilization.

This will be a more difficult challenge. Atrocities against human beings create a class of human victims; they divide our species and by doing so generate their own opposition. The victims can describe their suffering in language that all of us—including the victimizers—can understand. Atrocities against animals, however, do not divide the human race; to the contrary, they unite us. Whether you enjoy the taste of eggs and sausage, the look and feel of leather shoes, or the sight of tigers bounding through flaming hoops, or you look toward a cure for cancer, animal exploitation offers something for everyone. And to add insult to injury, the victims cannot plead their own case; they cannot describe their suffering or show us how the world looks—and how we appear—from within the slave quarters to which we have consigned them. For this, they have to depend on the conscience and good will of those who benefit from their exploitation. It is as if African slaves had been dependent on Southern plantation owners to speak out on their behalf.

Rights and Welfare

The history of our tyranny over animals includes the history of efforts to defend them against our despotism. Over the course of our story, we will encounter these efforts in two forms. In the first, animal advocates are concerned with our *treatment* of animals, and in the second with our *use* of animals.

The former, known as *animal welfare*, does not challenge our right to exploit animals—or even to kill them—for our own purposes, but argues that we should do so "humanely," which generally means that we should strive to cause animals as little suffering as possible *so long as that does not impede our use of them.* The animal welfare philosophy holds that humans are qualitatively superior to animals in ways that entitle us to enslave and murder them for our own benefit, but that our own moral superiority calls us to inflict upon them as little suffering as we are able without overly inconveniencing ourselves.

The latter, usually known as *animal rights* and sometimes *animal liberation,* challenges our right to use animals at all, arguing that animal exploitation is unjust and oppressive in the same way and for the same reasons that human exploitation is unjust and oppressive. The animal rights position is captured in the motto of People for the Ethical Treatment of Animals (PETA): "Animals are not ours to eat, wear, experiment on, or use in entertainment." The animal rights philosophy holds that there is a moral equality between humans and nonhuman animals that makes the enslavement and slaughter of animals as unjust and immoral as the enslavement and slaughter of human beings.

Alert readers will note that I do not use "animal rights" in the technical sense that implies acceptance of natural rights philosophy.

Rather I use it to designate the belief that exploiting animals for human benefit is morally wrong and should be forbidden by law. The term has acquired this common-language meaning, and when I intend to refer to natural rights philosophy, I will say so.

I use the phrase "animal protection" to encompass both animal rights and animal welfare.

We usually think of animal welfare as having a long history and animal rights as being a radical new philosophy that grew out of it. But when we look at the origins of animal protection—in ancient India, Greece, and Israel—we will see that the opposite is true. The first demands made on behalf of animals were not for their "humane" treatment while they were being exploited, but for an end to their exploitation. What we today call "animal rights" came first; "animal welfare" was a compromise worked out by society between unregulated animal abuse and the demand that animal exploitation be ended. Animal protection began as animal rights; only over time was it worn down into animal welfare.

The Evolution of Animal Protection

In the course of our story, we will see animal protection pass through four stages: 1) a philosophical or theological position held by a small number of thinkers; 2) the tenet of an affinity group, usually religious, that requires—or at least encourages—compliance by its members; 3) a public movement, more or less organized, that attempts to ease the plight of animals on a broad scale; and 4) the consensus of a society that enforces compliance by custom and law.

Stages One and Two have been with us for twenty-five hundred years. Stage Three does not appear until nineteenth-century England. From England, it has spread around the globe and is with us today in the form of organizations like the Royal Society for the Prevention of Cruelty to Animals, PETA, and The Humane Society of the United States.

From its beginnings in ancient India through the eighteenth century, the history of animal protection is the history of the ideas that eventually gave birth to the animal protection movement. From the nineteenth century to the present it is the story of the movement itself, as social reformers strive to weave those ideas into the fabric of society. To phrase it another way, from ancient India through the eighteenth century, animal protection history is intellectual history; from the nineteenth century forward, it is political history.

Apart from an abortive attempt to create a cruelty-free society in ancient India, Stage Four has existed only as the dream of a better future.

In the Beginning Is the Word

Just as social and economic equality for women required the creation of gender-inclusive language, moral equality for nonhuman animals requires the creation of species-inclusive language, a point made by Joan Dunayer in her book *Animal Equality*. It is too early to tell just how animal-inclusive language will look in its final form, but the driving principle is this: Moral equality for animals requires that we accept them as persons and group them in our minds with human beings rather than with inanimate objects. As sentient beings, they share with us what is most important. The great dividing line is not between human and nonhuman, but between sentient and insentient. That is why I refer to animals as "he" and "she" rather than "it," and use the relative pronouns "who" and "whom." For the same reason, I try not to use the words "person," "persons," or "people" in any context where they explicitly distinguish humans from animals. Animals are people, and all people are animals.

Moral equality for animals also requires that the same fact be described by the same term whether the subject is human or nonhuman. If human beings "eat," then animals must "eat," not "feed." If human beings "love," animals must "love," not "imprint upon." Likewise, if the caging of human beings is called "imprisonment" and their forced labor "slavery," then the caging of animals must be called "imprisonment," and their forced labor "slavery." At first, the application to animals of terms customarily reserved for human beings may be jarring, just as to an earlier generation the appellation "Ms." was jarring when it began replacing the time-honored "Miss" and "Mrs." But a distinct vocabulary for animals forms part of the cloak of invisibility that we cast over our nonhuman relatives. It distances them from us and implies that they have a lesser worth.

Some advocates object to the use of the word "animals" to mean all animals other than humans, and I understand their concern. Their preferred alternative, "nonhuman animals," does make the point that humans are animals, and I use it occasionally when that point is germane to what I am saying. But I do not use it in most situations. "Human animals" and "nonhuman animals" still divides the world into two classes of sentient beings—us and everybody else, with us as the focal point—and so I think its usefulness in combating speciesist habits of thought is less than some would have us believe. As yet, at least, there is no good alternative to "animals" when it is necessary to refer to all sentient beings other than humans.

"Vivisection" is a word that is widely misused by animal exploiters in an attempt to discredit the animal rights movement. Etymologically, "vivisection" refers to surgical procedures conducted on living animals, human or nonhuman, for research or teaching. And not surprisingly, experimenters who do not use a scalpel—like those who squirt caustic cleaning fluid into the eyes of rabbits—try to limit the use of the word to actual surgical procedures. But the meaning of a word is not restricted to its derivation. If it were, "to educate" would mean "to lead out," and "personable" would describe someone capable of wearing a mask.

In common parlance, "vivisection" refers to all experiments conducted on nonhuman animals, whether surgical or not, a usage sanctioned by no less an authority than the Encyclopaedia Britannica, which defines "vivisection" this way:

> Operation on a living animal for experimental rather than healing purposes; more broadly, all experimentation on live animals.[2]

Since "vivisection" is a word of enormously negative connotations, restricting it to surgical procedures excludes many of the most sadistic experiments conducted on animals (see Chapter 12). Therefore, I shall use "vivisection" in the broader sense of "all experiments conducted on living nonhuman animals."

Editorial Note:
In writing *The Longest Struggle*, my aim has been to describe the important trends and events—and show the historical threads that connect them—without getting bogged down in a plethora of details or an endless catalog of advocates, groups, and campaigns. This means that, of necessity, there have been omissions, and I regret every one. *Everyone who has ever advocated for animals, and every group that has worked on their behalf, is important.* Every activist, every caregiver plays a vital role. And the fact that some who are acknowledged as leaders—past and present—may not be mentioned here does not mean that I think they are unworthy of mention. If an advocate, group, or campaign is missing that you believe should be included, or is given less space than you feel they have earned, I am sure you are right. But had I given every leader, group, and campaign the credit they deserve, "the longest struggle" would be the reader's effort to make it to the end of the book.

1

The Roots of Evil

For the last half-century, the popular media have been mesmerized by the "hunting hypothesis." According to this theory, early hominids depended on hunting for their food and clothing. But the animals they hunted were faster or stronger than our ancestors, and so these protohumans could survive only by being smarter than their prey and by hunting in groups. Therefore, evolution selected for greater intellectual ability combined with voice boxes that could articulate complex instructions and responses. And voila! the result was us, the "apex of evolution," the smartest, most all-around superior creatures the planet had ever seen.

Concocted in the 1950s by an Australian anatomist named Raymond Dart, the hunting hypothesis was popularized a decade later by Robert Ardrey, a Hollywood scriptwriter. In a series of best-selling books including *African Genesis* (1961) and *The Hunting Hypothesis* (1976), Ardrey convinced much of the world that we are, in his memorable phrase, "killer apes," predestined to violence—and planetary dominance—by our evolutionary background.

As popular as Ardrey's books were, the hunting hypothesis soon came under attack within the scientific community. In 1971, feminist anthropologist Sally Slocum published an article entitled "Woman the Gatherer: Male Bias in Anthropology" in which she pointed out that the hunting hypothesis ignores half of the human race and assumes that it was men's behavior exclusively that determined our evolutionary path. Not so, said Slocum, who argued that our evolutionary course was determined less by men hunting than by women rearing children and gathering food, both of which occupations required communal cooperation and high intelligence.

Slocum's hypothesis draws support from the fact that in "hunter-gatherer" societies, the gathering is more important than the hunting. The diet of hunter-gatherers was plant-based, with meat as an occasional supplement. Therefore, the gatherers (the women) were, in fact, more important to the survival and evolution of the species than the hunters (the men). As Jane Goodall explains:

> Today it is generally accepted that although the earliest humans probably ate some meat, it was unlikely to have played a major role in their diet. Plants would have been a much more important source of food. This is true of almost all the hunter-gatherer peoples whose way of life lasted into the last century.[1]

Throughout the 1970s and '80s, a new generation of anthropologists demonstrated that hunting hypothesis advocates, including Dart and Ardrey, had grossly misread the fossil record. At the same time, field primatologists like Goodall, Dian Fossey, and Birute Galdikas were discovering that our closest relatives are not the vegetarian pacifists that we had always believed them to be. Other primates also hunt, fight, and even engage in warfare; and that being the case, the hunting hypothesis simply cannot explain why we evolved to dominate the planet and they did not.

By 1993, Matt Cartmill, professor of biological anthropology at Duke University, could characterize the hunting hypothesis as "a flimsy story" which had "collapse[d] during the 1970s," leading him to wonder why it had been "accepted for so long by thoughtful scientists." In the public mind, of course, it had not collapsed, only in the scientific community. Beliefs sometimes survive less by their truth than by the degree to which they reinforce our fantasies. And while scientists may have understood that the killer ape theory portrayed us as "sick, disordered animals," to laypeople it proclaimed that science had proved us to be the rightful masters of all we survey, king-of-the-hill of planet Earth. Among the public, the primary objection to evolution had been—and in some religious circles, still is—that Darwin's theory took away our uniqueness as human beings and reduced us to just another animal. The hunting hypothesis gave us back our unique status—and did it in the name of evolution.[2]

In 2005, in *Man the Hunted,* anthropologists Donna Hart and Robert W. Sussman pulled the hunting hypothesis inside out by arguing that our ancient ancestors were actually prey animals rather than predators, and that it was the need to escape stronger and faster predators that led to our intellectual ability and language. Needless to say, the popular media were not nearly as enthralled with this unheroic view of human origins as they had been with the hunting hypothesis.

The Crime with no Beginning

Even though hunting did not set our ancestors on the path to humanity, it is nevertheless true that one of our earliest relationships to other animals was predator to prey. As Professor Cartmill puts it:

> It is a safe bet that our australopithecine ancestors were hunters in a broad sense: that is, they sometimes killed and ate other animals, just as chimpanzees and people do today. And since people today are more predatory than chimpanzees, it is another safe bet that hunting took on an increased importance during the course of our evolution from a chimpanzee-like ancestor.[3]

Thus, the killing of nonhuman animals for food and clothing is a crime that had no beginning. We practiced it before we were human, brought it with us as we trudged down the evolutionary trail, and expanded on it as we became progressively more human.

For decades, it was believed that humans were distinguished from other animals by our use of tools. That, we now know, is untrue.

Many animals, from primates to birds, fashion and use tools. It does seem true, though, that hominids are set apart from other animals by the conception, construction, and widespread use of a certain type of tool: the weapon. As Hart and Sussman point out, as long as we had to depend on our own bodies, we were mediocre predators at best; but as prey, we were every predator's dream. We were slow, awkward, limited in our mobility (poor climbers, poor swimmers, clumsy jumpers, and absolutely unable to fly) and weaker than the flesh eaters who might find a nice human thigh or upper arm a satisfying dinner. At this early point in our history, we had no more impact on the lives of other animals than gorillas and chimpanzees do today.

That all changed with the invention of the weapon. In the old west, the six-shooter was called the great equalizer, because someone who was small and weak had as good a chance in a gunfight as someone who was big and strong. But prehistoric weapons were not equalizers; they were dominators, because we were the only species who used them.

The first weapons were probably clubs—in the form of broken-off tree limbs—and stones, picked up off the ground and thrown at their victim. These were of some help in warding off predators and hunting small prey animals such as ancestral squirrels and rabbits, but overall, throwing stones and swinging clubs did little to advance the fortunes of hominids.

The first weapon invented rather than discovered seems to have been the sling, the simplest form of which was a long narrow strip of cloth that the hunter folded once lengthwise. Picking it up with both ends held tightly together in one hand, he placed a stone in the fold and then twirled it around and around above his head. When he released one end of the sling, the stone flew out at a high rate of speed. In the hands of a skilled hunter, a sling is surprisingly accurate at close range, but the windup motion often startles the prey, reducing its value as a hunting weapon.

The weapon that began to create a new balance of power among species was the spear. With spears, our ancestors could defend themselves against most predators, and by hunting cooperatively in groups they could encircle and kill large prey animals, such as wild cattle, sheep, goats, and even bears and elephants. The invention of the spear marks the beginning of the hominids' transformation from gatherers who were almost exclusively vegan,[4] to hunter-gatherers who increasingly killed other animals for food, clothing, implements (made of bone, horn, and antler), and housing (tents made of skins).

The earliest known spear was found embedded in the side of an elephant killed around 250,000 years ago. Discovered in Germany, it was a shaft carved from the wood of a yew tree with a whittled point that had been case hardened over fire. The earliest known example of a sharpened flint spearhead—found buried in the head of a bear near Trieste, Italy—dates from around 100,000 years ago.[5] Although a flint tip added to the penetrating power of the shaft, mostly it tore muscles and blood vessels, causing greater pain, crippling, and internal bleeding. Then as now, large animals whose bodies were punctured by spears or arrows rarely died immediately. They suffered agonizing, terrifying deaths over hours or days from exsanguination, dehydration (from being unable to walk to water), or infection. Spear and bowhunting technique is—and has been from the beginning—to impale the victim, who immediately takes off running for her life, and track her until she collapses.

Next in the march of lethal technology came a small spear launcher with no moving parts called the atlatl (pronounced at-LAT-ul, sometimes known as a "spear thrower"). Usually made of wood or antler, about two feet long and just thick enough to grip comfortably, an atlatl has a tiny perpendicular prong on one end that fits into a notch on the back end of a long spear. The two are held together in one hand—the atlatl parallel to the shaft of the spear—and whipped forward in a running overhand throwing motion similar to that employed by a modern javelin thrower. At the top of the motion, the spear is released and the atlatl propels it forward with a range and velocity that the unaided human arm could never approach. The first known atlatls date from around 30,000 years ago, but if the use of antler was a relatively late development, as I suspect it was, the atlatl could easily be much older. Under most conditions, wood rots and leaves no traces.[6]

The weapon that decisively shifted the balance of power between humans and other animals was the longbow. For killing all but the largest animals, such as mammoths and elephants, the longbow is as far superior to the spear and the atlatl as the rifle is to the longbow itself. A longbow can be loaded, fired, and reloaded quickly and without the overhand throwing motion that alerts intended victims to the danger; the arrow travels at a higher velocity and on a flatter trajectory than a spear, making it almost impossible to evade; and most importantly, a longbow can be aimed with a degree of precision that a spear—no matter how it is launched—cannot begin to approach.

Exactly when the bow and arrow were introduced is uncertain. Some archeologists would set the date as far back as 40,000 to 50,000 years ago, but this is probably too early. Its first known appearance in Europe is around 8000 BCE.

One of the cruelest of all hunting weapons is rarely thought of as a weapon at all: fire. In colonial days, both native Americans and European settlers practiced fire hunting, as did Africans until well into the second half of the twentieth century—using flaming spears or arrows to set grasslands ablaze, burning the large animals, such as elephants, who were grazing there so severely that they died of their injuries or could be easily killed. By its nature, fire-hunting leaves no evidence for archeologists, but we may be confident that fire had not been long under the control of our prehistoric ancestors before they began using it as a hunting weapon.

*   *   *

Around 40,000 years ago, humans began to occupy Australia, which they found teeming with large mammals and reptiles, all of whom, according to Jared Diamond, suddenly "became extinct shortly after humans reached Australia." Likewise, when humans first settled North and South America, they found their new lands filled with large mammals like the wooly mammoth. Again, within a short time, most species of these large animals had gone extinct. The coincidence seems too great to be accidental, and while some anthropologists have proposed climatic reasons—a drought in Australia, the end of the Ice Age in North America—these explanations are not convincing. There was no drought in the Pacific Islands, which lost their large mammals when they were invaded by the same humans who invaded Australia; and wooly mammoths had made it through several previous Ice Ages without a problem. It seems clear that we began our career as exterminators of entire species a full 40,000 years ago.[7]

The Tyranny of Human Beings

The enslavement of animals did have a beginning, but one so far beyond the reach of history that it is lost to us forever. There is no incident to which we can point and say, "This is the first instance of a human community practicing animal slavery." Likewise, there is no group of whom we can say, "This is the society that first enslaved animals. The rest of us learned it from them." At every spot on the globe—east to west, north to south—we emerge into history as systematic exploiters of animals. All of the most ancient civilizations of which we have found evidence were built on the enslavement and slaughter of animals, who were used for food, clothing, labor, transportation, entertainment, and religious sacrifice. But exactly how this came about, we do not know. Of the theories that abound, most are nonsense and all are guesswork.

One theory that keeps showing up like the proverbial bad penny would have us believe that animals volunteered to be enslaved ("domesticated" is the euphemism that is typically employed) so that they could enjoy the protection and sustenance provided by herders and farmers. According to this theory, there is a kind of social contract between enslaved animals and their human owners—originally entered into freely by both parties—under the terms of which we provide them with food, shelter, and safety, and in return they allow us to kill them to satisfy our own needs. Why a contract entered into several thousand years ago should be binding today on descendents of the original parties many generations removed is a question for which the proponents of this theory have no convincing answer. But in fact, we never need to reach this question. Unsupported by evidence, the "volunteers for death" theory is a self-serving justification for modern-day animal slavery and slaughter projected backward in time so that it can masquerade as legitimate scholarship. It is the interspecies equivalent of claims that African slaves were happy in their servitude because it spared them the risks and uncertainties of freedom.

The earliest form of animal agriculture was pastoralism: herding, initially sheep and goats, then cattle, and finally horses. Unlike modern animal slavery, which is organized around a fixed-site prison—a barn, a corral, a fenced pasture—ancient pastoralism was nomadic. Herders cycled with the seasons, high country in summer, low in winter, as they followed the pasturage.

Pastoralism is incompatible with large-scale plant agriculture. For one thing, livestock and crops don't mix; the former have a frustrating tendency to trample or eat the latter. The two can exist side by side only in the presence of effective fencing, and, for obvious reasons, nomads don't like to build fences. Small gardens—some grain for bread, a few vegetables—are the closest to farming that pastoralists can come. To this day, in traditional societies, nomads are not farmers and farmers are not nomads.

Herding evolved out of the nomadic migrations of hunter-gatherers in temperate or dry climates. (In most tropical regions, the year-round abundance of plant and animal life make the nomad's annual circuit unnecessary.) Gatherers in search of growing plants would need to follow a cycle much the same as sheep, goats, and cattle, and so the early hunter-gatherers found themselves migrating along the same routes as these other herbivorous animals. They were, so to speak, traveling companions.

At some point, in some way that we do not know—and about which it is more fun than informative to speculate—the humans learned that there were benefits to bringing under their control the animals who were migrating beside them. These included an ample supply of meat and skins without the hardship, danger, and uncertainty of hunting; milk, cheese, and butter; wool; and body warmth against the cold—something to be valued during windy, snowy winters. Labor and transportation came later, first from dogs, who were useful for hunting and herding; then from oxen, yaks, camels, and llamas; and finally from donkeys and horses, who were not broken until sometime around 3000 BCE, give or take a thousand years.

* * *

The use of animals for labor and transportation ratcheted the cruelty of their enslavement up several notches. Previously, animals' enslavement had been mostly passive, that is, it consisted largely in preventing them from doing many of the things they did by nature, such as form their own societies and make their own decisions about where to live and when to migrate. It might even be more accurate to refer to pastoral servitude as "imprisonment," rather than "slavery." Being forcibly prevented from responding to the inborn demands of your nature is a terrible torture, as any human prisoner can tell you. But being turned into a slave laborer is worse.

Work is not a biological imperative of herbivorous animals; it is alien to their nature. They graze; they do not labor. When they are forced to work, it does violence to everything that they are. To break an animal to the yoke, the harness, or the saddle is to crush the animal's innermost self. What is broken is the animal's soul. It is true that most arrive at some sort of accommodation with their servitude, just as most human slaves reach an accommodation with theirs—it is a way of maintaining one's sanity—but they are broken nonetheless, and their lives—like the lives of all slaves—are drenched in the pain of living contrary to their nature.

From this juncture forward, the "domesticated" animals had lost control over their own lives and from birth to death were totally under the dominion of their slavemasters. This is the moment at which the words that George Orwell put into the mouth of a wise pig named Old Major became true: "Is it not crystal clear, then, comrades, that all the evils of this life of ours spring from the tyranny of human beings?"[8]

It is at this point that human society became fundamentally different from the societies of other species, and it becomes proper, therefore, to begin calling it civilization. "Civilization" is what we call our break with nature, and the critical step in that break, the step that made all of the subsequent steps possible, was the enslavement of animals by the first pastoralists. All human civilizations have been built on animal slavery and systematic animal killing, and those early herders were the first slaveholders and the first slaughterers.

Where and when pastoralism first emerged is a matter of some confusion and conjecture. Pastoral peoples don't leave much behind to remind us of their existence. But clearly, pastoralism was well established around the globe by the time of the first agricultural revolution, which occurred roughly 9,000 to 10,000 years ago, give or take a millennium or two.

Farms and Cities: The Neolithic Revolution
No doubt humans at various places around the globe had been planting a few seeds here and there and harvesting the plants for thousands of years. And over time, these would have developed into what we would call gardens. But large-scale plant agriculture depended on breaking animals to labor. And agriculture in turn ratcheted the suffering of animals up another notch. Previously, they had only been required to haul and carry, which was burden enough in itself; but with the arrival of farming, they also had to spend long days plowing and threshing, and they had new burdens to haul in the form of crops that had to be carted to market. Furthermore, human beings had now begun to live almost entirely on food produced by animals, either through their labor in the fields or by the taking of their bodies and their lives. This would not change until the tractor was invented 10,000 years later.

And there was worse to come. Agriculture created a large food surplus. For the first time in human history, the supply of available food could support more people than were needed to produce it. And it is a law of nature applying to all species that a food surplus leads to a population increase—which in this case became a population explosion. Scholars estimate that just before the agricultural revolution, around 8000 BCE, there were only about four million human beings worldwide, a number that had remained relatively stable for tens of thousands of years. By the beginning of the historical era, around 3000 BCE, that number had more than tripled to fourteen million. A mere thousand years later, in 2000 BCE, it had nearly doubled to twenty-seven million.[9] The human population has been growing ever since and now stands at just over six billion.

The creation of a large human population that was not needed to produce food had three results, all of them disastrous for animals. First, more humans meant more animals enslaved and slaughtered for food, skins, labor, sacrifice, and entertainment. Second, the division of labor on a large scale became possible for the first time in human history. Entire classes of full-time craftspeople, merchants, bureaucrats, priests, and soldiers arose who plied their trades while living on food produced by others. In turn, these occupations were themselves supported by animal labor, which led to a further increase in the number of animals—especially oxen, camels, donkeys, and horses—enslaved for work, transportation, and warfare.

Finally, the surplus population and the rise of specialization led to the creation of cities, and cities represented the final step in the alienation of animals from their own inherent natures. Animals who were brought into cities for labor and transportation, or (primarily chickens and ducks) to serve as convenient sources of meat and eggs were deprived of all semblance of their natural world.

The rise of cities set the pattern for animal slavery and slaughter that human societies have followed down to the present. The entire history of human civilization is the story of animal abuse remarkably unchanged through the centuries. Depending on the degree to which a society was urban or agrarian, the level of abuse might be somewhat higher or lower, but the basic structures of animal exploitation are the same today as they were ten thousand years ago. In fact, as our story proceeds, the only major changes that we will see in the broad patterns of human treatment of animals will be: (1) the widespread elimination of animal sacrifice, which began in India during the sixth century BCE and occurred in most of the West early in the Common Era; (2) the reduction in animal labor brought about by the invention of mechanical sources of power during the Industrial Revolution; (3) the widespread use of animals in medical and scientific experiments, beginning in the Renaissance; (4) the transformation of farms from prisons into concentration camps made possible by the discovery of antibiotics in the twentieth century; and (5) the creation of genetic engineering and transgenic animals in the late twentieth century.

Religious Sacrifice

The primary subjects of the cave paintings left by the Paleolithic tribes of Europe are not, as we might expect, human beings. The first artists—who lived around 15,000 years ago, plus or minus two or three thousand years—devoted themselves almost exclusively to painting wildlife, including scenes of hunting. Since these were hunter-gatherer peoples living at the tail end of the last great Ice Age, when gathering was still difficult and hunting was more important to the community than in warmer climates, it seems reasonable to conclude that cave paintings were intended to serve as props for religious ceremonies—somewhat on the order of altar paintings or stained glass windows—that were conducted to assure a successful hunt or to express thanks for one.

As part of these ceremonies, it would be natural for early hunters to begin offering a portion of the dead animal's flesh as a gift to be enjoyed by the higher powers who had given them success. From there, it was a series of short steps to offering a piece of hunted meat to enlist the aid of the gods in overcoming whatever obstacle the community was facing and to maintain their goodwill against the unforeseen. The offering was not the purpose of the killing. Animals were killed for food and skins and a piece of their flesh offered in thanks. Thus, animal sacrifice was rooted in fear—in this case, fear that the hunt would fail. The gods must be propitiated or calamity would befall the community. From its earliest inception, religion was enlisted in support of the murder of animals.

Herding was a more secure source of food than hunting, but it still had its share of uncertainties and potential disasters, relating mostly to weather, injury, and disease. And so when early humans took up the herding life, they did not give up their religions and the sacrifices that were central to them. Only now the animals whose flesh was offered to the gods were raised, not hunted, and they were slaughtered, not ambushed. In fact, many ancient societies seem to have had a taboo against eating animal flesh unless a portion of it had first been offered as a sacrifice. This taboo survived well into historical times and is recorded in the Bible.[10]

When and why animals began to be slaughtered specifically to be offered as sacrifices, we do not know. The practice probably began during the pastoral age, based on a desire to offer sacrifices not specifically connected with the slaughter of an animal: arrival of the birthing season, for instance, the beginning of a long trek, or some more personal event, like a wedding or a human birth or death. In all likelihood, the ritually murdered animal was still eaten, but there had been a subtle shift in the relationship between the ritual and the food.

With the emergence of cities, there arose temples and a class of priests to administer them. These temples were not the serene, comforting houses of worship that we know today. The principal function of ancient religion was to mollify the gods through sacrifice; the first temples were built as venues for sacrifice, and the first priests were technicians who knew the sacrificial liturgies that would assure the gods accepted the offerings and were well disposed toward the donors. If early doctors were barbers, early priests were butchers, and ancient temples were first and foremost abattoirs. This approach to religion extended deep into the historical period. In fact, It survived in Judaism until the destruction of the Jerusalem Temple—which was one of the largest slaughterhouses in the ancient world—in 70 CE. In the Classical world, animal sacrifice survived until Christianity took control of the Roman Empire and abolished it in the fourth century.

In Islam and some schools of Hinduism, it is still practiced, although on a reduced scale. Otherwise, sacrifice survives mostly in religions of African derivation, such as Santeria.

As the World Turns

By the dawn of history, around 3000 BCE when writing was invented, the origins of animal abuse had long been forgotten. Animal exploitation seemed so natural to our first visible ancestors that they never even thought about it. In the world's most ancient literatures, there are no defenses of animal exploitation because there was no occasion to defend what everyone took for granted. It was not until religious rebels in India, Israel, and Greece challenged animal slavery and slaughter that anyone bothered to craft a defense for it.

This challenge came during what historians call the "Axial Age," a remarkable period of about 600 years, falling roughly between 800 and 200 BCE, that saw the emergence of the major ethical and philosophical ideas that have shaped civilization down to the present. During these six centuries, human understanding of such fundamental issues as the nature of the universe, virtue, truth, the purpose of human life, and the organization of society changed more radically than at any time before or since.

In this brief period, human thought was literally swung about on its axis by thinkers like Confucius and Lao Tzu in China; Mahavira and the Buddha in India; Zoroaster in Persia; the Later Prophets in Israel; and Pythagoras, Socrates, and the Seven Sages in Greece. It was also during the Axial Age that the Vedas, the Upanishads, the *Bhagavad-Gita*, *Mahabharata*, and the Hebrew Scriptures were put into substantially their present form.[11] It is not too much to say that the idea of the primacy of love in human relations (as opposed to greed and fear), the notion that the function of government is to improve the lives of its citizens and not just to assure the dominance of one clan or tribe over others, and belief in reason as the best guide to human conduct all date from the most remarkable centuries in human history.

Animals shared in this revolution in human understanding as Mahavira, the Buddha, the Hindu sages, the Later Prophets, and Pythagoras used the ideas of the Axial Age to challenge the enslavement and slaughter of animals. Although this inconvenient fact is generally overlooked—part of the cloak of invisibility cast over animals and their suffering—the great spiritual pioneers of the Axial Age included animals within their moral universe, and they spoke out courageously against the two most egregious forms of animal abuse—religious sacrifice and meat eating.

2

The Challenge of *Ahimsa*

I n India, historical memory begins with a military conquest. Around 1700 BCE, warlike Indo-European nomads from the steppes of southern Russia began pouring over the Hindu Kush Mountains to conquer and subjugate an indigenous people who had created one of the most advanced societies in the ancient world, but one which had apparently been weakened by a series of natural disasters. Over a period of two or three hundred years, the light-skinned invaders, who called themselves *Aryans*, "the finest," "the exalted," "the noble," subjugated the local populations, dark-skinned people known as Dravidians whose descendents can still be found throughout southern India.

Wherever they went, Indo-Europeans were noted for three things: ruthless ferocity, horses, and cattle. They were the first people to break horses to the saddle and harness, probably around 3000 BCE, making the horse the last animal to be enslaved on a large scale. A warlike people, they wasted no time in forcing horses into military service, both as cavalry and for drawing chariots, an Indo-European invention.

Cavalry—invented by the Aryans sometime before 2000 BCE— continued to be the backbone of armies until World War I. But in a war that saw the introduction of motorized armored units and machine guns, horses were useless and helpless. Over eight million horses were killed on the Western Front alone,[1] nearly equaling the nine million human soldiers who were killed on both fronts. Four thousand years of being sacrificed in battles in which they had no interest and no stake finally came to an end in an equine bloodbath on the fields of France.

Returning to the Aryans: they were cattle herders who had left their home on the Russian steppes for reasons that are lost to our view. The ultimate pastoralists, they organized their community life around their cattle, measured wealth and status in cattle, worshipped gods who were personified forces of nature, and were always eager to destroy anything or anyone who stood between them and good pasturage with fresh water. But when they made themselves masters of India, all of this changed.

Pastoralists can conquer other peoples, and often do, but they cannot rule them. They are hit-and-run raiders who can exact tribute from defeated nations by threatening future raids, but they cannot administer conquered peoples without giving up their nomadic way of life. Faced with this reality, the Aryans who conquered India abandoned pastoralism and became a ruling class.

Archeologists tell us that the people they ruled, the Dravidians, had been urban, prosperous, and sophisticated. But beyond that, we know little about them; the only writings they left behind were brief commercial records, and these have resisted all efforts at translation. To what extent their civilization, which dated back to at least 3000 BCE, enslaved and killed animals is not known. But we do know that the society the Aryans created following the conquest was a typical ancient society founded on the enslavement and killing of animals for food, clothing, labor, transportation, and religious sacrifice.

The Men Who Said No

This was the way things stayed for a thousand years. Then, around 600 BCE, Indian society was transformed by a spiritual revolution known as the "Renouncer" Movement (in Sanskrit, *srmana*, pronounced shrih-MAH-nah), so called because its adherents renounced society and retired to the forest for a life devoted to meditation and yoga. Where archaic Hinduism (the religion of the Aryan

conquerors when they crossed the Hindu Kush) had based its
notions of right and wrong, good and evil, on ritual purity aimed at
propitiating some fairly capricious deities, the Renouncer concept of
good and evil was grounded firmly in the commonsense notion of
sentience. Pleasure and happiness are good, pain and suffering are
bad. Actions that cause happiness are virtuous; actions that cause
suffering are evil.

In other words, to the Renouncers, ethical behavior was moral
behavior. To us, this is so obvious that it sounds trivial. But in the
Axial Age it was revolutionary. Archaic Hinduism was based on obe-
dience and ritual, and its leaders were priests who knew the secret formulas that must be used if sacrifices were to be successful in
mollifying the gods. By contrast, Renouncer religion was based on
morality, and its leaders were teachers who had thought deeply about
the best ways to avoid causing suffering to oneself and others. In the
pattern of opposition that we will see played out again in Israel, the
Aryan priests (known as Brahmins) ruled by fear while the
Renouncer teachers (known as yogis) led by love.

The Renouncers taught that the consciousness of every sentient
being is immortal, and is reincarnated from one body to another and
one species to another according to its karma. This means that animals are not merely *like* us, they *are* us. The same individual could be
a Brahmin priest in one life and a pig in the next, a wealthy member
of the merchant class in the following life, and a chicken after that.
The Renouncers opposed Hinduism's notorious caste system (originally imposed by the Aryans as a way to keep the Dravidians in line)
and animal exploitation on identical grounds: they cause suffering to
sentient beings.

The goal of life, according to the Renouncers, is to gain liberation
from this endless cycle of birth and death in a world of suffering by
achieving union with a higher level of reality, where we will experience pure being, pure consciousness, and pure joy without end. This
liberation, the Renouncers believed, could only be attained by developing wisdom and compassion through the practice of meditation,
yoga, and moral behavior.

First, Do No Harm

One of the most important figures in the Renouncer movement was Vardamana Mahavira (599–527 BCE), the historical founder of Jainism. Mahavira taught that there is no greater evil than to harm or kill a sentient being. Therefore, he made nonviolence, or *ahimsa*—a Sanskrit word meaning "no harm" or "not harming"—the first and most important of the Five Great Vows of Jainism as well as the first and most important of Jainism's twelve ethical rules for laypeople. According to Pravin K. Shah of the Jain Study Center of North Carolina:

> Nonviolence is the foundation of Jain ethics. Lord Mahavir says: "One should not injure, subjugate, enslave, torture or kill any living being including animals, insects, plants, and vegetables." This is the essence of religion. It embraces the welfare of all animals.

Mahavira based his doctrine of *ahimsa* on compassion and taught that we should not inflict on others suffering that we would not want to experience ourselves:

> As it would be for you, so it is for those whom you intend to kill. As it would be for you, so it is for those whom you intend to tyrannise over. As it would be for you, so it is for those whom you intend to torment. In the same way (it is for those) whom you intend to punish, and to drive away. The righteous man who lives up to these sentiments does, therefore, neither kill nor cause others to kill (living beings).[2]

In other words, "Do unto others as you would have them do unto you."

Unlike Christianity, however, Jainism has from the very beginning applied this principle to animals. Mahavira stated explicitly that we have the same ethical duties to animals that we have to human beings.

> All sorts of living beings should not be slain, nor treated with
> violence, nor abused, nor tormented, nor driven away.³

When Mahavira said "all sorts of living beings," he meant *all sorts
of living beings*. Jains believe that everything that exists contains the
universal life force, including plants, rocks, and water, and is, therefore, in some sense a living being entitled to respect. Rather than ani-
mate and inanimate, they divide the world into sentient and
insentient beings, the former including everything that Western science groups into the animal and plant kingdoms, including microscopic organisms, while the latter is limited to minerals: rocks, sand,
water, and so on. Sentient beings are classified according to the number of senses they possess. What we would call the "higher animals"—
mammals, birds, etc.—have the full complement of five senses, while
insects are believed to have three or four; worms and grubs two; and
plants only one (touch). Mahavira taught that the more senses beings
have, the more intensely they can suffer. Therefore, in order to reduce
as much as possible the suffering they cause, Jains are instructed to
eat only single-sensed beings (plants) and dairy products.

To avoid harming living beings, Jains will go to what may seem
extraordinary lengths. As we just saw, all Jains are supposed to be
strict vegetarians, although in today's world there are some—mostly
living outside of India—who no longer follow this instruction.
Because travel involves killing—bugs on the windshield, for
instance—Jains are often reluctant to travel. But once again, in the
modern world this practice seems to be falling by the wayside.
Following instructions given by Lord Mahavira himself, Jain monks
strain their drinking water through a cloth in an effort to avoid killing
the tiny, unseen organisms who live in the water; and when walking,
they often gently sweep the ground in front of them with a soft whisk
to move to safety any small insects who might be in their path. In
India, Jains are famous for the veterinary hospitals that they have
maintained throughout their history. For two and a half millennia,
the followers of Lord Mahavira have upheld a standard of compassionate action on behalf of animals that is unequaled anywhere.

Buddhism

The Buddha (566–486 BCE) was a younger contemporary of Lord Mahavira who lived and taught in the same region of Northeastern India. Like Mahavira, he made *ahimsa* the foundation of his ethical system and extended its full protection to all sentient beings, although he did not include plants in this category and his attitude toward microorganisms is unclear. The Buddha taught that, "All beings fear before danger, life is dear to all. When a man considers this, he does not kill or cause to kill."[4] And he applied the first and most important of his Five Precepts, "Do not kill," to all sentient beings, not just humans, while forbidding his followers to engage in any occupation—such as hunter, butcher, or fishmonger—that brought suffering or death to animals.

Although the Buddha practiced and taught vegetarianism, the funeral fires of his cremation had hardly cooled when a contingent of Buddhist monks began constructing sophistries to justify meat eating.[5] As a result, throughout its history Buddhism has been divided about equally between vegetarians and meat eaters. Chinese Buddhism, notably Chan and Pure Land, has always boasted the highest proportion of vegetarians, followed by the Theravada Buddhism of Sri Lanka and Southeast Asia. Faced with a short growing season and poor soil, Tibetans have generally relied on a meat-based diet. Even so, there has always been a vegetarian tradition in Tibetan Buddhism, exemplified by famous teachers like Shabkar and Patrul Rinpoche. In exile in India and the West, where a vegan diet is easy to follow, most Tibetans have continued to eat meat. This, however, is beginning to change, especially among the younger generation. Three groups founded by young lamas, The Universal Compassion Movement, Tibetans for a Vegetarian Society, and Tibetan Volunteers for Animals, which enjoy the support of the Dalai Lama, actively promote a vegetarian and even a vegan diet in the Tibetan exile community.

The Dalai Lama has always commended a vegetarian diet as an expression of Buddhist compassion. Except for a few months in the early 1960s, however, he has not practiced it himself with any consistency, having been told by his doctors to eat meat because of a liver damaged by hepatitis B. For decades, he was vegetarian every other day as a balance between his compassion for animals and the advice of his doctors.[6] But on April 6, 2005, speaking at a conference in New Delhi on the protection of wildlife, the Dalai Lama announced, "When in Tibet we have also popularized the concept of vegetarianism and we did create an impression on the minds of the people. Lately I have also turned to a vegetarian diet."[7]

Two hundred years after the passing of Mahavira and the Buddha, Ashoka Maurya (reigned 274–236 BCE) ruled a sizable empire from the ancient prophets' home country of Magada in northeastern India. Although born a Jain, Ashoka does not seem to have been spiritually inclined until one day when, returning home from a war that he had provoked, he was horrified to see the suffering, death, and destruction that his military adventure had precipitated. He converted to Buddhism—Jainism, curiously enough, has sometimes been more tolerant of war, tending to view it as a form of self-defense—and announced that he would henceforward devote his reign to the well-being of all who lived within the ambit of his power—human and nonhuman alike.

Ashoka was as good as his word. He demobilized his army until it was little more than a border guard and launched large-scale charitable undertakings that created the closest thing the ancient world ever knew to a welfare state. He founded and maintained an extensive chain of hospitals for humans and animals, including wildlife, as well as a network of inns and resting stations where travelers and their animals could find food, water, and shelter. He forbade hunting, and banned meat eating on many holidays. He all but eliminated the slaughter of animals for the royal kitchen, and generally seems to have gone as far toward ending all killing of animals as he dared without provoking a popular uprising or a coup from within the palace. The Mauryan Empire under Ashoka is the first and one of the very few instances in world history of a government treating its animals as citizens who are as deserving of its protection as the human residents.

Unfortunately, upon Ashoka's death his heirs quickly reversed his compassionate policies and returned the Mauryan Empire to business as usual.[8]

Hinduism

During the Axial Age, the principles of *ahimsa*, vegetarianism, and animal protection entered Hinduism by way of the Renouncer movement, transforming it into the religion that we know today.

The earliest Hindu scripture, *The Rig Veda*, which contains material dating back to the Aryan invasion, is a chant book for religious rituals, most of which involved animal sacrifice. Pre-Renouncer Hinduism showed little sensitivity to the suffering of animals, but by the time the great Hindu epic *Mahabharata* was composed—sometime around 400 BCE—there had been a radical change in attitude. Echoing Lord Mahavira and the Buddha, *Mahabharata* commends *ahimsa* in language that anticipates Jesus and Hillel the Great by four centuries: "One should never do that to another which one regards as injurious to one's own self." On the subject of meat eating, *Mahabharata* does not mince words. "The meat of other animals is like the flesh of one's own son. That foolish person, stupefied by folly, who eats meat, is regarded as the vilest of beings."[9]

The Laws of Manu, an extensive collection of Hindu precepts that probably dates from the second century BCE, urges *ahimsa* toward all living beings. "He who does not seek to cause the bonds of suffering and death to living creatures, but desires the good of all beings, obtains endless bliss." Applying this explicitly to meat eating, *The Laws* continue: "Meat can never be obtained without injury to living creatures, and injury to sentient beings is detrimental to heavenly bliss; let him [the spiritual practitioner] therefore shun the use of meat."[10]

Hindu concern for the suffering of animals reaches its full flowering in the *Tirukural*, a long didactic poem in the Tamil language of Southern India dating from about 200 CE. In the chapter on "Abstaining from Meat," we find:

Riches cannot be found in the hands of the thriftless, / Nor can compassion be found in the hearts of those who eat meat. (252)

If you ask, "What is kindness and what is unkind?" / It is not killing and killing. Thus, eating flesh is never virtuous. (254)

If the world did not purchase and consume meat, / There would be none to slaughter and offer meat for sale. (256)

When a man realizes that meat is the butchered flesh / Of another creature, he must abstain from eating it. (257)

All that lives will press palms together in prayerful adoration / Of those who refuse to slaughter and savor meat. (260)[11]

From at least the time of *Mahabharata* until quite recently, vegetarianism was a widespread practice among high-caste Hindus, especially Brahmins, although it was less popular among lower castes. But in the modern world, opposing forces are breaking up this ancient pattern. On one side, the influence of the West has led many high-caste Hindus to take up meat eating. From the other direction, the Hindu Renaissance movement—which is growing rapidly in both India and the diaspora—is urging Hindus of all castes to adopt a compassionate vegetarian diet as an obligatory Hindu practice.

Monks and spiritual seekers who practice yoga and meditation according to the Hindu philosophy of Vedanta—which is the quintessentially Hindu form of *srmana* spirituality—are vegetarian, although even vegetarian Indians, conditioned by the centuries-old tradition of cow protection, have great difficulty appreciating the suffering and death represented by milk.

Despite this bias toward milk and cheese, some contemporary Hindu spiritual leaders, appalled by the cruelties of factory farming, are beginning to break with tradition by speaking out on behalf of a vegan diet. Notable among these is Dada J. P. Vaswani, who is famous throughout the Hindu world for his charitable and educational work among the poor. A lifelong vegetarian, in 2003 Vaswani told a reporter for the magazine *Hinduism Today*, "I now take soy milk instead of cow's milk because the cows are very cruelly treated in factory farming. Ever since I learned about it nine or ten years ago, I gave up milk. I believe it's the food of violence."[12]

Throughout its history—at the very least, from the time of the Aryan conquest—India has relied on animals for labor and transportation, a practice to which Mahavira and the Buddha did not object. Horses and elephants were also used in war for both battle and transport until motorized vehicles replaced them in the twentieth century. Hunting, especially birds, deer, and tigers, was a popular pastime among the wealthy until recent years, when overhunting had driven many species—including the tiger—to the brink of extinction.[13]

3

The Challenge Comes West

From India, the idea of animal protection traveled along the trade routes to the West, where it was introduced to the Hellenic world by one of the most fascinating and mysterious figures of antiquity. Today Pythagoras of Samos, who taught around 520 BCE, is all but forgotten, remembered mainly for the theorem in plane geometry that bears his name. But in the ancient world, he was a giant who exerted a powerful influence on religion, philosophy, ethics, science, mathematics, and music theory. Even today, the influence of Pythagoras is felt by way of Plato, who incorporated so much of the Samian's metaphysics into his own philosophy that some commentators refer to Plato as a Pythagorean.

Born and raised on the Eastern rim of the Aegean Sea, where his curiosity could be whetted by merchants and other travelers from distant lands, the young Pythagoras visited Egypt—and probably Persia—where he absorbed the ideas of the Renouncer movement that had been brought west with the great caravans: the illusory nature of the phenomenal world, the unity of all life, *ahimsa*, reincarnation, karma, and the possibility of gaining liberation from this world of suffering through spiritual practices such as meditation. These ideas, organized into his own unique amalgam, he taught to the disciples that he recruited into a mystical religious society that flourished until Christianity took charge of the Roman Empire 900 years later.

Pythagoras taught that all sentient beings possess identical souls, and that the soul, not being physical, is immortal. After the death of one body, the soul is reborn in another, not necessarily of the same species. On this basis, and out of compassion for the suffering of animals, Pythagoras forbade the eating of meat, instructing his followers in plain language to "Abstain from eating animals." Although some ancient commentators, unwilling to give up their meat, interpreted this to mean that one should not try to argue with fools, both the statement and its intent seem perfectly straightforward.[1] That Pythagoras did, in fact, teach a vegetarian diet is widely attested by later writers, and throughout antiquity Pythagoreans remained vegetarians. In fact, from ancient times until the word "vegetarian" was coined around the middle of the nineteenth century, a meatless diet was known in the European languages as a Pythagorean diet.

In his long masterpiece, *Metamorphoses*, the Roman poet Ovid (43 BCE—17 CE), affirms that Pythagoras "was the first to ban the serving of animal food at our tables," and has him condemn meat eating in harsh terms:

> O my fellow-men, do not defile your bodies with sinful foods.... The earth offers a lavish supply of riches, of innocent foods, and offers you banquets that involve no bloodshed or slaughter.... Alas, what wickedness to swallow flesh into our own flesh, to fatten our greedy bodies by cramming in other bodies, to have one living creature fed by the death of another![2]

These words are the literary invention of Ovid. But they reflect the teachings of the Pythagorean Society and of Pythagoreans in the first century, and there is every reason to believe that these teachings originated with Pythagoras.

Again reflecting the attitude of Jainism and Buddhism, Pythagoras was forthright in condemning the animal sacrifice that was the primary component of most ancient religions. "Never sacrifice without meal," was a well-known Pythagorean maxim, which was sometimes interpreted as an injunction to promote farming and sometimes as a command to his followers to offer only plant, and never animal, sacrifices.[3] Since we know that Pythagoreans offered plant-based sacrifices, often in the form of dough molded into effigies of sacrificial animals, the latter interpretation is clearly correct. Ovid's Pythagoras describes his attitude toward animal sacrifice in this vivid and moving description of ancient atrocity:

> Not content with committing such crimes [hunting, raising animals for slaughter, and eating meat], men have enrolled the very gods as their partners in wickedness, and suppose that the divinities in heaven take pleasure in the slaying of patient bullocks! . . . [At the altar, the victim] hears, without understanding, the prayers of the priest, and sees the corn it has cultivated sprinkled on its forehead, between its horns. It is struck down and stains with its blood the knives that it may have seen beforehand, reflected in the clear water. At once the lungs are torn from its still living breast, that the priest may examine them, and search out the purpose of the gods, revealed therein. And then, so great is man's hunger for forbidden food, you mortals dare to eat that flesh! I beg you, heed my warnings and abstain! Know and understand that when you put the flesh of slaughtered oxen in your mouth, the flesh you eat is that of your own labourers.

After telling us that Pythagoras forbade meat eating, Ovid remarks sadly that these were "wise words, indeed, but powerless to convince his hearers."[4]

Economic Vegetarians

The words of Pythagoras and his followers were powerless because the habits they wanted to change were so deeply ingrained. Greek and Roman society was founded on animal flesh, animal sacrifice, and animal labor, to which the Romans added animal entertainment. Although availability varied over time and place, cattle, sheep, goats, pigs, and chickens were the animals most killed for their flesh. Milk and cheese from cows and goats were popular, as were eggs.

Most of the Greco-Roman world was temperate to tropical, and since the ancients had no way to make ice, they could only store meat by salting or drying it, and they could not store eggs or dairy at all. In some areas, especially at higher elevations, springs would have provided natural refrigeration. But access to these would have been limited, as would their storage capacity and the length of time they would protect animal products from spoiling. Those who lived near high mountains could bring down ice and snow, but this was not practical on a large scale and was generally done only by the rich who had slaves to do the work and whose villas were conveniently situated.

The ancients shipped grain, fruit, and vegetables long distances—during the Empire, for example, Egypt was the city of Rome's principle grain supplier—but locally raised animals were the source of meat and dairy products. In earlier times, these were small family farms; later they were large plantations owned by the wealthy and worked by slaves: humans, oxen, donkeys, and horses, with dogs serving as herders and guards.

Because of the lack of refrigeration, meat was expensive, which made it a favorite luxury of the rich, and a prized treat for the poor. The banquets and dinner parties of the wealthy were orgies of gluttony featuring multiple courses of meats and cheeses. For everyone else, the main course at every meal—and often the only course—was bread, supplemented whenever possible by olives, a few vegetables, or a little fruit. Meat had a powerful hold on the Classical imagination, but it seldom found its way into the stomachs of most Greeks and Romans.

Slaughterhouses of Worship
We think of houses of worship as serene, comforting places where we hear inspirational messages, sing hymns, and commune peacefully with God. But the most important and most frequent ritual in Classical paganism—the equivalent of the Catholic mass or the

Protestant worship service—was animal sacrifice. Ancient temples were abattoirs adjacent to pens and cages filled with angry, terrified, squalling, screaming, bellowing, bleating, pissing, shitting cattle, sheep, goats, and birds waiting to be taken onto the killing floor that was the heart of the temple. The altar was a chopping block for the commission of ritual murder. The priest's primary role was to serve as a butcher who killed while chanting the sacred formulas that would assure the deity's acceptance of the offering. At the end of a service in which they sent the prayers of their parishioners heavenward on the smoke from the seared flesh of a murdered animal, their hands and vestments were covered with blood and they stank with the mortal terror and violent death of their victims. Classical paganism was a cult of mass killing.

Most ancient temples were also businesses. Worshippers would pay a fee for sacrifices, in addition to which they would either donate the animal to be killed, or they would kick in some extra money and the priests would purchase the victim. In a typical sacrifice, once the animal had been killed, the butcher-priests would lay him out on the altar and dress the meat. Most often, a small portion would be offered to the deity; some would be set aside for the priests and their families; and the rest would be sold for a profit. Temples were the meat markets of the Greco-Roman world. In many Roman cities, the only place you could find meat that had not been offered to a pagan deity was a kosher butcher shop run by Jews.

I Cannot Lay My Burden Down
The use of animals as slave laborers, which had begun with the rise of pastoralism and intensified with the Neolithic Revolution, continued unabated for more than ten thousand years—until the Industrial Revolution, when cheaper, more efficient, and more convenient sources of power made animal labor obsolete in the developed world. Oxen, donkeys, and horses were used throughout the Greco-Roman era for plowing land, threshing grain, turning stone mill wheels that ground grain into flour, and a variety of other tasks that required

power. They were also used for heavy hauling. Anything that would be moved by airplane, truck or rail car today, if it existed in the Classical world, was hauled by an ox, donkey, or horse. Donkeys and horses were ridden—horses by the rich, donkeys by the middle class; everyone else walked.[5]

Following Aristotle, Greeks and Romans believed that we had few, if any, ethical duties to slaves, human or nonhuman, and so they were made to work long days—the entire period of daylight, seven days a week, was the standard in the Roman Empire[6]—and fed as cheaply as possible, which meant small quantities of poor quality food. There were no animal welfare laws in the Classical world, and so the only constraint on animal abuse was the economic need to keep a slave laborer healthy enough to work as long as possible.

There were certainly owners who grew fond of their animal slaves and treated them with greater kindness than economics required, but the Greeks and especially the Romans were comfortable with cruelty as a part of everyday life to an extent that we would find appalling, and so we may safely assume that working animals lived short, miserable lives of overwork, undernourishment, lack of rest, exposure to the elements, and regular beatings. When they were no longer able to work, animal slaves were simply slaughtered.

Spectator Sports

The origin of chariot racing is lost in antiquity. There is a chariot race in the *Iliad*, and chariot races were a regular feature of Greek athletic festivals, including the Olympics. The Romans also loved chariot racing, and every city of any size in the Classical world had a racetrack, known in Greek as a hippodrome and in Latin as a circus, a narrow oval course around which two-horse and four-horse chariots raced for several laps. Crashes were a regular occurrence on the crowded courses and horses as well as drivers were frequently crippled or killed—which was a large part of the races' attraction to Roman sports fans, who were even more addicted to violence, pain, and death than American sports fans. The chariot race in the 1959 Charlton

Heston movie, *Ben-Hur*, in which drivers cut each other off and force one another into the wall at reckless speeds, causing multiple pile-ups that kill both drivers and horses, is an historically faithful portrayal of a Roman chariot race.

It was the Romans who introduced large-scale animal fighting to the world. At coliseums around the Empire, generals and politicians staged spectacles for the entertainment of the public in which human beings fought human beings, human beings fought animals, and animals fought one another, either singly or in groups and to the death. In order to impress the people and advance their own political ambitions, sponsors strove to outdo one another in the extravagance of the spectacles they put on. When the Coliseum in Rome—which was to ancient bloodsport what Yankee Stadium is to baseball and Wembley is to soccer—was dedicated by the Emperor Titus in 80 CE, more than five thousand animals died in "combat" in a single day.[7]

In the annals of Roman bloodsport, we find only one redeeming anecdote. In 55 BCE, the Roman general and politician Pompey the Great sponsored spectacles that included the slaughter of elephants by armed men. The Roman crowd—people who had come there to enjoy watching humans and animals kill one another—was so moved by the anguished cries of the wounded and dying animals that they shouted insults at Pompey for his cruelty.[8] This was the first popular protest against animal cruelty known to history, and so far as we know, it was never repeated in the ancient world. Except for this spontaneous outburst, no popular movement on behalf of animals ever developed in the Western world before the nineteenth century.

Socrates' Rooster and Plato's Shoes

Other than Pythagoras and a Pythagorean named Empedocles, none of the major pre-Socratic philosophers condemned meat eating or animal sacrifice. Modern animal advocates sometimes assert that Socrates himself was a vegetarian and an opponent of sacrifice, but there are no statements attributed to him that support those claims and no statements to that effect by ancient commentators.

In fact, according to Plato, Socrates' last words—spoken to his friend Crito as the numbing chill of the poison was climbing up his body—were "Crito, we ought to offer a cock to Asclepius. See to it, and don't forget." "No," replied the faithful Crito, "It shall be done."[9] Furthermore, in his *Memoirs of Socrates*, the philosopher's good friend Xenophon defends the martyred philosopher against the charge of atheism by pointing out that, "Everyone could see that he sacrificed regularly at home and also at the public altars of the state."[10] Both Plato and Xenophon describe dinner parties attended by Socrates at the homes of wealthy friends, where the menu would certainly have included meat, without suggesting that he ate differently from any of the other guests. And when discussing Socrates' lifestyle, Xenophon observes that he ate only small amounts of food, but never says that he refused to eat meat. In fact, Xenophon gives the clear impression that Socrates paid very little attention to food and ate whatever he was served, but in tiny portions.

A somewhat better case can be made for Plato, since in both *The Republic* and the *Laws* he prescribed a vegetarian diet for the citizens of his ideal state. Unfortunately, the reason he put forward had nothing to do with concern for animals. Like everyone in the ancient world, Plato considered meat a luxury, and he believed that a luxurious lifestyle led to indolence, cowardice, and a general breakdown in the civic virtues. Therefore, he mandated vegetarianism as a way to promote good citizenship. For the same reason, regarding shoes as a luxury, Plato required his ideal citizens to go barefoot. Ancient sources sometimes identify Plato as a vegetarian, but none of these were his contemporaries, and it is not clear whether their authors knew for a fact that he ate no meat, or were making an assumption based on the vegetarian passages in *The Republic* and the *Laws* and the obvious Pythagorean influence in Plato's philosophy. Whether Plato was a vegetarian is of little importance to us, however, since there is no evidence in his writings and no reports by other ancient writers that he was an advocate for animal protection.

What Goes Up but Never Comes Down?

If Socrates and Plato failed to condemn our crimes against animals, they also never made any serious effort to defend them. The task of crafting a response to Pythagoras fell to Plato's star pupil, Aristotle (384–322 BCE).

Pythagoras had attacked the killing of animals for food and sacrifice on two grounds: that we all have identical immortal souls that transmigrate from one species to another; and that animals are sentient beings who suffer from our mistreatment of them. Aristotle attempted to undercut both of these arguments. First, he argued that the soul is not an immortal entity distinct from the body, but is created when the elements necessary for life come together in the proper balance and under the right conditions. And when those elements fall out of balance, the body dies and the soul ceases to be. In other words, Aristotle made the ancient equivalent of the modern argument that life and consciousness are byproducts of the body's electrochemical processes.

Being a function of the bodies that gave rise to them, the souls of creatures with different kinds of bodies are themselves different, and not all souls are of equal value. In fact, Aristotle postulated a rigid hierarchy of beings based upon the kind of soul they possess. At the bottom were plants, which have vegetative souls, able to grow and reproduce, but not conscious. Then came animals, who have sensitive souls, able to experience physical sensations and emotions, and capable of thinking on a practical level—able to solve the simple problems of daily life such as finding food and escaping from danger. At the top were human beings, who alone possess rational souls, and are thereby able to engage in abstract thought, such as pondering the meaning of life or trying to define goodness, truth, and beauty—in other words, the kind of discourse that philosophers like Aristotle pride themselves on.

Finally, Aristotle explained that it is a universal law of nature that the lower exists to serve the higher. Thus, animals, having a lower form of soul, exist to serve human beings. He sums up his position this way:

Plants exist for the benefit of animals, and some animals exist for the benefit of others. Those which are domesticated serve human beings for use as well as for food; wild animals, too, in most cases, if not in all, serve to furnish us not only with food, but also with other kinds of assistance, such as the provision of clothing and other aids to life. Accordingly, if nature makes nothing purposeless or in vain, all animals must have been made by nature for the sake of men.[11]

As incredible as it seems, this is still the primary argument used to defend the enslavement and slaughter of animals: *All animals must have been made by nature for the sake of men*. To put it in language that we will encounter later, only human beings are ends in themselves. We are the only beings on earth who exist to satisfy ourselves. All other creatures, including animals, are merely means by which we humans can attain our ends. Our worth lies in ourselves. The worth of animals lies in their usefulness to us.

A second line of reasoning that Aristotle pursued to deny that we have ethical duties to animals was that moral responsibility arises out of the fellowship (or friendship) that exists among members of a community. Since friendship depends upon shared interests, we can have friendship only with other rational beings; therefore, we have no ethical responsibilities to animals. This notion was almost immediately refuted by his successor as head of the Lyceum (as Aristotle's school in Athens was called). Theophrastus (372–287 BCE) pointed out that we and animals share the same sensory world, similar emotions, and at least to some degree, reason.[12] Along with shepherds, cowherds, and guardians of companion animals the world over, Theophrastus recognized that we could most certainly enjoy friendship with nonhuman animals.

Despite Theophrastus, Aristotle's denial of rationality to animals and insistence on restricting friendship to human beings was picked up and embellished by the Stoics, one of the most influential schools of philosophy in the Greco-Roman world. Stoic philosophers relied on the fact that only rational beings can be held responsible for their behavior; therefore, they claimed that moral duties arise out of the natural community of interest—which they called "fellowship"—that exists among rational beings as a result of their mutual ability to hold one another responsible for their actions. Thus, we have moral duties only to other members of the community of rational beings. These are ideas that we will encounter a bit farther on in the Christian philosophies of Augustine and Thomas Aquinas, while the Stoic notion of mutual accountability is sometimes seen as a precursor to the social contract doctrine of Enlightenment philosopher Jean-Jacques Rousseau. Some Stoics were vegetarian, but out of a dislike for luxury rather than concern for animals.[13]

For a Little Piece of Meat

The classical world's most impassioned plea for ethical vegetarianism came from the essayist and biographer Plutarch (*c.*45–*c.*125 CE). In two essays entitled "On the Eating of Flesh," he defends Pythagoras' condemnation of meat eating in terms reminiscent of modern animal rights rhetoric:

> Are you not ashamed to mingle domestic crops [grains, fruits, and vegetables] with blood and gore? You call serpents and panthers and lions savage, but you yourselves, by your own foul slaughters, leave them no room to outdo you in cruelty; for their slaughter is their living, yours is a mere appetizer.[14]

> It is certainly not lions and wolves that we eat out of self-defense; on the contrary, we ignore these and slaughter harmless, tame creatures without stings or teeth to harm us....[15]

> For what sort of dinner is not costly for which a living creature loses its life? Do we hold a life cheap?[16]

For the sake of a little flesh, we deprive them of sun, of light, of the duration of life to which they are entitled by birth and being.[17]

In an essay entitled "On the Intelligence of Animals" (usually mistranslated as "On the Cleverness of Animals"), Plutarch argues that animals are highly intelligent and, in fact, rational beings, supporting his claim with numerous anecdotes, some accurately reporting the behavior of different species, some fanciful.

Plutarch fully understood the challenge that he had taken up in trying to persuade people to give up meat. It is all but impossible, he said, "to extract the hook of flesh-eating, entangled as it is and embedded in the love of pleasure."[18]

* * *

The last hurrah of animal advocacy in the classical world occurred only a few years before the triumph of Christianity erased the notion of animal protection from the West for more than a thousand years. In the third century of the Common Era, the Neoplatonist philosopher Plotinus (205–270) and his student Porphyry (234–305) gave new voice to the arguments of Pythagoras condemning meat eating and animal sacrifice. Porphyry's long essay *On Abstinence from Animal Food* was written to a Roman senator named Castricius Firmus, a one-time disciple of Plotinus who had begun eating meat when he converted to Christianity. Thus, one of the last skirmishes between paganism and Christianity was fought over the Pythagorean diet.

In *Abstinence*, Porphyry attacked Aristotle head-on. First, he argued from observation that animals are, in fact, rational. On this basis, he turned Aristotle's own argument against him by pointing out that if you believe (as did Aristotle and most Greek and Roman philosophers who came after him) that we have moral duties to rational beings, then we obviously have moral duties to animals. He then proceeded to dispute Aristotle's claim that there is a qualitative difference between the souls of animals and human souls. To Porphyry, animals and humans are "kindred" beings, who have far more in common, in terms of sentience, emotions, and reason, than they have separating them. "He may justly be considered as impious," Porphyry declared, "who does not abstain from acting unjustly toward his kindred." But ultimately for Porphyry, as for so many animal advocates since him, it came down simply to compassion. "For [animals] are naturally sensitive, and adapted to feel pain, to be terrified and hurt."[19] And therefore, we have a moral duty not to terrify and hurt them.

4

Judaism Crafts a Compromise

The Bible's first mention of animals comes in the first chapter of the first book, where the creation story uses the same Hebrew phrase to refer to all sentient beings without distinction, whether human, land animal, bird, sea creature, insect, or worm. That phrase, *nephesh chayah* (pronounced roughly NEF-esh hi-YAH), means "living soul."[1] Although Genesis is plainly telling us that human beings and animals have identical souls, our English Bibles— from the old familiar King James Version to the current bestselling New International Version—almost without exception translate *nephesh chayah* one way when it refers to an animal and another way when it refers to a human being. One popular subterfuge is to translate *nephesh chayah* as "living being" when it refers to animals and "living soul" when it refers to humans; another is to translate it "living creature" when it refers to animals and "living being" when it refers to humans.

At the time of creation, Genesis reports that God gave these instructions to Adam and Eve:

> Be fruitful and multiply, and fill the earth and subdue it; and rule over the fish of the sea and over the birds of the sky and over every living thing that moves on the earth.[2]

The Hebrew verb (*radah*) that the New American Standard Bible translates "rule over" is translated in the King James Version as "have dominion over," which is why the notion that God gave us the right to use and abuse animals however we want is referred to as "dominionism." But that is not what this verse says. *Radah* is the verb typically used in the Hebrew Scriptures to refer to the authority of governments and monarchs over their citizens.[3] We expect government officials to use their authority for the good of those over whom they exercise it. Rulers who abuse, enslave, and murder their citizens for their own enrichment, enjoyment, or convenience we invariably condemn as unjust and unfit. There is no reason to judge our dominion over animals by any other standard.

Viewed in that light, the grant of dominion can be seen as a summons to humankind to establish worldwide a regime like that of Ashoka, which took responsibility for the wellbeing of all who lived at its mercy, human or animal. And in fact, Jewish commentators have typically viewed dominion as a commandment to treat animals with kindness. It is primarily Christian authorities who have treated it as divine permission to abuse and kill animals whenever we like, however we like, without regard for their lives or their suffering.

Meatless in Eden

The mythologies of the ancient world tell of a long-ago epoch when *ahimsa* ruled the world. Crime and war were unknown; humans and animals were vegetarian. No one killed anyone else—not for food, not for gain, and not from anger. The Greek poet Hesiod described the people of this age of peace as "a race made all of gold," from which it has come to be known as "the Golden Age."[4] Porphyry summed up his case against meat eating by saying that, "We should imitate those that lived in the Golden Age . . . because they were satisfied with the fruits of the earth."[5]

The Biblical version of the golden age is the Garden of Eden, which Genesis portrays as a paradise in which no creature harmed another. In the Garden, God commanded Adam and Eve—and with them, all living creatures—to follow a vegan diet.

Then God said, "Behold, I have given you every plant yielding seed that is on the surface of the earth, and every tree
which has fruit yielding seed; it shall be food for you; and to
every beast of the earth and to every bird of the sky and to
every thing that moves on the earth which has life, I have
given every green plant for food." And it was so.[6]

The expulsion of Adam and Eve from the Garden of Eden did not
abrogate the vegan commandment, which remained in effect until
after the flood. When Noah and his family emerged from the ark, God
told them that human beings were now, for the first time, allowed to
eat the flesh of animals. This permission is accompanied by a chilling
statement:

The fear of you and the terror of you will be on every beast
of the earth and on every bird of the sky; with everything
that creeps on the ground, and all the fish of the sea, into
your hand they are given. Every moving thing that is alive
shall be food for you; I give all to you as I gave the green
plant.[7]

This revisionist commandment is a direct rebuttal to the earlier
claim that God had mandated a vegan diet. In the first passage, we are
introduced to a peaceful world in which God instructs us to treat all
living creatures according to the principle of *ahimsa*. In the second,
we see a violent world in which God authorizes us to follow our
appetites and fears into cruelty and murder against our weaker fellow
creatures.

Slitting Throats in the Name of God

It is the latter view that guided mainstream Judaism throughout the
Biblical era, as we can see by looking at the issue that dominated the
ancient Jewish debate about animal protection: religious sacrifice.

According to Genesis, the first human to offer an animal as a sacrifice was Adam and Eve's son Abel, and the Hebrew Scriptures report that the two founding prophets of Judaism—Abraham and Moses—conducted animal sacrifice.[8] But it was not until the erection of the first Jewish Temple, around 960 BCE, that sacrifice could be practiced on the massive scale that characterized establishment Judaism for the next thousand years. At the dedication ceremony, King Solomon presided over the slaughter of 22,000 cattle and 120,000 sheep and goats.[9] From then on—with a timeout for the Babylonian Exile (586–c.458 BCE)—sacrifices took place daily until the Romans destroyed the Temple in 70 CE.

There were the "official" sacrifices, which included daily sacrifices, weekly sacrifices (known as "sabbaths"), monthly sacrifices (known as "new moons"), sacrifices for holy days, sacrifices for the health of the king, for success in war, for prosperity, for good crops, for rain, and for any other need or occasion that the king or high priest might perceive. And as if these weren't enough, there were also "private" sacrifices sponsored by individuals for ritual purification, forgiveness of sin, expiation of legal guilt, health, the sanctification of marriages and births, thanksgiving, to solemnize a vow, and for a host of other reasons; there were few occasions in Jewish life that did not call for a sacrifice.

By the tens of thousands, Jews came every year to the Temple, and by the hundreds of thousands, cattle, sheep, goats, and doves were slaughtered. The Temple precincts were surrounded by stockyards. In the heat of Jerusalem, the stink of urine and feces must have been gut wrenching. And there could have been no escape, even in prayer, from the screams of animals being slaughtered or the stench of their blood and fear. Like their pagan counterparts, the priests who officiated at these ritual killings were first and foremost butchers, and the Temple was a slaughterhouse.

This holocaust (the word originally referred to animal sacrifice) continued until the Jews of Palestine revolted against their Roman rulers. Facing the most awesome military force the Western world had ever seen, the rebellion was doomed, and in 70 CE, Roman soldiers razed the Temple, which has yet to be rebuilt. Since sacrifice could take place only in the Temple, it came to an unceremonious halt and has never been resumed.

As I have already remarked, animal sacrifice is based upon fear, the belief that God (or the gods) will visit suffering upon you if you do not mollify him (or her or them) with gifts of death. But there was also within Judaism a minority tradition, which arose during the Axial Age, that rejected fear and taught that the foundation of righteousness is love. Its leaders were never in control of the official "state" religion. They never ran the Temple, they never held high religious or government office, they never had the power to define orthodoxy, and so they left no history of their movement. They were outsiders, "voices crying in the wilderness"—protesters, we might call them today—banging on the doors of the Temple demanding that a religion based on fear be replaced by one founded in love. The story of Biblical Judaism is the story of the unending struggle of those who would lead by love against those who ruled by fear.

Mercy, Not Sacrifice

Even if they never wrested control of the official cult from the fearmongers, those Axial Age figures that I think of as the Prophets of Love still managed to exert enormous influence on Judaism by liberally seeding the Hebrew Scriptures with an exalted spiritual and ethical message. It was one of their ranks whose vision of *ahimsa* in the Garden of Eden we quoted earlier. It was also one of their number who embedded among Leviticus' bloody instructions for every kind of animal sacrifice imaginable a principle of kindness as pure as any ever expressed: "You shall love your neighbor as yourself."[10]

Undoubtedly the most eloquent and influential of the Prophets of Love were the so-called Later Prophets,[11] who called the Jews to righteousness beginning about 780 BCE and continuing until shortly after the Babylonian exile. At once spiritual teachers and muckraking crusaders for social justice, the Later Prophets attacked the political and religious establishment, condemning kings and priests as cruel and greedy oppressors while demanding justice for widows, orphans, and the poor. They performed the role in ancient Israel that humorist Finley Peter Dunne called upon newspapers to play in modern America: they comforted the afflicted and afflicted the comfortable.

Like the Renouncer teachers in India, the Prophets of Love based their ethical system not on ritual, but on sentience, and their campaign was for an end to the oppression of all who were able to suffer, including the animals who were slaughtered for sacrifice. In terms that are straightforward and unmistakable, several of the Later Prophets extended the call for justice and compassion to animals by demanding an end to animal sacrifice.

> "What are your multiplied sacrifices to me?" says the LORD. "I have had enough of burnt offerings of rams and the fat of fed cattle; and I take no pleasure in the blood of bulls, lambs, or goats. When you come to appear before Me, who requires of you this trampling of my courts? [*I.e.*, Who told you to march all these cattle, sheep, and goats through the precincts of the Temple on their way to slaughter?] . . . [E]ven though you multiply prayers, I will not listen. Your hands are covered with blood. . . . Cease to do evil, learn to do good; seek justice, reprove the ruthless, defend the orphan, plead for the widow." (Isaiah 1:11–16)

> For I did not speak to your fathers, or command them in the day that I brought them out of the land of Egypt, concerning burnt offerings and sacrifices. But this is what I commanded them, saying, "Obey My voice, and I will be your God and you will be My people, and you will walk in the way which I command you, that it may be well with you." (Jeremiah 7:21–23)

> For I desire mercy, not sacrifice, and acknowledgement of God rather than burnt offerings. (Hosea 6:6)

These are not just condemnations of sacrifice, they are flat denials that God had ever commanded sacrifices to be offered, despite the numerous passages in the Hebrew Scriptures that describe those commands in bloody, stomach-churning detail. The Prophets of Love did not regard the teachings of the Prophets of Fear as divinely inspired. Before the destruction of the Temple, there was a great rift in Judaism that today is all but hidden from our view, and one of the principal issues over which the two sides fought was animal sacrifice.

In ancient Judaism, meat eating was closely associated with sacrifice. At least as recently as the days of King Saul (c.1000 BCE) and probably much later, Jews were permitted to eat meat only from an animal who had been offered to God.[12] As late as 70 CE when the Temple was destroyed, the connection between sacrifice and meat eating remained so strong that the rabbis seriously discussed whether Jews were still permitted to eat meat.[13] It seems almost certain, therefore, that when the Later Prophets condemned animal sacrifice, they were also condemning meat eating, and that this was understood perfectly well by their contemporaries. From this, we may conclude that the minority strain in ancient Judaism—what we may think of as "Progressive Judaism"—was at least vegetarian, and quite probably vegan, adhering to the diet prescribed by God in the Garden of Eden.

In Israel, as in India and the Classical world, there is no evidence that anyone ever objected to the use of animals for labor and transportation so long as they were well treated. Ancient civilization without animal labor would have been as unthinkable as modern civilization without oil or electricity. Therefore, the notion of freeing animals from work may simply have been inconceivable. Or, the defenders of animals may have believed that domesticated animals were happy so long as they were well fed, not overworked, and not beaten. In any event, around the ancient world, animal slaves carried out their eternal labors while none of their defenders called for their release.

The Biblical Compromise

In India and the Greco-Roman world, the two sides of the animal debate remained endlessly locked in their unequal struggle. Jains, Buddhists, and progressive Hindus maintained their perpetual challenge to the majority practices of meat-eating and sacrifice. But although they were unable to abolish those practices beyond their own circles, at least those circles encompassed large segments of Indian society. A majority of Indians continued to eat meat, but a very large minority did not, and over time animal sacrifice was marginalized except in Nepal, where it remains a mainstream Hindu practice. In the Greco-Roman world, the Pythagoreans were able to attract to their ranks only a handful of philosophers and spiritual seekers. They had no effect on society at large. In Israel, however, events followed a different course, as Judaism took the thesis of animal exploitation and the antithesis of animal rights and created a synthesis that I think of as the Biblical Compromise.

Today, we call this compromise "animal welfare." The rabbis who finalized and formalized it in the Talmud called it *tsar baalei hayyim* (pronounced roughly TSAR bah-ah-LAY hi-YEEM, spelling varies), "the suffering of living beings." Jews could use animals for food, clothing, labor, transportation, and so forth, but they must treat them with kindness and compassion while they were alive and kill them as quickly and painlessly as possible when that time came. The primary Biblical basis for *tsar baalei hayyim* was Deuteronomy 25:4, "You shall not muzzle the ox while he is threshing." The point of muzzling the ox was to keep him from eating any of the grain that he was threshing. The point of the commandment was the cruelty of forcing an animal to work for hours with his face just inches from tantalizing food that he cannot enjoy. In one stroke, this verse, and the doctrine that was built on it, permits the exploitation of animals but forbids cruelties that are not essential to it. These same two principles are also enshrined elsewhere in the Hebrew Scriptures, including the Ten Commandments, which require that animals, as well as humans, rest from their labors on the Sabbath.[14]

With the destruction of the Temple, the focus of the discussion

about our behavior toward animals shifted from sacrifice to the use
of animal products for food. Here, the Compromise took the form of
a complex set of rules known as *kashrut*. These rules, which are elab-
orations on a simpler set of regulations found in various places in the
first five books of the Hebrew Scriptures, regulate in minute detail
every aspect of choosing and slaughtering animals for food, and
preparing, serving, and consuming animal products. Generally, the
sages of the Talmud, and the great commentators who came afterward, agreed that *kashrut* had been established as a constant reminder
that animal food was different from plant food because it so often
required the killing of a *nephesh chayah*, a living, conscious soul.[15]
Meat eating incurs guilt; it had been a concession by God to the weak-
ness and stubbornness of humankind. A vegan diet is automatically
kosher, and subject to no restrictions, because it does not carry the
guilt of enslaving and slaughtering living souls.[16] The final step in the
formulation of the Biblical Compromise was to give meat eating the
stamp of divine acquiescence, while denying it God's enthusiastic
support.

*   *   *

The rebellion that resulted in the destruction of the Temple was a
murderous affair, with rival Jewish groups slaughtering each other
and the Romans slaughtering everybody in sight. One result of this
massacre was the effective elimination of both extreme camps in the
debate over animal sacrifice and meat eating. Before the rebellion, the
Pharisees—a moderate, centrist group with affiliations to both
Judaisms, Progressive and Official—had been the largest Jewish
denomination. Afterward, it was the only Jewish denomination of
any size or influence. Pharisee scholars saved Judaism by rebuilding it
in their image, adapting their moderate beliefs and practices to the
world as they found it after the failure of the rebellion, and codifying
those beliefs and practices, including the compromise of *tsar baalei
hayyim*, in that great, encyclopedic handbook of Jewishness, the
Talmud.

Centuries later, the Biblical Compromise would become the model for the welfare philosophy that dominated animal protection in Europe and North America from the Enlightenment through the first three-quarters of the twentieth century.

The Heritage of Abraham

Of the other two great religions that evolved from Jewish history and teaching, Christianity—as we shall see in a moment—abolished animal sacrifice, but for centuries rejected the Biblical Compromise (although it has now accepted it). Islam did just the opposite: from the beginning, Islam accepted the Compromise while enshrining animal sacrifice in its rituals. Down to the present, the festival of Eid-al-Adha, which celebrates the Hajj, the pilgrimage to Mecca that every Muslim whose circumstances permit is required to make at least once, is observed in the ritual slaughter of vast numbers of animals, mostly sheep. The Koran explicitly endorses meat eating, but the Hadith—didactic stories from the life of Mohammad that Muslims consider authoritative—are emphatic in their demand that animals, both wild and domestic, be treated with kindness.

5

Jesus vs. Aristotle

J esus had very little contact with animals. He did not, for example, use animals for transportation. A week before his crucifix-
ion, he rode a donkey from the village of Bethany on the Mount
of Olives to Jerusalem—a distance of about a mile and a half—for the
specific purpose of fulfilling a prophecy about the coming of the
Messiah, an event which Christians celebrate as Palm Sunday. But on
all other occasions, he is reported to have walked, even on his jour-
neys between Jerusalem and Galilee, nearly a hundred miles each way.

It would also appear that he did not sacrifice animals. The gospels
record numerous occasions on which Jesus taught in the Temple
(invariably getting into an argument with the teachers of Official
Judaism), but they record no instance in which Jesus or his disciples
offered a sacrifice. And Matthew reports that Jesus twice quoted with
approval the passage that I cited in the previous chapter in which the
prophet Hosea condemns animal sacrifice: "For I desire mercy, not
sacrifice, and acknowledgement of God rather than burnt offerings."
"If you understood this," Jesus told the representatives of Official
Judaism with whom he was debating, "you would not condemn the
innocent," referring to the innocent animals condemned for sacrifice,
and by extension, food.[1]

In an incident known as the "Cleansing of the Temple," Jesus
approached the open-air market where vendors sold sacrificial animals to worshippers and moneychangers plied their trade. Suddenly
losing his temper, Jesus overturned the tables of the moneychangers,

released the caged doves, and drove away the cattle and sheep, shouting, "It is written that my father's house shall be called a house of prayer, but you have turned it into a den of thieves."[2] Obviously, Jesus was outraged by the commercialism that permeated the Temple cult. But something else angered him as well, even though from a distance of two thousand years, it may not stand out as clearly.

Jesus' statement as he trashed the market was a quotation from Jeremiah, the same passage in which, as we saw in the last chapter, the prophet condemns animal sacrifice.[3] By driving away the sacrificial animals while quoting from a passage in the Hebrew Scriptures that condemns sacrifice, Jesus was launching a direct assault on sacrificial religion. He was attacking the religion of fear in the name of the religion of love. The Cleansing of the Temple was history's first direct action to liberate animals, and Jesus was the first animal liberator.

From its earliest beginnings down to the present, Christianity, both Jewish and gentile, has condemned sacrifice. But it soon lost sight of concern for the sacrificial animals, which had been a driving force behind the Later Prophets' attack on ritual cruelty. From the first century of the Common Era, Christian teaching has been that sacrifice had, indeed, been commanded by God, but was superseded by God's sacrifice of his only begotten son.[4] Therefore, sacrificing animals would demonstrate a refusal to accept God's grace and a lack of faith in Jesus.

Was Jesus a Vegetarian?

With its knack for outrageous slogans that turn out to be true, PETA has been proclaiming for several years that "Jesus was a vegetarian." Every social movement that comes down the pike tries to reinvent Jesus in its own image, but there is a far better case for a vegetarian Jesus than is generally recognized.[5]

First, the gospels never tell us that Jesus ever ate any animal product except fish. Only one gospel, Luke, tells us that he ate fish, and only once, after the resurrection, when he is said to have eaten a small morsel to demonstrate to his doubting disciples that he had been resurrected in the body as well as the spirit. Even so, there is good reason to believe that a later editor added this incident to Luke at a time (probably in the second century) when the Church was trying to stamp out the widespread belief that Jesus had been resurrected only in the spirit, not the body.[6]

Three of the four gospels describe the Last Supper as a Passover seder, and the Hebrew Scriptures prescribe lamb as the seder's main course. Therefore, it is widely assumed that Jesus must have eaten lamb. But the gospels never suggest that lamb was present. To the contrary, they give the clear impression that it was replaced by bread. The assumption that Jesus, who is often portrayed in the Bible as flouting ritual laws, such as those against working on the Sabbath, must have eaten lamb because that was the prescribed main course, is baseless.

Ancient Christian sources describe several of Jesus' closest disciples as following a strict vegan diet, including Simon Peter, Matthew, Thomas, and Jesus' brother, James the Just, who became the leader of the Christian community following Jesus' death. There is no disciple who is described as eating meat other than fish. This would suggest that veganism—perhaps with the exception of fish, which they may not have recognized as sentient—was the practice of Jesus' family and the religious movement he formed. And, in fact, ancient Christian sources tell us that the early Jewish Christians (known as *Ebionim*, "the Poor"), who had learned their practices directly from Jesus, were vegetarian.

Jesus was among the greatest of the Jewish Prophets of Love. He was a successor to the Later Prophets, and an advocate of the minority outlook that we have called Progressive Judaism. This made him heir to a compassionate tradition within Judaism that opposed the killing of animals for sacrifice or food. He openly attacked animal sacrifice, both verbally and by direct action, and is never reported as eating animal products (with the possible exception of fish). His closest followers were vegan, and for three centuries his Jewish followers were at least vegetarian and probably vegan. There is very good reason to believe that Jesus was a vegan who taught animal protection.

While Jewish Christianity remained true to its vegetarian origins until it vanished in the fourth century, gentile Christianity quickly turned carnivorous, leading us to ask: What went wrong?

Does God Care about Animals?

What went wrong was Paul, the diaspora Jew who, in the decades following the execution of Jesus, laid the groundwork for the spread of
Christianity to the gentile population of the Mediterranean world.
Paul came from a wealthy family with connections throughout the
Roman Empire, and had received an excellent Greek education. He
never met Jesus and was never an adherent of Progressive Judaism. In
fact, before his conversion, he had been a Pharisee from the conservative wing of the party that was aligned with the priests who ran the
Temple. Paul had even held a job in the Temple bureaucracy—enforcing the orthodoxy of Official Judaism by prosecuting Progressives.

While traveling from Jerusalem to Damascus armed with arrest
warrants for Ebionim, Paul experienced a vision of the risen Christ
that convinced him that Jesus was the Messiah. Apparently, Paul's
work as a prosecutor had made him familiar enough with the views
of the Progressives to know that even after his conversion, he did not
share them. Instead of going to the movement's leaders in Jerusalem
for instruction in his new faith, he deliberately avoided them and
spent the next several years in solitude working out his beliefs on his
own. Years later, he would brag that he had not learned his doctrine
"from any man," but that it had been revealed to him directly by
Christ in heaven, and therefore was of greater authority than the
teachings of the Ebionim.[7] Thus, Paul's teachings were not based
upon the teachings of Jesus, nor upon the teachings of those who had
been his closest companions, but upon his own blend of Greek philosophy, popular Greek religion, and Official Judaism, attached to the
belief that the Messiah was none other than Jesus of Nazareth. This
strange mixture he attributed to divine inspiration.

On the subject of animals, Paul's Greek education came to the
fore, leading him to reject not only the teachings of Progressive
Judaism, but the Biblical Compromise as well. We have seen that the
heart of the Compromise was the doctrine of *tsar baalei hayyim*,
based on Deuteronomy 25:4, "You shall not muzzle the ox while he is
threshing." Paul quotes this verse, and asks, "God is not concerned
about oxen, is He? Or is He speaking altogether for our sakes? Yes, for

our sake it was written."[8] He then goes on to interpret this verse as an allegory meaning that—contrary to Jewish practice at the time—preachers should be paid for their work.

On this basis, gentile Christianity abandoned the Jewish view that animals are God's sentient creatures, living souls who need and deserve our compassion and care, and adopted the Aristotelian view that animals are a lower order of being to whom we have no moral duties. In its consequences, Paul's preference for Aristotle over Judaism and Jesus was one of the most appalling moral choices in the history of Western civilization.

Paul was fully aware of the implications of his doctrine that God does not care about animals. "Eat anything that is sold in the meat market without asking questions for conscience' sake," he told his followers, and then quoted Psalm 24:1, "For the earth is the Lord's, and all that it contains."[9] Elsewhere, Paul concedes that a vegetarian diet is not a sin, but argues that it is not a virtue either.[10] Animals simply had no place in Paul's moral scheme; they were a matter of indifference. His personal view on meat eating seems to be that God put cattle, sheep, goats, and pigs (Paul rejected *kashrut*, at least for his gentile converts) on earth so that humans could enjoy their flesh, and it would show disrespect to our creator to reject His gift.[11]

"A Major Kind of Thing"

Despite Paul, there has always been a minority tradition of vegetarianism and concern for animals in the Church, especially in the east, where it was no doubt influenced by lingering memories of the vegetarianism practiced by Jesus and the apostles. A number of the early Church fathers, including Clement of Alexandria (d. *c.*215), Tertullian (*c.*160–*c.*240), and the so-called Desert Fathers—fourth-century mystics and monastics—were vegetarian, out of varying proportions of compassion for animals and a desire to avoid luxury. The last major Church figure to advocate vegetarianism was Jerome (340–420), who taught that Christians are obliged to do everything in their power to live as if they were already living in the Kingdom of

Heaven, which Jerome believed would be a re-creation of the Garden of Eden, right down to the vegan diet.

The Church, however, firmly rejected the vegetarian tradition. Paul had set the course of Christian thought for the next 1500 years. Throughout this millennium and a half, mainstream Christianity offered no solace to animals, as theologians took it for granted that Paul and Aristotle had settled the issue of our relationship to them. God (who took the place of Aristotle's "nature") had put animals here for us to use as we saw fit, and that left nothing more to discuss.

The most influential theologian of the Latin Church in the ancient world was Augustine (354–430), bishop of Hippo on the Mediterranean coast of what is now Algeria. In his younger days, Augustine had been a devotee of Manichaeanism, an eclectic Middle Eastern religion that practiced—for theological reasons even more arcane than Jerome's—vegetarianism. On becoming a Christian, he resumed eating meat and attacked abstention from it as a prideful rejection of God's gifts.

Following Paul, Augustine accepted Aristotle's hierarchy and gave it a Christian interpretation: "A human being is a major kind of thing, being made 'in the image and likeness of God' [Genesis 1:26–27] not by virtue of having a mortal body but by virtue of having a rational soul, and has thus a higher status than animals."[12] This led him to conclude that we have no direct moral duties to animals, as he explains in his masterpiece, *The City of God*.

> [W]hen we read, "You shall not kill," we assume that this does not refer to bushes, which have no feelings, nor to irrational creatures, flying, swimming, walking, or crawling, since they have no rational association with us, not having been endowed with reason as we are, and hence it is by a just arrangement of the Creator that their life and death is subordinated to our needs.[13]

JESUS VS. ARISTOTLE   55

The Dark Ages

By contrast with the Classical Age that went before and the Renaissance and Enlightenment that came after, the period between about 500 and 1400 is known as the "Dark Ages." But, comparatively speaking, for animals the Dark Ages were actually something of a bright spot. The triumph of Christianity had put an end to religious sacrifice and to mass murder for public amusement in the coliseums (except for bullfighting in Iberia and parts of southern France), thereby sparing millions of animals from suffering and violent death.

Otherwise, things went on pretty much as before. Cows, pigs, goats, sheep, and chickens were still kept in perpetual imprisonment and slaughtered for food and leather. Horses, donkeys, and oxen were still used as slave labor, and horses now rode into battle carrying knights who were wearing armor that added an additional fifty or sixty pounds to their burden. Hunters still pursued wildlife with spears, bows, and snares, and by the late Middle Ages, game species, especially deer, had been so overhunted that scarcity was a serious problem. Still, a surprising number of Christian monks and nuns are reported to have protected animals from hunters, including Carileff (c.400), Aventine of Gascony (c.440), Monacella (c.600, the patron saint of rabbits and hares), Anselm of Canterbury (1033–1109), and Godric of Finchale (d. 1170).[14] These medieval saints were the first hunt saboteurs, releasing animals from snares and placing their own bodies between the hunters and their prey.

On the other hand, compared to Christian Europe, the Classical world, including the fiercely repressive Roman Empire, had been a model of intellectual freedom. The Church ruthlessly eradicated all non-Christian religions, including Pythagoreanism,[15] and with them any vestiges of animal advocacy. The only vegetarians were the occasional monks who were imitating the asceticism of the Desert Fathers. No medieval theologian expressed any doubts about our right to enslave and slaughter animals.

"Animals Are Not Our Neighbors"

The most important of the medieval theologians was Thomas Aquinas (1225–1274), who remains to this day the pre-eminent philosopher of the Catholic Church. Aquinas' great contribution was a comprehensive synthesis of Christian doctrine and the philosophy of Aristotle.

Aquinas accepted Aristotle's hierarchy of souls, ignoring the inconvenient fact that the Bible describes only one kind of soul, the "living soul" shared by humans and animals, but not plants. On the subject of killing animals, he cites with approval a somewhat abbreviated version of the passage from Augustine that I quoted above. "When we hear it said, 'Thou shalt not kill,' we do not take it as referring to trees, for they have no sense, nor to irrational animals, because they have no fellowship with us. Hence it follows that the words, 'Thou shalt not kill' refer to the killing of a man."[16] As we saw earlier, this notion that moral duties depend upon "fellowship," which in turn depends upon reason, derives from Aristotle and the Stoics, not from Judaism or Jesus.

Aquinas then proceeds to give the Aristotelian/Stoic doctrine of fellowship a Christian spin. "The love of charity extends to none but God and our neighbor," he tells us. "But the word neighbor cannot be extended to irrational creatures, since they have no fellowship with man in the rational life. Therefore charity does not extend to irrational creatures."[17] In other words, animals are not our neighbors within the meaning of "You shall love your neighbor as yourself," and Christians have no direct obligation to treat them with kindness or show concern for their welfare.

This raises the obvious question of the numerous passages in the Hebrew Scriptures that command us to treat animals with respect and compassion. Aquinas is, of course, aware of those passages, and he has an answer ready. "God's purpose in recommending kind treatment of the brute creation is to dispose men to pity and tenderness toward one another."[18]

Despite these categorical statements, Aquinas does leave slightly ajar one door that the modern Catholic Church views as opening onto love and compassion for animals. "Nevertheless," he tells us, "we can love irrational creatures out of charity, *if we regard them as the good things that we desire for others, in so far, to wit, as we wish for their preservation, to God's honor and man's use*; thus too does God love them out of charity."[19] It is legitimate to feel love for animals, provided that this love is really a way of expressing thanks to God for placing animals here so that we can eat their flesh, drink their milk, wear their skins, and so on. We may not, however, love animals for their own sake, and in no event should we allow our love for animals to interfere with their enslavement and killing to satisfy human desires.

The Catholic Church held tenaciously to Aquinas' position until well into the twentieth century, even though—as we shall see in a few moments—Protestant and secular Europe had long ago adopted the Biblical Compromise. In 1863, the British Royal Society for the Prevention of Cruelty to Animals requested a charter from Pope Pius IX to open a branch in Rome.[20] But the Pope declined, on the grounds that allowing it might create the impression that human beings have moral duties to animals.[21] By the mid-twentieth century, however, the Catholic Church was moving to catch up with the rest of Europe by edging toward the Compromise ever so carefully. The *Catholic Encyclopedia*, published in 1948, tells us that:

> Societies for the protection of animals may be approved insofar as their objective is the elimination of cruelty to beasts. Not, however, insofar as they base their activities, as they sometimes do, on false principles (attributing rights to animals . . . or alleging a duty of charity, which in the Christian sense of that phrase, cannot obtain).[22]

By the century's end, in the wake of Vatican II, the Church had adopted the Biblical Compromise as its official position and admitted that we have at least some direct moral duties to animals, although these are severely circumscribed by human convenience. Despite this movement, the Church remains adamantly opposed to any hint of moral equality for animals. The universal Catechism prepared under the direction of Cardinal Josef Ratzinger—now Pope Benedict XVI—and issued by Pope John Paul II in 1992, states the Catholic version of the Compromise this way:

> 2416 Animals are God's creatures. He surrounds them with his providential care. By their mere existence they bless him and give him glory. Thus men owe them kindness. We should recall the gentleness with which saints like St. Francis of Assisi or St. Philip Neri treated animals.[23]

> 2417 God entrusted animals to the stewardship of those whom he created in his own image. Hence it is legitimate to use animals for food and clothing. They may be domesticated to help man in his work and leisure. Medical and scientific experimentation on animals is a morally acceptable practice, if it remains within reasonable limits and contributes to caring for or saving human lives.

> 2418 It is contrary to human dignity to cause animals to suffer or die needlessly. It is likewise unworthy to spend money on them that should as a priority go to the relief of human misery. One can love animals; one should not direct to them the affection due only to persons.

Putting Brother Ass in his Place

It is impossible to talk about animals and Christianity without discussing Francis of Assisi (1181–1226), the best known of the Catholic Church's patron saints of the animals. Contrary to popular opinion, Francis was not a vegetarian, and the Rule of the Franciscan Order, which he founded, is not and never has been vegetarian, although there are many individual Franciscans who are.[24]

According to Francis' principal biographer, Bonaventure (1221–1274), the guiding theme of Francis' life was to glorify God by practicing extreme asceticism and mortification of the flesh. In fact, Bonaventure's *Life of Saint Francis* leaves little doubt that Francis starved himself, beat himself with whips, deliberately chilled himself in the snow, and otherwise abused his body to the point that he destroyed his health and brought on an early and agonizing death. Reading Bonaventure's descriptions of Francis' mortifications, I had the horrifying sense that I was watching a man commit suicide in slow motion, under the delusion that his self-destruction was pleasing to God.

Bonaventure describes Francis' attitude toward his body this way. "He used to call his body Brother Ass, for he felt it should be subjected to heavy labor, beaten frequently with whips, and fed with the poorest food."[25] Forget his body for the moment—that was at least his to do with as he pleased—but if this is the way that Francis believed donkeys should be treated, and if he considered the word "ass" or "donkey" a term of contempt, he does not deserve to be called a saint, much less granted patronage of the animals.

Bonaventure tells us that Francis' daily diet was just a few bits of bread, and perhaps some herbs or thin soup. The point was not to avoid the flesh of animals, but to avoid giving his body anything that it might find filling or satisfying. When he was sick, however, as he often was due to the punishments he constantly inflicted on "Brother Ass," he would relent and eat meat, vegetables, and other nourishing food. Once he had recovered, he would repent his "lapse" and castigate himself publicly—not for eating the bodies of murdered animals, but for giving in to his body and letting it get the better of his will.

On the available evidence, Francis seems to have had little genuine concern for animals. The point of the numerous stories connecting him to animals is not that he treated them kindly, but that he was so holy that he could talk to them and they would obey him. In the Middle Ages, this was regarded as more a sign of piety than of empathy or compassion. Thus, when he preached, birds stopped singing and listened to the sermon. When Francis bought lambs waiting to be sold for slaughter and set them free, it was not because he felt compassion for their suffering, but because they reminded him that Jesus was the Lamb of God ... and on and on in that vein. Francis of Assisi did not see animals as sentient beings who were important in their own right. He saw them as lessons that God had placed on earth to teach piety to human beings.

There is a beautiful saying attributed to Francis that is widely circulated in animal protection circles. It goes, "Not to harm our humble brethren is our first duty to them, but to stop there is not enough; we have a higher mission: to be of service to them whenever they require it." When a source is given (which is rarely), it is Bonaventure's *Life of Saint Francis.* Unfortunately, it is nowhere to be found there. It is almost certainly apocryphal.

Here I Stand, but Not with the Animals

In 1517, Martin Luther (1483–1546) started the Protestant Reformation by raising objections to ninety-five points of Catholic teaching and practice. The Church's dim view of animals was not among them. In fact, Luther accepted Aquinas' view that the Bible's injunctions against cruelty to animals are intended to teach us kindness toward other human beings; "otherwise, it would seem to be a stupid ordinance ... to regulate something so unimportant."[26] Throughout his life, Luther ate meat and hunted with the North German princes who were his patrons.

John Calvin (1509–1564), on the other hand, drew his teaching on animals directly from the Hebrew Scriptures, and as a result taught a Christian version of the Biblical Compromise. "True it is," he said, "that God hath given us the birds for our food, as we know he hath made the whole world for us." As far as it goes, that is the traditional Pauline/Thomist position. But then Calvin invokes the compromise by telling us that this gift came "with the condition that we should handle [the animals] gently." [27]

Luther appears to have believed that animals will be present in heaven. Although this is not particularly well attested, it is probably true, because that is what is taught in the Bible, both in the Hebrew

Scriptures and the letters of Paul.[28] It is very well attested that John Wesley (1703–1791), the founder of Methodism, held this belief. In a sermon entitled "The General Deliverance," Wesley rejected the Aristotelian/Thomist assertion that animals are not rational beings.

> What then is the barrier between men and brutes? The line which they cannot pass? It was not reason. Set aside that ambiguous term: Exchange it for the plain word, understanding: and who can deny that brutes have this? We may as well deny that they have sight or hearing.[29]

Wesley assumes, however, that in fact there is a morally significant difference between animals and humanity—what he calls "the line which they cannot pass"—which he defines as the ability to know and obey God. Just as human beings fulfill their purpose in creation by serving God, animals fulfill theirs by serving human beings. In effect, John Wesley defines humans as gods for the animals. And although he was a vegetarian on-and-off for much of his later life, that was for reasons of health rather than ethics—Wesley suffered from a digestive disorder and found a vegetarian diet helpful.

Wesley had no objection to using animals for food, clothing, labor, and transportation, because God had created them for our use in the first place. He realized that this caused them suffering, but he salved his conscience with the thought that:

> *In recompense for what they have suffered*, when God has "renewed the face of the earth" and their corruptible body has put on incorruption, they shall enjoy happiness suited to their state without alloy, without interruption, and without end.[30]

That is precisely the consolation that Southern preachers offered African slaves.

Initially, the Protestant Reformation did little to help animals. Later, however, in the eighteenth and nineteenth centuries, it would be Protestant clergy who would initiate the Western world's first animal protection movement. And, by bringing an end to a suffocating regime of thought control that had kept Europe an intellectual backwater for a thousand years, the Renaissance and the Reformation together ushered in the Enlightenment, and the Enlightenment gave birth to the ideas that would inspire the modern animal rights movement.

6

Secular Offerings to a Savage God

With the exception of the Pythagoreans, and a few intellectuals like Plutarch and Porphyry who were influenced by them, the classical world had rejected Pythagoras' challenge to animal exploitation and accepted Aristotle's rebuttal. The triumph of Christianity in the fourth century ratified that choice, imposed it upon Europe by force, and extended it through the Middle Ages. Eventually, however, the Church's monopoly on European thought was loosened by the Renaissance (c.1400–c.1650) and the Reformation (1517–c.1600), and these, in turn, led to the Enlightenment (c.1650–1789), which finally returned freedom of thought to Europe.

The conventional wisdom of historians has it that the Renaissance replaced the theocentric world of the Middle Ages with the anthropocentric world that endures to the present day. Or, to put it another way: during the Renaissance, we stopped obsessing on God and began obsessing on ourselves. This attitude was summed up by the English Enlightenment poet Alexander Pope, who said, in his *Essay on Man* (1734):

Know then thyself; presume not God to scan.
The proper study of mankind is man.

No one exemplifies this outlook better than Leonardo da Vinci (1452–1519), one of the foremost painters, sculptors, and engineers in an era that excelled in painting, sculpture, and engineering. And yet, alone among his peers, Leonardo extended himself beyond the anthropocentrism that was the age's most salient feature. A lifelong vegetarian out of compassion for the suffering of animals, he sometimes purchased birds and set them free.[1]

While he never spoke out publicly against animal enslavement and slaughter, Leonardo's views were known to his contemporaries, and in his *Notebooks*, he expressed with great eloquence his distress at the suffering we inflict upon animals. "We make our life the death of others," he said, and "From countless numbers [of cows, pigs, sheep, and goats] will be taken away their little children and the throats of these shall be cut, and they shall be quartered most barbarously."[2]

Some historians refer to the Renaissance, Reformation, and Enlightenment as a "little axial age," but from the animals' point of view, the comparison is not deserved. The Axial Age included animals. The Renaissance, Reformation, and Enlightenment all but ignored them. In fact, the elevation of the search for knowledge to a position above all other virtues led to the creation of a new nightmare for animals: vivisection.

The Rise of Vivisection

The founder of Western medical science, Hippocrates of Cos (*c.*460–*c.*380 BCE), worked entirely by observing living human patients and performing autopsies on human beings who had died. He did not experiment on nonhuman animals, living or dead.[3] Insofar as we know, the first scientists to engage in vivisection were a school of physicians in Alexandria who experimented on both humans (usually condemned criminals) and animals (who were guilty only of falling into the clutches of humans) around the middle of the third century BCE.[4] A strong belief that the gap between humans and nonhuman animals was too great for humans to derive much benefit from studying other species kept vivisection from becoming widespread in the ancient world.

The great exception to this rule was Claudius Galenus of

Pergamum (130–200 CE), known to us as Galen, a court physician to the Roman Emperor Marcus Aurelius, who experimented on a wide variety of living animals in an effort to learn how the body is constructed, how it functions, and how disease progresses.[5] Following Plato, Galen believed that the world and everything in it was the work of a single creator, which commended him to later generations of Christians, and his enormous treatises on anatomy, physiology, and disease were the standard of knowledge until well into the Renaissance. In fact, when researchers found that their observations differed from Galen's (a common occurrence; Galen was often wrong), they generally assumed that they were mistaken and trusted Galen instead.

The medieval focus on otherworldly matters, combined with the belief that Galen had discovered everything there was to know about anatomy and physiology, meant that very little medical research was conducted in Europe during the Middle Ages, and most of that was in pharmacology, primarily herbalism and alchemy. With the Renaissance, however, things changed. The intense interest in anatomy that we see in Renaissance painting and sculpture was also expressed in science and medicine, as researchers began conducting experiments to expand the boundaries of our knowledge.

Much of the science and literature of the classical world had been lost to Europe since the collapse of the Roman Empire. More had been preserved in the Islamic world, which, from the eighth century until the sixteenth, represented the pinnacle of science and philosophy. Returning Crusaders brought this learning back to Europe— including previously unavailable works by Aristotle and Galen—where, in the hands of scholars like Roger Bacon (c.1214–1294), an English Franciscan monk who was a contemporary of Thomas Aquinas, it revolutionized European thought. In fact, it was this infusion of classical and Muslim learning from the Islamic world that created the Renaissance, and transformed Europe into the most advanced and powerful society of the seventeenth through the twentieth centuries.

Inspired by Aristotle and the work of Arab philosophers, Roger

Bacon is credited with creating the modern scientific method, based on empirical observation under carefully controlled conditions. And in the realms of anatomy and physiology, empirical observation meant dissection or vivisection. And since law, custom, and religious taboos made experiments on human beings, living or dead, all but impossible, researchers turned to nonhuman animals, who enjoyed the protection of neither church nor state.

The vivisection of animals was popularized by Andreas Vesalius (1514–1564), who made his reputation by refuting Galen's description of the heart. The University of Padua, where Vesalius taught, was soon the major European center for the study of anatomy and physiology. Among those who traveled to Padua to learn vivisection from the heirs of Vesalius was an English medical student named William Harvey (1578–1657). Galen had not realized that the blood circulates through the arteries and veins.[6] He thought that arteries contained air and the blood filling the veins did not circulate, but oscillated in a short back-and-forth motion, much like the tide. Blood, Galen believed, was continually being absorbed into the body's tissues to provide nourishment and energy, with new blood constantly generated to replace it. Back in England, Harvey cut open living, conscious animals—anesthetics had not yet been discovered—primarily dogs, cats, and rabbits, to demonstrate that the arteries carry blood, not air, and that the veins and arteries comprise a single closed system through which the blood circulates and recirculates continuously, with the heart serving as a pump.[7]

Although Muslim doctors had understood this for at least three hundred years,[8] in Europe it was a momentous discovery that tipped the balance in the debate between traditionalists who believed in the authority of Galen and upstart Baconites who advocated the experimental method. From Harvey forward, vivisection would spread relentlessly across Europe, until by the nineteenth century it had become the standard, universal method for investigating and teaching anatomy and physiology, with hundreds of thousands of animals, from frogs to primates, sacrificed every year on the altar of knowledge and human health.

God's Robots

The spread of vivisection created a problem for French philosopher, mathematician, and mercenary soldier René Descartes (1596–1650). But it was not the problem we might expect. Physiologists like Harvey, whom he admired, were demonstrating that animals were remarkably similar to human beings. But as a devout Catholic, Descartes believed that human beings were unique. How could the uniqueness, and the unique worth, of humanity be preserved in the face of Renaissance science?

In his *Discourse on Method*, published in 1637, Descartes fell back on an old argument to which he added a new twist. The mind, he noted, unlike the body, is immaterial; it is not subject to the laws of physics and chemistry, and thus it is entirely separate and distinct from the body. Bodies, he argued, can exist and function without minds, and minds can exist and function without bodies. As an example of a body that functions without a mind, he cited a mechanical clock, which can keep track of time as well as perform other functions—such as operating the complex moving *tableaux* that were a popular feature of Renaissance clocks—without being either intelligent or conscious. Such machines Descartes called "automatons."

Since death and decomposition take place in accordance with physical laws, they are themselves physical phenomena; therefore, mind is by definition immortal and survives the death of the body. There is nothing terribly original in this part of Descartes' argument. It is a variation on an ancient belief, espoused by many religions, that has become known to historians as "the ghost in the machine."

Descartes identified this "ghost" with the "rational soul" of Aristotle and Aquinas, which exists only in human beings. But unlike his predecessors, he made the rational soul the seat not only of abstract intelligence, but of sentience and consciousness as well. The "sensitive soul" that Aristotle and Aquinas had assigned to animals as the locus of sentience and practical intelligence, Descartes reduced to mere physical reflex that operated like the gears and rigging of a mechanical clock. To the potential objection that animals are far too complex and perform functions far too intricate to be automatons,

Descartes replied that if mere mortals can make a machine as mechan-
ically complex and functionally intricate as a Renaissance clock, surely
God could fashion machines that were infinitely more so.

Descartes summarized his position this way:

> These natural automata are the animals.... Thus my opinion
> is not so much cruel to animals as indulgent to men ... since
> it absolves them from the suspicion of crime when they eat
> or kill animals.[9]

In short, where Aristotle had attempted to justify the enslavement
and slaughter of animals by basing the entitlement to moral consideration on something other than sentience, Descartes pursued the
same goal by denying that animals are sentient.

A Few Rays of Enlightenment

The Enlightenment introduced the ideas that still govern Western society: freedom of inquiry and belief, government as a means to promote the welfare of the people, the primacy of the individual, and reason as the surest path to individual happiness and a benevolent, nurturing society. Although, like the Renaissance, the Enlightenment was strongly anthropocentric, a few of its leading lights applied these principles—at least in some degree—to animals.

"They Nail Him on a Table"

The early trailblazers in this new way of looking at society were a small group of French writers who became known, even in English, as the *philosophes*. Perhaps the foremost of these was the flippant social critic Voltaire (1694–1778). In his *Philosophical Dictionary* (1764), Voltaire directly rebutted Descartes' claim that animals are mere automatons upon which physiologists could experiment with moral impunity. His comments in the entry for "Animals" are worth quoting at length.

> It is such a shame and it is so shallow to say that animals are machines lacking consciousness and feeling, who simply act repetitively, and who are incapable of learning or improving themselves.

Is it because I can talk to you that you conclude that I have feelings, memories, and thoughts? Well then, I won't talk to you. You can watch me go into my house and search for a document. In obvious distress, I dash upstairs, hurry back downstairs, going from room to room until I suddenly remember that I had put it in my desk. And when I find it, I read it happily. You will conclude from this that I have experienced feelings of distress and happiness, and that I have memory and consciousness.

Now take the case of a dog who has lost his master. He searches the streets with mournful cries. Finally, he goes home, upset, anxious, and goes upstairs, downstairs, from room to room until he discovers the master that he loves in his study. The dog shows his happiness by yipping, jumping about, and rubbing against his master.

Barbarians seize this dog, who brings us such great friendship. They nail him on a table, and they dissect him alive to show you his mesenteric veins.[1] You see in him all the same sense organs that are in you. Tell me this, mechanist,[2] has nature provided animals with all the means of feeling in order that they won't have feelings? Do they have nerves for the purpose of not transmitting sensations to the brain? There is no way we can believe that nature has created such a senseless contradiction.[3]

The Social Contract

Another leading *philosophe*, Jean-Jacques Rousseau (1712–1778), advocated a vegetarian diet for children and women who were nursing, on the grounds that this was healthier for the child. He also believed that ingesting meat leads to cruel and aggressive behavior, apparently because of some inherent quality in the meat itself.[4] But although he quotes Plutarch at length on the cruelty inherent in animal flesh, and expresses revulsion for meat, his concern comes across more as squeamishness than compassion. Although you sometimes read that Rousseau was a vegetarian, he was not. Nor were any of the leading *philosophes*, although Denis Diderot—the moving spirit behind the *Encyclopedia* that was their most important manifesto—is reputed to have experimented briefly with a Pythagorean diet.[5]

Rousseau advocated kindness toward animals in these words describing the character of the fictional young pupil in his pedagogical novel *Emile*:

> Emile ... will never set two dogs to fight. He will never set a dog to chase a cat[6].... The sight of suffering makes him suffer, too; this is a natural feeling. It is one of the after effects of vanity that hardens a young man and makes him take a delight in seeing the torments of a living and feeling creature.[7]

But even so, Rousseau teaches his teen-age Emile to hunt as a way to keep his mind off sex. "I would not have the whole of Emile's youth spent in killing creatures," he tells us. "And I do not even profess to justify this cruel passion; it is enough for me that it serves to delay a more dangerous passion."[8] The idea that hunting distracts you from sex is a bizarre notion that was current from the classical world through the Renaissance. Renaissance essayist Michel de Montaigne subscribed to it, and suggested that the "ecstasy" of drawing down on the prey is so intense that it drives all other thoughts from your mind.[9] Perhaps, for some; but I hunted as a teen-age boy, and I can assure you that hunting did not keep my mind off sex. In fact, sex frequently took my mind off hunting. That Rousseau considered sex "a more dangerous passion" than killing suggests that animals were not very high on his moral priority list.

* * *

Rousseau's most influential contribution to Enlightenment thought was his elegant formulation of social contract theory. "Man is born free, and everywhere he is in chains," the ringing declaration that opens his book *The Social Contract*, became a motto of revolutions around the world. Originally conceived as a defense of the sovereignty of the people, social contract theory—or contractarian theory, as it is sometimes called—has been widely employed (although not by Rousseau himself) to defend human tyranny over everyone not of our species.

Stripped down to its basics, social contract theory works something like this. I want to kill you and steal your house, your car, and your money. But I am also afraid that you may kill me and steal my house, my car, and my money. So I go to you with a deal. "If you will respect my life and property, I will respect your life and property. This way, we can both live in safety and enjoy peace of mind." If you agree, then we have a contract, and each of us has certain rights that arise from that contract, namely the right not to be killed and robbed by the other.

When it is just you and I, this works fine. But even simple societies are too large and complex for this kind of individual contract to be anything other than an invitation to chaos, and so a third party enters the contractual arrangement: the state. Instead of contracting with each other, we all contract with the state to protect us from predatory neighbors and provide us with certain other forms of assistance (roads and airports, for example). In return for these benefits, we agree not to attack or rob our neighbors, to pay taxes, and to obey other rules established for the common good. Our rights as citizens arise from our participation in this contract. We agree to be bound by the contract not by signing a document, but by living in the society and enjoying its benefits—what is sometimes called "implied consent." People who violate the contract are assessed a penalty in the form of judicial punishment, which today is usually a fine or a prison term.

Since rights derive from participation in the contract, it can be argued that only participants in the contract have rights. Animals cannot even be made aware of the contract, much less abide by it; therefore, according to some social contract theorists, they have no rights; they may be used and abused however we please.

Contemporary English philosopher Roger Scruton supports hunting, fur farming, meat eating, and vivisection on the grounds that, "if animals have rights, then they have duties, too."[10] Since animals cannot fulfill these duties, according to Scruton, they have no rights.

This misuse of social contract theory was anticipated and refuted by Rousseau himself, who said in the Preface to his *Discourse on the Origin of Inequality*:

> [S]o long as [a person] does not resist the internal impulse of compassion, he will never hurt any other man, or even any sentient being except on those lawful occasions when his own preservation is concerned and he is obliged to give himself the preference. By this method also we put an end to the time-honored disputes concerning the participation of animals in natural law: for it is clear that, being destitute of intelligence and liberty [by "liberty," Rousseau means what later philosophers would call "autonomy," the ability to make independent decisions and act on them], they cannot recognize that law; as they partake, however, in some measure of our nature, in consequence of the sensibility with which they are endowed, they ought to partake of natural right; so that mankind is subjected to a kind of obligation even toward the brutes. It appears, in fact, that if I am bound to do no injury to my fellow creatures, this is less because they are rational than because they are sentient beings: and this quality, being common both to men and beasts, ought to entitle the latter at least to the privilege of not being wantonly ill-treated by the former.[11]

Rousseau allows that there are moral duties that fall outside the scope of the social contract, and that we owe these duties to animals, but precisely what they are, he does not tell us. Clearly, he thinks they are less than the duties we owe other human beings, and he leaves us with the impression that they are nothing more than protection from being "wantonly ill-treated," in other words, a disappointingly weak version of the Biblical Compromise.

At least Rousseau recognized, as some of his descendents do not, that the social contract is not the basis of morality; it is a way of organizing society and a mechanism for enforcing morality when people are inclined to act in immoral ways. The contract does not determine morality; morality determines—or ought to determine—the terms of the contract. Morality, in fact, arises from a far more profound source than any social compact, and it is applicable to a broader spectrum of behavior and a wider universe of beings than those encompassed by it. Morality arises from compassion for the suffering of others, and it excludes from its protection no being able to suffer.

This limitation of contract theory is also acknowledged by the twentieth century's most influential contractarian, Harvard political philosopher John Rawls. While Rawls believed that justice derives from the social contract, he recognized that morality as a whole does not. And so Rawls, like Rousseau, denies that contract theory provides a basis for denying ethical treatment to animals. He clearly believes that we owe animals some kind of duties, but exactly what they are and why we owe them is beyond the scope of contract theory, and he is no more willing to speculate about them than Rousseau.

> Last of all, we should recall here the limits of a theory of justice [contract theory]. Not only are many aspects of morality left aside, but no account is given of right conduct in regard to animals and the rest of nature. A conception of justice is but one part of a moral view.... *The capacity for feelings of pleasure and pain and for the forms of life of which animals are capable clearly imposes duties of compassion and humanity in their case.* I shall not attempt to explain these considered beliefs. They are outside the scope of the theory of justice, and it does not seem possible to extend the contract doctrine so as to include them in a natural way.[12]

Although they bowed politely in the direction of kindness to animals, the *philosophes*—with the exception of Voltaire—made little effort to promote their wellbeing. "Lip service" is the phrase that leaps to mind. By and large, like Rousseau, they regarded compassion for animals as one of the lesser virtues, to be practiced when it was convenient, and scuttled when it conflicted with human interests. And so it was left to the English Enlightenment—and to one English philosopher in particular—to lay the groundwork for the modern animal rights movement.

Can They Suffer?

Like their French counterparts, most British Enlightenment philosophers made soothing noises about kindness to animals and quickly moved on to more important matters. David Hume (1711–1776), for example, approved of our using animals for food, leather, and other human purposes, so long as in the process we favored them with "gentle usage," a remark that prompted Peter Singer to observe that:

> "Gentle usage" is, indeed, a phrase that nicely sums up the attitude that began to spread in this period: we were entitled to use animals, but we ought to do so gently.[13]

"Gentle usage" is also, of course, an apt description of the Biblical Compromise, which, once the Catholic Church's rejection of it could no longer be enforced on the larger society, quickly bounded to the forefront of European thinking about animals. And why not? It had everything going for it. It was taught in the Bible; it gave us a sense of virtue; and it allowed us to go on enjoying the fruits of slavery and slaughter.

The exception to this sugar-water approach to the suffering of animals was Jeremy Bentham (1748–1832), the founder of utilitarianism. Bentham effected a revolution in ethics, first by focusing on sentience as the source of entitlement to moral consideration, and second by emphasizing the results of an action rather than its motivation. Moral and immoral are very simple matters, Bentham said, and they are defined entirely by pleasure and pain/happiness and suffering, terms that he sometimes used interchangeably. A moral act is one that leads to happiness and an immoral act is one that causes suffering. Since a single act often affects many sentient beings and may cause happiness for some and suffering for others, the moral choice in any situation is the one that leads to the "greatest happiness for the greatest number." This requires that we compare the pleasure and pain of different individuals and try to balance, say, intense pain for two individuals against mild pleasure for two hundred, an operation that is sometimes referred to as "utilitarian calculus" or "utilitarian arithmetic." Since there is no way to do utilitarian calculus with any precision, it is here that the application of a simple principle begins to get complicated, and different schools of utilitarianism have different ways of approaching this problem, none of which need concern us here.

Two points are especially important for the application of Bentham's utilitarianism to our treatment of animals: First, there are no qualitative distinctions to be made among various types of pleasure and pain. Pleasure and pain may be more or less intense, but all pleasure of equal intensity and duration is to be given equal weight in the utilitarian calculus, and the same is true of pain. Intellectual pleasures are not to be valued over physical, nor sophisticated enjoyments over simple. As Bentham put it, "Quantity of pleasure being equal, pushpin is as good as poetry."[14] This means that the fact that our pleasures (or at least some of them) may be more intellectual and subtle than those of nonhuman animals does not entitle us to assign ourselves a higher value in the calculus.

The second point is that all beings who can experience pleasure and pain are said to have "interests," which is to say that they have an interest in experiencing pleasure and avoiding pain. And all beings with interests are entitled to have those interests given equal consideration in the workings of the utilitarian arithmetic. As another well-known dictum of Bentham's has it, "Each to count for one, and none for more than one." Thus, utilitarian ethics is absolutely egalitarian.

No sentient being counts for more in the moral equation than any other sentient being.

Bentham's most important work, *An Introduction to the Principles of Morals and Legislation*, published in 1789, contains the most portentous footnote in the history of philosophy. In it, Bentham explicitly includes animals in utilitarianism's moral universe. I shall quote it nearly *in toto*.

If the being eaten were all, there is very good reason why we should be suffered to eat such of them as we like to eat: we are the better for it and they are never the worse. They have none of those long-protracted anticipations of future misery which we have. The death which they suffer in our hands commonly is, and always may be, a speedier, and by that means a less painful one, than that which would await them in the inevitable course of nature. But is there any reason why we should be suffered to torment them? Not any that I can see.... The day *may* come, when the rest of animal creation may acquire those rights which never could have been withholden from them but by the hand of tyranny. The French have already discovered that the blackness of the skin is no reason why a human being should be abandoned without redress to the caprice of a tormentor. It may come one day to be recognized, that the number of legs, the villosity of the skin,[15] or the termination of the *os sacrum*, are reasons equally insufficient for abandoning a sensitive being to the same fate. What else is it that should trace the insuperable line? Is it the faculty of reason, or, perhaps, the faculty of discourse? But a full-grown horse or dog is beyond comparison a more rational, as well as a more conversable animal, than an infant of a day, or a week, or even a month old. But suppose the case were otherwise, what would it avail? the question is not, Can they *reason?* nor, Can they *talk*? but, Can they *suffer?*[16]

Bentham opens with a pernicious factual error that is a common-place even today—although why that should be the case I cannot for the life of me understand. Do people have so little experience with animals? Do they simply not pay attention? Or, to echo Ralph Ellison's insight, do they look at an animal and see their own precon-ceptions instead? The end of the footnote indicates that Bentham understood that animals are intelligent and communicative. So why does he assume, in common with a large segment of the human race, that they cannot anticipate "future miseries?"

My companion cats, who are used to being taken to the doctor in carriers, run and hide the moment a carrier makes an appearance. But in the doctor's office, once the exam is over, they hurry back into the carrier of their own accord. Clearly, they are anticipating both the future misery of a doctor's appointment and the future pleasure of returning home. Dogs who have been beaten with a stick will either cower and whimper or brace and snarl when someone approaches them with a stick.

There is some truth to Bentham's claim that animals in the wild often die a more painful and drawn-out death than they experience at our hands, but that hardly exculpates us for killing them to satisfy our appetites. After all, it is also true that we human beings often die a more painful and drawn-out death than we would experience if someone simply shot us. But that is no excuse for shooting us, espe-cially while we are still healthy. Once Bentham's factual error con-cerning animals' lack of a future sense is corrected, his defense of killing animals for food and convenience collapses.

Up until now, there is nothing remarkable in Bentham's footnote. He has simply been regurgitating commonplace speciesist cant. But when he moves from death to suffering, everything changes, and the sentences that follow are, to my mind, the most remarkable passage in the literature of the Enlightenment. In rapid-fire order, Bentham asserts that animals have "rights," describes our treatment of them as "tyranny," calls for the enactment of laws to shield them from our tyranny, and draws a moral equivalency between human slavery and the enslavement of animals. The world had seen nothing like it since Porphyry.

But Bentham is not finished. He caps his achievement by challenging Aristotle, the Stoics, Aquinas, Kant, and all of those who would deny rights to animals based on reason, language, self-consciousness, autonomy, or any other morally irrelevant factor. The fundamental principle of utilitarianism holds that morality is entirely a function of pleasure and pain; all other considerations are beside the point. Bentham applies this principle without flinching; he lets the chips fall where they may. And the utilitarian chips fall on the side of our having moral responsibilities to animals that are no different and no less important than our responsibilities to other human beings.

Jeremy Bentham had sounded the battle cry for animal rights—although no one would realize it for nearly two hundred years. While utilitarians debated "more important" issues such as whether we should strive to maximize pleasure or minimize pain—the utilitarian equivalent of "How many angels can dance on the head of a pin?"—Bentham's footnote drew little attention. Then in 1975, a young utilitarian philosopher named Peter Singer took up Bentham's call in a book that he called *Animal Liberation*. But that is a story for a later chapter.

The Categorical Imperative: No Animals Need Apply

The philosophy of the Enlightenment finds its culmination in the work of Immanuel Kant (1724–1804), who has joined Plato, Aristotle, Descartes, and a very few others in the ranks of those who have individually and dramatically changed the Western philosophical dialogue. The influence of his system of ethics is so pervasive that, even today, new ethical theories are often described according to their points of agreement and disagreement with Kant.

Kant regarded morality as a matter of immutable natural law, valid everywhere and in every situation, an absolute so absolute that not even God could change it. As intelligent beings with freedom of choice, we have a duty to obey this natural law, and moral behavior consists entirely in fulfilling this duty. Kant referred to this moral law as the "categorical imperative," by which he meant that it defines the principle according to which everyone everywhere should act at all times and in all circumstances. For different purposes, Kant stated the categorical imperative in three different ways. The statement that concerns us, commonly known as the "humanity formula," is this: "Act in such a way that you treat humanity, whether in your own person or in the person of any other, always at the same time as an end, never merely as a means."[17] Human beings, in Kant's view, are rational (capable of abstract thought), self-conscious (aware of themselves as distinct, continuing beings), and autonomous (able to make decisions for themselves and act upon them). These three qualities enable them to formulate and pursue goals for themselves as discrete, independent beings; therefore, they must always be treated as ends in themselves, never merely as a means to someone else's ends. As for animals, Kant believed that although they were able to suffer, they were not rational, self-conscious, or autonomous; therefore, they were suited only to serve as means by which others—human beings—could achieve their own ends.

Kant was perfectly aware of what this meant for nonhuman animals.

But as far as animals are concerned, we have no direct duties. Animals are not self-conscious and are there merely as a means to an end. That end is man. We can ask, "Why do animals exist?" But to ask, "Why does man exist?" is a meaningless question. Our duties toward animals are merely indirect duties toward humanity.... [Kindness to animals] helps to support us in our duties towards human beings, which are bounden duties.... Tender feelings toward animals develop humane feelings toward mankind.... Vivisectionists, who use living animals for their experiments, certainly act cruelly, although their aim is praiseworthy, and they can justify their cruelty, since animals must be regarded as man's instruments; but any such cruelty for sport cannot be justified.... Our duties toward animals, then, are indirect duties toward mankind.[18]

There are two obvious weak points in Kant's denial that we have direct moral duties to animals. The first is that he separates morality from sentience. The idea—popular with so many philosophers intent on excusing our crimes against nonhuman animals—that only beings who are rational, self-conscious, and/or autonomous are entitled to moral treatment is utterly without foundation. It can be asserted, but never demonstrated, either logically or experientially. Its charm lies entirely in its convenience for the human race. On the other hand, the idea that all sentient beings are entitled to moral treatment can be demonstrated by an appeal to the most fundamental experiences of all—fear and pain.

The second weak point in Kant's denial that we have direct moral duties to animals is that it depends on his claim that animals are not rational, self-conscious, or autonomous. Modern scientific investigation is demonstrating that at the very least the more complex animals, including all of the vertebrates and many invertebrates, are all three of those things. And when Kant's factual error is corrected, Kant's approach to ethics leads ineluctably to the conclusion that we do indeed have direct moral duties to animals, as demonstrated, for example, by modern animal-rights philosopher Tom Regan (see Chapter 16).

As Jeff Sebo observes in a paper published in the *Animal Liberation Philosophy and Policy Journal*, "Kant is not always the best interpreter of his own theory,"[19] a point with which few Kant scholars would disagree. Sebo points out that Kant was both a racist and a sexist, but that no one believes that Kantian ethical theory supports racism or sexism. "Rather," he concludes, "[w]e simply accept that we should distinguish 'Kant the man' from 'Kantianism the theory.' "[20] And that, Sebo suggests, is what we need to do with regard to Kant's low view of animals.

Overall, we are left with the impression that Kant never took the trouble to apply his genius to the question of animal suffering. He just took the majority opinion of philosophers since Aristotle and recast it in the terminology of his own system. In English, the *Lectures on Ethics* (which contains his views on animals) is 253 pages long;

only one and a half of those pages are devoted to our duties toward animals, not much more than he devotes to our moral duties toward demons and other disembodied spirits. Animals didn't matter to Kant, and he wasn't about to waste time or energy on them.

8

"Pain Is Pain"

The first genuine animal protection law that we know of in the Western world—enacted solely for the good of animals, without some ulterior motive such as the protection of property—was the so-called "Massachusetts Body of Liberties." Composed in 1641 by a Puritan clergyman, Nathaniel Ward, who had also trained in England as a lawyer, it was the first official code of law in New England. Two of its one hundred and twenty-three provisions apply to animals.

Of the Brute Creature

92. No man shall exercise any tyranny or cruelty toward any brute creature which is usually kept for man's use.

93. If any man shall have occasion to lead or drive chattel [livestock] from place to place that is far off, so that they be weary, or hungry, or fall sick, or lame, it shall be lawful to rest or refresh them, for competent time, in any open place that is not corn [any crop], meadow, or enclosed for some peculiar use.[1]

Nathaniel Ward, Puritan divine–*cum*–attorney-at-law, applied the Biblical Compromise as he found it in the Hebrew Scriptures to the Massachusetts colony. Liberty Number Ninety-Two echoes Proverbs

12:10, "A righteous man respects the soul of his animal," and establishes the two general principles of the Compromise. Animals may be enslaved and killed for human purposes, but they must be treated with as much kindness as is possible under the circumstances. Liberty Number Ninety-Three captures the spirit of Biblical rules requiring that livestock not be overworked and that they be given adequate food, water, and rest.

Intriguingly, the first person to apply the word "rights" to animals was not a secular Enlightenment philosopher, but a Christian mystic, Thomas Tryon (1634–1703), who anticipated Jeremy Bentham's use of the word by nearly a century.[2] A self-educated shepherd and hatter, Tryon was a devout Behmenist, a follower of the German Protestant mystic Jacob Boehme (1575–1624).[3] An ethical vegetarian and pacifist, Tryon was a prolific writer on subjects ranging from diet to theology. In *The Countryman's Companion*, published around 1683, Tryon put these moving words into the beak of a rooster:

> But tell us, O Man! We pray you tell us what injuries we have committed to forfeit? What law have we broken or what cause given you, whereby you can pretend [claim] a right to invade and violate our part, and our natural rights, and to assault and destroy us, as if we were the aggressors, and no better than thieves, robbers and murderers, fit to be extirpated out of the creation.[4]

In his *Autobiography*, Benjamin Franklin tells us that as a teenager he came across a book by Tryon and was inspired to adopt a vegetarian diet.[5] The legendary cheapskate seems to have been moved entirely by a desire to cut his food budget and improve his own health, and he does not mention the suffering of animals as playing any part in his decision. In any event, Franklin did not stick with it, and little more than a year later we find him eating meat again, an appetite he indulged for the rest of his life.[6]

The Sin of Cruelty

With one important exception (Lewis Gompertz, whom we shall meet in Chapter 9), the modern animal protection movement was begun by English Christians, largely but not exclusively Protestant clergy, who were intent on bringing the Biblical Compromise forward into the modern world.

Great social movements never have a single starting point. They are born in the confluence of many trends, and each putative beginning turns out to have antecedents. But if I had to pick a single event from which to date the modern animal welfare movement, it would be the publication in 1776 of *The Duty of Mercy and the Sin of Cruelty to Brute Animals* by Reverend Doctor Humphrey Primatt, an Anglican priest.[7] Primatt died young and wrote only one book, an impassioned appeal for the Biblical Compromise, which he states this way:

> And first, as it is a universal practice, it shall be taken for granted that man has a permission [from God] to eat the flesh of some animals, and consequently, to kill them for food or necessary use. But this permission cannot authorize us to put them to unnecessary pain or lingering death.[8]

Primatt's importance lies not so much in his advocacy of animal welfare—others before him had done that—but in the heartfelt passion of his plea and his firm grounding of it in the sentience of non-human animals, anticipating Jeremy Bentham by more than a decade. And, as we shall see in a moment, *The Duty of Mercy* led directly to the creation of the world's first organized animal protection movement.

> Superiority of rank or station exempts no creature from the sensibility of pain, nor does inferiority render the feelings thereof the less exquisite. Pain is pain, whether it be inflicted on man or on beast; and the creature that suffers it, whether man or beast, being sensible of the misery of it whilst it lasts,[9]

suffers *evil*; and the sufferance of evil, unmeritedly, unprovokedly, where no offence has been given, and no good end can possibly be answered by it, but merely to exhibit power or gratify malice, is cruelty and injustice in him that occasions it.[10]

Three of *The Duty of Mercy's* five chapters appear to be edited versions of sermons that Primatt had delivered from the pulpit.[11] These chapters draw extensively on the Bible, and are heavily footnoted with citations of chapter and verse. *The Duty of Mercy* is a deliberate and direct Christian refutation of the claim maintained from Paul through Augustine and Thomas Aquinas to Martin Luther that we have no direct moral duties to animals.

Primatt's argument builds to a conclusion that is profoundly and unabashedly Christian, and one of the most eloquent calls for compassion toward animals ever proclaimed.

> Make it your business, esteem it your duty, believe it to be the ground of your hope, and know that it is that which the Lord doth require of thee—*to do justly, to love mercy, and to walk humbly with thy God.* See that no brute of any kind, whether entrusted to thy care, or coming in thy way, suffer through thy neglect or abuse. Let no views of profit, no compliance with custom, and no fear of the ridicule of the world, ever tempt thee to the least act of cruelty or injustice to any creature whatsoever. But let this be your invariable rule, everywhere, and at all times, to *do unto others as, in their condition, you would be done unto.*[12]

Like his contemporary Jeremy Bentham, Primatt believed that animals live in an eternal present, with no memories of past joys, and no anticipation of the future. He also believed that they have no concept of death, and therefore, no fear of it.[13] Thus, for him as for Bentham, cruelty to animals consists entirely in causing them pain, while killing them painlessly is not cruel.

In Primatt's religious argument, as in Bentham's and Kant's secular arguments, this gross factual error is all that sustains the justification of killing animals for human use. Once we acknowledge the obvious, that animals anticipate the future and have a sense of a continuing self, just as we do, Bentham's greatest happiness principle, Kant's categorical imperative, and Primatt's Golden Rule no more allow the killing of animals for food than they allow the killing of humans for food. When the factual mistake is corrected, Primatt has made the case not for animal welfare, but for animal rights, and has made it most forcefully. After all, which of us, if we were in the situation of animals, completely dependent on the mercy of beings whose power over us is absolute, would want to have our lives cut short so our legs could be fried as drumsticks for someone's picnic lunch?

Most animal advocates writing specifically as Christians— Humphrey Primatt included—believed that they were thrusting with a sword they were forbidden to drive home. They felt commanded by God to advocate and practice kindness to the animals we exploit. But they felt equally commanded by God not to go beyond this incidental kindness by trying to eradicate any cause of animal suffering that also brought with it benefits to humans. And so, except for the occasional Thomas Tryon, Christian animal advocates replicated the Bible's half-heartedness and inconsistency. This bondage to the Bible is why the animal protection movement in the modern world, unlike its ancient antecedents, began as animal welfare rather than animal rights.

The Compromise Crosses the Ocean

On the west bank of the Atlantic, Humphrey Primatt's call was taken up by Herman Daggett, a Presbyterian minister, Christian educator, and author, in language that suggests he may have been familiar with *The Duty of Mercy*. In 1791, Daggett delivered a lecture at Providence College entitled "The Rights of Animals: An Oration,"[14] which—apart from the Massachusetts Body of Liberties—is the earliest call for animal protection in America that I am aware of.

While acknowledging that God has given us the right to "take away their lives, or deprive them of their privileges, without the imputation of blame," in order to eat their flesh or when they interfere with our way of life, Daggett argues forcefully against harming animals in any other circumstance:

> That they are sensible [sentient] beings, and capable of happiness, none can doubt: That their sensibility of corporeal pleasure and pain is less than ours, none can prove. And that there is any kind of reason, why they should not be regarded with proportionable tenderness, we cannot conceive.... [L]et us call into view a rule of judging, instituted by a divine Philanthropist, and oracle of wisdom, in the days of Julius (Tiberius) Caesar. 'That we do unto others as we would have them do unto us'; i.e. in a change of circumstances. This is a maxim that approves itself to the reason and conscience of every man.... And it must extend to all sensible beings, with whom we have any dealings, and in whose situation we are capable of imagining ourselves to be.... Let this rule, therefore, be faithfully applied, in every case, and cruelty to animals would no longer be indulged.[15]

In America, as in the mother country, the animal welfare movement would arise in a society that had been prepared for it by Protestant clergy applying principles that they found in the Bible.

A Footnote to History: Kindness for the Sake of Cruelty

The first animal protection laws in modern Europe were enacted in 1635 by the English military governor of Ireland, Thomas Wentworth, First Earl of Strafford. Strafford's laws forbade pulling the wool off sheep and tying plows to horses' tails. As Strafford's life gives no other evidence of concern for the suffering of animals—or anyone else, for that matter—we have to look for some other motive, and, in fact, we do not have to look far. Strafford was a Celtophobic tyrant whose administration was dedicated to depriving the Irish of their national customs and character and assuring their subservience to England. Therefore, we may presume that the real motive behind these laws was not to protect animals from abuse, but to force the Irish to farm in the English style.[16] Strafford was later beheaded for trying to subvert the power of Parliament and return Great Britain to absolute monarchy.

9

"Harassing the Lower Orders"

I n England during the 1700s, two forces came together to transform, almost overnight, an agricultural society that had hardly changed since the Norman Conquest. First, the development of overseas markets and the creation of mass production, made possible by the steam engine, enabled manufacturing and finance to replace farming as the best means to accumulate wealth. Second, the seizure of public farming and grazing land by large private landowners—a process known as enclosure—uprooted hundreds of thousands of yeoman farmers and peasants, plunging them into sudden and unfamiliar penury, and sluicing them into cities like London, Liverpool, and Manchester in search of work in the new manufacturing industries.

A new class of industrialists and financiers, whose wealth was not based on land—and whose interests were different from those of the aristocracy and landed gentry—emerged to create a new center of power that often saw this "middle class," as it came to be known, challenging the policies and prerogatives of Britain's traditional rulers. At the same time, the rural farmers, peasants, tradespeople, and merchants whose livelihoods had been destroyed by industrialization and enclosure found themselves living in squalor in tenement slums rife with disease, alcohol, and violence. Several families were often crammed into a single room—men, women, and children together because they had no money for larger quarters. Hunger was a way of life. Poverty, child labor, and sixteen-hour days put education out of the reach of most children of the new urban poor.

Wrenched from the countryside where their forbears had lived for generations, adrift in the proletarian ghettos of bloated cities, their extended families shattered, growing up illiterate, and forced to live and die in abject and hopeless poverty, it is small wonder that the English working classes developed some fairly disagreeable habits. Alcoholism, brawling, street crime, domestic violence, prostitution, and language and manners that offended the sensibilities of the comfortable were commonplace.

Times of traumatic social dislocation are often the occasion for outbreaks of religious fervor, and England during the Georgian and Victorian eras was no exception.[1] Here, it took the form of evangelicalism, both within the Church of England and in the so-called "nonconformist" churches that were growing in popularity among the middle and lower classes, such as the Baptist and Methodist denominations.

Just as in America today, evangelicals in Georgian and Victorian England insisted on seeing the problems of society in terms of morality, and morality in terms of personal behavior. The idea that the immoral behavior of individuals might be provoked by the far more immoral behavior of political and economic institutions was alien to them. If people were poor or unemployed, it was because they were lazy and parasitic, not because there were more workers than jobs and industry paid starvation wages. If children were illiterate, it was because their mothers were off drinking and whoring when they should be staying home and tending to their children, not because they could not afford to go to school. If the poor were sick, it was not because they were undernourished and could not pay for decent health care, and there was no public sanitation in their neighborhoods; it was because of their dissolute life style. If the poor sometimes picked pockets and shoplifted, it was not because they were desperate and had no other means to feed themselves and their families, it was because they were immoral and given to sin. If they brawled, it was not because they were carrying a heavier burden than they could bear, it was because they drank. And if they drank, it was not to escape the wretchedness and hopelessness of their lives; it was because they were weak and wicked.

It was a classic case of "blame the victim." The greedy, rapacious behavior of the rich—especially the industrialists and their political allies—kept the working classes mired in illiteracy and destitution. But the social reformers, inspired by evangelical Christianity, insisted on seeing the plight of the poor as the result of their lack of Christian "manners" rather than the predatory nature of unregulated capitalism. And so, England's social reformers insisted on reforming the poor and not the rich. They expended enormous amounts of time, energy, and money on campaigns to persuade the poor to stop drinking, stop beating their wives and children, stop stealing, brawling, and cursing, and start attending chapel regularly, where they would find the spiritual strength to mend their ways. And while the reformers often engaged in charitable relief projects to provide food, clothing, and medicine for the objects of their attentions, there was also a strong concern that too much charity would make the poor dependent and destroy whatever initiative, pride, and self-reliance they might have. Despite ample evidence to the contrary, the reformers continued to believe that if the poor reformed their behavior, they would all find well-paying jobs and live happily ever after. Social welfare programs, they believed, would make the problem worse, not better. And so the wealthy, the churches, and the government lectured and preached at the poor, instead of helping them.

Lewis Gompertz, a Jewish campaigner for slaves, women, the poor, and animals, recognized this aspect of his evangelical comrades' moral fervor. The language may have a bit of an old fashioned flavor, but Gompertz' condemnation of blaming the victim and his recognition that an individual's character flaws can be caused by his social disabilities—seem to come straight out of Lyndon Johnson's Great Society:

> [I]t is a very injurious, though a prevalent mode of reasoning, where virtue and happiness are invariably linked

together, and vice and misery [poverty].... This appears indeed a shrewd and harsh method of stopping the mouth of complaint, and of forcing back the virus of a suffering object ... upon its own wounds. It has frequently been asserted by authors...that "no man is miserable [poor] but by his own fault." But what good purpose this slander on the unfortunate can accomplish, is difficult to discover, as is also how the idea can appear correct. And even in cases where it *may* be his *fault*, what is *fault* but *infirmity*?[2]

Unlike Gompertz, the majority of the animal advocates that we will meet in this and the following chapter—Richard Martin, Thomas Erskine, Arthur Broome, T. Fowell Buxton—saw the issue of cruelty to animals as a facet of their campaign to help the poor by reforming their morals. For them, the Biblical Compromise was primarily a matter of morality rather than compassion. The distinction here is subtle, and the two elements overlap, but placing so much emphasis on the morals of the perpetrators made it easy to campaign only against those whose morals were known to be lax, while failing to recognize the crimes of those who were held up as models of Christian rectitude.

Protecting the Pleasures of the Rich

Among the titled aristocracy and landed gentry, animal cruelty as amusement took the form of "hunting" (*i.e.*, hunting in which the killing is done by dogs, usually against foxes, deer, or small game) and "shooting" (hunting in which the killing is done by the hunter, usually against birds). Hunting and shooting were ancient and cherished traditions that the aristocracy and landed gentry held sacrosanct. They were off-limits to reformers, and the reformers were more than willing to behave with the discretion and tact that were expected of Christian English gentlemen.

The cruel pastimes that were most popular with the working classes were animal fighting—usually roosters or dogs—and baiting, in which an unfortunate animal—a bear, if one was available, but more often a bull—was chained to a tree or pole, and dogs were set on him while onlookers took bets on things like how many dogs would die before they killed the bull.

In the ancient world, the animal protection debate had been waged over religious sacrifice and meat eating, practices which generally cut across class lines, and were actually more the province of the rich than the poor. But in early nineteenth-century England, the debate was most often triggered by the cruelties indulged in by the poor, and scorned by the rich as "vile" and "vulgar." It was not until the late twentieth century that the cruel amusements of the rich came under serious attack. In fact, until Frances Power Cobbe launched her campaign against vivisection in 1863, animal welfare was a minor skirmish in the class struggle that was transforming Britain from an agricultural oligarchy into an industrial democracy. Only a few lonely individuals, most of whom were not Christians—such as the atheists Percy and Mary Shelley, and the Jew Lewis Gompertz—were unbiased by this class warfare, calling for an end to all forms of animal enslavement and slaughter. Otherwise, animals were very much pawns in a game being played by humans.

The Victorian Revolution

Coinciding with these traumatic social changes during the late Georgian and the Victorian eras was an equally dramatic change in the way people viewed animals. Concern for the wellbeing of animals had been widespread in ancient India and Israel, and had attracted philosophers and mystics in the Greco-Roman world, although it made little, if any, headway in Classical society at large. But from the triumph of Christianity until the Reformation, thoughts of animal welfare all but vanished from the West, although the Biblical Compromise remained strong in the Islamic world and in Judaism. The Reformation and Enlightenment brought the Compromise to the center of Western thinking about animals, but it was not until late in the eighteenth century that this concern began to spread beyond philosophers and religious thinkers.

The beginning of the nineteenth century saw the development in England of the world's first broad popular movements for animal protection. Historians looking at this phenomenon generally ascribe it to what they like to call a "sentimentalization" of animals. Since "sentimentality" is generally considered to be a false, or at least excessive emotion, the implication is that the Victorian concern for animals was some sort of aberration that needs to be accounted for by sociological or psychological factors.

Numerous theories have been offered; two of the most popular are displacement and the "humanization" of pets. The displacement theory is based on the fact that middle-class Victorians suddenly found themselves face-to-face with visible, massive, abject poverty in the industrial cities, an experience that England's prosperous classes had been largely spared until now. They felt a natural sympathy for the plight of the poor, but believed they could do little about it, and so they assuaged their consciences by transferring their sympathy to nonhuman animals. There are, I think, several things wrong with this theory. First, in the face of intransigence from both the upper and lower classes, Victorian campaigners were not able to do much about animal suffering either, making animal welfare a singularly ineffective conscience-salver. Second, many of the leaders in the campaign against animal cruelty were also leaders in the campaigns against human slavery and the oppression of women, and on behalf of the poor, suggesting that what we are seeing is not displacement, but a broad, inclusive compassion for all who suffer. Finally, the displacement theory presumes that human beings are inherently more worthy of compassion and protection than animals, and hence it is based on a speciesist bias.

It is often said that the Victorian era saw the beginning of animals serving as companions for human beings. But this is not strictly true. The ruling classes have always kept companion animals, and farmers and peasants have always enjoyed companionship with their animals, even though the animals were kept primarily for their utility. With the growth of an urban middle class in Victorian England, however, there was for the first time a large number of people who had little opportunity for close companionship with animals. I believe that our desire for friendship with other species of sentient beings is as deep and natural as our desire for friendship with other human beings, and so in the Victorian Age, the keeping of companion animals— "pets"—became a widespread phenomenon among the classes who shaped public opinion and policy.

Since neither the lives, the prosperity, nor the dinners of companion animal–guardians depended on the enslavement and slaughter of their animals, Victorians were freed to acknowledge and act upon their natural, universal feelings of empathy and sympathy for animals.

The notion that animals lack the characteristics to make them satisfying companions for human beings, and that we can enjoy friendship with them only by imaginatively endowing them with traits that in reality belong only to human beings, is a speciesist bias that is contrary to easily observed fact. The Victorians did not "humanize" animals. They recognized—even if in an incomplete and somewhat muddled way—that the traits which bind all species of sentient beings together are more extensive and important than the traits that isolate one species from another. Once the conflicts of interests that impeded these feelings from being acknowledged and expressed were removed, natural compassion could rise to the fore. We will see this process take another great step forward in the latter half of the twentieth century, when the end of human dependence on animal labor clears the way for the creation of the modern animal rights movement.

(A Few) Animals Come to Westminster

The first animal protection bill ever debated by a legislature was a proposed ban on bull-baiting introduced before the House of Commons on April 18, 1800, by a Scottish Member of Parliament named William Johnstone Pulteney. Pulteney's bill was opposed by no less a figure than George Canning, who would go on to become Foreign Secretary during the Napoleonic Wars and even, for a brief period before his death, Prime Minister. Canning called it the "most absurd bill" ever introduced in the House of Commons, and claimed that bull-baiting made Britain a stronger country by giving "an athletic, vigorous tone to the character of the class engaged in it."[3] Most likely, Canning hoped that as long as the lower classes could vent their frustrations on animals, they wouldn't vent them on the upper classes. Pulteney argued passionately for his bill, but on April 24, 1800 it was defeated by two votes, forty-three to forty-one.[4]

By focusing on animals in sport and entertainment, Pulteney's bill had provoked a marriage of convenience between the upper and lower classes that blocked its passage. Sir Thomas Erskine (1750–1823), a famous and flamboyant Edinburgh lawyer, tried to avoid this roadblock by targeting farmed animals.

One of the leading lights of British political life, Lord Erskine was at the height of his power in 1809 when he introduced in the House of Lords a bill making it illegal to beat a horse, donkey, ox, sheep, or pig (a list that pointedly omitted bulls and bears). Hoping to gain support among the upper classes, he proposed to prosecute only the person who actually committed the abuse, usually a poor employee, while ignoring the person of wealth who was the animal's owner and the offender's employer.

But to his credit, Erskine's purpose went deeper than outlawing a specific form of cruelty. For thirty years, he had been a close friend of Jeremy Bentham, and he shared Bentham's view that animals should have legal rights. As he said in a speech to the House of Lords:

> Animals are considered as property only. To destroy or abuse them, from malice to the proprietor, or with an intention injurious to his interest in them, is criminal, but the animals themselves are without protection; the law regards them not substantively; they have no rights.... [It is] that defect in the law which I seek to remedy.[5]

Thanks to Erskine's sponsorship, the bill passed the House of Lords with no great difficulty. But when it reached the Commons, William Windham, who had joined Canning in his opposition to Pulteney's bill nine years earlier, turned Erskine's class-warfare strategy against him by pointing out that his bill would convict employees but not their employers, and would impose a crippling fine on a poor tenant farmer who whipped a recalcitrant plow horse, but would ignore a wealthy landowner who ran his horse to death during a fox hunt.

> If the bill were passed, said Windham, Members would show themselves "the most hardened and unblushing hypocrites that ever shocked the feelings of mankind. The bill ought to be entitled, not 'A Bill for preventing cruelty to animals,' but 'A Bill for harassing and oppressing certain classes among the lower orders of the people.'"[6]

The charge of class warfare worked, in part because it was by no means entirely false. Where Pulteney's bill had failed by two votes, Erskine's failed by ten. Needless to say, Windham's concern for the "lower orders" was nothing more than demagoguery. He would have been every bit as opposed to a cruelty bill that treated the upper and lower classes equally; he would just have had to think up a new excuse for his opposition.

From Pulteney and Erskine, the baton passed to one of the most colorful characters in the history of English politics, "Humanity Dick" Martin. Born into an ancient landowning family in County Galway, Ireland, Richard Martin (1754–1834) was an affable, lovable rogue with a heart of gold and a gunpowder temper. His other nickname was "Trigger Dick," after his fondness for dueling. Although his parents were Catholic, they raised their only son Protestant so that when he grew up he could enter the Irish Parliament (for which only Protestants were eligible) and work for Catholic emancipation.

In 1777, Richard Martin entered the Irish Parliament, just as his parents had planned, and remained there until 1800, when it was dissolved into the British House of Commons in the wake of the Irish insurrection of 1798. He served in the Commons until 1826, when he was removed on a charge of election fraud. Losing his seat stripped him of parliamentary immunity from arrest, and since he was wanted on bad debt charges—although he still owned land, he had given away his liquid assets to various charitable causes—he skipped to France, where he died in 1834.

As a young man at Cambridge, Martin had become friends with George, Prince of Wales, heir apparent to the British crown, and the two remained close after the Prince ascended the throne as King George IV. Because of Martin's generosity and his tireless work on behalf of Catholics, slaves, the poor, and animals, his friend the king took to calling him "Humanity Dick," and when the popular press picked it up, the nickname stuck.

One of Richard Martin's first votes in the British Commons had been in support of William Pulteney's baiting law. Nine years later, he had voted for Lord Erskine's cruelty law. Then in 1821, Martin introduced an anti-cruelty bill of his own, one that forbade "wantonly beating, abusing, or ill treating" large farm animals, including horses, sheep, cattle, mules, and donkeys. The bill passed the Commons by a vote of forty-eight to sixteen, the first animal protection bill to do so, but this time, despite the support of Erskine, it failed in the House of Lords.

But nobody had ever called Humanity Dick Martin a quitter, and the following year, he introduced his bill again. This time it passed both Houses, and on July 22, 1822, "An Act to Prevent the Cruel and Improper Treatment of Cattle," or "Martin's Act," as it came to be known, was given royal assent by its sponsor's good friend, King George IV. For Lord Erskine, the passage of Martin's Act would be the last hurrah; he died in 1823.[7]

Martin's Act provided that any citizen could bring charges before a local magistrate, a fact which essentially placed cruelty prosecutions in the hands of the public and eventually led to the peculiar circumstance of private humane societies being chartered by legislatures to make arrests and bring criminal charges in cases of animal cruelty, a practice that still endures in much of the world.

A lawyer, Martin brought the first charges under his own law, against a London street vendor named Bill Burns whom he accused of beating his donkey. Determined not to lose, Martin insisted on bringing the donkey into court so the judge could see the animal's scars. This led to jokes in newspapers and music-halls, created the legend that Humanity Dick had brought a donkey into court to testify, and earned Bill Burns the ignominy of being the first person ever convicted of violating the rights of a nonhuman animal.

Until he left the House of Commons, Richard Martin continued introducing new bills that would ban bull- and bear-baiting. In one House or the other, they were all defeated. By the sheer force of Martin's personality and Erskine's influence, the two friends had achieved what no one had thought possible. Martin's Act provided few enough animals with little enough legal protection, but it was still more protection at the bar of justice than animals had seen since the days of Ashoka. But now Erskine was dead, and Martin met his match in the House of Commons' newest rising star, the future Prime Minister Robert Peel, a foxhunter of legendary stature who cut his oratorical teeth defending cruelty to animals.[8]

Societies for the Prevention of Some Cruelties to Some Animals by Some People

Inspired by Humphrey Primatt's *The Duty of Mercy and the Sin of Cruelty to Brute Animals*, Reverend Arthur Broome (*c.*1782–1837), vicar of the Church of Saint Mary in London, came to see the protection of animals as his Christian duty. The passage of Martin's Act, with its reliance on the public for enforcement, showed him how this duty could be discharged. On June 16, 1824, Reverend Broome assembled a group of Britain's leading social reformers, including Richard Martin, to form an organization that would investigate and prosecute animal cruelty cases. Broome's minutes of that first meeting tell us that:

> At a meeting of the Society instituted for the purpose of preventing cruelty to animals, on the 16th day of June 1824, at

Old Slaughter's Coffee House, St. Martin's Lane: T F Buxton
Esqr, MP, in the Chair,

It was resolved:
That a committee be appointed to superintend the
Publication of Tracts, Sermons, and similar modes of influ-
encing public opinion ...

Resolved also:
That a Committee be appointed to adopt measures for
Inspecting the Markets and Streets of the Metropolis, the
Slaughter Houses, the conduct of Coachmen, etc.- etc.... [9]

Thus was born the world's first animal protection organization,
the Society for the Prevention of Cruelty to Animals—which in 1840
would receive the patronage of Queen Victoria and be rechristened
the Royal Society for the Prevention of Cruelty to Animals.[10] Among
the "tracts, sermons, and similar modes of influencing public opinion" that the Society published (or reissued) in its early years were
Humphrey Primatt's *The Duty of Mercy* and Lord Erskine's speech to
the House of Lords defending his 1809 anti-cruelty bill. The "measures for inspecting the markets and streets of the metropolis," etc.,
were, of course, for the purpose of enforcing Martin's Act.

In its early years, the RSPCA was both an evangelical organization
that was part and parcel of the Christian social reform movement,
and a rigidly conservative body that never strayed far from its upper-
crust origins. Its founding members were prominent evangelical cler-
gymen, lawyers, members of Parliament, a city councilman, and a
doctor. This was the flower of society, not the grassroots, and they
pursued animal welfare as it was conceived by the wealthy and powerful, which meant that the cruelties of the upper classes were exempt
from scrutiny. Richard Martin was an avid bird hunter, had been
when he served in the Commons and continued to be afterward.
Fowell Buxton, the lawyer and Member of Parliament who chaired
the first meeting at Old Slaughter's Coffee House, was a lifelong

shooter, who once killed five hundred birds in a single week to win a bet.[11] It is no wonder that the Society did not condemn hunting or shooting any more than it condemned meat eating. The only known vegetarian among the founders was Lewis Gompertz, who, being Jewish, was also the only founder who was not a Christian, a circumstance that would soon lead to a shameful incident of bigotry by the Society.

Quickly realizing that the Committee Members, all being men of affairs, had no time to roam the city in search of cruelty cases to prosecute, the board hired an "inspector"—or, as we would say today, a "humane officer"—to do that work. The cases were so numerous that soon there was a full-fledged investigating staff. In 1832, the first year the Society kept statistics, they successfully prosecuted 181 cases of animal cruelty, or about one every other day.[12] In 1838, one of their inspectors, James Piper, became the first person in history known to have given his life for animal protection, when he was beaten to death by a gang of cockfighters in Middlesex.[13] But office space, inspectors, and prosecutions all cost money, and:

> By January 1826, the Society was nearly £300 in debt....
> Worse was to come. Arthur Broome—being responsible for
> the debts of the Society—was thrown into prison in January
> 1826.... Lewis Gompertz ... and a few friends [including
> Richard Martin, who was himself being pursued by financial
> disaster] hastily collected enough money to pay the debts,
> and Mr. Broome was released.[14]

But as the Society began to attract favorable publicity, it also attracted donors, and by the time it received the patronage of Queen Victoria in 1840, it was respectably in the black.

The First Animal Rights Activist
In his day, Lewis Gompertz (1779–1865) was a highly regarded inventor, best known for a device that forms part of a lathe, called an

"expanding chuck." His great passion, however, was animal rights. In 1824, the same year that he helped found the SPCA, he published *Moral Inquiries on the Situation of Man and of Brutes*, in which he broke free of the Biblical Compromise by advocating a vegan diet and overcame the British Blind Spot by opposing hunting and shooting. Not wanting to benefit in any way from the enslavement and suffering of animals, Gompertz refused to travel by horse or mule-drawn conveyance, which meant that everywhere he went in London, he walked. (The first London subway line opened in 1863, two years before his death.) Beyond London, he was limited to places within walking distance of a railway station. It is entirely reasonable to call Lewis Gompertz the first modern animal rights activist. And he was a living rebuke to the meat-eating, hunting, shooting, and carriage-riding gentlemen who ran the SPCA, a fact that would soon cause him difficulties.

Gompertz became Secretary—which is to say, the day-to-day manager—of the SPCA in 1828, when Arthur Broome either resigned or was removed for reasons that are not clear, but probably related to his health and finances. Richard Ryder speculates that he may have been depressed following his imprisonment. If he wasn't, he was probably depressed over the constant infighting that seems to have been a permanent feature of life on the governing board.

One particularly vicious skirmish took place in 1832. Ryder describes it this way:

> [Lewis Gompertz] fell out with two other members of the committee, Dr. John Fenner and the Reverend Thomas Greenwood. Fenner and Greenwood attacked Gompertz on three grounds: first, because he used "informers" (i.e. the society's inspectors) to prosecute offenders [using informers was considered ungentlemanly behavior]; secondly for his professed "Pythagoreanism," by which was meant his advocacy of a vegetarian diet; and thirdly, because he was not a Christian. In the summer of 1832, the SPCA committee resolved to suspend the inspectorate [it did not stay sus-

pended for long] and insisted that "the proceedings of this Society are entirely based on the Christian Faith and Christian Principles."[15]

The SPCA was run by Christian gentlemen with respectable positions in British society—and, for all practical purposes, this was Victorian society in its least attractive aspects: priggish, sanctimonious, hypocritical—even if its eponymous monarch was still five years from the throne. They were not about to sit quietly by and let a Jew—and a Jew who was flirting with the pagan cult of Pythagoreanism, at that—lecture them on the immorality of their favorite foods and pastimes.

Gompertz either resigned or was removed from the SPCA—it seems to have been a "you can't fire me, I quit," kind of affair—and founded his own organization, the Animal's Friend Society, where he began publishing the world's first animal protection periodical, called *The Animal's Friend, or the Progress of Humanity.* The Animal's Friend Society, which Gompertz continued to operate until poor health forced his retirement in 1848, was, as we might expect, more aggressive than the RSPCA, and was instrumental in getting a nationwide ban on baiting and animal fighting enacted in 1835.

10

The Great Meddler

The son of a socially prominent New York family, Henry Bergh (1813–1888) spent his early life on a grand tour of Europe, idling in the salons of the aristocratic and the artistic. While he was dallying in Europe, President Lincoln appointed him First Secretary of the American Legation in St. Petersburg, a job for which he was eminently qualified because it consisted mainly in schmoozing Russian courtiers. It was in the Czarist capital that Henry Bergh found his calling, not as a diplomat, but as an advocate for the powerless.

The catalyst was the sight of horse-cart drivers mercilessly beating their overloaded animals. Legend has it that:

> One day in 1863, a St. Petersburg droshky driver was merrily lashing his horse in the Russian manner. Suddenly a smart carriage pulled alongside and Bergh, who was First Secretary of the U. S. Legation, bellowed to his coachman, "Tell that fellow to stop!" Obediently the droshky driver dropped his whip. First Secretary Bergh nodded approval and set out in pursuit of other inhumane drivers.[1]

It is not certain that this story is literally true, as Henry Bergh was a larger-than-life figure who proved to be a magnet for legends. It is, however, entirely in character, as there are numerous well-attested stories of Bergh accosting cart and carriage drivers on the streets of

New York—where more than 200,000 draft horses labored every day[2]—a habit that earned him the nickname "the great meddler."

When southerner Andrew Johnson, who had succeeded Lincoln in the presidency, declined to reappoint the New York aristocrat, Bergh returned home by way of London, where he spent several weeks consulting with Lord Harrowby, who was then president of the RSPCA. On February 8, 1866, he held a meeting in New York's Clinton Hall, an old opera house that had been converted into a library, where he addressed a large gathering of the city's movers and shakers. "This is a matter purely of conscience," he told his audience. "It has no perplexing side issues. [He meant that animal cruelty is not a partisan political issue.] It is a moral question in all its aspects."[3]

New York already had an animal cruelty statute, passed in 1828, as had several other states, including Massachusetts (1835), Connecticut (1838), and Wisconsin (1838),[4] but these laws had no specific enforcement mechanism, and police and prosecutors were reluctant to devote scarce time and resources to acts that most of them did not consider a crime in the first place. Recognizing this, Henry Bergh looked to the British model, and lobbied the New York state legislature for a double-barreled approach: the creation of an animal protection society chartered by the state, and an animal cruelty law that granted enforcement powers to this new organization.

Since Bergh had had the foresight—and the clout—to line up support from a wide spectrum of New York's leadership community, his proposals sailed through the legislature in record time. On April 10, 1866, the charter was approved, and on April 19, an animal protection statute was enacted that granted the newly-minted American Society for the Prevention of Cruelty to Animals the authority to enforce it.[5]

From that point on, Henry Bergh was a human dynamo. He spent more time in slaughterhouses and on the streets of New York than in the office. He campaigned against live pigeon shoots, which were popular among upper-class "sporting men." In 1867, he created the first ambulance for draft horses who went down in the street. In 1875, he installed a newly-invented sling that allowed horses to be lifted into and out of the ambulance more easily and without causing them additional pain. He created a network of water fountains around Manhattan so that the horses who pulled the carriages, wagons, and streetcars could relieve their thirst. He even leaped from a skylight into a dog-fighting pit to arrest the proprietors.[6]

But most of all, Henry Bergh set an example that moved humans all across the country to show at least a bit of mercy to their nonhuman slaves. On April 27, 1866, Colonel M. Richards Muckle (pronounced muck-lay), a Philadelphia businessman, published a notice in the *Philadelphia Evening Bulletin* that he was organizing a society in the City of Brotherly Love similar to the ASPCA. But his proposal stalled when he was unable to secure a charter from the legislature. In 1867, he joined forces with Caroline Earle White (1833–1916), a prominent Quaker feminist and peace activist who had been talking to Bergh about founding an SPCA in Philadelphia, and together they were able to obtain the needed charter. The Pennsylvania Society for the Prevention of Cruelty to Animals was born on June 21, 1867. In 1869, White, understandably unhappy with the subordinate role in which women were cast, created the Women's Branch of the PSPCA, of which she was the first president.[7]

In 1868, George Thorndike Angell (1823–1909), a Boston attorney and well-known philanthropist, read a newspaper article about a long-distance horse race (such races were popular in the nineteenth century) in which two horses named Empire State and Ivanhoe collapsed and died after being forced to run forty miles in two and a half hours, each with two riders on his back and without stopping for rest or water. Outraged, Angell wrote a letter to the editor of a Boston newspaper asking like-minded people to join him in opposing cruelty to animals. That was the beginning of the Massachusetts Society for the Prevention of Cruelty to Animals, now known as MSPCA-Angell.[8]

George Angell believed that animals—at this juncture his particular concern was horses—needed a book that would rouse public opinion against cruelty to animals the way *Uncle Tom's Cabin* had rallied opposition to slavery. When he read *Black Beauty*, by English author Anna Sewell (1820–1878), he thought he had found what he was seeking. Written for adults who owned, worked, or cared for horses, *Black Beauty* was an eloquent plea to treat horses with kindness and consideration for both their physical and emotional wellbeing. (That we now consider it a children's book shows how we devalue animals by treating their personhood as a fairy tale rather than a serious moral issue.) In 1890, Angell published the first American edition of *Black Beauty* and sent 216,000 copies free of charge to legislators, newspaper editors, educators, and other opinion leaders around the country. He subtitled his American edition, *The Uncle Tom's Cabin of the Horse*.[9]

Within a few years, SPCAs had been established in other large cities, and by mid-twentieth century, they were a ubiquitous—if long overdue—feature of American life.

A Window onto Slavery

In a society committed to covering animal slavery and slaughter in a cloak of invisibility, the activities of groups like the ASPCA are often the best windows we have onto the reality of animal slavery. If one of the ASPCA's first needs was for an ambulance for draft horses who had been overworked until they collapsed, we can conclude that working horses literally to death was a common practice; otherwise, given the plenitude of needs, the ambulance would have been lower on Henry Bergh's wish list. If the ASPCA had to install water fountains around Manhattan (followed by fountains in other boroughs), we can conclude that draft horses had to work long hours, in heat and cold, without a drink. If the Pennsylvania SPCA had to campaign for streetcar rails to be oiled to reduce friction and ease the horses' burden, and had to fight for a requirement that working horses be blanketed in winter,[10] we can conclude that draft horses were regularly worked without regard for their comfort, health, or safety. It was cheaper to work a horse until she literally fell in her harness and could not get up again, and then sell her for glue or soap, than it was to feed and care for her properly during her working life. Historian Diane Beers reports that:

> During the late nineteenth century, approximately twenty-five thousand streetcar horses died from overwork annually in the nation's largest cities. Typically, a driver would simply unhitch a dead animal and deposit the body along the curb.[11]

Draft horses that collapsed in harness but were still alive often met the same fate: dumped at the curb and left to die, uncared for, uncomforted, in the heat or the cold, the rain or the snow, with busy people bustling by with no time to spare a minute for a dying horse who had given her life for their convenience.

Horses and mules on small family farms fared better than horses in the city, but even they were sold for slaughter when they grew too old or sick to work.

When Is a Shelter Not a Shelter? When It's a Slaughterhouse.

The most controversial activity of the ASPCA—and eventually of SPCAs and Humane Societies around the country—began in 1894, six years after Bergh's death, when the Society took over the city of New York's "animal control" program—which had previously been handled by city workers—in the hope of improving the horrific conditions that prevailed in the animal shelters of the day. Under the terms of their contract with the city, the ASPCA would "collect" homeless dogs and cats, take them to shelters which the Society would maintain, and either adopt them out or kill them. The city financed this arrangement with fees for dog (and eventually cat) licenses.[12]

A generation earlier, New York and the ASPCA had set the national pattern for animal cruelty laws and their enforcement. Now, they created a system for dealing with homeless companion animals that spread across the United States during the first half of the twentieth century. Today, there are between four thousand and six thousand shelters for lost or homeless companion animals,[13] most of them operated by local organizations that, with a certain Orwellian panache, style themselves Humane Societies or Societies for the Prevention of Cruelty to Animals.

I say "Orwellian," because during the twentieth century, these groups killed the great majority of the unfortunate animals who came into their "shelters." Until quite recently, they did not keep statistics, and even now their figures are incomplete and unreliable, but a sophisticated guess would be that since the ASPCA became an animal control agency in 1894, animal shelters in the United States have killed more than a billion healthy, adoptable dogs and cats, sometimes because there really were no homes for them, sometimes because it was cheaper and more convenient to kill them than go to the trouble and expense of running an aggressive adoption program and caring for the animals until they found homes.

To this day, most American animal shelters are slaughterhouses for dogs and cats; only secondarily are they genuine shelters and adoption agencies. The primary concern of the people and political institutions that set their policies and control their budgets—by which I mean mayors, city managers, city councils, county commissioners—is to get homeless animals off the street and keep them off. And since caring for animals costs money, and homeless animals don't vote, the cheapest and surest way to accomplish this is to kill them. Most shelters keep homeless animals no more than two or three days; hardly any do longer than two weeks. However the individual workers may feel about it—and many of them genuinely love the animals and suffer terrible job-induced stress—their mission in the eyes of those who pay their salaries is to eliminate a public nuisance as cheaply as possible.

It is important to understand that these shelters do not exist in a vacuum. They are an essential component in an integrated system of companion animal supply and disposal, created to protect the profits of the suppliers—breeders and pet stores—and of the ancillary industry that has grown up around them—pet supply companies,

trainers, and associations of "fanciers," to use their own term, that
sponsor dog and cat shows.

The system works like this. Breeders, pet stores, and fancy associations prosper by treating animals like any other consumer product,
to be marketed and sold based on their physical and psychological
characteristics, rather than treated as individuals worthy of love and
respect simply because they are sentient beings. Breeds are to dogs
and cats what models are to television sets and automobiles and styles
are to clothing. They are inducements to buy, deliberately created to
keep money flowing into the coffers of suppliers.

Cars, televisions, and clothing are disposable. In fact, disposability
and a disposal mechanism are essential to any consumer-driven system. Old, out-of-date, unfashionable, or worn-out models must be
gotten rid of to make room for new ones. For cars, we have used car
lots and junkyards; for TV sets and clothing, we have thrift shops,
dumpsters, and landfills. For dogs and cats, we have animal shelters.
The primary purpose of animal shelters is to provide a disposal
mechanism for homeless and unwanted animals, and to do it in a way
that they do not clog up the supply chain and cut into the profits of
the suppliers. Breeders, pet stores, and fancy associations—despite
their pious mouthings to the contrary—do not want animals adopted
from shelters in large numbers, because that would reduce the number of animals they can sell. From their perspective, every animal
adopted from a shelter is one that is not bought from a breeder or pet
store, and therefore, they want as many animals as possible who go
into shelters to be killed. And throughout the twentieth century, the
shelter system accommodated them.

In the mid-twentieth century, the newly-created Humane Society
of the United States, founded by people who were genuinely appalled
at the number of dogs and cats being killed in shelters, began urging
that "pet owners" have their companion animals spayed or neutered
as a way of reducing input into the system and thereby reducing the
volume of output. An aggressive public education campaign aimed at
the general public, at state and local officials, at the staff of local animal shelters, and at veterinarians has, to a large degree, been success-

ful. HSUS estimates that today, seventy-two percent of "owned dogs" (that is to say, dogs who have a home with a human guardian) and eighty-four percent of "owned cats" are spayed or neutered.[14]

Even so, HSUS estimates that animal shelters kill three to four million homeless dogs and cats every year while adopting out an equal number. *Animal People*, a magazine for the animal protection community, estimates that shelters kill an average of 4.4 million animals a year.[15] These estimates, as appalling as they are, are almost certainly optimistic. From 1994 through 1997, The National Council on Pet Population Study and Policy, an organization representing veterinarians, breeders, and welfare groups, conducted surveys of animal shelters. These surveys revealed that more than sixty percent of all animals entering shelters during that period were killed, including roughly fifty-six percent of dogs and seventy-two percent of cats.[16] A healthy dog going into an American animal shelter had less than a fifty-fifty chance of coming out alive, while a healthy cat had barely one chance in four. If I entered an institution knowing that the staff were likely to kill me within a few days, I would not think of that establishment as a "shelter." I would think of it as a death camp.

Thinking Like a Mountain—or a Homeless Dog

Had he been born twenty years earlier, Michael Mountain might have been a hippie in Haight-Ashbury. As it was, the British expatriate, Oxford dropout, world-class backpacker, and anti-vivisection campaigner found his way to Kanab Canyon, at the southern edge of Utah. There, smack-dab in the middle of the desert, he and nineteen likeminded friends founded Best Friends Animal Sanctuary to be a place where no animal would be killed simply because he was unlucky enough to be without a home.[17] They were determined to create a shelter that would be a refuge for homeless animals, not a junkyard for the convenience of greedy animal breeders and irresponsible pet owners.

When Best Friends opened in 1982, there were already a number of what would soon become known as "no-kill" shelters scattered around the country—small, local facilities maintained for the most part by dedicated volunteers who kept them going at great personal sacrifice. But if you are looking for a single, discernible starting point for the no-kill shelter movement, the creation of Best Friends is an obvious choice. Best Friends' dedication to the animals, their insistence on the highest standards of care, and their uncompromising opposition to the slaughter of discarded companion animals was combined with a remarkable business and media savvy to make Kanab Canyon the capital of the no-kill world.

Its advocates like to refer to the no-kill movement as a "revolution," and, in fact, its leaders intend to overhaul America's companion animal system from top to bottom by restricting breeding; promoting spay/neuter, both by public education and by legislation; eliminating restrictions on companion animal guardianship in apartments and condominiums; repealing laws and neighborhood association rules that limit the number of companion animals in a household; promoting trap, neuter, and release programs for feral cats; and limiting killing in shelters to animals who are terminally ill and suffering, or who represent a danger to other animals or to human beings. Thus, most no-kill organizations are a combination of shelter, veterinary service, adoption agency, public education office, and lobbying agency on behalf of homeless animals. How many no-kill shelters now exist is not known with any precision, but the number is believed to be around 250 and climbing. Nearly all of them are still small, privately funded groups staffed by volunteers.

A second milestone in the no-kill movement was the founding of Alley Cat Allies in Washington, D. C., in 1990 by Louise Holton and Becky Robinson. Through an aggressive public education campaign, Alley Cat Allies popularized Trap, Neuter and Release (TNR; now most often referred to as Trap, Treat, and Return, or TTR) as a humane way of dealing with the feral cat populations that exist in every city and town. Under TTR, feral cats are humanely trapped, spayed or neutered, inoculated against rabies and other feline diseases, treated for any health problems they may have, and released back into the neighborhood where they were trapped. In many cases, volunteers provide food and makeshift shelter for the colony and monitor the health of its members. In this way, cats who are not adoptable because they cannot be socialized to humans, and cats for whom there are no homes, can live out their natural lives in peace.

In 1994, San Francisco became the first major city in the world to officially adopt the no-kill philosophy when the San Francisco SPCA announced that it would no longer euthanize animals simply because there were no homes for them. By agreement with San Francisco Animal Care and Control, a city agency that performs the traditional animal control functions, any "adoptable" dog or cat whom the ACAC cannot place in a good home is transferred to the SPCA for placement through one of its several adoption programs.[18] And while San Francisco has not entirely eliminated killing, it has reduced the number of homeless animals killed every year from sixty-five thousand to two thousand.[19]

Across the country, more and more localities have begun the process of transitioning to the no-kill philosophy, including New York, which has set a goal of becoming entirely no-kill by 2015.[20] New York acted after criticism from no-kill advocates led the ASPCA—whom they accused of being too eager to kill and too reluctant to pursue aggressive adoption programs—to relinquish its animal control function in 1995. A nonprofit group receptive to the no-kill philosophy called Animal Care and Control of New York City now carries out animal control in New York.

Both directly and through the pressure that it has put on traditional Humane Societies and SPCAs to pursue more aggressive adoption and spay/neuter policies, the no-kill movement has dramatically reduced the number of companion animals killed in shelters in the United States, from an estimated seventeen million in 1987[21] to around six million in 2005.

Tragically, many animal protection organizations have resisted the no-kill philosophy, including PETA, The Humane Society of the United States, the ASPCA, and most local SPCAs and Humane Societies. Their concern is that if all the shelters in the country became no-kill, many would devolve into prisons in which animals would be warehoused for years in conditions of severe deprivation. Given the number of dogs and cats born every year, and the state of many shelters today—especially in parts of the South and in many rural areas—this is not an idle fear. But until pressure is put on the system, it will never change, and until the system changes, millions of animals will continue to be killed for convenience.

In fairness, these groups are to be commended for aggressively promoting spay-neuter and bans on puppy-mills and the sale of live animals in pet stores. HSUS and ASPCA support TNR, but PETA advocates live-trapping feral cats and taking them to a local animal shelter—where they will likely be euthanized.[22] PETA also runs a euthanasia program which in 2004 killed over two thousand dogs and cats from shelters in rural North Carolina, a practice which PETA defends by pointing out, accurately, that the animals involved are living in horrific conditions in these shelters, are often sick or injured, are not receiving medical care, and are facing certain death, since the shelters do not run active adoption programs. Although I do not find this argument persuasive, there is no doubt that PETA and its employees who carry out the program are acting from a compassionate desire to relieve suffering.

I understand the argument that death is preferable to a life of utter, unrelieved misery. For some, such as those with terminal illnesses that cause severe pain and disability, I am sure it is true, and when our own companion animals are in that situation, my wife and I take them to the doctor to be euthanized as what we hope and believe is an act of mercy. But it is also true that living beings hold life irrationally dear, and cling to it desperately in ways and for reasons that defy dispassionate understanding. Our attachment to life is a matter of passion, not reason, and we should always respect this deepest instinct of living beings and be very reluctant to take the lives of those who cannot communicate their wishes. What seems eminently reasonable to those who are not about to die can be the ultimate horror for those who are.

11

The Pit of Despair

William Harvey's discovery of the circulation of blood in 1616 had assured the ascendancy of vivisection in medical research. But while the knowledge gained from experiments on living animals replaced the myths that had dominated physiology since ancient times, it did not lead immediately to the betterment of human health. In fact, the first major practical achievement of modern medical science, the smallpox vaccine—developed by English physician Edward Jenner in 1798—was arrived at entirely through clinical testing.[1]

Prophets of a Cruel God

At the beginning of the nineteenth century, the center of the vivisection movement shifted from Italy to France when Paris physiologist Xavier Bichat established a set of standardized principles for conducting experiments on animals.[2] Intended to assure results that could be replicated by other scientists, Bichat's principles appeared to put vivisection on a solid scientific foundation, and thereby heightened its respectability in the broader research community.

Bichat's work was taken up by another Frenchman, François Magendie (1783–1855), a legendary figure whose impact on medical science was so great that one prominent medical historian, Carl Lichtenthaeler, has divided the history of modern medicine into two eras, with Magendie as the watershed.[3] Magendie claimed to have been the first to show that sensory nerves and motor nerves are separate from one another. But to his chagrin, British researcher Charles Bell had made the same discovery. Bell accused his French rival of stealing his work, and a first-class international academic name-calling contest ensued. Bell's charge has never been resolved, and eventually the scientific establishment played Solomon by dubbing the discovery the "Bell-Magendie Law."

Magendie's most significant contribution, however, for which there is no question that he deserves full credit, was to the methodology of research physiology. Working at the College of Medicine in Paris, and at France's leading school of veterinary medicine in nearby Alfort, François Magendie invented mass-production vivisection. Aware of the variations in results that can be caused by individual differences among animals, he would conduct the same experiments over and over on many individuals, an approach that set the stage for the imprisonment, torture, and killing of hundreds of millions of animals in laboratories over the next two centuries. In just two sets of experiments related to the Bell-Magendie Law, he tortured and killed eight thousand dogs.[4]

Magendie's mantle was passed to his student, Claude Bernard (1813–1878), who is remembered today primarily as a philosopher of science. But in his own day, Bernard was famous for his work in physiology, a pursuit he took up after losing a competition for a position on the faculty at the College of Medicine in Paris.[5] As a physiologist, Bernard's principal method—almost his only method—was vivisection, which he believed to be the proper way to apply the experimental method to physiology. As a philosopher, Bernard claimed that science is not merely a methodology for describing the physical world, but that it is a system of values that can be called upon to justify behavior that might be condemned by other, competing, values. "Science," he proclaimed, "permits us to do to animals what morality forbids us to do to our own kind."[6]

This belief that science can in some mystical, undefined way make imperative as well as descriptive statements is at the heart of what is known as "scientism," the faith in knowledge as the ultimate good and science as the guide to the only authentic form of knowledge. Bernard was one of the earliest exponents of scientism, although he seems to have been only dimly aware of the direction in which he was traveling. He was not led to vivisection by a prior belief in scientism; he wandered into scientism as a way of defending vivisection against its critics. Here is Bernard invoking scientism to defend experiments on conscious, suffering animals:

> The physiologist is not an ordinary man: he is a scientist, possessed and absorbed by the scientific idea that he pursues. He doesn't hear the cries of the animals, he does not see their flowing blood, he sees nothing but his idea, and is aware of nothing but organisms which conceal from him the problems he is wishing to resolve.[7]

Scientism is not science, and scientistic statements are not scientific statements. Bernard's assertion that "Science permits us to [vivisect] animals" can survive none of the tests by which science evaluates a proposition. It does not describe a phenomenon that can be observed and measured; it cannot be empirically tested; and it cannot be falsified, either empirically or logically. It is, in fact, a statement of values, not a statement of fact. It carries all the scientific weight of a proposition like "God has commanded me to slay the infidels," or "God wants me to kill abortion doctors." Although he seems not to have known it—as we shall see in a moment, self-awareness was not Claude Bernard's strong suit—Bernard was making a confession of religious faith that substitutes Science for God. Belief in the supremacy of knowledge over all other values—including compassion and morality—is itself a value. Scientism allows scientists to cloak their own personal, unexamined motivations in the mantle of science.

The unacknowledged personal motivation behind Bernard's passion for vivisection was glimpsed by Dr. George Hoggan, a British physician who worked with him for a while before becoming disgusted and quitting. In a letter addressed to the London *Morning Post,* Hoggan described Bernard's attitude:

The idea of the good of humanity was simply out of the question and would be laughed at, the great aim being to keep up with or get ahead of, one's contemporaries in science even at the price of an incalculable amount of torture needlessly and iniquitously inflicted on the poor animals....[8]

The frustrated professor of medicine was pursuing knowledge for the sake of his bruised ego—with no thought of doing good and no regard for the suffering he inflicted. The man they had said wasn't good enough to teach medicine was now acclaimed as a hero of science who knew more than the most respected medical professors in the world. And he owed it all to vivisection.

Death on the Altar of Science

Some of Magendie's and Bernard's victims were elderly cavalry horses, who had lived through wars in the service of France only to be rewarded by an agonizing death in the laboratory.[9] No doubt their fate was similar to the horror inflicted on other horses by Bernard's students:

> On August 8, 1863, the Paris correspondent of *The Times* [of London] reported: "At the veterinary college at Alfort, a wretched horse is periodically given up to a group of students to experimentalize upon. They tie him down and torture him for hours, the operations being graduated in such a manner ... that sixty and even more may be performed before death ensues." Sometimes an eyeless, hoofless,[10] eviscerated beast was shot if the experiments had not already killed it; at other times the students wandered off when their curiosity was satisfied and left their victim to the knacker [someone who buys old, injured, or exhausted livestock, slaughters them, and sells the meat and skin].[11]

But their favorite victims were dogs. Again, Dr. George Hoggan:

> I think the saddest sight I ever witnessed was when the dogs were brought up from the cellar to the laboratory.... they seemed seized with horror as soon as they smelt the air of the place, divining, apparently, their approaching fate. They would make friendly advances to each of the three or four persons present, and as far as eyes, ears, and tail could make a mute appeal for mercy eloquent, they tried it in vain.[12]

By mid-century, chloroform, the first practical anesthetic, had come into widespread use; laudanum, an opium derivative, had been known to relieve pain since the Renaissance, and morphine had come into use as an analgesic in the 1820s. Magendie, however, refused to use any of these, on the grounds that his studies of the nervous system required the animals to be fully conscious so that he could observe their reactions.[13] Bernard was especially familiar with anesthetics, having written a paper on them, but he shared the view of his mentor and used anesthetics only when they were necessary to keep his victims from struggling.[14]

And struggle they did. A doctor who watched Magendie work described a dog's desperate efforts to escape his torment:

> Magendie, alas! performed experiments in public, and sadly too often at the College de France. I remember once, among other instances, the case of a poor dog, the roots of whose spinal nerves he was about to expose. Twice did the dog, all bloody and mutilated, escape from his implacable knife; and twice did I see him put his paws around Magendie's neck and lick his face.[15]

Galen had conducted his butchery in public, and had even charged admission. His shows were popular with the same people who flocked to the Coliseum to watch animals and humans tear one another apart. Resurrecting the tradition, Magendie and Bernard also opened their tortures to the public and as a result became famous throughout Europe. They were among the first modern celebrities of science.

It turned out, however, that Claude Bernard was less popular in his own home than in his laboratory. In 1869, his wife became so outraged at her husband's cruelty—he conducted experiments at home, and is even said to have brought mutilated animals into the bedroom so that he could wake up during the night and observe them—that she left him to found an anti-vivisection organization and sanctuary for homeless dogs and cats. Bernard was reportedly outraged at her effrontery. I first heard this story years ago in a class on the philosophy of science at the University of Maryland. It was, the professor assured any of us who might be so tiresomely bourgeois as to sympathize with Mme. Bernard, an example of the burdens that great minds have to put up with from the inferior people who surround them. Historians of science hold her in such contempt that very few biographical sketches of Claude Bernard even report her name, dismissing her simply as "Bernard's wife." But it was she who took a stand for the higher value—compassion—and it is her name, not her husband's, which deserves to be known and honored. She was born Françoise-Marie Martin, and her friends called her Fanny.

Living Test Tubes

The first direct improvement to human health as a result of vivisection came from the work of Louis Pasteur (1822–1895), a Bernard protégé who used animals to develop vaccines against anthrax and rabies, diseases caused by bacteria.

Microorganisms had been discovered by Dutch scientist Anton van Leeuwenhoek, who first observed them through a primitive microscope in 1676. No one paid much attention, however, until 1844, when Agostino Bassi, an entomologist employed by the Italian silkworm industry, suggested that Leeuwenhoek's tiny creatures caused diseases in animals and humans. Pursuing Bassi's insight, German physician (and vivisector) Robert Koch was the first to isolate and identify pathogens that cause specific diseases in humans: anthrax in 1877, tuberculosis in 1882, and cholera in 1883. In 1905,

Koch won the Nobel Prize in medicine for his work on tuberculosis, but it was left to Pasteur to put Koch's discoveries to clinical use.

Between them, Koch and Pasteur added a whole new dimension to vivisection and created modern animal experimentation. Up until now, vivisectors, including Magendie and Bernard, had simply cut animals open to find out how their bodies worked. Koch pioneered the use of animals as living laboratory equipment and developed the methodology still used by researchers seeking to identify pathogens. "Koch's Postulates," as they are known, call for the researcher to look for a microbe that is present in every individual who has the disease being investigated but is not commonly found in healthy individuals. The researcher isolates that microbe and grows it in a Petrie dish, a process called "culturing." She then injects the cultured microbes into healthy laboratory animals to see if they develop the disease. Finally, the researcher kills the animals and necropsies them to see if the microbe is still present. If the animal develops the disease and the microbe is still present in the dead animal, the researcher can conclude with a high level of confidence that she has identified the pathogen that causes the disease in question.[16]

Like Bernard, Pasteur did not start out to be a physiologist. But unlike his mentor, it was success, not failure that led him into vivisection. Louis Pasteur started out as a chemist working in the milk, wine, and silk industries, where he identified the organisms that cause spoilage, fermentation, and two destructive silkworm diseases.[17] When he realized that liquids like wine, beer, and milk could be made safe by heating them in sealed containers to kill the microbes they contained, the process of pasteurization was born.

In the 1860s, a cholera epidemic swept across Europe, hitting Paris especially hard, and France's top scientific minds, including Bernard and Pasteur, were assembled to combat it. They failed—the epidemic eventually burned itself out, as epidemics do when too many of their victims either die or develop natural immunity—but two events occurred that were critical to the future of vivisection. Pasteur's attention turned toward human disease, and he became friends with

Claude Bernard, who encouraged him to pursue Bassi's and Koch's germ theory of disease using animal models.[18]

From this point on, Pasteur adopted Koch's methodology. But he also followed Magendie's and Bernard's mass-production approach to vivisection, and this led him to a key discovery that took him beyond Koch's Postulates and vastly multiplied the number of animals killed in medical research. If you injected microbes into an animal, recovered them, re-injected them into a different animal, recovered them again, re-injected them into yet another animal, and so on, eventually you arrived at an animal upon whom the microbe conferred immunity, not illness. Pasteur had no idea why this was so—antibodies would be discovered by German researcher Paul Ehrlich in 1896—but he realized that he had stumbled upon a more sophisticated version of the principle by which Edward Jenner had created a smallpox vaccine: A weakened form of the agent bearing the disease confers immunity.[19]

Microbes are tiny predators who compensate for their miniscule size by entering the bodies of their prey and attacking from within. Koch and Pasteur were setting packs of microscopic hunters to destroy the internal organs of their previously healthy victims. But as brutal as it was, loosing deadly microbes on dogs, cats, rabbits, and horses worked. In 1881, Pasteur successfully demonstrated a vaccine for anthrax, and four years later he successfully used a rabies vaccine on a nine-year-old boy who had been bitten by an infected dog. The science of immunology was born, and the shape of vivisection was set for decades to come, as the bodies of millions of animals were turned into living test tubes for isolating and working with pathogens.

It is not too much to say that by finding solutions for rabies and anthrax, Pasteur won over the European and North American public to vivisection. Pasteur's accomplishments convinced the public that the vivisector was their friend and protector. Vivisection would prevent and cure the most horrible diseases, and to ban it would be to condemn themselves and their children to the risk of sickness and early death. It was a price people were not willing to pay, and—as we shall see in the next chapter—they gradually, quietly, with no great fuss, began ignoring campaigns against vivisection in ever-greater numbers. Almost single-handedly, Louis Pasteur destroyed the anti-vivisection movement by making the vivisection debate a matter of choosing between the lives of animals and the lives of human beings.

Over the following decades, the creation of vaccines for dreaded diseases like diphtheria and tetanus established vivisection as a growth industry and led an ever-increasing number of animals into the torture chambers and execution cells of science. During World War II, vivisection received another boost when scientists belatedly recognized the potential of penicillin—discovered serendipitously by British biologist Alexander Fleming in 1928—and began a frantic search for other "wonder drugs," as antibiotics were called. Although animals played no role in the discovery of antibiotics, they were—and still are—widely used in testing them. In fact, the efficacy of penicillin was first demonstrated on mice because there was as yet no method for synthetically producing it, and sufficient quantities could not be gathered for testing on more than a handful of human beings.

Five Million Primates Died for Our Polio
Toward the end of the nineteenth century, the industrialized world began to be ravaged by recurrent epidemics of poliomyelitis. With each passing decade, the outbreaks grew worse, until by the early 1950s there were tens of thousands of new cases every summer in the United States alone. The peak was reached in 1952, when America experienced fifty-eight thousand severe polio infections.[20] Summer became known as "polio season," and every autumn found thousands more children—and a few adults—paralyzed. The image of the tank respirator, or "iron lung" as it was christened in the press, in which children whose chest muscles were paralyzed by polio would have to spend their entire lives, haunted every American family.

Propelled by a mounting public terror, the medical community marshaled its resources and launched what public relations officers today would call a "war on polio." In fact, it turned out to be a war on primates. Researchers had discovered in 1910 that nonhuman primates can contract polio (which most other animals cannot), and that they and humans can pass the disease to one another.[21] And so, from the 1920s on, monkeys, primarily rhesus macaques, but also chimpanzees, African green monkeys, and other species, were much in demand in laboratories across North America and Europe. According to medical historian Anita Guerrini, "The population of rhesus macaques in their native India plummeted from an estimated five million to ten million in the 1930s to fewer than two hundred thousand by the late 1970s."[22]

Because polio is a viral disease, antibiotics were useless against it, and so scientists focused their efforts on creating a vaccine. This meant a return to the methods of Koch and Pasteur, with one exception: until the 1930s, scientists were unable to culture viruses, so initially they grew the polio virus by injecting it into the spines of living monkeys and allowing it to grow in their spinal fluid. The monkeys, of course, contracted the disease, and their suffering ended only when the scientists killed them and ground up their spinal matter to be injected into the spines of other doomed monkeys. Later, scientists learned to grow the virus in the kidney fluid of monkeys. When it became possible to culture viruses, this practice became less common, but monkeys were still sacrificed by the hundreds of thousands every year to test vaccines, and later, to produce them.

No comprehensive records were kept, but most estimates are that well over one million monkeys were tormented, infected, and killed in our war on polio, and the number is probably closer to five million.[23] Success came in 1955 when a killed virus vaccine developed by American physician Jonas Salk was approved for public use. Two years later, the feared summer epidemics were a thing of the past. The monkeys' nightmare, however, was far from over, as living monkeys were now used to manufacture the vaccine. If the public at large had any doubts about vivisection, the Salk vaccine ended them.

Harry Harlow: The Vivisector as Sadistic Rapist

At the same time that vivisectors were testing antibiotics and creating a polio vaccine, they were also branching out into other fields, most notably psychology, where their favorite victims were rats, mice, and pigeons (because they were small, easily handled, and cheap), and primates (because they were so much like humans physically and mentally).

The leading early figure in the extension of vivisection to psychology was Harry Harlow (1906–1981), an American psychologist who set out to apply the principles of experimental science to the question of love. Harlow was not some caricature of a mad scientist working in feverish isolation in an out-of-the-way little laboratory, scorned by the scientific community. For more than three decades—from the 1930s into the 1970s—Harry Harlow dominated experimental psychology. In 1931, he founded the Psychology Primate Laboratory at the University of Wisconsin, which he headed until 1964, when it merged with the Wisconsin Regional Primate Laboratory and he became director of the combined institution. Honored with too many awards to list, including the National Medal of Science, the highest recognition the United States offers for scientific achievement, Harlow was a member of the prestigious National Academy of Sciences, and served a term as president of the American Psychological Association. Even today, he is praised as a brilliant and courageous pioneer who put psychology—long derided as a "soft" discipline—on a firm scientific footing.

Like Jonas Salk, Harlow used rhesus macaques, although thankfully in far smaller numbers. He chose macaques because they are able to move about and grasp things with their hands almost from the moment of birth, and therefore, they can clearly express attractions and aversions through their behavior—show fear and love from the time they are a few hours old. As it turned out, macaques were also tragically suited to Harlow's purposes because they form deep and long-lasting emotional bonds with their mothers, siblings, and playmates. Harlow described his feelings for his subjects in the stark language that was typical of him:

The only thing I care about is whether a monkey will turn out a property I can publish. I don't have any love for them. I never have. I don't really like animals. I despise cats. I hate dogs. How could you love monkeys?[24]

Harlow was obsessed with the idea of maternal deprivation, possibly because he felt that his own mother had denied him her love when he was a child.[25] Over more than thirty years, he performed hundreds of variations on the same theme: deprive an infant of a mother's love and see what happens. He started out by taking newborn macaques from their mothers and giving them two dolls as substitutes, one of which was soft and cuddly, the other made of harsh chicken wire, and observing their emotional and social development. As time went on, the procedure became more elaborate and more sadistic. Harlow gave the infants heated "mothers" and chilled "mothers," mechanical "mothers" who cuddled them and mechanical "mothers" who stuck pins in them, squirted water on them, or attacked them in other ways, often unpredictably. He put baby macaques alone in a cage and subjected them to sudden loud noises, bright lights, and other frightening stimuli. Unsurprisingly, all of the deprived and assaulted infants suffered emotional damage, usually severe and often permanent. Finally, in his *pièce de résistance*, Harlow imprisoned baby macaques in tiny solitary confinement chambers—he called them "pits of despair"—for months at a time. These poor creatures went totally, irreversibly insane, and no amount of affectionate contact afterward could restore them to anything resembling normalcy.

In females, one common effect of being raised by what Harlow called an "evil mother," a mechanical surrogate that repulsed or attacked the infant, was an unwillingness to mate, and so when Harlow wanted to mate one of these monkeys (in experiments to see what kind of mother she would be), he would fasten her into a stereotaxic device—a mechanical restraint that renders an animal entirely unable to move—and either artificially inseminate her or allow a male macaque to mate with her. He called his victims "hot mamas," which they certainly were not, and the stereotaxic device a "rape rack," which is exactly what it was.

Harlow's defenders cannot plead ignorance on his behalf. He understood that he was inflicting intense emotional suffering on vulnerable infants and children—suffering that was often lifelong and debilitating. The whole point of Harlow's research was to obtain results that could be extrapolated to human beings. His experiments were premised on the belief that macaques are emotionally similar to humans. Otherwise, his results—from his own point of view—would have been worthless. As for his contributions, he is credited with discovering the importance of maternal love and positive social interactions in the development of a strong, healthy personality, something that had been common knowledge since prehistory.

In the case of Harry Harlow, the scientific community in general, and the psychology professions in particular have a lot to answer for. Everyone knew exactly what Harlow was doing. He broadcast the details of his experiments in books, articles, and lectures that were widely distributed in the professional community. But while some scientists criticized his methods as unjustifiably cruel, the scientific world as a whole heaped praise upon him, appointed him to prestigious academic posts, and hung medal after medal around his neck. The American science establishment richly rewarded Harry Harlow for his cruelty, and by doing so encouraged him to continue in it and encouraged subsequent generations of young scientists to pursue animal cruelty as the high road to professional glory.[26]

12

Requiem for a Little Brown Dog

The anti-vivisection movement was born in Victorian England as a reaction to the work of Magendie, Bernard, and their imitators on the continent. Even so, it was slow getting started, largely because of a perception—for the most part accurate—that experiments on conscious animals were relatively rare in Britain and that vivisection was a "foreign" problem.

There had been a brief spurt of activity in 1824, when François Magendie paid a visit to London, where he gave the kind of public demonstrations that had made him a star in Paris. To Magendie's surprise, the physicians and journalists who attended were appalled at what they saw. They were accustomed to the work of his antagonist Charles Bell, the leading British medical researcher of this era, who emphasized anatomy over physiology, and therefore, concentrated on the dissection of human and non-human cadavers. When he did carry out vivisections, Bell usually stunned the animal first.[1] Although public sentiment against vivisection was slowly building in England and on the continent, no serious anti-vivisection movement would form until Frances Power Cobbe exploded onto the scene in 1863.

The Rights of Man and the Claims of Brutes
Descended from generations of English landed gentry, Frances Power Cobbe (1822–1904) was born and raised in County Dublin, Ireland.

For three hundred years, her family had been wealthy and influential pillars of the British Army and the Church of England; her great-great-grandfather had been the Anglican archbishop of Dublin.[2]

In 1863, at the age of 40, traveling with her lifelong companion, Welsh sculptor Mary Charlotte Lloyd, Cobbe visited Aix-les-Bains in the foothills of the French Alps to "take the waters," as the saying went, for a broken ankle that was slow to heal. There she learned of Claude Bernard and his atrocities. Outraged, she promptly wrote an essay entitled "The Rights of Man and the Claims of Brutes" which she sent off to a childhood friend of her brother's, historian James Froude (rhymes with "loud"), who was editor of *Fraser's Magazine for Town and Country*, a general-interest magazine with a wide readership that often represented the views of middle-class social reformers. *Fraser's* published the article, and at the age of forty-one, Frances Power Cobbe had found her mission in life.

Anticipating spending time with friends in Italy after completing her therapy at Aix, Cobbe had secured an appointment as Italian correspondent for the London *Daily News* before she left England. Now she learned that a German physiologist named Moritz Schiff, working just across the Alps in Florence, was performing experiments on live animals that were every bit as horrifying as those conducted by Bernard.[3] Cutting short her stay in France, she hurried on to Florence, from where, in December 1863, she filed a story with the *Daily News* that unloaded on Schiff with both barrels.

Cobbe's next step was to circulate a petition among Florentine high society, both Italian and international—Florence was a favorite wintering spot for what today would be called the "jet set"—on which she obtained seven hundred and eighty-three signatures, including fifty members of the Tuscan nobility, in the first known use of a petition drive in the cause of animal protection.[4]

Cobbe submitted her petition to Schiff, who threw it in the trash, but not before responding to it point by point in a letter to Florence's leading newspaper, *La Nazione*. Cobbe dashed off a reply, but *La Nazione* refused to run it, and she was reduced to pleading with the editors to let her place it as a paid advertisement. *La Nazione* ran her ad, but Cobbe's campaign against Schiff was effectively over. Schiff's letter unleashed an avalanche of venomous attacks on Cobbe, portraying her as a silly, meddling English spinster who was trying to bring Italian science, about which she knew nothing, into disrepute.

To understand the vehemence of the attacks on Cobbe, we have to put them in the context of the times. Until the middle of the nineteenth century, Italy was a hodgepodge of small, backward feudal states ruled either by the Catholic Church or—like Tuscany—by a reactionary aristocracy. The political unification of the peninsula was engineered by modern Italy's three national heroes, Giuseppe Mazzini, Camillo Cavour, and Giuseppe Garibaldi, as part of what was known as the *Risorgimento* ("Resurgence"), an intellectual, political, and cultural movement to bring Italy into the modern era. The word *Risorgimento* was deliberately chosen to echo *Rinascimento* ("Renaissance") and promised a return of lost glory, with Italy once again taking its rightful place as the intellectual, artistic, and cultural leader of Europe, the Renaissance resurgent. Tuscany had been added to the growing collection of unified Italian states just two years earlier, in 1861, following a plebiscite and over the protests of the aristocracy. From 1865 until Rome was brought into the Republic in 1870, completing the unification, Florence would be capital of the newly united Italy. It was thus at the center of the turmoil that was remaking Italian society.

In this atmosphere, Schiff—although a German—was able to present himself as a hero of the new Italy who was putting Italian research on a par with the most advanced science in the world. He made much of the fact that the Italian signatories of Cobbe's petition were reactionary aristocrats opposed to the unification of Italy and the *Risorgimento* in general, and that the foreign signatories were members of a wealthy cosmopolitan—and equally reactionary—leisure class whose sympathies were with the aristocrats, not the Italian people.[5] Thus, Schiff was able to portray Fanny Cobbe as a modern-day defender of feudalism whose real agenda was to throw a monkey wrench into the machinery of Italian progress.

Back in England, stung to the quick by the personal nature of the attacks on her, Cobbe withdrew for several years from active campaigning against vivisection, which she regarded as primarily an issue in continental Europe. But the situation in England was changing, and these changes would draw Fanny Cobbe back into the fray.

Continental Vivisection Comes to England

European medical and veterinary training changed little between the Middle Ages and the nineteenth century. Students studied medical texts, attended lectures, dissected the occasional cadaver, and shadowed doctors as they went about their tasks in a kind of apprenticeship. Under the influence of Magendie and Bernard this changed radically on the continent beginning in the 1820s. First-hand experience in the laboratory now became the core of medical and veterinary training. And in both instances, this meant vivisection. Students learned about the body and its functions by cutting up living animals, with lectures and textbooks serving to explain what they were seeing. There are no reliable statistics, but the number of animals tortured and killed in laboratories and classrooms skyrocketed.

England was much slower to adopt the new model of medical and veterinary training, but by the 1860s, English scientists were eager to catch up with their continental colleagues, who regarded them as hopelessly backward. In 1870, the Royal College of Physicians, which licenses doctors in the U.K. and sets standards of medical practice (much like the American Medical Association in the U.S.), updated the examinations for medical students and M.D. candidates to place greater emphasis on physiology. Medical schools were suddenly scrambling to add vivisectors to their faculties so their students would be prepared for the new exams.

The growing popularity of continental-style vivisection in England energized Fanny Cobbe. She drew up a petition calling for the strict regulation of vivisection and urging the RSPCA to be proactive in prosecuting all vivisectors who engaged in painful experiments upon animals. In the wake of her Italian experience, she was sensitive to the charge of being opposed to science, and so she did not demand the abolition of vivisection, but only an end to experiments that caused the animals pain. As she had in Florence, Cobbe circulated her petition among the social, political, and intellectual elite—to whom her wealth and her family's status gave her access—and obtained over one thousand signatures, including those of historian Thomas Carlyle and art critic John Ruskin.

Charles Darwin refused to sign, concisely summarizing the three arguments commonly used by defenders of vivisection: the potential benefits to humanity, the need for England to keep up with the rest of Europe (an English echo of the argument in Florence), and the unfairness of picking on scientists while the upper classes continued to kill and maim animals for sport (a variation on the class-warfare argument of a half-century before).

> I believe that Physiology will ultimately lead to incalculable benefits, and it can progress only by experiments on living animals. Any stringent law would stop all progress in this country, which I should deeply regret.
>
> I cannot but be struck by the injustice with which physiologists are spoken of, considering that those who shoot birds for mere pleasure, cause by wounding them manifold more suffering than do the physiologists (beside the indirect suffering of traps); yet the sportsmen are not blamed, while physiologists are spoken of as "demons let loose from hell."[6]

Nevertheless, Darwin was not entirely of one mind about vivisection. In his 1872 book, *The Expression of the Emotions in Man and Animals*, Darwin had recognized that animals have rich interior lives and that they can experience intense suffering, both physical and emotional. In a letter to physiologist Edwin Ray Lankester, he expressed his ambivalence:

> You ask about my opinion on vivisection. I quite agree that it is justifiable for real investigations on physiology; but not for mere damnable and detestable curiosity. It is a subject which

makes me sick with horror, so I will not say another word about it, else I shall not sleep to-night.[7]

Darwin took the position that English social reformers had generally been taking toward animals for the past fifty years. They were willing, even eager, to attack fringe practices carried out by marginalized members of society—like bull-baiting or animal experiments conducted by amateur, unaffiliated researchers. But they were unwilling to condemn mainstream practices carried out by persons of substance and position in society—like hunting or animal experiments conducted by university professors. In short, they regarded animal protection as an issue of secondary importance which must never be allowed to interfere with the established order of society.

The Woman Who Experimented on Claude Bernard

It was while this political maneuvering was going on that Anna Kingsford entered the fray. Anna Bonus Kingsford (1846–1888) was born in London to a prosperous shipbuilder of Italian ancestry and an Irish/German mother. A delicate and sickly child, Annie, as she was known throughout her life, had a reputation in her family for what we would call ESP, including the unsettling ability to foresee someone's death.

On New Year's Eve, 1867, at the age of twenty-one, Annie eloped with her cousin, an Anglican seminary student named Algernon Kingsford—on whom she imposed a stipulation unheard of at the time. In what amounted to a Victorian pre-nup, she insisted on being free to pursue her own interests and live her own life. Kingsford agreed and was as good as his word. Although they lived apart for a number of years, and she spent most of her time in the company of another man, novelist and psychic Edward Maitland, the couple shared a genuine—if unorthodox—bond of loyalty and love, and Algernon never failed to support Annie in all of her undertakings—some of which were positively scandalous for the wife of a priest of the Church of England, including a conversion to Catholicism.

Kingsford's psychic abilities led her to spiritualism—which enjoyed wide popularity throughout the Victorian era—and she became acquainted with most of the leading mystics of her day, including Annie Besant (1847–1933), who was also an active social reformer, a founding member of the socialist Fabian Society, and a campaigner for women's rights, animal rights, trade unions, universal education, vegetarianism, and Indian independence. Another friend was Helena Blavatsky, founder of the Theosophical Society, which presented Eastern mysticism, primarily Tibetan Buddhism, in Western dress. Eventually Kingsford turned away from Theosophy to form her own organization, the Hermetic Society, which looked to the traditions of Western, rather than Eastern, mysticism. For the remainder of her life, she was a regular figure at séances and other spiritualist demonstrations and a prominent public advocate of the reality and power of the psychic world. Believing that animals have souls and that enslaving and killing them is sinful, Kingsford followed the example of her friend Annie Besant and in 1872 became a vegetarian.

In that same year, she bought a London magazine, *The Lady's Own Paper*, to provide a forum for her views on social reform, especially women's rights. Although *The Lady's Own Paper* was severely underfunded and soon went belly up, Kingsford's articles earned her introductions to the leading lights of England's social reform movements, one of whom was Fanny Cobbe. Ever on the lookout for a new platform, Cobbe submitted an article on vivisection that moved Kingsford so profoundly she took up the cause as her own. Before long, she had gained a reputation as an articulate and persuasive speaker on the anti-vivisection circuit.

Being a woman in the Victorian era and having neither wealth nor social position, Kingsford realized that she needed a credential to establish herself as a serious voice in the anti-vivisection movement, and so she decided to become a doctor. Since English medical schools would not admit women, Kingsford traveled to Paris and studied at the notorious College of Medicine, where Claude Bernard lectured. Remarkably, through a combination of extraordinary intelligence, fierce willpower, and feminine charm—which she did not hesitate to unleash on her male chauvinist professors—she completed the entire course of study without having to perform a single vivisection. She graduated in 1880, and Dr. Kingsford returned to England, where she became the second female physician in English history.[8]

At medical school, an instructor described experiments in which Bernard had roasted conscious animals alive in an oven designed so that he could observe the animals' death. Kingsford was so revolted that she began an experiment of her own—in psychic assassination, focusing her energy on a wish for the vivisector's death. Two months later, Bernard died (after an illness of nearly a decade), and Kingsford told her companion, Edward Maitland, "Woe be to the torturers.... I will make it dangerous, nay, deadly, to be a vivisector. It is the only argument that will affect them. Meanwhile, thank God the head of the gang is dead."[9]

Convinced that she could cause the death of vivisectors and was justified in doing so to end their crimes, Kingsford turned her attention to Bernard's successor, Paul Bert. It took almost ten years, but Annie Kingsford was nothing if not persistent, and when Bert died in 1886, she wrote in her diary, "I have killed Paul Bert, as I killed Claude Bernard; as I will kill Louis Pasteur if I live long enough.... it is a magnificent power to have, and one that transcends all vulgar methods of dealing out justice to tyrants."[10]

Her qualification that she would kill Louis Pasteur "if I live long enough" was prescient. In November 1886, Kingsford visited Louis Pasteur's laboratory as part of her psychic campaign against him. While in Paris, she caught cold, and never regained her strength. In February 1888, she died of consumption (presumably tuberculosis complicated by pneumonia) at the age of forty-one.[11] The last years of her life had been dedicated to promoting spiritualism, advocating for vegetarianism and against vivisection, and providing free medical treatment to the poor.

The Victoria Street Irregulars

While Kingsford was studying in Paris, back in England Fanny Cobbe

was stirring up a hornet's nest. In January 1875, Cobbe's petition calling for the regulation of vivisection was delivered to the RSPCA. The
Royal Society appointed a committee, dithered, waffled, wrangled
over irrelevant side issues, and ultimately did nothing, partly because
they did not want to appear to be standing in the way of British science, and partly because, like the proper Victorian gentlemen they
were, they were still unwilling to take a stand against hunting and
shooting.

Shortly after Cobbe's disheartening presentation to the RSPCA, a
British physician, George Hoggan, who had studied with Claude
Bernard in Paris, published the letter in the London *Daily Post* that I
quoted in the previous chapter. In February, George Jesse—a retired
civil engineer famous in his own day as a stereotypical English eccen-
tric—became the first person to organize a serious campaign for an
absolute ban on animal experiments, when he founded the Society
for the Abolition of Vivisection (SAV). Other groups opposed to vivisection soon sprang up all across Britain.

In the meantime, Cobbe and Hoggan joined forces and decided
that the time had come to move beyond petitions and letters to the
editor, and go straight for legislation. Cobbe drafted a bill, which was
presented to the House of Lords by Lord Henniker, that would
require vivisection laboratories to be licensed, would make them subject to inspection, and would require that the animals be anesthetized
unless that would defeat the purpose of the experiment. Every painful
experiment on an unanesthetized animal would require a separate
license.

This was mighty thin soup, but even so, the medical profession
was having none of it. Backed by Darwin and Thomas Henry Huxley,
a prominent Darwinian and popularizer of science (as well as grand-
father of novelist Aldous Huxley), they submitted an alternate bill
that would grant vivisectors blanket five-year licenses and immunize
them from prosecution under Martin's Act. Neither bill passed.
Parliament studied and debated the proposals with great intensity,
but was careful to take no action on them.

Faced with a blathering Parliament and a feckless RSPCA, in 1875

Cobbe and Hoggan moved to put opposition to vivisection on a more secure footing by creating an organization to rally the troops and lead the charge. The Victoria Street Society—named for its location—began with the limited goal of regulating vivisection with a view toward reducing the suffering of its victims. But over time, the refusal of the scientific community to accept any meaningful regulation convinced Cobbe that this was a futile strategy. If scientists were going to fight regulation as fiercely as they would fight abolition, why settle for half measures? To make matters worse, the Victoria Street Society was coming under attack from groups like George Jesse's SAV that were committed to abolition, and equated regulation with betrayal.

The final blow came in 1876, when Queen Victoria made it known that she wanted to see vivisection regulated. After more thrashing about, Parliament finally amended Martin's Act to specifically cover experiments on animals. The Cruelty to Animals Act was a compromise piled on top of a compromise. It required experimenters to be licensed annually and provided that experiments could be performed on living animals only for the advancement of science or the prolongation of human life, not for demonstration or teaching purposes—unless the vivisector had the support of a recognized scientific organization, such as a medical school. Thinking—correctly—that the Act did little more than provide protective covering for vivisectors, Cobbe was furious, and for the next two years pressured the directors of the Victoria Street Society to make the complete abolition of vivisection the group's official goal. When they did, in 1878, George Hoggan and a number of other charter members resigned.

In addition to guiding the Victoria Street Society, Cobbe continued to write and speak in a style that was designed to shock an apathetic public into action while exposing the lies of the vivisectors. In 1877, she printed and distributed throughout London two thousand flyers and posters featuring gruesome illustrations from textbooks on vivisection. She was roundly attacked for sensationalism and a lack of good taste—cardinal sins for a woman in Victorian England. Even George Jesse, in an act of moral cowardice that detracts from his courage in calling for the complete abolition of vivisection, wrote letters to London newspapers and to Charles Darwin publicly condemning the posters.

But Cobbe was not to be intimidated. Two years later, she published a twenty-page pamphlet entitled *Bernard's Martyrs*. Drawing heavily on text lifted directly from Bernard's latest book, *Leçons de Physiologie Opératoire* (*Lessons in Surgical Physiology, i.e.* vivisection), Cobbe described in intimate detail the horrors of Bernard's laboratory. Even more to the point, she illustrated *Bernard's Martyrs* with the vivisector's own horrific illustrations. Again, she was met with a storm of protest.

The Struggle of the Titans

In 1880, when Anna Kingsford was preparing to return home from Paris, medical degree in hand, she wrote her friend Fanny Cobbe to enlist her help in re-entering the inner circle of London's progressive opinion leaders, from which she had been absent for seven years. This was a request that Cobbe—a popular hostess among London's liberal elite—was in a unique position to fulfill at no cost to herself. All she had to do was include Kingsford in the social evenings (the *soirées*, as the English still called them) that she regularly hosted at her London home, and suggest to one or two of her friends that they add the new doctor to their guest lists as well. And yet, Cobbe flatly refused, on the grounds that since Kingsford was a wife and mother, she had an obligation to eschew public life and stay at home caring for her husband and daughter. Worse than that, Cobbe guaranteed that Kingsford would be excluded from polite London society by launching a vicious gossip campaign portraying her as a tart who had deserted her husband and child to lead an immoral life with another man in Paris.

There was just enough appearance of truth in the charge to give it substance in Victorian eyes. Edward Maitland had joined Kingsford in Paris shortly after her arrival and remained with her—with the express approval of her husband—until the two returned to England in 1880. Although the relationship appears not to have been sexual, this was outrageous behavior for a married woman in Victorian

England. Even so, as a woman who traveled everywhere with a female "companion," to whom she was every bit as bonded emotionally as Kingsford was to Maitland, Fanny Cobbe was throwing stones from inside a glass house. But she got away with it. In Queen Victoria's London, social rank was everything. Cobbe had it; Kingsford did not. And so, despite the medical degree for which she had worked so hard and endured so much, Anna Kingsford was denied access to the company of London's progressive elite.

Despite her reputation as a feminist, Cobbe was much more the straitlaced Victorian than her modern admirers like to admit. And she genuinely believed that married women should stay out of public life, a view she expressed frequently in lectures, essays, and books. Even more surprisingly, her split with Kingsford seems to have owed a great deal to Cobbe's hostility to a vegetarian diet. Although estranged from organized religion, Cobbe accepted the Biblical Compromise lock, stock, and barrel, and regarded vegetarianism as a violation of God's will. She was adamant that it must not be linked in the public mind with opposition to vivisection.

But there were also less ideological reasons for Cobbe's attacks on Kingsford. Fanny Cobbe was a strong, often overpowering personality, and she did not brook competition, especially from other women. While Kingsford looked upon Cobbe as an ally and a mentor until the older woman turned on her, Cobbe seems to have regarded Kingsford as a rival from very early on.

The anti-vivisection movement was now split into four major factions, with splinter groups too numerous to describe, all of which refused—as a matter of high principle—to cooperate with one another. One faction, led by George Hoggan, a physician who did not want to impede the progress of medical science, favored the regulation, but not the abolition of vivisection. Another, led by George Jesse, called for the abolition of vivisection, but condemned tactics that might upset people or appear to be in bad taste. The third, led by Cobbe, favored the abolition of vivisection and pursued it by tactics intended to jolt the conscience of the public. And the fourth, led by Anna Kingsford, Annie Besant, playwright George Bernard Shaw

(1856–1950), and (from the mid-1880s) Henry Salt, whom we shall meet in the next chapter, campaigned for an end to all cruelty to animals, including killing them for food and science.

The Lost Cause

With Britain in the forefront, popular sentiment against vivisection grew throughout the 1870s all across Europe. It seems likely that, had the question been put to a popular vote, the U.K. at least, and possibly the Scandinavian countries, might have banned vivisection outright. But vivisection was not put to a popular vote, and the scientific establishment was able to convince the political leadership that opposition to experiments on animals was opposition to science and the modern era. Caving in to the forces of ignorance and superstition, which were led by obscurantist religious fanatics like Cobbe and Kingsford, would deny humanity the golden age that science was on the verge of ushering in, and would relegate England to the status of an intellectual backwater, a relic from the Dark Ages. With some notable exceptions—like John Ruskin, Matthew Arnold, and Shaw—this argument always impressed England's intelligentsia, and as education became more democratic, more and more people came to support vivisection as part and parcel of the endless progress being promised by science and technology.

From the beginning, Fanny Cobbe—who was, in fact, deeply distrustful of science—had compromised her own case by claiming that vivisection could never result in gains to human health. The differences between humans and animals were too great, she said, for experiments on animals to advance human health. For a while, it seemed as though she might be right. But before long, Louis Pasteur's creation of a rabies vaccine appeared to demonstrate that vivisection could reveal the answers to any number of human plagues. In the public mind, Louis Pasteur had discredited Fanny Cobbe, and with her the entire movement against vivisection.

Finally, Claude Bernard—and following him, vivisectors all across Europe—closed his laboratory to the public and began giving demonstrations only to sympathetic audiences of serious students of physiology. Out of sight, out of mind. With the horrors of vivisection now hidden from public view, it grew harder to arouse indignation at the cruelty. And when Fanny Cobbe tried to let people look inside the laboratories by reprinting and distributing descriptions and illustrations from Bernard's own texts, it was she, not Bernard, who was assailed from all sides—including her own colleagues—for breaches of decorum and good taste.

Under these circumstances, opposition to vivisection gradually declined. Attempts to strengthen the 1876 Act became an almost annual ritual, but they all failed. In 1882, the scientific community struck back by creating the Association for the Advancement of Medical Research (AAMR), to which all of Britain's leading vivisectors belonged, including medical hero Joseph Lister, who, although he had discovered the principle of antisepsis by clinical trial, nevertheless supported vivisection. The AAMR soon convinced the Home Secretary, who was responsible for administering the Act of 1876, to allow them to take over the process of reviewing applications and issuing licenses to vivisectors. The bank robbers were now guarding the vault, and the last miserable little shred of protection for animals had been ripped from the 1876 Act.

*   *   *

As victory began drifting farther and farther out of reach, Fanny Cobbe began to self-destruct. One of the staff members of the Victoria Street Society was Mildred Mary Coleridge, the thirty-six-year-old daughter of the Lord Chief Justice of the British Empire, and the grandniece of poet Samuel Taylor Coleridge. Somehow, Cobbe became aware of a budding romance between Mildred and another staff member, Charles Warren Adams (the two were later married) and told the Lord Chief Justice, who was a personal friend, that Adams had seduced his daughter in a Victoria Street office. Exactly what motivated Cobbe to this piece of madness is uncertain, but Mildred's brothers Bernard and Stephen, who were leading members of the VSS, had been agitating for the Society to abandon its hard-line stance and return to its original policy of campaigning for the regulation rather than the abolition of vivisection. Cobbe, who as the Kingsford affair showed, had a taste for using gossip to eliminate challenges from rivals, may have been hoping to neutralize the brothers Coleridge by slandering their sister in a way that would make it appear as though she was defending the family's honor. Be that as it may, the Coleridge family never forgave Cobbe her meddling, and Mildred's brothers would later play a key role in Cobbe's fall from grace at the Victoria Street Society.

For his part, Adams retaliated by suing the Society for unpaid royalties on a book and several newsletter articles that the VSS had published. Vivisectors had a field day with the ensuing notoriety, and when the Court ruled in Adams' favor, the Society's directors made it clear that they intended to put Cobbe on a very short leash. Unable to accept this, Fanny Cobbe gave up her active management role in the Victoria Street Society in 1884, and withdrew to Mary Charlotte Lloyd's country house in the north of Wales. Her withdrawal, however, was more strategic than sincere, and she still exercised considerable, although diminishing, influence behind the scenes, and published monthly articles in the Society's newsletter, *The Zoophilist*. Despite losing control of the VSS, Cobbe continued to be the public face of opposition to vivisection by publishing—independently of the Society—numerous articles, pamphlets, and books, including her autobiography and *The Modern Rack: Papers on Vivisection*, a compendium of her views on the subject nearest and dearest to her heart.

In 1895, the Victoria Street Society changed its name to the National Anti-Vivisection Society (NAVS), signaling a break with the Cobbe past. In 1898, Bernard and Stephen Coleridge, who had risen in prominence since Fanny Cobbe's retreat to Wales, finally persuaded the Society's national convention to endorse a campaign for the regulation of vivisection, for all practical purposes abandoning abolition and making Cobbe's fall from power complete. Immediately, Cobbe severed all connections with NAVS, withdrew her financial support, and at the age of seventy-five, created a new organization, the British Union for the Abolition of Vivisection (BUAV), to pursue a campaign for the complete abolition of experiments on animals.

Although both organizations survived, the world's first modern animal rights campaign, which Cobbe had inaugurated in 1863 with her articles on Claude Bernard and Moritz Schiff, was effectively over. It would struggle on, kept on life support by a cadre of dedicated activists, but it would represent no threat to vivisection.

In 1904, Fanny Cobbe died suddenly of heart failure, having lived long enough to see her British Union for the Abolition of Vivisection established on a viable footing even as the cause it promoted receded farther into the margins of public consciousness.

Coming to America

In 1851, John Call Dalton, a graduate of the Harvard Medical School who had spent the previous year in Paris studying physiology with Claude Bernard, was appointed professor of physiology at the University of Buffalo, where he conducted what are believed to be the first experiments on living animals in the United States. In 1855, Dalton was elected to the chair in physiology at the College of Physicians and Surgeons in New York, one of the nation's most prestigious medical schools, from where he promoted the spread of vivisection to medical schools throughout the U.S.

By 1871, the demand for experimental subjects had grown to the point that surgeons in Philadelphia turned to the shelter run by the Pennsylvania SPCA as a cheap and convenient source of animals. The Society refused to accommodate them, but the idea endured, and by the 1940s, states had begun enacting "pound seizure" laws, which required animal shelters to surrender their unadopted dogs and cats to laboratories and medical schools. These would not be successfully challenged until a campaign led by Henry Spira forced the repeal of New York's pound seizure law in 1979. (See Chapter 16.)

In 1883, Caroline White—the Quaker activist who had co-founded the Pennsylvania SPCA—founded the American Anti-

Vivisection Society (AAVS) on the model of the Victoria Street Society. Originally, the group campaigned for the regulation of vivisection, but proposed federal legislation was crushed by fierce opposition from the medical community, leading White—like Cobbe—to conclude that if scientists were going to fight regulation as hard as they would fight abolition, she might as well go directly for what she really wanted.[12] White's mentor on animal protection issues, Henry Bergh, who was outraged by Dalton's experiments on animals at the College of Physicians and Surgeons, had several bills introduced in the New York state legislature, none of which became law.

Following Bergh's death in 1888, the ASPCA quickly lost interest in vivisection as the Society became more conservative and more tightly focused on homeless dogs and cats.[13] In fact, beyond a few visionary leaders, like Bergh, White, and George Angell, the American animal welfare movement showed little interest in protecting animals who were being tortured and killed in laboratories and classrooms.[14] In 1877, twenty-seven humane organizations established the American Humane Association, a coalition created to campaign for the enforcement of laws requiring that farmed animals be given food, water, and rest while they were being transported.[15] In 1900, the AHA sponsored an international conference of animal welfare groups that "formally expelled all antivivisectionist organizations."[16] In 1908, Henry Bergh's nephew, an officer of the ASPCA, advocated a system of voluntary agreements between scientists and animal welfare advocates that would "not interfere with the legitimate and necessary workings of science."[17] In 1914, delegates to the national convention of the AHA, representing most of the American animal welfare movement, told observers from the medical establishment that the American Humane Association and its constituent organizations intended to "leave vivisection alone."[18]

Fiercely opposed by the scientific, medical, and business communities, and betrayed by the very people who should have been its strongest supporters, the antivivisection movement in the United States never got off the ground. The popular support that developed in Britain during the 1870s failed to materialize on this side of the

Atlantic, despite heroic efforts by Caroline White and others. The creation of the National Anti-Vivisection Society in 1929 gave the movement a shot in the arm that helped keep it alive until help could arrive in the second half of the century. But until the creation of the Humane Society of the United States in 1954, opposition to vivisection remained a fringe movement, without allies in either the social justice or the animal welfare communities.

Footnote to History: A Monument to a Little Brown Dog

In 1903, Leisa Schartau and Lizzie Lind-af-Hageby, two Swedish women studying medicine at University College London (English medical schools had by now begun admitting women) published a book called *The Shambles* [slaughterhouse] *of Science* in which they recounted one horror story after another of vivisections they had witnessed in the course of their studies. One of these described "a small brown dog of the terrier type" whose neck had been cut open without anesthesia to demonstrate to students that the pressure exerted by the saliva gland is greater than the pressure of blood. The dog showed scars from having been cut open before, and during the demonstration, the students laughed at him and joked about his struggles and cries. At the end of the demonstration, he was killed by a student who stabbed him in the heart with a knife.[19]

Stephen Coleridge, who now held Fanny Cobbe's old job of Honorary Secretary—chief operating officer—of NAVS, publicly accused the vivisector, Dr. William Bayliss, of violating the 1876 Act. Bayliss sued for libel, and after a sensational trial amply covered in the press, won. But the "little brown dog," as the London newspapers dubbed him, had become a celebrity. When the London *Daily News* asked its readers to send in contributions to reimburse Coleridge, the paper received donations totaling more than twice the amount of damages he had been assessed.[20]

In 1906, the International Anti-Vivisection Council—an umbrella organization that included NAVS and BUAV—received permission from the town council of Battersea, a London borough on the south bank of the Thames, to erect in Battersea Park a memorial in the form of a drinking fountain for both humans and dogs, atop which stood a bronze statue of the little brown dog. A plaque read:

> In Memory of the Brown Terrier Dog done to Death in the Laboratories of University College in February 1903, after having endured Vivisection extending over more than two months and having been handed from one Vivisector to another till Death came to his Release. Also in Memory of the 232 dogs vivisected at the same place during the year 1902. Men and Women of England, how long shall these things be?[21]

London medical students decided to fight back by staging protests at Battersea Park. These led to counter-protests by opponents of vivisection, and clashes between the two sometimes ended in street fighting—known as the "Brown Dog Riots"—that had to be broken up by police. Eventually, residents of Battersea, tired of the disorder, elected a more conservative borough council, which, before dawn on March 10, 1910, had the memorial removed under cover of darkness. Since it has never been found, historians believe it was destroyed. A new statue on a concrete plinth, bearing a reproduction of the original plaque, was erected on the site in 1985.[22]

13

Ahimsa Returns to the West

I n the nineteenth century, materialism and faith in reason dominated European intellectual life. But they did not eradicate the ages-old belief that beyond the physical world there is a higher reality in the form of a transcendent, immaterial realm that represents the ultimate truth—a truth that can be approached better by feeling and intuition than by logic and reason. Among those inclined toward religion, this belief took the form of mysticism and spiritualism. Among those not inclined toward religion, it found expression in romanticism. By honoring emotion and intuition, mystics and romantics often opened themselves to empathy and compassion for all sentient beings in a way that rationalists and scientists typically did not—witness Anna Kingsford and Annie Besant.

The Fall from Grace

Modern Western mysticism derives largely from the work of Swedish theologian Emanuel Swedenborg (1688–1772), who experienced dreams and visions that he believed transported him directly into heaven, where he was taught by Christ, angels, and other spiritual beings.

Swedenborg's theology was based upon his doctrine of *correspondences*, which holds that patterns of reality in the physical world "correspond to," or imitate, patterns of reality in the spiritual realms. Drawing on the passage in Genesis (1:29–31) in which God institutes a vegan diet, Swedenborg said that meat eating corresponds to the fall from grace in the Garden of Eden and was, therefore, the point of entry of sin and suffering into the world.

Swedenborg did not, however, require his followers to keep to a vegetarian diet, holding that in our present fallen state, meat eating was permitted to us, as Genesis also reports (9:1–3). Whether Swedenborg himself ate meat is uncertain, and although he specifically rejected Descartes' claim that animals are automatons, he showed little concern for their suffering.

Swedenborg lived for a number of years in London, and was perhaps more popular in England than anywhere else outside of his native Sweden. By the beginning of the nineteenth century, the Swedenborgian "New Church," as it was called, was a fixture in several English cities, including Salford, a medium-sized industrial city bordering Manchester, where the pastor was a former Anglican curate named William Cowherd (1763–1816).

One Sunday morning, Cowherd—who had had a stormy relationship with the Swedenborgian leadership for several years over various matters of New Church doctrine—announced to his congregation that, despite Swedenborg's teaching to the contrary, authentic spirituality required a vegetarian diet for reasons of compassion toward God's sentient creation as well as for physical, mental, and spiritual health. The congregation got up and walked out, and in response, Cowherd—in 1809—organized the first vegetarian institution of any size or influence in the West since the demise of the Pythagorean Society fifteen hundred years earlier: the Bible Christian Church.[1] Cowherd's new denomination required that its members be vegetarian, and his church served free vegetarian meals to Salford's poor. In 1812, Martha Harvey Brotherton, a leading figure in the Church, published what may be the Western world's first vegetarian cookbook, entitled *A New System of Vegetable Cookery*.[2] In 1816, Cowherd died and Martha Brotherton's husband, Joseph (1783–1857) succeeded to the leadership of the Church.

The following year, William Metcalfe (1788–1862), who had been a close associate of Cowherd, led a group of forty-two Bible

Christians across the Atlantic, where the Church took root in Philadelphia, Boston, and other cities. There, Cowherd's doctrine of vegetarianism for physical and mental health—although not his message of compassion for animals—caught the attention of Sylvester Graham (of the eponymous cracker) and John Harvey Kellogg (of cereal fame), who would go on to play key roles in the creation of the American vegetarian movement. In both America and England, the Bible Christian Church enjoyed a promising early growth spurt followed by a long period as a small but stable institution. Then it began to quietly shrivel up until it vanished without a trace during the Great Depression.

The vegetarian movements that were born in the Axial Age had been first and foremost animal protection movements. Their goal had been to stop the killing of animals for human benefit, and vegetarianism was merely the necessary means toward that end. William Cowherd had taken a holistic approach to a vegetarian diet, teaching that it was essential to physical, mental, and spiritual health, and to reduce the innocent suffering of animals. By contrast, Sylvester Graham and John Kellogg were concerned exclusively with human health—both physical and mental—and they created a health-based vegetarian movement that separated itself from animal protection. As this is an animals' history, I will trace only the wing of the vegetarian movement that remained solidly connected to compassion.[3]

A Supereminence of Pain

The Romantic Movement was a secular counterpart to mysticism and spiritualism, although in some, such as poet and artist William Blake (1757–1827), mysticism and romanticism combined. Blake was deeply influenced by Swedenborg, and the word most often used to describe his work is "visionary." A vegetarian, he often spoke out in his poems against cruelty to animals.

The high point of the Romantic Movement in literature is represented by poet Percy Shelley (1792–1822) and his wife Mary (1797–1851), author of *Frankenstein.* Mary's mother, Mary

Wollstonecraft Godwin (1759–1797), who died following her daughter's birth, had been a feminist pioneer; and her father—radical political philosopher William Godwin (1756–1836)—had given Mary an excellent formal education while steeping her in his and her mother's progressive ideas.

Although Godwin was not a vegetarian and showed no interest in the plight of animals, he regularly entertained in his home the leading progressive thinkers of the day, a few of whom, such as literary historian Joseph Ritson (1771–1803) and vegetarian advocate John Frank Newton (1770–1827), believed that animals should benefit from social reforms as much as humans. It was at these *soirées* that young Mary Godwin became acquainted with Percy Shelley (although they had met earlier in her father's bookstore) and with the ethical vegetarianism that they practiced their entire adult lives. Influenced by Godwin and his friends, both were militant atheists, feminists, socialists, and advocates for the poor and disempowered of all classes, races, and species.

In 1813, Percy published *Queen Mab*, a long narrative poem to which he appended numerous footnotes, some of which were actually short essays. One of these he expanded into a booklet entitled *A Vindication of Natural Diet*, in which he put forward the secular counterpart to Swedenborg's argument that eating meat represented the fall from grace. When at some point in our distant past we began killing animals and eating their flesh, Shelley said, we infected ourselves with physical and spiritual illnesses that afflict us down to the present. Human health and happiness and the creation of a nurturing society depend on re-establishing humankind's original—and uniquely moral—vegetarian diet. Shelley felt so deeply about this that he portrayed animal enslavement and slaughter as nothing less than Satanic: "The supereminence of man is like Satan's, a supereminence of pain."[4]

Meat eating, or more precisely, the murder on which it depends, is the fundamental crime of humanity, the crime from which all of our other crimes, and most of our sorrows, flow. "The advantage of a reform in diet," he tells us, "is obviously greater than that of any other.

It strikes at the root of the evil."[5] Abolish meat eating, and we will not only wipe out animal cruelty, we will also be on our way to ending poverty, class differences, crime, disease, capitalism, and war.

In Mary Shelley's masterpiece, the monster—who represents natural innocence untarnished by society—is vegetarian, while the obsessed scientist who creates him—representing the greed and lust for knowledge at all costs that have corrupted modern society—is a meat eater.[6]

The Unforeseen Fruits of Empire

In 1757, Robert Clive—at the head of a private army authorized by the British government and paid for by the British East India Company—defeated Siraj ud Daulah, the last independent ruler of Bengal, inaugurating nearly two centuries of British colonial rule over India. Gradually, a cadre of English administrators, soldiers, businessmen, missionaries, adventurers, and scholars became the new Indian ruling class.

During the Axial Age, Indian philosophy had traveled along the trade routes to the Classical world, where Pythagoras repackaged it. In the nineteenth century, Indian thought returned to the West, carried this time by the guardians of empire, where it was repackaged in Europe by German philosopher Arthur Schopenhauer (1788–1860) and in America by the New England Transcendentalists.

Boundless Compassion—With Time Out for Lunch

During most of the nineteenth century, Immanuel Kant was still the dominant philosopher in Europe. For the most part, Schopenhauer considered himself to be a Kantian, but he took strong exception to Kant's ethical system. As we saw in Chapter 7, Kant considered ethics to be a matter of duty—the duty of every rational being (*i.e.*, every normal human being) to obey a moral law that was so absolute— "categorical," in Kant's term—that not even God could change it. Schopenhauer thought this was nonsense. Consciously reflecting the outlook of Hinduism and Buddhism, he believed that ethics should be based upon compassion and loving-kindness toward others.

> Boundless compassion for all living beings is the surest and most certain guarantee of pure moral conduct, and needs no casuistry. Whoever is filled with it will assuredly injure no one, do harm to no one, encroach on no man's rights; he will rather have regard for everyone, forgive everyone, help everyone as far as he can, and all his actions will bear the stamp of justice and loving-kindness.[7]

Like the Hindu and Buddhist teachers from whom (through books) he learned this fundamental ethical principle, Schopenhauer applied it to animals.

> It is asserted that beasts have no rights; the illusion is harbored that our conduct, so far as they are concerned, has no moral significance, or to put it in the language of these codes [the ethical systems of European philosophy], that "there are no duties to be fulfilled towards animals." Such a view is one of revolting coarseness, a barbarism of the West, whose source is Judaism.[8]

Attributing the notion that animals are without moral significance to Judaism, rather than to Greek philosophy and Christian theology, is, as we have seen in earlier chapters, bizarrely off the mark. It is, in fact, a reflection of the anti-Semitism that distorts Schopenhauer's work. A bit farther on, for example, he refers to the notion that animals exist solely for human benefit as "Jewish stench,"[9] which is both factually ridiculous and morally repugnant. Despite the protests of his apologists, Schopenhauer bears a portion of the guilt for the rise of National Socialism by virtue of his open and irrational hatred of all Jewish influences, real and imagined, on European intellectual life. He was also a misogynist who believed that women were innately inferior to men and inherently untrustworthy. While his

thought occupies a place in the history of animal protection that cannot be overlooked, Schopenhauer is hardly the poster boy for universal compassion and loving-kindness that he might appear to be at
first glance.

But to continue:

> Compassion for animals is intimately connected with good-
> ness of character, and it may be confidently asserted that he,
> who is cruel to living creatures, cannot be a good man.

> Europeans are awakening more and more to a sense that
> beasts have rights, in proportion as the strange notion is being
> gradually overcome and outgrown, that the animal kingdom
> came into existence solely for the benefit and pleasure of man.
> This view, with the corollary that non-human living creatures
> are to be regarded merely as things is at the root of the rough
> and altogether reckless treatment of them, which obtains in
> the West. To the honor, then, of the English be it said that they
> are the first people who have, in downright earnest, extended
> the protecting arm of the law to animals.[10]

Despite these noble sentiments, Schopenhauer was not a vegetarian, and he saw no moral impediment to killing animals for food.

> For the rest, we may observe that compassion for sentient
> beings is not to carry us to the length of abstaining from
> flesh, like the Brahmans [Hindus]. This is because, by a nat-
> ural law, capacity for pain keeps pace with the intelligence;
> consequently men, by going without animal food, especially
> in the North, would suffer more than beasts do by a quick
> death, which is always unforeseen; although the latter should
> always be made still easier by means of chloroform.[11]

The great irony here is that the anti-Semitic Schopenhauer ends
up by advocating the Biblical Compromise, a Jewish creation.

His "natural law" by which "capacity for pain keeps pace with the intelligence" is a naked assertion that he clothes in not one shred of evidence. It is a dishonest piece of sophistry whose sole purpose is to reconcile Schopenhauer's grand vision of boundless compassion for all sentient beings with a most uncompassionate eagerness to rob innocent animals of their lives because he enjoys the taste of their flesh.

The Death-Set Eyes of Beasts

The first great flowering of American intellectual life—apart from the burst of political genius that had given birth to the country— took place in Boston and Concord late in the first half of the nineteenth century. Influenced by Swedenborg, by way of Kant and Romanticism, the New England Transcendentalists—who included figures like Ralph Waldo Emerson (1803–1882), Nathaniel Hawthorne (1804–1864), Bronson Alcott (1799–1888), and Henry David Thoreau (1817–1862), also looked directly to ancient Indian Scriptures for inspiration. They believed in a higher reality, which the individual could approach intuitively, but not rationally; and here in the lower realm—to which they devoted the bulk of their attention—they were committed to social justice. Vehemently opposed to slavery, the Transcendentalists played leading roles in the abolitionist movement.

It seems fair to say that the Transcendentalists saw America as a new departure for humanity, a hopeful, unprecedented step on our species' path of spiritual, moral, political, and social improvement. Their aim was to provide intellectual underpinning, encouragement, and—where needed—correction to this noble American experiment. By and large, however, they did not see our treatment of animals as an issue of any great importance to their quest, and they were meat eaters—with one important exception.

A. Bronson Alcott (1799–1888)—who pioneered the liberal pedagogical principles that would guide American education in the twentieth century—had become a vegan early in life. Apparently, he came to veganism on his own, although he was supported and encouraged by Sylvester Graham, with whom he was acquainted, and by his cousin, Dr. William Alcott, a physician who was one of the leading voices in the vegetarianism-for-physical-and-mental-health movement that enjoyed a considerable vogue through much of the nineteenth century. Unlike Graham and cousin William, however, Bronson Alcott saw compassion for animals as a value in its own right—for the sake of the animals—as well as part and parcel of the physical, mental, and spiritual improvement of humanity.

Although he never ate meat himself, Alcott did for a while buy it for his wife (who later became a vegan), leading him to write one of the most moving passages in all the literature of animal protection as he recalled a visit to the butcher shop:

> Death yawns at me as I walk up and down in this abode of skulls. Murder and blood are written on its stalls. Cruelty stares at me from the butcher's face. I tread amidst carcasses. I am in the presence of the slain. The death-set eyes of beasts peer at me and accuse me of belonging to the race of murderers. Quartered, disemboweled creatures suspended on hooks plead with me. I feel dispossessed of the divinity. I am a replenisher of graveyards. I prowl, amidst other unclean spirits and voracious demons, for my prey.[12]

And once, when Emerson was pontificating on the evils of cannibalism while carving a roast, Alcott made the point that all meat eating is cannibalism by asking his host, "But Mr. Emerson, if we are to eat meat at all, why should we not eat the best?"[13]

In 1843, Alcott founded a vegan, pacifist, utopian socialist community just outside of Concord called Fruitlands, where it was said that he was so committed to nonviolence that he would not kill the worms who spoiled apples. But inadequate funding, a poor harvest, a cold winter, and internal dissension forced Fruitlands to close after just seven months.[14]

In 1838, English admirers of Bronson Alcott founded a vegan

utopian community in Surrey, not far from London. Originally known as Ham Common, from the grounds on which it was situated, it was renamed Alcott House following a visit by Bronson Alcott himself. In 1847, Alcott House and the Bible Christian Church, still under the leadership of Joseph Brotherton, played the leading roles in organizing the conference that founded the Vegetarian Society, of which a Bible Christian, James Simpson, was the first president.[15] By calling itself the "Vegetarian Society" rather than the "Pythagorean Society," the founders hoped to disabuse the Christian public of the notion that vegetarians formed some kind of exotic, pagan religious cult.

The conferees did not, as is sometimes claimed, coin the word "vegetarian;" it had been around for some time. But their adoption of it led to "vegetarian" replacing "Pythagorean" as the common term for a diet without meat.[16] One popular story would have it that "vegetarian" was derived from the Latin word *vegetus*, which means "lively," "fresh," or "vigorous," but there is no evidence to support this. The International Vegetarian Union calls the story a "myth" and points out that:

> In the early 1850s the magazine representing the [Vegetarian] Society had quite clearly defined it as: *'Vegetarian—one who lives on the products of the vegetable kingdom'.*[17]

It seems likely that "vegetarian" was derived from "vegetable" in the same way that "fruitarian" is derived from "fruit," or "Trinitarian" is derived from "trinity."

*   *   *

At the urging of William Metcalfe, who was still in touch with Bible Christian leaders in England, the first American Vegetarian Convention was held on May 15, 1850, in New York's Clinton Hall—where sixteen years later, Henry Bergh would lay the groundwork for the creation of the ASPCA. Organized by Metcalfe, Bronson Alcott, and Sylvester Graham, the Convention founded the American Vegetarian Society, with Alcott as president, and Metcalfe and Graham among a cadre of vice presidents large enough to run a major corporation—nine, to be exact, no doubt chosen to mollify the various factions that were present and assure that the new organization got off to a harmonious start.[18]

Despite the fact that Alcott and Metcalfe personally believed in animal protection for the sake of animals—as well as for other reasons—the proceedings of the Convention show very little attention being paid to the sentient beings whose flesh was the whole point of the gathering. Even when the cruelty of slaughter is decried, it is most often in terms of the deleterious effect that it has on the intellect and sensibilities of the butchers and the meat eaters—and through them on the society as a whole—rather than in terms of the suffering that it causes animals. Historians Karen and Michael Iacobbo offer this description of the resolutions passed by the Convention.

> Therefore, they resolved: anatomy, physiology, and chemical analysis of plant and animal substances show that humans are meant to eat plants; Paradise [the Garden of Eden], made by God for people, was vegetarian; human beings only eat animal flesh because they are in a degraded spiritual condition since the biblical Fall; to return to Paradise's conditions of purity, people must cease to kill and eat animals; plants provide proper nutrition; human senses of smell, taste, and sight prefer plants and grains to "the mangled carcasses of butchered animals;" flesh eating leads to other unnatural desires, whereas vegetable eating leads to serenity and strength; the flesh eater, unlike the vegetarian, can never enter into certain intellectual and moral delights; that cruelty "for the mere purpose of unnecessary food, or to gratify depraved appetite, is obnoxious to the pure human soul, and repugnant to the noblest aspects of our being;" . . . [and] promoting the vegetarian cause is an opportunity to elevate one's fellow human beings.[19]

These resolutions, while laudable in many ways, are breathtaking in their anthropocentric messianism. They represent a decision by the founders to present vegetarianism to the public, not as an instrument of simple compassion and common sense that would save countless animals from slaughter and improve human health, but as a crusade to reform human nature and redirect society. It is no wonder that to most people, vegetarians seemed more self-righteous than righteous, and vegetarianism took on the aspect of just another one of the addle-brained schemes that abounded on both sides of the Atlantic for creating heaven on earth, like anarchism or eugenics.

In 1862, in the midst of the Civil War, William Metcalfe died. The American Vegetarian Society did not long survive him, nor did the dream of a vegetarian nation.

The Destiny of the Human Race—But with Any Luck, Not in My Lifetime

Beyond Alcott, the leading Transcendentalists did not apply the nonviolence they had learned from Hinduism and Buddhism to animals. Emerson, Hawthorne, and Thoreau were not vegetarians, and their writings pay no more than pious lip service to animal suffering.

Here is Thoreau on the vegetarianism that he commended but did not practice:

> Is it not a reproach that man is a carnivorous animal? True, he can and does live, in a great measure, by preying on other animals; but this is a miserable way,—as anyone who may go on to snaring rabbits and slaughtering lambs may learn,—and he will be regarded as a benefactor of his race who shall teach man to confine himself to a more innocent and wholesome diet. *Whatever my own practice may be*, I have no doubt that it is a part of the destiny of the human race, in its gradual improvement, to leave off eating animals, as surely as the savage tribes have left off eating each other when they came in contact with the more civilized.[20]

The contrast between Thoreau and Bronson Alcott—both of whom recognized that meat eating is wrong—could not be more striking. Alcott took personal responsibility for his behavior and modified his diet to remove the cruelty from it. Thoreau tried to avoid personal responsibility for his behavior by treating the end of animal cruelty as a matter of the "gradual improvement" of humanity over centuries or millennia, rather than as a personal moral issue.

While living by Walden Pond, Thoreau fished frequently, ate what he caught, with no visible qualms of conscience, and complained that Walden Pond was a poor fishing site.[21] He also dined regularly at the homes of his friends, where he ate meat without hesitation. Thoreau did not hunt—he gave up hunting as a young man—but looked back upon it fondly and joined Rousseau in regarding hunting as an essential part of a boy's education.[22]

A Missionary among Savages

Henry S. Salt (1851–1939) was born in India, the son of an officer in the British colonial army. Sent back to England as an infant, educated at Eton and Cambridge, he taught at Eton until 1884, when he retired to a cottage in Surrey to devote himself to writing and social advocacy. While teaching at Eton, he had been converted to vegetarianism by his brother-in-law, J. L. Joynes, now forgotten, but in his lifetime a well-known socialist, pacifist, and social reformer. A prolific writer, Salt wrote numerous essays and books on animal rights, including *A Plea for Vegetarianism and Other Essays* (1886) and *Animals' Rights Considered in Relation to Social Progress* (1892), in which he advanced most of the primary arguments that are now used in defense of animal rights.

With Hinduism, Buddhism, and Schopenhauer, Salt argued that morality consists in acting out of compassion toward all sentient beings, human and nonhuman, in everything we do. He argued passionately against hunting and shooting, against all forms of vivisection, against raising and slaughtering animals for food and clothing, and in favor of vegetarianism.

Salt called his philosophy of life "humanitarianism," by which he meant human rights and animal rights taken together as one indivisible whole. Deeply influenced by Shelley, he said apropos of *Queen Mab*:

> For when the oneness of life shall be recognized, such practices as blood-sports will be not only childish but impossible; vivisection unthinkable; and the butchery of our fellow-animals for food an outgrown absurdity of the past.[23]

Even so, Salt did not make Shelley's mistake of supposing that vegetarianism was a cure for all the world's ills.

> [N]or will man's responsibility be diminished by ... [the] contention that vivisection, or sport, or flesh-eating, as the case may be, is the one prime origin of all human inhumanity. We want a comprehensive principle that will cover all these varying instances....[24]

In 1891, Salt founded the Humanitarian League to advance his philosophy—it survived until 1920—and he was active in the Vegetarian Society for most of his life. But it was as the author of arguments such as these that Henry Salt made his greatest contribution to animals' rights:

> When we have grasped the great central fact about animals, that they are in the full sense our fellow-beings, all else will follow for them; and we shall know, and act upon the knowledge, that in the words of Howard Moore, author of that memorable book *The Universal Kinship*: "They are not conveniences but cousins."[25]

> ... almost every conceivable form of cowardly slaughter is practised as "sportsmanlike" and commended as "manly". All this, moreover, is done before the eyes and for the example of

mere youths and children, who are thus from their tenderest years instructed in the habit of being pitiless and cruel.[26]

That those who are aware of the horrors involved in slaughtering, and also aware of the possibility of a fleshless diet, should think it sufficient to oppose "scriptural permission" as an answer to the arguments of food reformers is an instance of the extraordinary power of custom to blind the eyes and the hearts of otherwise humane men.[27]

Henry Salt wrote his own eulogy, in which he gave this description of the credo by which he had lived:

... when I say I shall die, as I have lived, rationalist, socialist, pacifist, and humanitarian, I must make my meaning clear. I wholly disbelieve in the present established religion; but I have a very firm religious faith of my own—a Creed of Kinship I call it—a belief that in years yet to come there will be a recognition of brotherhood between man and man, nation and nation, human and subhuman, which will transform a state of semi-savagery, as we have it, into one of civilisation, when there will be no such barbarity of warfare, or the robbery of the poor by the rich, or the ill-usage of the lower animals by mankind.[28]

In an era when the popular heroes of empire were writing smug, patronizing memoirs of their own courage and sacrifice among the "primitive" peoples of Africa, Asia, and the Middle East, Henry Salt titled his 1921 autobiography *Seventy Years among Savages*. He had lived his entire life in England.

"The First Step"

After completing his second great masterpiece, *Anna Karenina*, in 1876, Russian novelist Count Leo Tolstoy (1828–1910) fell into a profound spiritual crisis. Feeling that life had no meaning, he searched the Christian, Hindu, and Buddhist scriptures for an answer to his malaise. Finally, he found it in the Sermon on the Mount (Matthew 5–7), in which—influenced by his studies of Indian thought—he discovered a gospel of boundless compassion and an absolute command to nonviolence, even in self-defense. Universal compassion and complete nonviolence were, Tolstoy believed, the message of Jesus to the world and the key to living in harmony with God's will. Applying this gospel consistently to all of God's sentient creatures, for the last decades of his life Tolstoy was a vegetarian who condemned hunting—which, like most of the old Russian nobility, he had previously enjoyed.

Tolstoy poured his outrage at the killing of animals for meat into the essay "The First Step" (1892), in which he described a vegetarian diet as the essential first step toward a moral—that is to say, a nonviolent—life.

> If he be really and seriously seeking to live a good life, the first thing from which [a person] will abstain will always be the use of animal food, because, to say nothing of the excitation of the passions caused by such food, its use is simply immoral, as it involves the performance of an act which is contrary to the moral feeling—killing; and is called forth only by greediness and the desire for tasty food.

"The Moral Basis of Vegetarianism"

Mohandas Karamchand Gandhi (1869–1948) was the son of a local official in the Indian state of Gujarat. Although his mother was extremely religious—in the Jain-influenced Hinduism of the region that emphasized nonviolence and vegetarianism—Mohandas, like the children of most prosperous Indian families, grew up admiring Western customs (although not Western imperialism) and wanting to adopt Western ways. As a young teenager, he occasionally ate meat out of his mother's sight, in the belief that eating meat made the English strong, while a vegetarian diet kept Indians weak.

In 1888, Gandhi traveled to London to study law. Before he left, however, his mother—who knew her son better than he realized—made him swear an oath, administered by a Jain monk, that he would consume no meat or eggs while he was away. Out of respect for his mother, Gandhi, who was not particularly religious at this point in his life, kept his vow, even though he found it a hardship. Then, he read Henry Salt's *A Plea for Vegetarianism*.

> From the date of reading this book, I may claim to have become a vegetarian by choice. I blessed the day on which I had taken the vow before my mother. I had all along abstained from meat in the interests of truth and the vow I had taken, but had wished at the same time that every Indian should be a meat-eater, and had looked forward to being one myself freely and openly some day, and enlisting others in the cause. The choice was now made in favor of vegetarianism, the spread of which henceforward became my mission.[29]

In addition to Henry Salt, Gandhi familiarized himself with the work of—and in many cases counted among his friends—the leading figures in the European vegetarian and anti-vivisection movements, including Anna Kingsford, whose book *The Perfect Way in Diet* he praised highly; Annie Besant, who was also active in the struggle to liberate India from British rule; and Leo Tolstoy, whom he admired and with whom he corresponded.

In 1931, Gandhi addressed the Vegetarian Society on the subject "The Moral Basis of Vegetarianism," urging the members to promote a meat-free diet as a bedrock moral issue, rather than a matter of human health. Since the Vegetarian Society had always been a more or less uncomfortable coalition between those concerned with human health and those who objected to the killing of animals, Gandhi's talk was a not very subtle rebuke to the human health faction. It was, in fact, a ringing call for the vegetarian movement to align itself with what Henry Salt—who was present when Gandhi spoke—had dubbed "animals' rights," and it presaged the vegan movement that would be inaugurated by Donald Watson thirteen years later.

> ... vegetarians had a habit of talking of nothing but food and nothing but disease. I feel that that is the worst way of going about the business. I notice also that it is those persons who become vegetarians because they are suffering from some disease or other—that is, from purely the health point of view—it is those persons who largely fall back. I discovered that for remaining staunch to vegetarianism a man requires a moral basis. For me that was a great discovery in my search after truth. At an early age, in the course of my experiments, I found that a selfish basis would not serve the purpose of taking a man higher and higher along the paths of evolution. What was required was an altruistic purpose.

Gandhi also cautioned against the self-righteousness that we have already remarked was a feature of the vegetarian movement.

> What I want to bring to your notice is that vegetarians need to be tolerant if they want to convert others to vegetarianism. Adopt a little humility. We should appeal to the moral sense of the people who do not see eye to eye with us. If a vegetarian became ill, and a doctor prescribed beef tea, then I would not call him a vegetarian. A vegetarian is made of sterner stuff. Why? Because it is for the building of the spirit and not of the body.... Therefore, I think that what vegetarians should do is not to emphasise the physical consequences of vegetarianism, but to explore the moral consequences.

Unlike most Indians who grew up in the tradition of cow protection, Gandhi recognized the problematic nature of milk—although he regarded it as a less serious issue than meat—but he drank it daily on his doctors' advice, saying:

I know we must all err. I would give up milk if I could, but I
cannot. I have made that experiment times without number.
I could not, after a serious illness, regain my strength, unless
I went back to milk. That has been the tragedy of my life.[30]

Earlier, I talked about the cloak of invisibility that protects our
oppression of animals. Nowhere is it spread more blatantly than
over Gandhi's vegetarianism. Volumes are written about Gandhi's
commitment to nonviolence in defense of poor and oppressed
human beings, but his equally strong commitment to nonviolence
in defense of oppressed animals is passed over in silence. Thomas
Merton, for example, edited a volume of Gandhi's sayings on
ahimsa and *satyagraha*, Gandhi's philosophy of nonviolent social
protest. The only comment on vegetarianism that he saw fit to
include is this one: "I have known many meat-eaters to be far more
non-violent than vegetarians."[31] Assuming that the quote is authentic, Merton must have searched long and hard to find that particular saying buried among Gandhi's myriad statements in support of
vegetarianism.

Vegan scholar and advocate Keith Akers notes that:

The motion picture epic "Gandhi" (which appeared in the
early 1980s) popularized the life and ideas of the Mahatma,
yet during the length of this otherwise excellent motion picture there was never a single reference to Gandhi's vegetarianism.[32]

And yet Gandhi himself saw vegetarianism as an integral part of
his philosophy and work. Gandhi student Arun Sannuti sums up the
importance of vegetarianism to Gandhi:

Gandhi's choice to become vegetarian started him on the
road towards ahimsa, renunciation, and finally, satyagraha
itself. Without it, he would have never realized the power of
morality and never would have become the Mahatma.

Reverence for Life

At thirty years of age, Albert Schweitzer (1875–1965) was a renowned organist, a musicologist whose study of Johann Sebastian Bach is still read, a Unitarian theologian who revolutionized our understanding of Christian origins, and a professor of philosophy and theology at the prestigious University of Strasbourg. But in 1905, he gave it all up to study tropical medicine and surgery and become a medical missionary in French Equatorial Africa. In 1913, the newly-minted physician journeyed to Lambarene, in what is now the Republic of Gabon, where he established a hospital for Africans. There, except for brief periods, he remained until his death at the age of ninety.

Steeped in the philosophy of Schopenhauer and the teachings of Hinduism and Buddhism—he wrote a lengthy study of *Indian Thought and its Development*—Schweitzer began searching for an ultimate moral principle that would express universal empathy for all living things. In 1915, it crystallized for him into the phrase "reverence for life," which came in a flash of inspiration while he was hitching a ride on a barge up the Ogooue River to Lambarene.[33] As he expressed it in *The Philosophy of Civilization*, published in 1923:

> I am life which wills to live, in the midst of life which wills to live.... Ethics consist, therefore, in my experiencing the compulsion to show to all will-to-live the same reverence as I do to my own.... It is good to maintain and encourage life; it is bad to destroy life or to obstruct it.[34]

In his memoir of his early life, Schweitzer made it clear that reverence for life applied fully and directly to nonhuman animals. "Because the extension of the principle of love to animal creation means so great a revolution for ethics, philosophy shrinks from this step."[35]

Even so, it was not until the last decade of his life that Albert Schweitzer adopted a vegetarian diet. When he did, however, it was with the kind of moral conviction that Gandhi had spoken of to the Vegetarian Society. According to his biographer, Erika Andersen, when he lay on his deathbed in Lambarene, his daughter tried to persuade him to take some beef broth in the hope of restoring his strength. With what were nearly his final breaths, Schweitzer refused.[36]

A Footnote to History: The World's Longest Life Sentence

Robert Clive, who founded the British Raj in India, owned four Aldabran tortoises—kidnapped from their island home in the Indian Ocean—who roamed the grounds of his estate in Bengal. When Clive returned to England in 1767, the tortoises were passed on to others. Three disappeared from history, but one, named Adwaitya ("The One and Only" in Bengali) passed away on March 23, 2006, having outlived his onetime colonial master by two hundred and thirty-two years, and the Raj itself by fifty-nine years. For Adwaitya, however, Indian independence did not mean freedom. Since 1875, under both British and Indian rule, he had been imprisoned in the municipal zoo at Calcutta. All told, Adwaitya endured captivity for roughly two hundred and forty-six of his estimated two hundred and fifty years of life, and at least a hundred and thirty-one of them confined in a zoo.[37]

14

One Step Forward, Twenty Steps Back

I n less than a century and a half, the Industrial Revolution accomplished what twenty-five hundred years of animal advocacy had never even attempted. It released animals from slave labor. Apart from a few isolated remnants, between 1800 and 1940 the use of animals to do humanity's heavy lifting came to an abrupt end in the industrialized world. A burden that had been placed on the backs of animals some ten thousand years ago was finally being lifted.

In 1765, Scottish engineer James Watt built the first working model of a steam engine that produced energy efficiently enough to have practical applications. By 1776, the first industrial (stationary) steam engines were in operation, and in 1804, the first steam-powered railroad engine began running in Wales. Three years later, the world's first steam-powered passenger train went into operation, also in Wales. By mid-century, railroads had replaced horse- and mule-drawn wagons, carriages, and barges for most over-the-road transportation of people and goods. But steam engines were too big and heavy, too hot and noisy, used too much fuel in the form of wood or coal, and required too long to heat up before a trip to be of much use for personal transportation or for local hauling within cities. And so local transportation remained the province of the horse and the mule until the early twentieth century.

In 1876, German engineer Nikolaus Otto built a four-stroke gasoline engine, the first internal combustion engine powerful and efficient enough for practical use. Another German engineer, Gottlieb

Daimler, realized that Otto's invention—smaller and lighter, cooler and quieter, quick starting, and needing less fuel than a steam engine—was ideal for powering smaller vehicles suitable for personal and local transport. In 1885, he developed an improved version of the gasoline engine, which he attached to a stagecoach, thereby creating the first automobile.

Henry Ford, an American engineer with the Edison Light Company, saw the growing popularity of "horseless carriages" and devised a method for building them quickly and cheaply by creating a production line, on which the equipment was stationary and the automobile being built moved along the line on conveyers. Ford later said that he had gotten the idea by watching the carcasses of slaughtered cattle being conveyed along the line at Chicago's Union Stock Yards. In 1908, Ford brought out the reliable and affordable Model T, of which he sold nearly a million a year for the next two decades. By the mid-nineteen-thirties, working horses and mules had become an unusual sight in the city streets of North America and Western Europe, as cars and trucks took over the transport of people and goods.

Steam-powered farm implements gained some popularity on large farms from the mid-nineteenth century on, but they were hot and clumsy to use, and difficult to keep supplied with fuel. Then in 1892, an Iowa inventor named John Froelich built the first practical gasoline-powered tractor. Before long, Ford, John Deere, and other companies were mass-producing tractors, and by World War II, horses and mules were still used only on small farms by old men who were unwilling to adopt the new technology, and by the very poor, who were unable to afford it.

"It's Your Misfortune"

From the victims' point of view, animal agriculture changed little from the Neolithic Revolution until the middle of the twentieth century. With only minor variations, farmers and ranchers followed the same basic model, regardless of when or where they lived. Animals were kept confined in fields where they could find food and water, and nature was allowed to take its course. Farmed animals were in prison: they were not able to manage their own lives and organize their own societies, and they were under a sentence of early death from the day they were born—but they were not yet in concentration camps.

The first signs of the coming change appeared in the 1850s, when the white seizure of the American West and the attendant destruction of the great buffalo herds that occupied it began opening up vast amounts of rangeland, suitable for cattle grazing and not much else, to exploitation by settlers hungry for land. The giant cattle ranches that were established in the third quarter of the nineteenth century got their start by supplying beef to the army that was engaged in destroying the Indians and occupying the West. During the Civil War and the intensified Indian wars that followed, the army's demand for beef accelerated. As the early cowboys told the calves, in a lullaby of death that they sang during roundups:

> You're gonna be soup for Uncle Sam's soldiers.
> It's "Beef, more beef," they always cry.
> Git along, git along, git along, little doaggies.
> You're gonna grow up to be beef by and by.
>
> Yippee ti-yi-yo, git along, little doaggies,
> It's your misfortune and none of my own.[1]

Supported this way by the army, the ranches soon grew productive enough to begin shipping beef back to the rapidly growing cities of the East and Midwest. The modern American diet—which is more meat-intensive than any diet in human history, apart from the Inuit—had its beginnings in the sudden, unprecedented availability of cheap beef, coupled with expanding populations of immigrants from Europe, who viewed meat as a sign of success. In the old country, only the wealthy could eat meat regularly; here in the Promised Land, even working people could afford the flesh of dead animals several times a week. Dudley Giehl observes, "The desire of the working class for meat is noted in a Democratic satire on Whig politics in 1842:

> And then your wages we'll raise high,
> Two dollars and roast beef."[2]

By the end of the century, the children and grandchildren of these immigrants would be eating meat three times a day every day of the week, and regarding it as their American birthright.

Given the numbers involved and the lack of good refrigeration, it was more efficient to ship cattle long distances to centralized slaughterhouses than it was to slaughter them locally and ship the dressed beef. And this involved a ratcheting-up of the cruelty entailed in animal agriculture. The method was to take the herds on a forced march—called a "cattle drive"—from the ranch to a railhead, where they would be loaded onto cattle cars and shipped east to the slaughterhouses, located in large Midwestern cities like Omaha, Kansas City, and Chicago.

Western cattle drives were not the leisurely meanderings of primitive herders; they were precisely what I called them, "forced marches," in which the object was to move the cattle to the railhead—which was most often several hundred miles from the ranch—as quickly as possible. Even so, at ten to twelve miles a day, which was as fast as a large herd of cattle could be driven, a typical cattle drive took up to three months of sheer torture for the animals.[3] Deaths were a daily occurrence, as animals who were weak or injured and could not keep up were either butchered for the cowboys to eat or left behind to die. Gradually, as the railroads spread through the West, the drives grew shorter, and by the late 1880s, they had become a thing of the past.

Once at the railhead, the exhausted animals were crammed into cattle cars for a trip to the slaughterhouse that would typically take two to three days or longer. Without food or water, and with no room to lie down, the cattle suffered even more on the way to the slaughterhouse than they had on the forced march to the railhead. Many died. All endured bleak, unspeakable agony.

Since cattle were typically shipped across state lines—and states are forbidden by the Constitution from regulating interstate commerce—state legislatures were powerless to come to the animals' rescue. And so, local Humane Societies and SPCAs, led by Henry Bergh and the ASPCA, turned their attention to Washington, and in 1873 they persuaded Congress to enact the first national animal protection law in the United States. The so-called "Twenty-Eight Hour Law" required that livestock being transported by rail or barge were given food, water, and rest every twenty-eight hours.[4]

It was little enough. But time was money, and in the second half of the nineteenth century, the railroads were among the wealthiest and most politically powerful entities in the country. They simply made no effort to comply, and the Department of Agriculture, which was charged with administering the Twenty-Eight Hour Law, failed to enforce it.

When the animals had been given no relief after four years, John G. Shortall, president of the Illinois Humane Society, brought together representatives from a number of state and local humane organizations to create the American Humane Association (AHA) for the specific purpose of gaining enforcement of the Twenty-Eight Hour Law. Although the AHA was able to defend the Law against legal challenges by the railroad and cattle industries, it failed in its primary purpose. The Department of Agriculture did not begin enforcing the Twenty-Eight Hour Law until 1905, under pressure from the rising tide of public outrage at conditions in the meatpacking industry that would lead to the Federal Meat Inspection Act the following year.

After a promising start, the American Humane Association quickly abandoned their activist stance, and by the mid-1880s, most of their efforts were devoted to working cooperatively with cattle ranchers, railroads, and meatpackers to "improve conditions." By the late 1890s, the staff of the AHA, which by now had been thoroughly co-opted by the industry, was reporting that most cattle shipping and meatpacking operations were "clean and humane," a claim that a federal investigation in 1906 would show had been a bald-faced lie. The delegates to the AHA's national convention in 1899 didn't believe it either, and rebelled against their own officers, demanding that the organization take a more aggressive stance toward the industry and toward enforcement of the Twenty-Eight Hour Law.[5]

Nothing changed, however, and the AHA continued to play its role of providing protective cover to the animal abuse industries until 1954, when four of its officers, led by Fred Myers, quit in disgust and created The Humane Society of the United States.[6] The American Humane Association was, you will recall, the group that in 1900 expelled those of its member organizations that campaigned against vivisection.

Today, the AHA—which now calls itself simply American Humane—remains little more than an industry front, taking aggressive stands only on issues that generate little controversy in the United States, like the Canadian seal hunt and animal fighting. As to farmed animals, their primary effort is the "Free Farmed" program, which puts American Humane's official stamp of approval on meat that comes from animals who were not raised in the intensive confinement conditions that will be described later in this chapter, so that "consumers can be guaranteed that the products they select come from animals who were raised and treated compassionately and humanely."[7] They do not promote vegetarianism, and fail to understand that innocent imprisonment and slaughter to satisfy our appetites is inherently inhumane and devoid of compassion.

The Great Chicago Death Camp

The old slaughterhouses of the Midwest could not handle the torrent of beef on the hoof that the railroads were bringing in to feed the growing appetite of the big cities. Relief arrived in 1865 in the form of Chicago's Union Stock Yard, a vast, sprawling complex of railroad terminals, holding pens for cattle and pigs, ramps and chutes for moving the doomed animals from the cattle cars to the holding pens and from the pens to the slaughterhouses, and finally, the slaughterhouses themselves—known in the euphemism of the industry as "packinghouses"—which were operated by several of the largest animal killing companies in the world, including Armour and Swift.

The Union Stock Yard, which Jeremy Rifkin calls a "disassembly plant," operated on what was then a novel principle. The equipment, and the employees who operated it, remained stationary, while the cattle who were being "disassembled"—killed, drained of their blood, disemboweled, skinned, and hacked into cuts of meat—were moved along by steam-powered overhead conveyers past each of the various work stations in the slaughterhouse. As with the railroads, time was money, and the motorized conveyer system made it possible to kill cows and hack them into edible little pieces faster than anyone had imagined possible. Profits soared, and the Union Stock Yard became the model for cattle-slaughtering operations throughout the Midwest and around the world.

Construction began in June 1865, and on Christmas Day of that same year, the world's largest and first fully mechanized, consolidated stockyard and slaughterhouse held its official grand opening. By 1900, the Union Stock Yard had taken the lives of four hundred million cattle.[8] Until the creation of high-volume chicken processing plants in the late twentieth century, the Union Stock Yard was the largest death camp that human beings had ever operated.

Inside was pure hell for animals and workers—stifling in the summer, freezing in the winter, every exposed surface slick with gore and filth, the air thick with the stench of blood and death, and the everlasting screams of animals—not yet dead but maimed by the knife and the saw—drowning out all other sounds. And while the public might not care a great deal about the fate of the animals, the labor movement cared about the workers. By the early 1900s, union leaders and muckraking journalists were campaigning for improved working conditions, and public pressure began building on Congress to regulate the meatpacking industry. Then, in early 1906, Upton Sinclair, a young socialist who wanted to remake the world through fiction, published *The Jungle,* a naturalistic novel about Lithuanian immigrants working in the Union Stock Yard. Sinclair had spent seven weeks living in the Union Settlement House—low-cost housing provided by the University of Chicago for workers and their families—interviewing stock yard employees and their wives and children.[9] His aim, as he described it himself, was to write "the *Uncle Tom's Cabin* of the labor movement."

Sinclair cared about the workers, not the animals, but it turned out that the public was more concerned about themselves than either the workers or the animals. *The Jungle's* horrific descriptions of conditions inside the slaughterhouses—including the carcasses of diseased animals being turned into meat for human consumption—struck terror into the hearts of meat-eating Americans. A public outcry over the safety of American meat led to an on-site investigation by a Presidential Commission—which found conditions very much as Sinclair had described them—and the passage, in June of that same year, of the federal Meat Inspection Act of 1906. Sardonically, the would-be Harriet Beecher Stowe of the labor movement remarked, "I aimed at the public's heart, and by accident, I hit it in the stomach."

The Meat Inspection Act required the health inspection of livestock prior to slaughter and of the meat after slaughter; it established sanitation standards for slaughterhouses and directed the U. S. Department of Agriculture to maintain a continual inspection regime. These measures made meat a lot safer and working conditions a bit better, but they did nothing for the animals. Now sometimes touted as a milestone in animal protection, the Meat Inspection Act of 1906 was actually an effort—largely successful—to preserve animal cruelty by protecting human beings from its consequences.

The Union Stock Yard closed in 1971, a victim of the decentralization that became the standard in the meatpacking industry during the 1960s. Unionization (it was easier to keep unions out of small plants), the increasing use of trucks as opposed to railroads (partly as a result of the Interstate Highway System, begun in the 1950s, and partly because trucks were still not covered by the Twenty-Eight Hour

Law[10]), and improved refrigeration had made smaller plants scattered about the country more economical than huge, consolidated operations. An industrial park now stands on the site. But the ornate stone arch that formed the main entrance, erected in 1879, has been preserved by the city of Chicago—proud of its reputation as "hog butcher for the world"—as an historical landmark.

With the creation of industrial packinghouses, the slaughterhouse was no longer the crimp in the meat production pipeline. Meat packers could kill and disassemble as many animals as the ranchers could ship. As the market for meat continued to grow, attention shifted to the raising of the animals, and the challenge became how to raise more animals faster with more usable meat per animal.

A Quantum Leap in Cruelty

The response to that challenge was slow in coming because it depended on two scientific breakthroughs that were not made until the twentieth century. But when it came, it abolished farms as they had existed since the Neolithic Revolution, and replaced them with factories in which animals were treated as raw materials to be turned into a finished product as quickly and cheaply as possible. The natural model for raising animals was out; the industrial model was in.

The first breakthrough was the discovery in 1908 by German chemist Fritz Haber of a process for extracting nitrogen, in the form of ammonia, from the air. Following refinements to the process by Haber's colleague, engineer and chemist Carl Bosch, mass production of nitrogen fertilizer began in 1913, making possible for the first time in history the large-scale, monocrop cultivation of grains like wheat and corn, which deplete nitrogen from the soil. Since industrial animal production requires that the animals be fed large quantities of grain (pigs are never allowed to forage; cattle are not allowed to graze during the final months of their lives), the invention of the Haber-Bosch Process for producing nitrogen fertilizer paved the way for factory farming, the immediate catalyst for which was the discovery of antibiotics.[11]

Industrial animal agriculture entails raising large numbers of animals in an unnaturally small space, a practice the industry calls "concentrated animal feeding operations" (CAFO). These are laboratory-perfect conditions for the proliferation of pathogens and the rapid spread of disease. Without antibiotics, herds and flocks kept in intensive confinement would be wiped out before the animals were old enough to ship to slaughter.

As we saw earlier, the first antibiotic, penicillin, was discovered by Scottish pharmacologist Alexander Fleming in 1928. Because penicillin was very difficult to obtain, however, Fleming's discovery was of little use until 1939, when scientists at Cambridge developed a procedure for mass-producing it synthetically. By the end of World War II, antibiotics were in wide use against everything from syphilis to tuberculosis, and following the war, scientists working in the field of animal husbandry discovered that the new wonder drugs could be used to prevent disease in farmed animals. By the 1970s, farmers realized that antibiotics would also stimulate muscle growth (i.e., meat production) and milk output. In contemporary farming, the routine treatment of healthy animals with antibiotics—and, in the case of cattle, the more recently developed synthetic growth hormones—is standard procedure.

The conversion of farms from prisons into concentration camps began slowly in the years following World War II and grew rapidly during the 1950s and '60s. The system works somewhat differently for different animals, but the fundamental principles are the same: 1) Control every aspect of the animals' nutrition and environment with a view to obtaining the most meat, milk, or eggs in the minimum time at the least expense; and 2) Make all animal care decisions based exclusively on cost-effectiveness—do not consider the welfare of the animals, as this will reduce the profit margin. The industry likes to tell the public that happy, healthy animals are better producers than sick, depressed animals, and so it is in the company's interest to promote good living conditions. This is a lie. In fact, the opposite is true.

Cows

Cattle endure the least oppressive form of intensive confinement. According to Jeffrey Moussaieff Masson, beef cattle:

> are weaned at six to 10 months of age, live three to five months on the range, spend four to five months being fattened on a feedlot, and are typically slaughtered at 15 to 20 months. Considering that their average lifespan is nine to 12 years, these animals live only a brief fraction of the time they were meant to live.[12]

All animals raised for food are killed before they have time to grow up. Steaks and burgers, bacon, sausage, and Chicken McNuggets are the flesh of children.

A feedlot is a large pen, usually outdoors with a concrete floor, in which several thousand beef cattle are held so they can be fed a special food mixture, including recombinant bovine growth hormone (rBGH), that will fatten them up quickly. Since the stomachs of cattle are meant to digest grass, the feedlot mixture causes diarrhea and a bevy of other gastric disorders. As you can imagine, feedlots are all feces, urine, flies, and the potent chemicals that are used to suppress disease under conditions that are pathogen paradise. A typical feedlot holds about five thousand cattle on ten acres of hoof-wounding, feces-covered concrete.

The cruelty required by commercial milk production is even worse. A cow is not a milk machine. She is a female mammal, and like other mammals, she only lactates when she has been pregnant. To keep a steady supply of milk coming, a cow has to be made pregnant every year of her adult life. And to keep the milk going to humans who don't need it, the calf who does must be deprived of it. Female calves are typically taken from their mothers a few days after birth; some are fed a milk substitute and eventually turned into dairy cows themselves; others are sold to be slaughtered for beef. About one in five male calves are taken from their mothers almost immediately after birth and confined in cages—known as "veal crates"—so narrow they cannot lie down, turn around, or lick themselves, the idea being to prevent them from developing muscle tone, which would make the veal less tender. They are then fed a diet completely lacking in iron, which, as you might expect, causes a severe iron deficiency anemia that leaves the muscle tissue white, the color favored by connoisseurs of veal. At just fifteen weeks old, still a baby, the veal calf is sent to slaughter. The remaining male calves are fed a synthetic diet and sold into beef herds.

Dairy cows are kept in a completely controlled environment. Whether they are held indoors on a concrete surface that damages their hooves, or outdoors in a small yard that turns to ankle-deep mud when it rains, they are not allowed to graze, but are fed a special formula that increases their milk output. After five or six years of constant pregnancy, twice-daily milking, and an improper diet, a dairy cow is exhausted—"spent" in the jargon of the industry—and sent off to slaughter.

Pigs

Pigs are the latest animals to fall under the yoke of factory farming. As recently as twenty-five years ago, most pigs were still raised on family farms in some kind of loose confinement. But in the 1980s and '90s, agribusiness moved in on the family pig farmer in a big way, and today giant factory farms holding thousands of pigs in crowded confinement sheds are the industry standard.

In nature, baby pigs are born in nests of leaves and soft straw lovingly made by their mothers. Factory-farmed pigs come into the world on the concrete floor of a farrowing pen. Farrowing pens and gestation crates are metal cages so narrow that the mother pig has no room to move around. She spends her adult life on twenty-two inches of hard concrete, first in the gestation crate being artificially inseminated and waiting to give birth, then in the farrowing pen having her babies and nursing them. When one family of babies is ready to be weaned, she is taken back to the gestation crate, impregnated again, and the cycle starts anew. After eight pregnancies, she is considered "spent" and sent to slaughter.[13]

At about three weeks of age, baby pigs are taken from their mothers and sent to a "finishing shed," where their lives are defined by concrete floors, cinderblock or corrugated walls, artificial light, and rank, nasty-smelling air. Most never see sunlight or feel the earth beneath their feet. None will ever be able to run and play, root in the ground, or roll in the mud, all activities that are born into the nature of pigs. Crammed in cheek by jowl with hundreds of their fellows, normally gentle, easygoing pigs turn vicious and begin biting one another's tails. Since this causes infection and lowers production, hog farmers routinely cut off the tails of their pigs without anesthesia. (Among free-ranging pigs, tail biting does not occur; it is a sign that overcrowding and unnatural confinement drive the pigs insane.) They are sent to slaughter when they reach 250 pounds, half their adult weight.

Chickens

Chickens make up nine billion of the ten billion animals killed every year in the United States for food. And they spend their short, doomed lives in the most horrific conditions of any farmed animal.

There are two distinct kinds of chickens: "broilers," who are raised for their flesh, and "layers," who are raised for their eggs. Both spend their entire lives inside a dark, foul-smelling building with no opportunity to see the sun, smell fresh air, walk around pecking at the ground, or take dust baths. Broiler chickens live on an open floor in an enclosed "confinement shed," where they are crowded to such a density that they typically are allowed only 115 square inches per bird, a space about ten by twelve inches, barely larger than a sheet of typing paper. Compare this to the fact that an adult chicken needs a minimum of 197 square inches to turn around, 138 square inches to stretch, 290 square inches to flap wings, and 172 square inches to preen, all basic biological activities.[14]

Laying hens get even less space. Most live in small wire pens, called battery cages, stacked horizontally and vertically in a confinement shed. A typical battery cage is twelve inches by eighteen inches and holds three or four chickens. The industry standard is sixty-seven square inches of living space per bird—about two-thirds the size of a sheet of typing paper—in which the chickens have to live out their entire lives.[15] But overcrowding is only one of the horrors that factory chickens have to endure. The poorly ventilated confinement sheds are gas chambers, filled with toxic ammonia from the urine of tens of thousands of chickens. One night in March of 2001, Miyun Park and three other investigators from the Washington, D.C. animal rights group Compassion Over Killing surreptitiously entered a laying hen confinement shed in nearby Maryland. Here is what they found:

> [W]e could smell the stench of thousands of pounds of excrement, disease, and death.... [W]e made our way through a manure pit on the ground level, walking between three-foot-high mounds of excrement extending nearly the length of two football fields. The dim light from our headlamps prevented us from accidentally stepping on the decomposing corpses of hens who had escaped their cages only to fall into the pit and die surrounded by manure. Still living birds wandered aimlessly around the pit [unable to get to food or water].
>
> We were surrounded by emaciated, featherless hens covered with excrement from those in higher cages. Countless hens were immobilized in the wires of the battery cages, caught by their wings, legs, feet, and necks, some alive, others dead.... In some of the cages we saw, hens were left to live with the decomposing bodies of their former cage-mates. We removed the rotting corpses, many of which had been left in the cages for so long that they were flattened to an inch.
>
> We filmed hens riddled with cysts, prolapses, infections, and bloody sores—some so weak they could barely lift their heads or drink the water we offered them.... [A]s veterinary care costs more than the bird is worth to the producer, they suffer without treatment.[16]

The Industrial Revolution released animals from forced labor. The scientific and technological revolutions that followed created a hell for animals that no one living earlier than fifty years ago could have imagined.

At this juncture, the best hope for farmed animals would appear to be not the vegetarian and animal rights movements, but the creation of meat grown *in vitro* from small clusters of cells. When this process, which is now in its infancy, is improved to the point that it mass-produces flavorful meat more cheaply than factory farms, animal agriculture will join animal labor as a thing of the past in the industrialized world. Paul Shapiro, founder of Compassion Over Killing (see Chapter 20) and director of the Humane Society of the United States' factory farming campaign, expects this to happen within his lifetime:

> I would be very surprised if we still had factory farming in fifty years. I think the meat people will be eating in fifty years will be mostly *in vitro* meat. It will happen the way digital photography replaced film and CDs replaced cassettes.[17]

Or the way automobiles replaced horses.

15

Heralds of Change

Following the collapse of the anti-vivisection campaign, the first half of the twentieth century was a time of retreat and retrenchment for animal protection advocates. The vegetarian movement, especially in the United States, continued to drift away from animal protection—more concerned with human health than with saving animals from suffering and death. But even so, animal protectionists often continued to affiliate with vegetarian groups simply because they were the only organizations around opposed to the eating of animal flesh.

Humane societies and SPCAs continued to spread, and by World War II there was one serving practically every city and county in the U.S. But like the ASPCA since the death of Henry Bergh, they concerned themselves strictly with the care and control of companion animals, and as we have seen, most were little more than disposal mechanisms for the unloved and the homeless. The first half of the twentieth century was not so much a time of conscious cruelty—such as we saw during the Roman Empire—as it was an era of ignorance and indifference to the plight of animals.

For ten thousand years, from the Neolithic Revolution until the twentieth century, animals had been integrated into the life of the human community to a degree that those of us living at the beginning of the twenty-first century can comprehend only by a long stretch of the imagination. As the nineteenth century drew to a close, nearly everyone, whether they lived in Manhattan or Otumwa, whether they were hansom drivers or accountants, stable hands or housewives, had contact with working animals almost every day of their lives. Most families and a large swath of workers were intimately acquainted with—and at some point in their lives responsible for the care of—the animals who pulled the carriages, buggies, carts, wagons, and other conveyances that moved people and goods around our cities and towns. This was a cruel companionship, but it was real. Day in and day out, everyone could see the animals' gentleness, their fatigue, and their pain. To live with the cruelty of animal labor and not be driven insane by it, people developed a callousness that kept them from caring too much.

Then, after ten thousand years—with the arrival of cars, trucks, trains, buses, and subways—animals disappeared from our lives in the space of about two generations. People whose grandparents had driven horses and mules were now driving automobiles and trucks. People whose grandparents had fed and combed and cared for living beings were pumping gas and changing oil. Animals and human beings were isolated from one another in a way that they had not been since deep in the prehistoric past.

Even on the farm, once animals no longer provided labor, the farmer's relationship to them changed. Animals ceased to be servants who worked alongside their masters. Now the only animals the farmer encountered were raw material, born to be killed, living out their lives in an industrial estrangement from the family that ran the farm, rarely seen unless it was time to feed them, milk them, ship them, or kill them, and even much of the feeding and milking was now done by machines.

As the saying goes, "Out of sight, out of mind." With animals out of sight, people no longer needed the callousness that had protected their parents from the pain of their own cruelty; and so, it was replaced by an indifference born of ignorance. It may well be that a generation of indifference had to intervene before a mass movement of compassion could be generated. Indifference based on ignorance, even willful ignorance, can be overcome with knowledge; callousness developed as a defense against compassion is harder to penetrate. I think that a full-blown animal rights movement that advocated the complete liberation of animals from human oppression could not have developed as long as human civilization—human survival even, at least in the numbers in which we have existed since the Neolithic Revolution—was dependent upon the slave labor of animals. You will recall that Axial Age animal advocates—including the Buddha, the Later Prophets, and Pythagoras—did not object to animal labor. Even in the Victorian Era, with its unprecedented outpouring of compassion for animals, it was only the occasional maverick, like Lewis Gompertz, who refused to ride in conveyances drawn by animals.

Veganism: *Ahimsa* in Modern Dress

The first hint that change might be in the air came in 1944, when Donald Watson (1910–2005) founded the Vegan Society in Leicester, England. Watson, one of the most remarkable, inner-directed spiritual pioneers in history, became a vegetarian at the age of fourteen, although he had never met a vegetarian in his South Yorkshire hometown. A year later, he left school to take up an apprenticeship, and throughout his adult life, until retirement, earned his living by teaching woodworking, first in Leicester, and later in Keswick, a small town in the Lake District where he lived until his death. A lifelong pacifist, Watson was a conscientious objector in World War II, and as a natural outgrowth of his commitment to nonviolence he extended his vegetarianism to embrace avoidance of all animal products.

When Watson decided to create a society to promote his philosophy of total abstention from animal products, he and his wife Dorothy began casting about for a name. Ultimately, they coined the word "vegan" (VEE-gun) to describe a lifestyle free of animal cruelty, constructed from the opening and closing letters of "vegetarian," "because," as he put it, "veganism starts with vegetarianism and carries it through to its logical conclusion."[1] In 1962, "vegan" appeared in the Oxford English Dictionary, and it now appears in most English-language dictionaries[2] and has been picked up in all of the European languages and the major Asian languages. Watson's word and his concept are a permanent part of the global culture. As for the Vegan Society, it remains an active organization.

Watson's efforts inspired Dr. Catherine Nimmo of Oceano, California, and Rubin Abramowitz of Los Angeles to form a Vegan Society in the United States in 1948. Primarily a correspondence circle among a small group of like-minded people, the first vegan society in the New World closed its doors in 1960 when the vegan cause was taken up by H. Jay Dinshah (1933–2000), the American-born son of Dinshah P. Ghadiali, a Parsee from Bombay (now Mumbai), India, and his wife, Irene Hoger Dinshah.[3] Although Parsees are not typically vegetarian, as a teenager Ghadiali had adopted—for ethical reasons and clarity of mind—the lacto-vegetarian diet of a Hindu neighbor, and Jay and his siblings were raised vegetarian. In his adult life, Jay Dinshah practiced a nondenominational spirituality based on *ahimsa* and influenced by the work of Gandhi and Schweitzer and the Zoroastrian threefold path of "good thoughts, good words, good deeds."[4]

In 1957, young Jay Dinshah visited a slaughterhouse and was appalled at the cruelty of killing innocent animals to appease human appetites. Shortly thereafter, he gave up all animal products when he discovered literature published by Donald Watson's Vegan Society. Three years later, in February 1960, Jay Dinshah founded the American Vegan Society (AVS) in Malaga, New Jersey, where he had been born and where, except for brief periods, he lived his entire life. The first dues-paying member was Catherine Nimmo. A few months after founding AVS, Jay married Freya Smith, and together they shaped and directed what would become America's pre-eminent vegan organization.[5]

Freya Dinshah is a soft-spoken woman of profound grace and gentleness whose modesty—the natural expression of her dedication to nonviolence—could easily be mistaken for shyness. Born and raised in England by vegetarian, pacifist parents—her father, like Donald Watson, was a conscientious objector in World War II—Freya got to know Jay Dinshah when they began a correspondence that included discussion of vegan philosophy and practice.

The Dinshahs saw the function of AVS to be "inspirational and motivational." By exposing the horrors of animal agriculture and preaching the gospel of *ahimsa*, they hoped to inspire the public to adopt a nonviolent lifestyle. From the beginning, their aim—like Watson's—was to return vegetarianism to the firm moral basis that Gandhi had urged on the Vegetarian Society three decades earlier.

For both philosophical and tactical reasons, the AVS style is deliberately low-key and non-confrontational, but that does not mean that AVS is willing to compromise on matters of principle:

> Vegan living is compassionate living. We don't look back to the family farm as being ideal. There is a strong concept today that what's bad about meat, dairy, and eggs is factory farming, but I don't think you could hold a brief for animal agriculture before factory farming. Slaughterhouses have always been a nasty business, whether they are big or small.[6]

Jay and Freya Dinshah were early pioneers in spreading the gospel of nonviolence toward animals. In 1964, the American Vegan Society published *Here's Harmlessness: An Anthology of Ahimsa*, a collection of articles on veganism from the Society's magazine, including pieces by such luminaries as Eva Batt, a leading figure in The Vegan Society in England, and Muriel, Lady Dowding, founder of Beauty Without Cruelty—a British nonprofit that campaigned against animal testing and fur—who would later be a contributor to *Animals, Men, and Morals* (see Chapter 16). In 1965, Jay Dinshah published a compendium of his philosophy entitled *Out of the Jungle: The Way of Dynamic Harmlessness*, which remains one of the best nonsectarian introductions to veganism as an expression of *ahimsa* that has ever been written. And from 1981 to 1983, *Ahimsa* carried a series of articles by Victoria Moran, which when published in book form in 1985 as *Compassion, the Ultimate Ethic: An Exploration of Veganism*, which demystified veganism for a whole generation of animal rights activists who were struggling with the complexities of adapting their lifestyle to their new philosophy. Appearing at a critical time, *The*

Ultimate Ethic played a crucial role in helping a movement in transition gain its bearings and its confidence.

*   *   *

In 1973, several representatives of American and Canadian vegetarian communities—including Jay Dinshah, Rubin Abramowitz, and Helen and Scott Nearing, longtime activists from Harborside, Maine—attended the biennial Congress of the International Vegetarian Union (IVU)—an umbrella organization of national vegetarian societies founded in 1908—held that year at a resort center near the coastal town of Ronneby, Sweden. They requested that the next Congress be held in North America, and were told that this could happen if they could guarantee an appropriate venue and assume responsibility for the work involved. When they made the necessary commitments, it was announced at the closing session that the next Congress would be held in the United States.[7]

The Nearings identified a suitable venue—the campus of the University of Maine at Orono, near Bangor—and the leadership of the North American vegetarian community set about creating an organization that could manage the logistics of the Congress in the short term, and, in the long term, serve as a clearing house and resource center for vegetarians and local vegetarian societies. Jay Dinshah was founding president of the North American Vegetarian Society (NAVS).[8] From the beginning, NAVS has taken a holistic approach to vegetarianism, and has been supportive of both the health and the animal-rights wings of the movement. For three decades, NAVS' annual Summerfest—under the guidance of Brian and Sharon Graff—has been the largest and most influential gathering of vegetarians in North America, and has provided a venue for animal activists as well as health and environmental advocates.

Held August 16 through 28, 1975, the IVU Congress brought together fifteen hundred vegetarians and vegans from around the world. For many of the future leaders of the vegan and animal rights movements in the United States, the Orono Congress—the first of its kind held in North America—was an inspirational, life-changing event. Alex Hershaft, an animal rights pioneer (some of whose contributions we will discuss in Chapter 17), told me that he was "totally blown away" by the Congress. According to Hershaft, just being on the campus with fifteen hundred vegetarians gave the participants—for the first time in their lives—a sense that they did not have to think of themselves as isolated and marginalized; they were part of a worldwide movement. In addition to the speakers, Orono provided activists from all over the country the first networking opportunity they had ever had. During those two weeks, Hershaft and other American animal rights people spent more time meeting in small groups, getting to know one another, and holding informal discussions than they did attending the official sessions.[9] The groundwork for much of what would soon become the American animal rights movement was laid in 1975 at the Orono Congress. But that is a thread we will pick up shortly.

Bridges to the Future

At the same time that a cadre of animal advocates was moving beyond the traditional concerns of their fellow vegetarians, another set of advocates was branching out from the traditional activities of the humane movement to create groups that would turn out to be precursors of today's animal rights organizations. Although they do not see themselves this way, I think of these groups as being "transitional organizations" between the older humane societies and SPCAs and the animal rights groups that would spring up in the '70s and '80s.

The earliest of these, the Animal Welfare Institute (AWI), was founded in 1951 by Christine Stevens, wife of Roger Stevens, a successful Broadway producer (*West Side Story, Cat on a Hot Tin Roof*) and Founding President of the John F. Kennedy Center for the Performing Arts in Washington, D.C. Disillusioned at the American Humane Association's cozy relationship with the vivisection industry, Stevens created AWI to campaign against animal experimentation, but soon widened the focus to include factory farming, the steel-jaw leghold traps used in the fur industry, commercial whaling, and the killing of great apes.[10]

Christine Stevens—who served as president of AWI until her death in October 2002—described her philosophy in terms that echoed Humphrey Primatt:

> The basis of all animal rights should be the Golden Rule: we should treat them as we would wish them to treat us, were any other species in our dominant position.[11]

And also like Primatt, AWI does not promote vegetarianism, but attacks factory farming while commending animal agriculture as practiced on family farms and encouraging consumers to support "sustainable" agriculture and "humane" slaughter. AWI likewise supports the regulation rather than the abolition of vivisection, and limits itself to proposing a ban on steel-jaw leghold traps while passing over other forms of hunting, fishing, and trapping in discreet silence.[12]

By far the largest of these "transitional organizations" is The Humane Society of the United States. You will recall that HSUS was created in 1954 by four staff members of the American Humane Association who were fed up with that organization's failure to protect animals from abuse. When the top management of the AHA censored articles in the Association's newsletter that were critical of the National Society for Medical Research, an industry group established to defend vivisection, they decided to defect and create their own group. Led by the newsletter's editor, a former journalist and public affairs specialist named Fred Myers, the dissidents resigned from AHA and, on November 22, 1954, created the National Humane Society, soon renamed the Humane Society of the United States.[13]

HSUS quickly dwarfed every other animal protection organization in both membership and resources, as it does to this day, and by the 1960s it had become the public face of animal welfare in the United States. Taking full advantage of its unique standing with the American public, it was instrumental in bringing companion animal

overpopulation to the forefront of public consciousness, in popular-
izing the spaying and neutering of companion animals, in providing
educational and training materials to managers and workers in animal shelters intended to help them reduce the suffering of their
inmates, and in educating the public on the compassionate care of
animals. HSUS vigorously opposed pound seizure, and campaigned
for legislation to regulate vivisection (but not abolish it), utilizing
undercover investigations to expose inhumane laboratory conditions
as early as 1963.[14]

The new animal protection groups formed in the '50s and '60s
expanded the concept of animal welfare beyond the traditional concern for companion animals to include wildlife (commercial whaling,
the Canadian seal hunt, endangered species, and leghold traps; even
sport hunting, which Fred Myers and HSUS strongly opposed), vivisection, and the treatment of farmed animals. In doing this, they
began to draw back the cloak of invisibility that society had cast over
animals; they sensitized the public to the suffering of all animals
and—often unintentionally—paved the way for the rapid growth of
the animal rights movement following the publication of Peter
Singer's *Animal Liberation* in 1975. And—often working in conjunc-
tion with environmental organizations—they were responsible for a
series of animal welfare laws including the Humane Slaughter Act
(1958), the Animal Welfare Act (1966), the Wild Free Roaming Horse
and Burro Act (1971), the Marine Mammal Protection Act (1972),
and the Endangered Species Act (1973).

Even so, the transitional groups never became the training ground
for the leaders of the animal rights movement that we might have
expected they would. With few exceptions, the pioneers of animal
rights came out of either the human rights movements of the '60s or
the vegetarian movement. The reason was meat. At least during their
early years, the transitional groups neither practiced nor preached
vegetarianism, and the women and men who would form the early
core of the animal rights movement were more comfortable around
people who refused to eat meat for whatever reason than they were

around people who professed their deep compassion for animals while they continued to enjoy the fruits of the slaughterhouse.[15]

Until 2005, when new president Wayne Pacelle established a vegan policy for all functions under the control of HSUS, meat was frequently on the menu at HSUS-sponsored luncheons, dinners, and working groups. In 1990, John Hoyt—who led HSUS from 1970 until 1997—had assured the members of the California Farm Bureau that no animal farmer need fear being put out of business by the Humane Society of the United States:

> We are not a vegetarian organization, and as a matter of policy do not consider the utilization of animals for food to be either immoral or inappropriate, a position that as you might expect earns us a great deal of criticism from various animal rights organizations.[16]

Indeed it did, and the fact that he would brag about this to a professional association of animal abusers goes a long way toward explaining the low esteem in which Hoyt and HSUS were held by animal rights activists during the era of his leadership. But as time went on, more and more staff members, especially the younger employees, did consider meat eating immoral, not to mention inappropriate in an organization that exists to help animals.

The Improper Bostonian
Perhaps more than any other individual, Cleveland Amory (1917–1998) represents the transition from animal welfare to animal rights. If Christine Stevens's Animal Welfare Institute was the first of the new transitional animal protection groups that sprang up in the 1950s and '60s, and the Humane Society of the United States was the largest and best known, Amory's Fund for Animals became the most successful at combining outreach to the mainstream public with increasingly aggressive animal rights positions.

Cleveland Amory came from an old and well-connected Boston

family with a history of caring for animals. His great-uncle was George Angell, who had founded the Massachusetts SPCA. Between 1947 and 1960, Amory published three best-selling ruminations on American high society: *The Proper Bostonians, The Last Resorts,* and *Who Killed Society?* For years, he was an editor at *The Saturday Evening Post* and the national Sunday supplement magazine *Parade*; he was the television critic for *TV Guide* and the cultural critic on NBC's *Today Show*, a job that he lost when he refused to stop speaking out against vivisection.

Increasingly, Amory began advocating for animals in his articles and columns, and by the 1960s, he was looking for ways to become involved in animal protection on a more systematic and full-time basis. In 1962, he joined the board of directors of the Humane Society of the United States. (He resigned in 1970 to devote full time to the Fund for Animals.)

In 1967, aided by Marian Probst—who had served for several years as his literary assistant—Cleveland Amory founded the Fund for Animals. Upon his death in 1998, Probst succeeded him as president and chair of the Board of Directors. A very private person who shuns the limelight and rarely gives speeches or interviews to the press, Marian Probst is unknown outside of the movement and little known within it, but for forty years she has been one of the most active and effective leaders in the animals' cause. Probst subsequently stepped down as president, although she remained chair of the Board, and nominated Michael Markarian, a Fund staff member since the mid-1980s, to succeed her. Following the merger of the Fund and HSUS in 2005, Probst became a member of the Board of Directors of HSUS and Markarian senior vice president for external affairs.

The Black Beauty Ranch

During the nineteenth century, prospectors used burros to pack in and out of the rugged country in the American southwest. Some of these burros got loose and ran away; others were simply turned out into the wild when their owners had no more use for them—either because they were no longer fit to work or because their owners had given up and moved on. Either way, by the middle of the twentieth century, there was a large population of wild burros living in the southwest.

In 1976, the National Park Service, considering the animals both an invasive species and a nuisance, announced a plan to rid the Grand Canyon of its burros by shooting them, slitting open their bodies, and letting scavengers pick their bones. Implementation of the plan was delayed by a public outcry, but the Park Service, supported by ranchers and the hunting community, was determined to proceed.

Then, early in 1979, just as the Park Service was about to begin the slaughter, Cleveland Amory threw a monkey wrench into the gears by announcing—to the astonishment of everyone involved, on both sides of the issue—that the Fund for Animals was prepared to rescue the burros and find them homes in private sanctuaries. The Park service wasn't interested, but Amory—who knew everybody who was anybody, as the saying goes—brought in an army of celebrities including Princess Grace of Monaco, Steve Allen, Glenn Ford, and Mary Tyler Moore to build up a groundswell of public opinion in favor of the rescue.

To do what the experts said was impossible, Amory hired a born-and-bred, dyed-in-the-cloth cowboy named Dave Ericsson. Ericsson had no truck with environmentalists or animal rights activists, but he could handle horses and burros a lot better than anyone in the AR community, and Cleveland Amory was always more concerned with results than political correctness. If this man could save the burros, Amory was going to use him, no matter what his personal philosophy was.

The burros were spotted from the air, then rounded up by Ericsson and his crew of cowhands, and airlifted out of the canyon one by one in a sling suspended from a helicopter flown by a former Vietnam chopper pilot named Dan O'Connell. Some of the burros had to be taken down the Colorado River on rafts to a place where there was room to bring the chopper in low. Remarkably—and this is a testament to Ericsson's and O'Connell's skill—none of the burros and none of the horses used in the roundup was injured. At the end of the rescue, the Fund for Animals had saved 575 burros at a cost of $500,000. Park Service plans for a burro shoot were permanently cancelled.

Now the question was what to do with the rescued burros. Two volunteers from Connecticut, Vicki and Allyn Claman, gave a temporary home to 400, and adopted them out to carefully vetted adopters who had to put up $400 for each animal to assure that no burro went to someone who intended to sell him. Others were adopted out directly, most to friends of Cleveland Amory and supporters of the Fund for animals, but there were still some who needed homes.

This brought into urgent focus an idea that Amory had been kicking around for years: the need for a permanent sanctuary for animals of all kinds who had nowhere else to go, a home of last resort for the abused and the abandoned. The Fund for Animals purchased an eighty-three acre ranch in Murchison, Texas, a village about an hour northeast of Dallas, just outside of Tyler.

Over the years, Black Beauty Ranch—now renamed the Cleveland Amory Black Beauty Ranch and operated by the Humane Society of the United States—has grown to 1300 acres. In addition to wild burros and horses, it has been home to thousands of animals, including elephants, chimpanzees, antelopes, and giraffes, all rescued from abuse or saved from an early death, and an entire village of prairie dogs that was marked for extermination to make room for a shopping mall. In creating a sanctuary to complement his advocacy, Cleveland Amory pioneered a trend within the animal rights movement that has been taken up with great success by newer organizations like Farm Sanctuary and United Poultry Concerns.[17]

The Guns of Autumn

The first animal taken in at the Black Beauty Ranch was a cat who crawled up to the ranch house while it was still being refurbished dragging a steel jaw leghold trap, probably set for coyotes, that had seized her by the leg. Torn and shattered, the leg had to be amputated, but Peg—named for "Peg O' My Heart," one of Cleveland Amory's favorite songs—lived for more than twenty years at Black Beauty.

It was entirely appropriate that the ranch's first resident should be a victim of trapping. From its creation, the Fund for Animals' primary focus had been on defending wildlife against human depredation. In 1974, Amory published a book entitled *Mankind? Our Incredible War on Wildlife*, which exposed the cruelty of hunting and trapping. The following year, *Mankind?* became the basis for a CBS television special, *The Guns of Autumn*, which for the first time brought the truth about hunting to the general American public.

Most hunting is done in rural areas by people who live on farms and in small towns; therefore, it goes on out of sight of the majority of Americans and tends to be ignored by most animal rights groups. Nevertheless, hunting and angling are the second leading form of animal slaughter in the United States, with 115,000,000 land animals and birds and 185,000,000 fish killed by hunters and anglers every year.[18]

Hunters like to describe their sport in terms of myth rather than reality. They invoke our prehistoric ancestors hunting to insure the survival of our species, intrepid frontiersmen carving a new nation out of the wilderness, and sturdy farmers going into the woods with a rifle so that their wives and children could be fed. The truth is that since the early twentieth century no one in the lower forty-nine has had to hunt to eat. Hunting in modern day America is a sport, pure and simple; people do it because they enjoy it; there are a lot easier and cheaper ways to get meat today than to go out and kill it yourself.[19]

Stripped of the mythology, hunting is a cowardly act of bushwhacking, killing the harmless and the helpless for pleasure. Hunters put on camouflage, sneak around in the woods, and shoot unsuspecting animals from ambush, or shoot them in the back while they flee in terror for their lives. Any way you look at it, there is nothing fair and sporting or noble and uplifting about it. It requires no courage—hunters are almost never in danger from the animals they hunt, and when they are it is invariably due to their own carelessness; after all, they have guns, and the animals are unarmed.

Counterattack

While an undergraduate at Yale, Wayne Pacelle—the future president of HSUS—had founded the university's first animal rights club. In 1984, he led club members on the first field protest against hunting (often referred to, following the British example, as "hunt sabotages") conducted in the United States—in which activists went into the woods to disrupt a hunt on land owned by Yale's School of Forestry. The protestors were arrested, but charges were later dismissed.[20]

The Yale hunt sabotage remained an isolated incident until September 18, 1989, when Pacelle, who was now the Fund for Animals' National Director, and Heidi Prescott, a wildlife rehabilitator, artist, counselor at a domestic abuse shelter, and volunteer at PETA, organized a hunt sabotage at the McKee-Beshers wildlife management area in suburban Montgomery County, Maryland. Pacelle and Prescott quickly organized other sabotages in Kentucky, Connecticut, Washington State, and Michigan, and before long, local groups around the country were conducting their own "hunt sabs."

On November 25, 1989, while taking part in a subsequent hunt sabotage at McKee-Beshers, Prescott—who had joined the staff of the Fund for Animals—went into the woods with a father and son who were hunting together. The father told the natural resources police that as Prescott walked along beside them, she rustled dead leaves with her feet and frightened away the deer. Cited for violating Maryland's hunter harassment law, which made it a misdemeanor to interfere with a lawful hunt, Prescott appeared in court, where she was sentenced to fifteen days in jail when she refused to pay a fine of five hundred dollars. "I don't believe that what I did was wrong," she told the court. "I believe that I had at least as much right to be on public land protecting animals as the hunters had to be on public land killing them."[21]

With two days off for good behavior, Prescott served thirteen days. She was the first person to serve jail time in the United States for violating a hunter harassment law.

By the mid-1990s, hunt sabotages had pretty well run their course. As laws and enforcement became more draconian, field protestors found themselves facing stiff fines and even extended jail time. And when the novelty wore off, the press stopped covering the protests, which stripped them of their usefulness in exposing the unseen atrocity of hunting to public view.

16

The Age of the Pioneers

T he new militancy that would characterize the animal protection movement for the next thirty years erupted without
warning, catching animal advocates and exploiters equally
unprepared. The site, of course, was England, where every advance in
the campaign for animal protection in the modern era had first
appeared. The issue was one that had been festering for 150 years—
hunting.

Opposition to hunting had been one of the issues that had separated Lewis Gompertz from his fellow directors of the RSPCA, and
Henry Salt's Humanitarian League had opposed hunting since its
founding in 1891. But the RSPCA continued to waffle, and in 1924,
two of its leading figures, Henry Amos and Ernest Bell, resigned to
organize the League Against Cruel Sports. By the late 1950s, the
League was engaging in occasional direct actions against hunting—
primarily by laying down trails of animal scent to lead the hounds
astray—but although this tactic generated publicity, it had only a nuisance effect on the hunts. In describing one of these direct actions on
August 4, 1958, the London *Daily Telegraph* used the word "sabotage,"
and the term "hunt sabotage" stuck as the name for direct action
against hunting.[1]

Then in 1963, John Prestige, a twenty-one-year-old journalist in
Devon—a center of League activity in the far southwest of England—
covered the story of a pregnant doe who had been run to ground and
torn limb from limb by hounds in the middle of a village. Disgusted

by what he learned, Prestige decided to follow the example of League activists and sabotage the hunts. To great fanfare in the press, he announced the founding, on December 15, 1963, of the Hunt Saboteurs Association. Two weeks later, on Boxing Day (December 26), the Hunt Saboteurs—Prestige and a few friends—set out piles of meat donated by a sympathetic butcher not far from where the South Devon Fox Hunt would be running their hounds. With well-timed bugles from hunting horns, they called the dogs to the meat and the hunt was over almost before it began.[2]

John Prestige was a master at garnering favorable media coverage, and his sabotage was massively reported in the British press. From the beginning, the Hunt Saboteurs captured the British imagination, and in a matter of months Hunt Saboteur Associations had sprung up around the country. Then things turned serious. Under pressure from landowners and other hunt supporters, police started to make arrests, courts imposed stiff penalties, and violence began to break out—with each side accusing the other of instigating it. While at the beginning, the violence appears to have been initiated by hunt supporters frustrated at the failure of the legal system to end the sabotages, there is no doubt that both sides contributed to it at various times.

The lines were drawn and neither side relented. For the next forty years—with some waxing and waning—raucous and sometimes violent confrontations between hunt supporters and saboteurs were a regular feature of English country life. Although the saboteurs did not directly end the hunts, they kept the issue on the public agenda and the pressure on the politicians. And they attracted two generations of British young people to the cause of animal rights. Among these new recruits was Ronnie Lee, who would take direct action to a new level, as we will see in Chapter 18.

Lord Houghton's Legacy

Following World War II, there was growing opposition to hunting within the Labour Party, whose strength was among industrial workers, trade unions, and progressive city dwellers, while the

Conservative Party, whose power base was in the countryside and among the privileged classes, supported hunting as a traditional feature of English country life.

In 1977, Douglas Houghton (Lord Houghton of Sowerby) attended an Animal Rights Symposium held at Trinity College, Cambridge. A longtime Member of Parliament who had held various cabinet posts in the government of Harold Wilson, Houghton was a power in the Labour Party. Two years earlier, he had resigned his seat in the Commons (he was then 76 years old) and had been promptly elevated to the House of Lords. For many years, Houghton had been an advocate for various animal protection measures, and he was concerned that the opponents of hunting were not taking good advantage of the opposition to animal cruelty within the Labour rank and file. At the Symposium, Houghton persuaded the leaders of the British animal protection movement to form a coalition that would speak with one voice in the political arena and make animal protection an issue that the parties would have to take a stand on.[3]

The British animal protection movement took Houghton's advice to heart and created the General Election Coordinating Committee for Animal Protection with Houghton serving as the first chairman. The Coordinating Committee published a manifesto entitled "Putting Animals into Politics," distributed leaflets, ran ads, and, most importantly, lobbied the party conventions on behalf of animal protection.[4]

Slowly, over the course of the next two decades, the campaign paid off. Although it still has a long way to go, the U.K. now has the most progressive legislation for the protection of farmed animals of any country in the world. As for hunting, the Coordinating Committee's political campaign was reinforced by the hailstorm of publicity generated by the Hunt Saboteurs. In 1997 the Labour Party came to power on a platform that included a ban on hunting with dogs. But out of fear of losing such votes as Labour had in rural areas, Prime Minister Tony Blair was reluctant to make good on his party's promise, and so he paid lip service while temporizing and resorting to parliamentary maneuvering to make sure a bill never actually became law.

A turning point came in 2002, when the Scottish Parliament passed the Protection of Mammals Act, banning hunting with dogs, which was widely viewed in Scotland as an English pastime with no deep roots in Scottish culture. Edinburgh's action put serious pressure on Labour, and in 2004, rank-and-file Labour members of Commons threatened a rebellion and forced the party leadership to move the ban on hunting to a vote. The bill passed easily, but was promptly vetoed by the House of Lords. Then, on November 18, 2004, the Speaker of the House of Commons invoked the Parliament Act (which gives the Commons the power to override vetoes by the House of Lords), and the Hunting Act of 2004[5] made hunting with dogs—including hunting for foxes, hares, deer, otters, and mink, all of which were traditionally hunted with dogs—illegal in England and Wales. After a series of legal challenges failed, the Act went into effect on February 18, 2005. Neither the Hunting Act nor the Scottish law bans what the British call "shooting" and North Americans would describe as hunting without dogs.

But the issue may not yet be settled. There are frequent reports of Hunts using fanciful legal reasoning to find "loopholes" in the Act or simply violating it outright, and local authorities appear reluctant to move against the Hunts, whose members typically include the most powerful landowners and businesspeople in the county. Although hunting has been widely reported throughout England, a year and a half after the Hunting Act went into effect, there have been no governmental prosecutions of hunters. Disgusted at the authorities' diffidence, the League Against Cruel Sports brought a private prosecution against huntsman Tony Wright after the Avon and Somerset police had refused to press charges. Supported by videotape of Wright signaling the hounds to pursue a fox, the League won the first-ever conviction under the Hunting Act on August 3, 2006.[6]

It is widely believed that hunters are thumbing their noses at the Act and trying to hold on any way they can until a Conservative government returns to power and revokes it. It has even been reported that several prominent Hunts have moved their hounds to

France, with the thought of returning them to England following what some are referring to as "the Restoration." But the faith of those who await the return of an *ancien régime* is not often rewarded, and it is by no means assured that a Conservative government could muster the votes to overturn the Hunting Act—or even that it would try very hard.

The Rights of Animals

During the 1950s, while factory farming was taking hold in Europe and North America, animal advocates stayed tightly focused on their traditional issues of companion animals, vivisection, and (in the U.K.) hunting. In fact, the movement barely noticed the industrial revolution in agriculture until 1964, when English activist Ruth Harrison (1921–2000) wrote an expose entitled *Animal Machines*.

Two years earlier, Rachel Carson had published *Silent Spring* to international acclaim, and although the two had never met, Harrison sent the American scientist a copy of the manuscript for *Animal Machines* with a request that she write a foreword. Appalled at what she read, Carson showed the manuscript to her friend Christine Stevens, founder of the Animal Welfare Institute, and asked if Harrison's book could possibly be accurate. Told that it was, Carson wrote the foreword, which assured *Animal Machines* a publisher and a wide audience.[7] While Harrison herself argued for the reform, rather than the abolition, of animal agriculture, her book became a call to action for advocates of putting an end to all animal enslavement and slaughter.

The following year, British feminist, antiwar activist, gay and lesbian advocate, novelist, and playwright Brigid Brophy (1929–1995) published a lengthy essay in the *Sunday Times* which she called "The Rights of Animals" in homage to Thomas Paine's *The Rights of Man*. Inspired by George Bernard Shaw, Brophy had become a vegetarian in the 1950s, and now she was telling the British public—over their traditional Sunday breakfast of bacon, sausages, and eggs—that our dominion over animals is profoundly unjust and must be radically redefined.

> The relationship of homo sapiens to the other animals is one of unremitting exploitation. We employ their work; we eat and wear them. We exploit them to serve our superstitions: whereas we used to sacrifice them to our gods ... we now sacrifice them to science....[8]

Although it would not reach the United States for another decade, the modern animal rights movement had begun.

The Oxford Group

As a clinical psychologist who had trained in the era of Harry Harlow, Richard Ryder had seen the brutal reality of animal experimentation at first hand, and he was determined to bring some much-needed change to his chosen profession. Unsure where to start, he began publishing letters to the editor in the London *Daily Telegraph*. The letters impressed Brigid Brophy, who got in touch with Ryder to suggest that since he was living in Oxford—he was serving as senior psychologist at Warneford hospital there—he should look up three post-graduate students in philosophy at the University who were wrestling with the ethics of our treatment of animals: Stanley and Roslind Godlovitch, husband and wife from Montreal, Canada, and London-born John Harris. He did, and before long the four were distributing leaflets against vivisection and hunting, and organizing small protests.[9]

One evening in 1970, while relaxing in a hot bath reflecting on the issue that was occupying more and more of his time and attention, Ryder hit upon the term "speciesism" to describe our attitude toward animals. Speciesism, he said, is "like racism or sexism—a prejudice based upon morally irrelevant physical differences."[10] He included his new coinage in a flyer that he wrote for one of the group's Oxford demonstrations, and before long, "speciesism" had become the core term—and the core concept—around which the animal rights movement would be organized.[11] In 1986, "speciesism" appeared in the Oxford English Dictionary. Animal rights had taken its place in the lineage of Western social justice movements grounded in the Enlightenment.

The Godlovitches, Harris, and Ryder were soon joined by two more post-doctoral students in philosophy, Stephen Clark and Peter Singer—the latter an Australian recently arrived at Oxford—along with a theology student named Andrew Linzey, who was then serving as secretary to the Oxford Vegetarian Society.[12] Known as the "Oxford Group," they became the driving spirit behind the incipient movement that Brigid Brophy had called into being.

In 1971, the Godlovitches and John Harris edited *Animals, Men and Morals,* a collection of thirteen essays whose authors included, among others, Roslind Godlovitch, Stanley Godlovitch, John Harris, Richard Ryder, Ruth Harrison, and Brigid Brophy. In the Introduction, the editors set forth what would become the credo of the animal rights movement for the next two decades:

> Once the full force of moral assessment has been made explicit, there can be no rational excuse left for killing animals, be they killed for food, science, or sheer personal indulgence.... Compromise, in the traditional sense of the term, is simple unthinking weakness when one considers the actual reasons for our crude relationships with the other animals. To argue that a lack of compromise is wrong-headed is merely to perpetuate various fantasies people have about the regard that should be had toward other species.[13]

In the Postscript—which is, in fact, the book's closing essay—philosopher Patrick Corbett sounded the same theme:

> [W]e require *now* to extend the great principles of liberty, equality, fraternity over the lives of animals. Let animal slavery join human slavery in the graveyard of the past![14]

Animal Liberation

The Oxford Group did not stay together long. Most were in Oxford only for the period of their post-doctoral work, and soon went their separate ways.[15] *Animals, Men and Morals* attracted no interest from the press and by 1973 appeared to be sinking into oblivion. Hoping to salvage it by creating a demand for an American edition, Peter Singer wrote an unsolicited review that he submitted to the *New York Review of Books*.[16] Surprisingly, given the subject matter, the *Review* published it on April 5, 1973. Calling the book "a manifesto for an Animal Liberation movement," Singer—who is a utilitarian—quoted the passage from Jeremy Bentham that was discussed in Chapter 7, and told his readers that:

> Surely Bentham was right. If a being suffers, there can be no moral justification for refusing to take that suffering into consideration, and, indeed, to count it equally with the like suffering (if rough comparisons can be made) of any other being.[17]

Singer's six-thousand-word essay was the world's introduction to the term "animal liberation" and to Singer's trademark argument, adopted from Bentham, that animals are entitled to have their interests given equal consideration with ours. It was also a sign that animal rights was about to leave Oxford to burst onto the world stage in New York, not simply as a philosophical argument, but as a full-blown social movement in the tradition of abolition, women's suffrage, the labor movement, feminism, and civil rights.

Singer's term at Oxford expired in June 1973, and in September of that year he joined the department of philosophy at New York University as a visiting lecturer. On the strength of his *New York Review of Books* article, the continuing education department asked him to teach a twelve-hour, non-credit course entitled Animal Liberation, which in 1974 he did, the first formal course on animal rights that had been offered anywhere in the world.

Singer was already hard at work on the book that would introduce animal rights to the world at large, and his notes became the lesson plan for his course.[18] Published in New York in 1975, *Animal Liberation* caused an instant sensation and remains the single most influential text in the history of animal rights. Its unique status is, I believe, the result of four factors: First, it is clearly and accessibly written. Peter Singer is an excellent writer, and non-academic readers are not put off by the book.

Second, Singer soft-pedals his utilitarianism—especially the more outrageous implications of utilitarian calculus—so that his utilitarian arithmetic looks to most readers like the commonsense argument that it is wrong to torture and kill innocent beings for the sake of our own appetites and convenience.

What went widely unnoticed until it was pointed out by American philosopher Tom Regan—and until Singer himself made it more explicit in his later writings, especially *Practical Ethics*—was that when Singer called for moral equality for humans and animals, he did not mean that animals' lives should be granted the same nearly absolute protection that we now grant humans' lives. Rather, he meant that in working the utilitarian calculus, we should grant equal weight to the interests of animals and human beings, which is quite a different matter, since in practice it would mean raising the protections granted to animals and lowering those granted to human beings until they meet somewhere in the middle.

The third reason for the historic impact of *Animal Liberation* is that Singer devotes a large portion of the book to descriptions of the suffering of animals on factory farms and in laboratories, and these were a revelation to the general public. *Animal Liberation* was as much journalistic exposé as philosophical argument.

And finally: the secret of success is always in the timing, and *Animal Liberation* was the right book at the right time. A public that had been prepared by the transitional groups in the United States and by Ruth Harrison, Brigid Brophy, and the Hunt Saboteurs in Britain, was primed to consider a reasoned, coherent argument against animal enslavement and slaughter.

I have never met anyone who entered the animal rights movement during its growth spurt from 1975 to the mid-'90s who does not claim *Animal Liberation* as a critical influence. For me—I entered the movement in 1987—reading *Animal Liberation* was a life-changing experience, akin to religious conversion. And it was the same with many of my friends. Down to the present, *Animal Liberation* has provided the roiling, contentious animal rights movement with a coherence that transcends ideology or strategy. Singer's book quickly became a kind of talisman, a banner around which animal rights advocates of all stripes could rally, even those who disputed his utilitarian rationale. *Animal Liberation* remains the most revered icon of the animal rights movement not because of its specific arguments— at least some of which most animal advocates do not support—but because its call to treat animals as our moral equals galvanized a generation to action.

The Case for Animal Rights

Animal Liberation had two primary impacts: it gave intellectual respectability and a tremendous impetus to the fledgling animal rights movement, and it created the discipline of animal rights philosophy as a subset of ethics. A number of philosophers are now producing important work in the field of animal rights, including, among others, Italian ethicist Paola Cavalieri, German philosopher Helmut Kaplan, Americans Steve Sapontzis, David DeGrazia, and Carol Adams, and Richard Ryder, whose *Painism: A Modern Morality* cuts through jargon and abstract theories to ground animal rights in a commonsense ethic based on compassion for all who are able to suffer.

But along with Singer himself, the most influential animal rights philosopher is Tom Regan, professor emeritus at North Carolina State University in Raleigh. In 1983, Regan published *The Case for Animal Rights*, in which he rejected Peter Singer's utilitarianism and built a case for animal rights based on the same natural rights philosophy that undergirds most of our thinking on human rights.

Natural rights philosophy teaches that everyone has certain inherent entitlements based on their possession of specific attributes. These entitlements are absolute and may not be abrogated unless the person forfeits them, or some portion of them, by failing to respect the rights of others. The principle of inflicting suffering on some to promote the happiness of others that underlies utilitarian calculus is anathema to natural rights philosophy.

When natural rights philosophy was first created—during the Enlightenment—its proponents were a little vague about who had rights. They talked grandly about "all men," *i.e.*, all human beings, but in practice they tended to favor a graduated scale with propertied white males at the top, poor white males next, white women next, and everyone else at the bottom of the heap with either no rights, or remarkably few. Animals were not even considered. Since then the ambit of natural rights has gradually expanded until now it is generally acknowledged to include all human beings.

In extending natural rights theory to animals, Regan had to identify the attribute on the basis of which we can ascribe rights to nonhumans. The trait that he chose is being "the subject of a life," *i.e.*, having an interior life that includes the ability to experience pleasure and pain and to conceive of oneself as a distinct continuing being. In Regan's view, a being can be sentient, but not the subject of a life. As we saw earlier, separating moral consideration from sentience can restrict the animals who are entitled to it. And, in fact, in the first edition of *The Case for Animal Rights*, Regan included only mammals, although he admitted the possibility that other kinds of animals might also belong. Over time, however, his view of which animals are, in fact, subjects of a life has broadened. More recently, in light of a growing body of scientific data, he has included birds and—with some hesitancy—fish. He is not, however, dogmatic about it and from the beginning has been open to widening the universe of beings with rights still farther as more information becomes available. An activist as well as a philosopher, Tom Regan is a well-known and widely admired figure within the animal rights movement.

The Animals Get Religion

In 1976, Reverend Doctor Andrew Linzey, an Anglican priest and former member of the Oxford Group, opened up an animal rights dialogue within the Christian community by publishing *Animal Rights: A Christian Perspective.* His subsequent books, most notably *Christianity and the Rights of Animals, Animal Theology,* and *Animal Gospel,* developed a compassionate and sophisticated theology of animal rights which remains a high point of Christian thinking about animal creation.

Pointing out that Christ presented himself as the servant of all who suffer and are in need, Professor Linzey argues that Christians must likewise become the servants of all who suffer. That is the true meaning of the *imitatio Christi,* the imitation of Christ to which all Christians are supposed to aspire. Christian ethics, as Linzey sees it, is the diametrical opposite of Aristotelian ethics, in which the lower exists to serve the higher. For Christians following the teachings and example or Jesus, the higher exists to serve the lower, and therefore becoming a Christian means transforming yourself into the servant of all who are less powerful, less fortunate, and less able to help themselves—including nonhuman animals, who are, in fact, the least powerful, least fortunate, and least able to help themselves of all God's sentient creation. "The uniqueness of humanity," says Linzey, "consists in its ability to become the servant species."[19] Thus, while Peter Singer and Tom Regan call for moral equality between humans and animals, Andrew Linzey tells us that the powerlessness of animals entitles them to moral priority. And just as Peter Singer created the discipline of animal rights philosophy, Andrew Linzey has almost singlehandedly created the discipline of animal rights theology.

In contrast to Linzey, however, the theologians who have followed in his wake have generally been timid and half-hearted about calling for an end to all animal enslavement and slaughter. But at least they encourage Christians to move in the right direction and challenge the traditional, mainstream Christian view of animals. Far more forthright and uncompromising is Reverend J. R. (Regina) Hyland, whose groundbreaking book *God's Covenant with Animals*—originally published in 1988 as *The Slaughter of Terrified Beasts*—builds a strong Scriptural case for veganism and animal rights.

In the Jewish tradition, animal rights has been pioneered by Dr. Roberta Kalechofsky, founder of Jews for Animal Rights, and Dr. Richard Schwartz, president of Jewish Vegetarians of North America, both of whom employ the Biblical and Talmudic teaching of *tsar baalei hayyim* (see Chapter 4) to argue for vegetarianism and animal rights. Kalechofsky has written *haggadot* (liturgies for the Seder) for a vegetarian Passover, and edited an informative and insightful collection of essays on Judaism and animals entitled *Judaism and Animal Rights: Classic and Contemporary Responses*. Schwartz is the author of *Judaism and Vegetarianism*, which has become the definitive work on vegetarianism and animal rights from a Jewish perspective.

Within the Christian and Jewish faith traditions, a number of groups have formed that are working hard to promote animal rights and vegetarianism, but in general, animal rights activists have avoided the subject of religion. The secular animal rights group that has done the most to reach out to religious communities is People for the Ethical Treatment of Animals, thanks to the influence of Bruce Friedrich, a devout Catholic who joined PETA in 1996 (see Chapter 20). In addition to their flamboyant "Jesus Was a Vegetarian" campaign (which they have not actively promoted since 2002), PETA has developed an impressive array of resources on animal rights in relation to Christian, Jewish, and Islamic teachings, and campaigns actively to promote animal rights in the context of religious faith and practice.

Animal Rights Hits the Pavement

Born in Belgium, Henry Spira (1927–1998) was as American as apple pie, one of the last in the long line of immigrants who helped nurture the American dream by bringing the European progressive tradition to the New World.[20] After coming to New York with his parents as a teenager, he finished high school and served a hitch in the Merchant Marine, where he became active in the Maritime Union. After a tour

in the Army, he went to work as a union organizer and then headed
south to be part of the new civil rights movement. Working in the
Montgomery bus boycott, Mississippi voter registration drives, and
the integration of restaurants and lunch counters in Florida, Henry
Spira learned the strategy, tactics, and politics of social justice campaigns on the front lines all across the deep South. In 1966 he took a
job teaching school in disadvantaged black and Latino neighborhoods in New York City.

In 1973, Henry Spira happened to come across a newspaper col-
umn by progressive political activist and folklorist Irwin Silber, sar-
castically describing Peter Singer's article in *The New York Review of
Books* as "evidence that the social collapse of capitalism gives rise to a
certain collapse of the intellect among some sectors of the bourgeois
intelligentsia."[21] To cut through the leftist jargon: Silber, like all too
many progressives since then, interpreted animal rights as proof that
the prosperous classes in our society were so determined to keep the
poor on the bottom of the heap that there was no cause too ridiculous for them to adopt before they would turn their attention to
oppressed human beings. But Spira didn't see it that way. His curiosity piqued, the former union organizer and civil rights worker read
Singer's piece for himself and began to think that perhaps:

> ... animal liberation was the logical extension of what my life
> was all about—identifying with the powerless and the vul-
> nerable, the victims, dominated and oppressed.[22]

Watching his companion cats, he began to see his dinner in a different light, wondering "about the appropriateness of cuddling one
animal after sticking a knife and fork into others." Then, he heard that
Peter Singer would be teaching a course in Animal Liberation at New
York University and decided to attend. In class and in conversations
with Singer after class:

> ... it all began to jell. The confluence of events included my
> activist background, the personal experience of living with

first one and then two cats, and the influence of Peter Singer.[23]

Henry Spira was a left-wing activist, and had been since his early days in the Merchant Marine. Philosophy, for him, was not a parlor game; it was a guide to action. His philosophy now told him that the exploitation of animals was wrong, and so he had to do something about it. The question was: What?

As he studied the literature sent out by animal protection groups, Spira became convinced that their strategy was all wrong. As he told interviewer Erik Markus:

> Organizations were sending their members information about atrocities and asking for money, and then the next month they'd send them more atrocities stories, and it wasn't really focused on changing anything. It was really focused on generating outrage, as if outrage alone could be productive. What we did was adapt the strategies of the human rights movement to the animal cause.[24]

In applying the strategies of the civil rights and labor movements to the animal cause, Henry Spira created the American animal rights movement and set the pattern that animal rights campaigns would follow for the next twenty years, a pattern that relied heavily on protests, demonstrations, marches, and picketing.

Again drawing on his experience in the labor and civil rights movements, Spira thought that the road to success was to conduct a focused campaign against a specific atrocity being carried out by an identifiable perpetrator. Deciding that vivisection was a logical place to start, he ultimately settled on experiments being conducted at the American Museum of Natural History in New York in which cats were being mutilated so that researchers could observe the effect that the mutilation had on their sexual behavior.

In June 1976, Spira sent a letter to Museum officials requesting a meeting to discuss the experiments. When they ignored it, he followed up with telephone calls—with the same result. He tried to interest the *New York Times*, but to no avail. Finally, he decided to resort to the tactic that had proven indispensable to both labor unions and civil rights activists; he decided—in the argot of the labor movement—to "hit the pavement." Henry Spira was going to picket the American Museum of Natural History.

In preparation, Spira published an article in *Our Town*, a weekly newspaper distributed around Manhattan free of charge, describing the experiments in graphic detail and asking readers to join him (and a small cadre of friends from Singer's class) in picketing the Museum that weekend. Begun in July 1976, the protest went on for over a year. Every weekend—Spira was still teaching school on weekdays—a growing number of protesters picketed the Museum, carrying signs and chanting slogans in the best traditions of 1960s protest movements. He issued press releases, and now that he had organized the first animal rights demonstration held in the U.S., the press paid attention; Spira attracted not just local, but national media coverage. He wrote members of Congress, who promptly contacted the National Institutes of Health (the funding agency for the cat experiments) to demand that they stop wasting the taxpayers' money on nonsense like the sex lives of injured cats. He distributed flyers and posters, he gave interviews, and he made a pest of himself in every way that he knew how.

After eighteen months of mounting pressure, the Museum notified NIH that it would not be requesting a renewal of the grant. It did, however, ask that the current grant be extended for a year to allow an orderly completion of work in progress. Under siege from the public and members of Congress, NIH refused, and at the end of August 1977 the American Museum of Natural History's cat laboratory lost its funding. By December, it had closed down completely. The first modern animal rights campaign had ended in victory. The Museum's president later told Cleveland Amory that Spira's campaign had cost the Museum one-third of its membership subscriptions.[25]

In terms of numbers, the victory may not have been large—the Museum experimented on about sixty cats a year—but in terms of impact, it was massive. Combined with the publication of *Animal Liberation*, Henry Spira's campaign brought animal rights into the public dialogue, inspired people around the country to take up the cause—over the next decade, small, local animal rights groups popped up in cities from coast to coast—and paved the way for bigger campaigns to come. It also changed forever the way the media and the public viewed the animal issue. Citing Helen Jones, one of the founders of the Humane Society of the United States and founder of the International Society for Animal Rights, social historians Lawrence and Susan Finsen report that during Spira's American Museum of Natural History campaign, "for the first time, the American press used the term *animal rights activists* rather than *animal lovers* in describing these events."[26]

*   *   *

From the American Museum of Natural History, Henry Spira went on to challenge New York state's pound seizure law (see Chapter 12), obtaining its repeal in 1979, and followed this up with a campaign against the safety testing of cosmetics on animals.

It was an article of Spira's faith that having a limited and precisely defined goal is essential to success. He saw huge, amorphous campaigns as invitations to failure. He would rather win a small, concrete victory that might set the stage for another small, concrete victory, and another, and another, than experience a grand, heroic loss that did not improve any animal's life. Thus, he had not campaigned against all vivisection, he had campaigned against one specific set of experiments being conducted at one institution. He had not campaigned against all use of dogs as vivisection subjects, only against the use of dogs taken from shelters in New York State. Following this principle, in taking on cosmetics testing Spira decided to focus initially on one company, Revlon, and on one procedure, the so-called Draize eye-irritancy test.

In 1938, alarmed by a rash of injuries caused by cosmetics and household chemicals—including several severe eye injuries—

Congress passed the Food, Drug, and Cosmetics Act (FDCA), which required the U. S. Food and Drug Administration (FDA) to set safety standards for cosmetics and personal care products. Manufacturers now had to tell the FDA how toxic their products were, under what circumstances they were toxic, and what kind of damage they caused. The fastest, cheapest, and most convenient way to get this information was to expose small animals to the chemical being evaluated and see what happened. Vivisection had been employed in product development since the late nineteenth century, but on a relatively small scale. As a direct result of the Food, Drug, and Cosmetics Act, however, safety-testing products on animals became standard procedure, and vivisection spread from the research laboratory into the manufacturing plant in a big way.

The FDA had problems, however, because every company devised its own tests, and there was no standard, industry-wide scale against which test results could be evaluated. To help resolve this situation, in 1944 an FDA toxicologist named John Draize developed a standardized test to measure the nature and extent of the damage that chemicals caused to the eye. The Draize test is—it is still in use—deceptively simple and unspeakably cruel. Rabbits are immobilized in body-hugging boxes and the chemical being evaluated is rubbed or squirted into their eyes. Over days or weeks, the victims are kept immobile while researchers observe the results. Most often, of course, the results are ulceration, excruciating pain, the destruction of the rabbits' eyes, and blindness. When the test is completed, the rabbits, now useless to the researchers, are killed. The FDA never issued a written regulation requiring the Draize test; but manufacturers quickly figured out that if they wanted their cosmetics and household cleaners approved, they had better provide the regulators with Draize test results.

Henry Spira believed that the Draize test was so widely used and so heavily relied upon by the Food and Drug Administration that a campaign for its immediate abolition would be futile. So while he made the abolition of the Draize test the ultimate goal of his campaign, he set a much more modest goal for the short term, one that he hoped would spell the beginning of the end for product testing on animals. He told Revlon that he wanted them to provide substantial funding for research into alternatives to the Draize test, promising that as soon as they did, the campaign against them would end.

As a result of his two earlier victories, Henry Spira was a hero in animal protection circles, and he could draw on a large, global network of anti-vivisection activists and organizations that were eager to work with a leader who had discovered the formula for success. Spira's own group, Animal Rights International, was never, in the words of Peter Singer, "much more than a letterhead that Henry could use when he was acting on his own behalf rather than as part of a coalition."[27] But the coalition that he built for the Revlon campaign—styled the Coalition to Stop Draize Rabbit Blinding Tests—was by far the most extensive that the animal protection movement had put together.

Created on August 23, 1979, the Coalition included over four hundred separate organizations, most of which had never worked together before (and never would again), including some of the giants of animal protection, most notably the Humane Society of the United States and the American Society for the Prevention of Cruelty to Animals, whose millions of members and healthy budgets gave the Coalition real clout in the media and the marketplace. Despite misgivings by some groups—notably HSUS, whose lawyers were afraid that as the coalition member with the deepest pockets they would be sued by Revlon—the coalition held together. Spira had been so successful in the past, where everyone else had failed, that "everyone wanted to be a part of the coalition even if they disagreed with what it was doing."[28]

Using press releases, mass mailings, video clips provided to television newsrooms, large demonstrations outside corporate headquarters in New York and in cities around the world, and paid advertising—spearheaded by a full-page newspaper ad designed free of charge by a high-octane Madison Avenue ad executive named Mark Graham—the Revlon campaign dwarfed anything that had ever been attempted on behalf on animals. Revlon was taking a beating in the press, and the price of their stock was declining. For the first time ever, animal rights was front-page news from coast to coast and across Western Europe.

Caught off guard, Revlon executives were in a state of shock. It had never crossed anyone's mind that the company should care about the welfare of laboratory animals. After a period of initial resistance followed by pointless negotiations that were mostly a delaying tactic while they got their act together, Revlon capitulated. They agreed to donate $750,000 over three years to The Rockefeller University—a prestigious center for biological research noted for the number of Nobel laureates on its faculty—to fund research on alternatives to animal testing for product safety. On December 23, 1980, sixteen months to the day from the promulgation of the statement of principles that marked the founding of the Coalition, Henry Spira held a press conference announcing the agreement.

The Coalition had won a significant victory: for the first time in history, a major corporation was spending money to reduce animal testing rather than expand it. The Revlon campaign was complete. Spira was ready to close the books on it and move on to the next campaign, just as he had after the Museum of Natural History.

Not everybody was ready to move with him, however. Some coalition members felt that all Spira had accomplished was to immunize Revlon against criticism while the company continued to use the Draize test. He had, they believed, been outmaneuvered by company officials who had bought their way out of trouble—and on the cheap, at that—without making any changes to the practices that were torturing and killing animals. It was at this point that Henry Spira's coalition—and with it the unity of the new animal rights movement—began to unravel.

The next target was Avon, which, having no wish to absorb the kind of public relations punishment that Revlon had endured, quickly agreed to make their own $750,000 contribution to the search for alternatives to the Draize test. Bristol-Myers was more pugnacious, taking the position that they would not submit to extortion. Stiffening opposition convinced still more coalition members that

Spira was wrong in not trying to force the companies to stop Draize testing. If the opposition would fight as hard against contributing to a research fund as they would fight against changing their testing practices, why not hold out for what they really wanted?

In November 1981, the Coalition agreed to Bristol-Myers' offer to contribute $500,000 to the research fund, and the initial phase of the product-testing campaign was over.

Spira continued to campaign against product testing, moving on to the so-called LD-50 ("Lethal Dose-50%") test, which was—and still is—used throughout the cosmetics and chemical industries. In the LD-50, small animals, usually mice or rats, but sometimes guinea pigs, hamsters, rabbits, cats, or dogs, have progressively stronger solutions of the chemical being evaluated forced down their throats to determine at what quantity and strength fifty percent of the animals will die within a specified time. But the grand coalition of the Revlon campaign had broken up, never to be re-created.

Henry Spira's strategy had been based on the concept of disciplined, tightly focused campaigns pursuing a limited objective. But, flushed with success, some of the growing movement's new leaders— filled with idealism but lacking Spira's experience in the arena of social justice—grew impatient. They believed that Spira was being too timid. He had demanded a little, and he had gotten a little. If he had demanded everything, they believed, he would have gotten everything. They considered anything less than a categorical demand for an immediate end to all animal testing to be a sell-out.

17

The Sixties' Last Hurrah

The Sixties—America's great age of social protest—had been ushered in by the Montgomery bus boycott in 1955, and driven forward by free speech movements, anti-war movements, civil rights movements, Black Power movements, and women's movements. Its spirit was sustained by sit-ins, freedom rides, marches, demonstrations, civil disobedience, and bonfires fueled by women's bras and men's draft cards. It was the age of the Southern Christian Leadership Conference, the Student Non-Violent Coordinating Committee, the New Mobilization Committee to End the War in Vietnam, the Students for a Democratic Society, the Black Panther Party, the Black Muslims, the National Organization for Women, and the Yippies. It was the age of Martin Luther King, Jr., Malcolm X, Stokely Carmichael, Huey Newton, Bobby Seale, Abbie Hoffman, Angela Davis, Mario Savio, Joan Baez, the Berrigan brothers, Kate Millett, and Germaine Greer. It was the age of "THE PEOPLE," an era of tremendous human energy—fueled by the belief that the young could create a world better than they had inherited. It was a time when all good things seemed possible.

By the time the animal rights movement was born in the mid-1970s, the spirit of social protest that had animated the last two decades was dying out in the broader society. The progressive organizations had either vanished, like the New Mobe and the SDS, or gone mainstream, like the SCLC and NOW. The hippies and Yippies of the '60s and early '70s were hard at work becoming the yuppies of the '80s, a transmogrification typified by Jerry Rubin, who reinvented himself as a businessman. In many ways, the early animal rights movement was an anachronism, as animal activists carried the spirit and tactics of the '60s into a new era of social and political conservatism.

This initial burst of idealism, energy, and fearlessness lasted for nearly twenty years—from 1975 until the early 1990s, when it finally burned itself out. From the point of view of activists, this was the golden age of animal rights—filled with enthusiasm and optimism, fueled by explosive growth within the movement, and by the emergence of animal issues as a serious topic for public dialogue in a way that had not been seen since the anti-vivisection debates in Victorian England. To be a part of the animal rights movement during these early years was to be infected with the belief that you could end the enslavement and slaughter of animals within a single generation, just as the civil rights movement had ended segregation in less than twenty years.

Just A-Lookin' for a Home

At the Orono Conference in 1975, Alex Hershaft met Nellie Shriver and Connie Salamone, two vegan activists who were struggling to establish an animal protection movement within the American vegetarian community. "These people didn't have a home," Hershaft told me, speaking of animal activists. "They were lonely and frustrated, because we [vegetarians] were the closest thing they had and we didn't understand them. The vegetarian movement in the United States had become basically a fellowship rather than a social action movement."[1]

During the next five years, Hershaft organized several vegetarian conferences in Pennsylvania and Washington, D.C. These provided the first regular forum for Salamone, Shriver, and activists affected by Peter Singer's *Animal Liberation* to speak out on behalf on animals. Finally, in 1980, Hershaft brokered a meeting that included himself; Shriver; Salamone; animal activist Richard Morgan; environmental and animal activists Doug Moss and Jim Mason, who had recently founded *The Animals' Agenda*, the world's first animal protection magazine to represent the entire movement rather than serve as the house organ for a particular group; Ingrid Newkirk and Alex Pacheco, who were in the process of creating People for the Ethical Treatment of Animals; and a handful of others in New York, where they began planning to build a broadly based animal rights movement within the vegetarian community.[2]

Their opportunity came the following summer at a holistic living conference at Cedar Crest College in Allentown, Pennsylvania. With a purpose and a plan, "the animal rights people took over and turned it into the first animal rights conference in the United States."[3] At Cedar Crest, the leaders of fledgling groups and activists who were preparing to form groups were able to network, compare notes, informally stake out their areas of primary interest and generally get ready to move onto the national stage. In the wake of the Cedar Crest Conference were formed Trans-Species Unlimited and Mobilization for Animals, two groups that are now long defunct but played key roles in the early years of the American animal rights movement, Alex Hershaft's FARM, and PETA as national organizations.[4]

One of those in attendance at Cedar Crest was Richard Morgan. Although practically unknown outside of the movement and now largely forgotten within it, Morgan was extremely influential in the early years of animal rights. He had been active in the anti-war and civil rights movements of the Sixties and was an advocate of Sixties-style campaigns on behalf of animals—complete with marches, demonstrations, sit-ins and civil disobedience. In 1980, he had formed a group called Mobilization for Animals, which focused primarily on anti-vivisection campaigns and gained headlines with its flamboyant protests. Although Mobilization for Animals faded from view in the mid-80s, early movement leaders like Alex Hershaft and George Cave speak of Richard Morgan in deeply respectful terms as a "pioneer" and a "mentor."

In 1980, George Cave was teaching writing courses at Penn State University in State College, Pennsylvania, when he came across Peter

Singer's article from the *New York Review of Books* and used it as an assignment for one of his classes. A philosopher by training, with an interest in ethics, he was intrigued "on a purely theoretical level" by Singer's argument for moral equality based on sentience, and began reading widely on the topic of animal rights. What he learned about the treatment of animals in laboratories and on factory farms turned his academic interest into a commitment to work for change. He formed a grassroots group in central Pennsylvania called Trans-Species Unlimited to communicate the idea of compassion and respect across the boundaries of species.[5]

Beginning in 1981, in the wake of Cedar Crest, Alex Hershaft put together a series of annual conferences organized specifically for animal rights activists, called the "Action for Life" conferences. After attending the first of these, in Atlantic City, George Cave decided to take his group national,[6] and for the next decade Trans-Species Unlimited was among the most active and best known animal rights groups in the country, taking on vivisection, fur, and factory farming.

TSU was one of the first groups to focus on the fur trade, and in 1984 Cave organized a sit-in at Macy's Department Store in Manhattan, complete with civil disobedience and arrests, which he called "Sit Down for Wildlife." The next year, Last Chance for Animals, a California group led by actor Chris DeRose and activist Cres Vellucci, joined with TSU in organizing Sit-Downs in New York and Sacramento. In 1986, the event was moved to the day after Thanksgiving—chosen because more fur garments are retailed on that day than any other day in the year—and renamed Fur Free Friday. In 1988, five thousand demonstrators marched down Fifth Avenue in New York, led by television personality and game show host Bob Barker.[7] Now coordinated by a coalition of groups including Last Chance for Animals and the Humane Society of the United States, Fur Free Friday events are still a fixture on the animal rights calendar in cities across the country.

By 1990, George Cave was feeling the strain of two full-time jobs, one as president of TSU and the other teaching at Penn State.[8] Compounding his stress, Cave had launched a campaign to publicize what he believed were the exorbitant salaries pulled down by the leaders of large national groups—which Cave saw as conservative welfare organizations that were accomplishing much less for animals than they should be—especially HSUS, where John Hoyt earned nearly $150,000 in 1989.[9] This drew the ire of a number of movement leaders and turned out to be the opening volley in a fratricidal battle between the "grassroots" and the "nationals" that would threaten to tear the movement apart in the mid-'90s.

Changing the name to Animal Rights Mobilization (ARM), Cave tried to withdraw from active leadership while transforming his group into an organization that would not conduct campaigns itself, but instead would serve as a clearinghouse for local grassroots groups, mobilizing activists across the country and providing them with the information and resources—flyers, videos, etc.—that they needed to conduct their own campaigns. The concept failed to gain traction, however, and ARM passed into history in the early 1990s.

The Great American Meatout

The Orono conference was not the first time Alex Hershaft's life had changed dramatically. As a small child in Warsaw, Poland, he had been herded by German soldiers, along with his parents and their fellow Polish Jews, into the Warsaw Ghetto. Fewer than ten percent of those who were sealed into the ghetto came out alive. Alex's father was killed, but he and his mother were among the lucky few. Smuggled out shortly before the final destruction of the ghetto, he hid out in Poland for the remainder of the war, and then spent five years in Italy in a camp for Displaced Persons (as people rendered homeless and stateless by Fascism and the war were called), before coming to the United States at the age of sixteen.[10] More than half a century later, Hershaft would say of his childhood nightmare:

> In the Warsaw Ghetto, I learned that human beings can treat other human beings like animals. From that, I concluded

that the only way to end all oppression is to eliminate the oppression of the most oppressed—nonhuman animals.[11]

In 1963, Hershaft became what he describes as a "closet vegetarian." The Orono and Cedar Crest conferences were his coming-out parties. Following Cedar Crest, Hershaft formed a group to campaign against factory farming, which he called the Farm Animal Reform Movement. (He later changed the name to FARM.)

FARM's first major campaign, begun in 1983, was World Farm Animals' Day, to be observed on Gandhi's birthday, October 2. Observed with peaceful demonstrations and candlelight vigils in about 400 cities around the world, it is a solemn commemoration of the loss of billions of lives every year to animal agriculture. As Hershaft told me, "World Farm Animals's Day is not a fun event. If the Meatout is like a wedding or a bar mitzvah, World Farm Animals's Day is like a funeral."[12]

The "Meatout" that Hershaft alluded to is "The Great American Meatout," held every year around March 20 and modeled on the "The Great American Smokeout," an anti-smoking campaign in which people are urged to give up smoking for one day as a way to encourage them to quit for good. The idea of a Meatout—in which people would give up meat for a day as a device for educating them about the cruelty of animal agriculture and encouraging them to go vegetarian—was suggested at a FARM brainstorming session by Walt Rave, a colorful and respected local activist from Takoma Park, Maryland. Hershaft jumped on it, and what began in 1985 with events in twenty-five communities has grown to over one-thousand events in twenty-eight countries around the world.[13]

Alex Hershaft had started out wanting to reform factory farming. But by the mid-'90s, he had come to the conclusion that the only morally adequate response to the enslavement and slaughter of animals for food was the abolition of animal agriculture. Since then, FARM has, in Hershaft's words, "worked strictly on abolition. The only productive solution is small steps toward abolition."[14] He feels especially good about FARM's "School CHOICE" program, which works to get vegetarian options into school cafeterias, and the Sabina Fund, inaugurated in 1999, which has awarded one hundred and fifteen grants of between $500 and $1,000 each to small grassroots groups to promote a vegan diet. The Sabina Fund is named in honor of Alex Hershaft's mother.[15]

"Animals Are Not Ours"

Born in England, Ingrid Newkirk moved to India when she was seven years old and her father, a navigational engineer, was seconded to the Indian government as part of the assistance that Great Britain continued to provide its former colony. When she was a teenager, the family relocated to the United States, and after completing her education, she took a brief turn training to be a stockbroker.

One day in 1969, Newkirk found a family of abandoned kittens, and concerned that they would starve to death, she did what any kindhearted person would do—she gathered them into a cardboard box and took them to a nearby animal shelter in suburban Montgomery County Maryland. Appalled at the filthy, crowded conditions she found at the shelter, Ingrid Newkirk then did what almost no one else would have done—she abandoned the prospect of a lucrative career in finance and took a job cleaning cages and bathing dogs in an animal shelter. Studying animal care at night, she worked her way up in the organization, making such improvements as she could. It was during this period that:

> I stopped eating animals virtually one species at a time; first snails (I was taking some home to cook and they tried to liberate themselves from the bag. They looked so pathetic, I felt like a heel and liberated them down the bottom of my garden); then lobsters and other shelled beings after picking a live lobster out and having him cooked (I've no idea why the penny suddenly dropped—perhaps it was the ... realization he'd been broiled alive for me); then pigs—when I was a law enforcement officer and found lots of farmed animals aban-

doned, most dead, one little pig alive. I finally put two and two together when I realized I was about to prosecute some people for cruelty to a pig, while going home to eat the pork chops in my fridge![16]

During this same period, Newkirk read *Animal Liberation*.[17] "Good grief," she thought:

THIS is what I really believe. Not that animals should be treated kindly, of course they should, but that they're not OURS to use. They are other nations. Other individuals. Just in other strange (to us) packages.[18]

Leaving Montgomery County, Newkirk became head of the animal shelter in neighboring Washington, D.C. (Her official title was chief of the Division of Animal Disease Control of the Public Health Administration.) There she met Alex Pacheco, a student at George Washington University who volunteered part-time at the shelter cleaning out the runs and generally trying to make the lives of the animals a little less bleak.[19]

Born in Joliet, Illinois, but raised in rural Mexico, where his parents—his father was a doctor, his mother a nurse—went to provide medical care to the poorest of Mexico's poor, Alex Pacheco attended high school back in the United States and then began studying for the Catholic priesthood. On summer break from college in 1978, he went to visit an acquaintance who had a summer job at a slaughterhouse and:

... witnessed the violent deaths of terrified dairy cows, pigs, and chickens. What I saw changed my life. Shaken by the slaughtering, I sought and joined the animal protection community. As a newcomer to the movement, I could not have been more fortunate than to find two brilliant activists, Nellie Shriver, founder of American Vegetarians, and Constantine Salamone, an artist, feminist, and animal rights activist. They became my teachers.[20]

Not long thereafter, he met Cleveland Amory, who was funding Paul Watson's *Sea Shepherd,* and asked to be taken on as a crewmember. Impressed by the kid's sincerity—Pacheco was only nineteen—Amory accepted him, and in 1979, Alex Pacheco sailed as a seaman aboard *Sea Shepherd.* This was the cruise on which *Sea Shepherd* rammed and sank the pirate whaling ship *Sierra* off the coast of Portugal (see Chapter 18), although Pacheco was not on board at the time of the ramming.[21]

After leaving *Sea Shepherd* in Portugal, Pacheco went to England, where he campaigned for several weeks with the Hunt Saboteurs before returning to the United States. Settling in Washington, D.C.—which was a kind of base of operations for Nellie Shriver and Connie Salamone—he enrolled at George Washington University and volunteered at the D.C. animal shelter on New York Avenue, where he met Ingrid Newkirk.

Determined to act on their newfound animal rights philosophy, in March of 1980, Newkirk and Pacheco founded People for the Ethical Treatment of Animals as a small, underfunded local group whose tiny membership was drawn largely from students at George Washington University and activists from the Vegetarian Society of D.C.

The Silver Spring Monkeys

The following year, fresh from the Cedar Crest Conference, Newkirk and Pacheco decided that Pacheco should spend his summer break working in a vivisection laboratory to learn first hand what went on inside.[22] The one he chose, almost at random from a directory of animal research facilities licensed by the U.S. Department of Agriculture, was the Institute for Behavioral Research—better known as IBR—a small private laboratory in nearby Silver Spring, Maryland.

In May, Pacheco applied for a job at IBR, claiming to be a college student (which was true) who was looking for laboratory experience over the summer break (which was also true, sort of). He was interviewed by IBR's principal investigator Edward Taub, a psychologist in the tradition of Harry Harlow, who was severing the spinal nerves that enabled monkeys to have feeling in their hands and arms—a process known as "deafferentation"—and then observing the effects that this had on their behavior. The effect was that the monkeys stopped using the deadened limbs, even though the physical ability to move them had not been impaired by the surgery. Taub claimed that if he could teach the monkeys to use the deafferented limbs again, the knowledge gained might be used to help human beings suffering from stroke or spinal cord injury.

Taub told Pacheco there were no paid jobs available, but offered him a volunteer position—a kind of unstructured internship—working for a student assistant named Georgette Yakalis. Pacheco accepted, and began his stint at IBR on May 11, 1981 with a guided tour of the facility conducted by Taub. It is best to let Alex Pacheco tell what he saw on that tour and in the days and weeks to come:

> I saw filth caked on the wires of the cages, faeces piled in the bottom of the cages, urine and rust encrusting every surface. There, amid this rotting stench, sat sixteen crab-eating macaques and one rhesus monkey, their lives limited to metal boxes just 17 inches wide. In their desperation to assuage their hunger, they were picking forlornly at scraps and fragments of broken biscuits that had fallen through the wire into the sodden accumulations in the waste collection trays below. The cages had clearly not been cleaned properly for months. There were no dishes to keep the food away from the faeces, nothing for the animals to sit on but the jagged wires of the old cages, nothing for them to see but the filthy, faeces-splattered walls of that windowless box, only 15 ft square....

> Twelve of the seventeen monkeys had disabled limbs as a result of surgical interference (deafferentation) when they were juveniles. Sarah, then eight years old, had been alone in her cage since she was one day old.... [T]hirty-nine of the fingers on the monkeys' deafferented hands were severely

deformed or missing, having been either torn or bitten off....
Many of the monkeys were neurotic.... Like a maniac, Sarah
would attack her [own] foot and spin around incessantly,
calling out like an infant.... Because of a long-standing
rodent problem, rat droppings and urine covered everything,
and live and dead cockroaches were in the drawers, on the
floor and around the filthy scrub tank [in the operating the-
ater]....

No one bothered to bandage the monkeys' injuries properly
(on the few occasions when bandages were used at all), and
antibiotics were administered only once; no lacerations or
self-mutilation injuries were ever cleaned. Whenever a bandage was applied, it was never changed, no matter how filthy
and soiled it became... Two monkeys had bones protruding
through their flesh. Several had bitten off their own fingers
and had festering stubs, which they extended toward me as I
discreetly took fruit from my pocket. With these pitiful limbs
they searched through the foul mess of their waste pans for
something to eat. ...[23]

Pacheco soon had the free run of the lab—along with a set of
keys—and was able to come in at night and on weekends, when he
could take pictures undetected. On at least one occasion, Pacheco
smuggled his camera in during the day and photographed a monkey
in a stereotaxic device—Harry Harlow's "rape rack," which holds an
animal absolutely immobile in whatever position the experimenter
desires, no matter how awkward or painful.

Pacheco's next step was to recruit experts to tour IBR with him
surreptitiously at night so that they could testify to conditions in the
laboratory. Geza Teleki and John McCardle were internationally
respected primatologists; Ronnie Hawkins was a medical doctor who
had worked with primates; Michael Fox was a veterinarian, author of
books on animal welfare, and a vice president of the Humane Society
of the United States.

The only actual animal rights activist in the group was Donald Barnes, who, as a civilian physiological psychologist with the U.S. Air Force for sixteen years, had conducted experiments in which monkeys were irradiated to determine the extent to which radiation sickness might affect the performance of pilots during a nuclear war. (This was the research on which the 1987 Matthew Broderick movie, *Project X,* was based.) In 1980, as Barnes puts it, "the blinders slipped off," and he recognized the immorality of the research.[24] Resigning his government position, he relocated to the Washington, D.C. area and became director of education for the National Anti-Vivisection Society. For the next twenty years, Barnes was a leading figure in the national animal rights movement and a popular speaker at conferences and conventions, until he returned home to San Antonio, Texas, where he works on local animal rights issues and enjoys a well-earned semi-retirement.

In late August, Pacheco and Newkirk presented Pacheco's evidence—including affidavits from the five experts and Pacheco's own affidavit, photographs, and notes—to representatives of the Maryland state's attorney's office and the Montgomery County police department. The state's attorney was eager to prosecute, and on the morning of September 11, the Montgomery County police, led by Detective Sergeant Rick Swain of the Silver Spring district and backed by a search warrant issued by Maryland Circuit Court Judge John McAuliffe, raided IBR.[25]

PETA had alerted the media. And at the prospect of the first police raid ever conducted on a vivisection laboratory, they showed up in force. By evening, the Silver Spring monkeys, who had suffered all their lives in anonymity and obscurity, were being seen in living rooms all across the country, and People for the Ethical Treatment of Animals—which a few hours earlier perhaps a hundred people had heard of—was a household name. Although they had little experience at this sort of thing, in the weeks and months that followed, Ingrid Newkirk proved to be a gifted strategist in working the media, and Alex Pacheco an effective spokesperson—coming across as sincere, modest but self-assured, and committed to the welfare of the monkeys. The intense media coverage, coming on the heels of Henry Spira's Museum of Natural History campaign and coinciding with his Draize campaign, burned animal rights into the consciousness of the American public and transformed PETA into the best-known animal rights group in the world.

The monkeys were seized by the police and—since the National Zoo refused to help—relocated under the supervision of Dr. Teleki to a specially constructed facility in the basement of the home of Lori Lehner, an adoption specialist at the Montgomery County animal shelter who was a friend of Newkirk. Taub quickly petitioned the court to have the monkeys returned to him, claiming that both his research and the animals' health had been endangered. Filed with his petition were reports of inspections by the U.S. Department of Agriculture finding "no infractions," or only "minor infractions" of USDA animal care standards at IBR. Impressed by the government reports, Taub's credentials, and the letters and telegrams of support that had begun pouring in from the scientific community—which was quickly closing ranks around one of its own—Judge David Cahoon granted Taub's motion and ordered the monkeys returned to him the following day.

But when the police went to pick up the monkeys, they were gone—vanished, as it were, into thin air. To this day, who took them and precisely where they were taken has never been revealed. In her book about the Animal Liberation Front, *Free the Animals*, Ingrid Newkirk says that the monkeys were transported in a moving van to a small, private sanctuary in Florida.[26] This had been widely rumored within the animal rights community for years before Newkirk published her book and appears to be true, rather than part of Newkirk's effort to disguise the identities of the people she writes about.

Lehner, who had spent the night in a hotel—she claimed to have received an anonymous telephone call advising her not to be home that night—was arrested and held in jail overnight. The next day, the charges were dropped for lack of evidence. In all likelihood, she had been locked up in the hope that going to jail would frighten her into revealing the whereabouts of the monkeys. So far as I have been able to determine, Lori Lehner was the first person in the United States to actually spend time in jail for animal rights. Newkirk and one other person were booked and released on their own recognizance before charges were dropped against them as well.

The public loves a good mystery—especially when it involves a dramatic, last-second rescue—and the monkeys' disappearance caught the country's imagination. With the media attention putting pressure on all parties, PETA negotiated an agreement with the police that if the monkeys were returned, they would not have to go back into Taub's torture chamber; a court hearing was scheduled to determine where they should go.

Judge Cahoon, however, had other ideas. Angered that his order had been defied, as soon as the monkeys were securely in police custody, he cancelled the hearing and ordered them returned to IBR. Within a week, one was dead—of a "heart attack"—and another had been severely injured. Out of patience now with both parties, the judge ordered IBR to turn the monkeys over to the federal agency that was funding the experiments, the National Institutes of Health. And so, they were transferred to NIH's primate quarantine center in nearby Poolesville, Maryland, which serves—it is still in operation— as both a vivisection laboratory and a holding facility through which primates pass on their way to laboratories around the country. While at Poolesville, one of the monkeys became paralyzed as a result of injuries incurred at IBR; as he was in severe, irremediable pain, he was euthanized. Another monkey's deafferented arm was gangrenous and had to be amputated. Taub objected to both actions on the grounds that the monkeys could still be useful to his research.

Taub and his assistant, John Kunz, were charged with multiple counts of animal cruelty and animal neglect. The trial in *Maryland v. Taub, Kunz* opened on October 27, 1981, with the defendants represented by a battery of lawyers led by attorneys from Washington's most prestigious and politically connected law firm, Arnold and Porter. The vivisection community would later claim that Taub exhausted his savings on attorneys' fees; animal advocates suspected that institutions supporting vivisection—believing, "Today Taub, tomorrow the rest of us"—had quietly covered most of his expenses, wanting to see Taub win, but not wanting to share in the negative publicity. The American Psychological Association, of which Harry Harlow was a past president, openly donated $10,000. The prosecution was conducted by Roger Galvin, a criminal prosecutor from the state's attorney's office.[27] Maryland District Court Judge Stanley Klavan presided.

Both sides made the expected arguments. There were no surprises. Galvin showed the court Pacheco's photographs and presented testimony from Pacheco, the five experts who had toured the facility, and other experts who told the court that Taub's practices were cruel, caused the monkeys "unnecessary suffering," *i.e.*, suffering not essential to the success of the research, and were not consistent with professional standards of care for primates. The Arnold and Porter lawyers introduced the passing grades that IBR had received on USDA inspections and presented expert witnesses who testified that conditions at IBR were consistent with industry practices, did not cause the animals unnecessary suffering, and that Taub was a respected scientist doing important research. Taub himself testified to the importance of his research, and his concern for the welfare of the monkeys, and he suggested that at least some of Pacheco's photographs had been staged and that someone—he did not say whom he suspected, but it was not hard to guess—had bribed the caretakers into letting filth pile up and conditions in the lab deteriorate while Taub was on vacation.

Taub's lawyers had had the good sense not to request a jury trial. They wanted this case decided by a judge on the fine points of the law, not by a jury whose sensibilities had been outraged by Alex Pacheco's photographs. Even so, they lost, but it was close. Of more than a hundred charges against Taub, Judge Klavan dismissed all but six, and these related to Taub's failure to provide veterinary care for six of the monkeys who the judge believed had needed it. Incredibly, the court ruled that the prosecution had failed to prove that Taub had otherwise mistreated the monkeys or caused them unnecessary suffering. John Kunz—who had not testified—was acquitted on all counts, as

Judge Klavan held that Taub, not Kunz, was responsible for obtaining veterinary care for the monkeys.

Taub appealed his convictions, and in June 1982, he was retried—this time before a jury—on the six charges on which he had been convicted. After two and half days of deliberation, the jury—which was not allowed by the court to hear most of the evidence in support of the original convictions—voted to convict Taub on one count and acquit him on the other five.

Taub appealed again, and the Maryland Court of Appeals in Baltimore dismissed the one remaining charge. On August 10, 1983, the court ruled that since Taub's research had been funded by the federal government, Taub and IBR were not subject to the Maryland anti-cruelty statutes, and the state, therefore, lacked the authority to prosecute him.

The criminal justice phase of the case of the Silver Spring monkeys was over. But the next decade would be devoted to legal wrangling over their fate, as animal advocates, led by PETA, Alex Hershaft, and Cleveland Amory, battled to have the surviving monkeys released to a primate sanctuary, and Taub, joined by much of the vivisection community, fought to have them returned to him. Caught between a rock and a hard place, NIH did what bureaucracies are uniquely equipped to do—they stonewalled everybody.

On June 24, 1986, they transferred the monkeys to the Delta Regional Primate Research Center, located just outside of New Orleans and operated under federal grants by Tulane University. When the monkeys arrived, a small group of activists held hands and formed a human chain across the road, symbolically blocking the entrance. They were quickly cleared out of the way by police and security guards.

Five of the monkeys had served as Taub's control group and had not been experimented upon. In 1989, in a deal brokered by Congresspersons Bob Dornan of California and Bob Smith of New Hampshire, these monkeys were transferred to the San Diego Zoo, leading to a bit of wry animal rights humor: "When does a zoo not feel like a prison?" "When you've done time at IBR."

The ten monkeys who remained never left Delta, despite repeated pleas to NIH to release them to a private sanctuary. The government's intransigence apparently stemmed from a desire to keep the public from seeing the extent of the brutality and mutilation that these animals had suffered. With the monkeys out of the public eye, NIH hoped that popular outrage—and the anti-vivisection sentiment it engendered—would die down. In the early 1990s, seven were subjected to further experiments and killed afterward. Two had died in the late '80s, and the one remaining, Sarah, may be presumed dead, although there has been no announcement from NIH.

Unnecessary Fuss

Overnight, PETA was established in the public mind as *the* animal rights group *par excellence*, a status it has maintained down to the present. Although from the beginning, Newkirk and Pacheco intended PETA to address all forms of animal enslavement and slaughter, in the early years, almost by default, the emphasis remained on vivisection.

In 1984, a local group called the Pennsylvania Animal Rights Coalition (PARC) became aware of research being conducted on primates by Dr. Thomas Gennarelli at the University of Pennsylvania in Philadelphia.[28] Funded by grants from NIH, Gennarelli was attempting to develop a scale for objectively measuring the severity of injuries from falls, automobile accidents, and so forth.[29] As part of this effort, he was trying to create a device—a high-tech variation on the captive-bolt pistol that is used in slaughterhouses—that would deliver a precisely calibrated blow to a primate's skull. As this torture machine was being perfected, Gennarelli would test it by fastening it to a monkey's head, administering the blow—which would often crack the animal's skull—and then recording the damage. Incredibly, the device was actually glued onto the monkeys' heads to hold it in place, and then removed with a hammer and chisel applied directly to their skulls, compounding the injury already inflicted. PARC and the Fund for Animals publi-

238 THE LONGEST STRUGGLE

cized the cruelty of Gennarelli's research, but made no headway in getting it stopped.

Then on May 28, 1984, members of the Animal Liberation Front broke into the laboratory and discovered sixty hours of videotape on which the researchers had recorded their own brutality and callousness. The monkeys were given repeated severe blows to the head which left them semi-conscious, disoriented, and unable to stand or walk while the researchers clowned around and made fun of their condition. The video showed the researchers smoking during surgery, leaving monkeys uncared for after they had been injured, and generally showing no concern for the animals' suffering.

The ALF sent the videotape to PETA, who used it to produce a thirty-minute video which they titled *Unnecessary Fuss*, a reference to a comment that Gennarelli had made to a newspaper reporter before the scandal broke to the effect that he tried to avoid publicity because it "might stir up all sorts of unnecessary fuss among those who are sensitive to these sorts of things."[30]

PETA, joined by a loose coalition of other groups, launched a major national campaign to shut down Gennarelli's laboratory. They distributed *Unnecessary Fuss* far and wide, they ran full-page ads in major newspapers, they urged Congress to deny funding to NIH until it rescinded Gennarelli's grant, and they organized demonstrations in Philadelphia, Bethesda, Maryland (headquarters of NIH), and around the country. Gary Francione, a law professor and animal rights advocate, negotiated with the University on behalf of the activists, but got nowhere. The coalition applied all the political pressure they could muster—in 1985, sixty members of Congress asked NIH to cancel Gennarelli's grant—and cranked up a deafening roar of negative publicity, but nothing worked. NIH and the University of Pennsylvania held tough.

On July 15, 1985—in what was probably the high point of Sixties-style activism for animals—a group of precisely one hundred and one activists,[31] led by Ingrid Newkirk and Alex Pacheco, walked into the eighth-floor offices of Dr. Murray Goldstein, Director of the National Institute of Neurological Disorders and Stroke (NINDS), the agency of NIH that was funding Gennarelli's research. The activists—who included Elliot Katz, a veterinarian who in 1983 had founded the animal rights group In Defense of Animals, George Cave, and Tom Regan—demanded that NINDS cancel Gennarelli's funding, they sat down all over the furniture and the floor, and they waited to be arrested for trespassing. Nothing happened. They were not there to take hostages, so they allowed the occupants of the offices to leave. They waited some more. Still nothing happened. Then, things did begin to happen, but not what anyone had expected. The lights went out and the air conditioning went up so high that the protestors, who were dressed for the hot and muggy Washington weather, were left shivering. (Fortunately, the windows could be opened.) The telephones stopped working and—since this was before the age of cell phones—the demonstrators had to smuggle in a bulky, early version of a portable telephone in order not to be isolated from the outside world. Slowly, it dawned on everyone that NIH intended to seal them off and wait them out.

As word of the sit-in spread, supporters gathered on the grounds of NIH outside the building.[32] Activists and press stayed around the clock. Nobody knew when something might break, and nobody wanted to miss it. Several lawyers—including Gary Francione and Roger Galvin, who was now in private practice—were allowed to shuttle in and out and negotiate on behalf of the protestors. Hidden in their pockets and briefcases, some carried food and personal care items to activists who had come expecting to be in the building an hour or two at most. The bathrooms and water fountains worked, but that was about all. PETA activist Sharon Lawson, who was coordinating the outside support, had to scramble around to find blankets for shivering demonstrators. One of the attorneys carried in a coil of rope that was later lowered from a window and used to haul up food. When NIH—which did not want to be accused of starving the demonstrators—agreed to allow food to be brought in, a small television set was concealed in a box of food so that Newkirk and Pacheco could stay abreast of the media coverage. On one occasion, Ingrid Newkirk was able to slip out of the building, appear on a morning television network news show, and slip back into the building undetected.

By not arresting them immediately, NIH had given the demonstrators an unexpected opportunity to win far more for Gennarelli's monkeys than just a quick burst of publicity, and they determined to make the most of it. No one would have resisted arrest—they had come expecting to be arrested—but NIH did not know that, and given the show of public and Congressional support for the monkeys and their cause, the Department of Health and Human Services— NIH's parent agency—was afraid to risk a pitched battle. And so, instead of being just a one-shot headline, the story ran for four days, and got bigger every day, because no one knew how the "standoff" would end.

Then without warning, on day four, it ended as suddenly as it had begun. Margaret Heckler, the former Republican Congresswoman from Massachusetts who was Ronald Reagan's Secretary of Health and Human Services, suspended Gennarelli's grant pending a full investigation of his practices. PETA's coalition had won. The Department of Health and Human Services would claim that Heckler's decision was based on an interim report issued by HHS investigators. Activists claimed that after months of refusing to look at *Unnecessary Fuss*, Heckler had finally watched the PETA video.

"I'd Rather Go Naked"
In a world that was growing blasé about demonstrations and street theater, PETA kept the issue of animal enslavement and slaughter before the public by being particularly imaginative. One stunt that PETA has updated to great effect is that old chestnut from vaudeville, a pie in the face. A few of the best-publicized facial pies from among hundreds that PETA has launched around the world will give a sense of how they have turned silly vaudeville shtick to a serious purpose.

In 1991, the Iowa Pork Queen got a tofu custard in the face while standing onstage in gown and tiara at the Iowa State Fair. In the full glare of Las Vegas stage lights, a young woman named Brandy DeJongh gained an immortality of sorts by catching a vegan chocolate in the kisser, moments after being crowned Miss Rodeo America 2000. Frank Perdue, serial killer of billions of chickens, got his pie—thrown by a woman wearing a chicken suit—at a meeting of the Board of Regents of the University of Maryland, of which he was a member. Other animal abusers who have received the PETA pie award include fashion designer Oscar de la Renta; Dan Glickman, Secretary of Agriculture in the Clinton administration; and Smithfield ham executive Raoul Baxter, who got his while delivering a speech at the World Pork Congress.

Fur protests have ranged from taking over the runway at fashion shows and unfurling anti-fur banners to bringing the bloody skinned carcasses of foxes to demonstrations at the opening of the New York Metropolitan Opera season—where society ladies traditionally show off their furs—with signs reading "This is the rest of your coat." Young, attractive "Tiger Ladies" have protested zoos and fur by crouching in small cages wearing a G-string and orange and black striped body paint.

In 2000, PETA launched a national advertising campaign aimed at college students suggesting that beer was a healthier beverage than milk. Called "Got beer?" as a parody of the dairy industry's "Got milk?" campaign—which featured pictures of celebrities with a white milk "mustache" on their upper lip—the parody went big-time when Mothers Against Drunk Driving claimed that PETA was encouraging college students to drink irresponsibly. PETA briefly withdrew the ads and made conciliatory gestures toward MADD, but when this failed to placate the anti-drunk driving group, they restarted the campaign. That same year, when Rudolf Giuliani was diagnosed with prostate cancer, PETA ran a picture of New York's mayor with a milk mustache and the caption "Got Prostate Cancer?" to illustrate their claim that dairy products can contribute to various forms of cancer. The national outcry against PETA made many times more people aware of the campaign against dairy products than the original ads.

PETA's most successful and longest running publicity gimmick is the "Naked" campaign. In its advertising mode, celebrities—most often high-fashion models or actresses, but also including men (basketball zany Dennis Rodman and rocker Tommy Lee, for example)—appear discreetly posed *au naturel* above the slogan, "I'd rather go naked than wear fur." In the campaign's protest mode, everyday activists—usually about equal numbers of both genders—hold "I'd rather go naked ... " banners in front of territory that their clothes would normally be expected to cover.

PETA's use of gimmicks has drawn criticism from some in the movement who believe that they trivialize the issue of animal suffering and give the public a negative image of the animal rights movement. "It's hard enough trying to get people to take animal rights seriously," one activist told me, "without PETA out there acting like a bunch of jerks." But it's hard to argue with success, and PETA is far and away the most successful cutting-edge animal rights organization in the world, in terms of both membership and spreading the animal rights message to the public at large—and has been for the past quarter-century. With a larger membership and bigger budget than most organizations that are less flamboyant, PETA took in $26,000,000 in donations in 2005, suggesting that the public is being attracted, not turned off, to animal rights by PETA's attention-grabbing shenanigans.[33]

The sharpest criticism of PETA from within the animal rights movement, however, is directed at the Naked campaign. Here, the argument is that PETA is exploiting women and contributing to gender stereotypes that have been used for centuries as instruments of female oppression. But over the years, Ingrid Newkirk has been consistent in her response. No one, she says, is being exploited. Everyone who participates (including Newkirk herself) is an uncoerced volunteer. Sexual attraction is a fact of life, and if it can advance the animals' cause, she makes no apologies for using it. And besides, Newkirk points out, nudity isn't always sexy; sometimes, it's just attention-getting.

The Battle of Hegins

The massive demonstrations and high-profile campaigns that characterized the animal rights movements during the early 1980s had focused on what might be called "urban issues," such as vivisection, fur, and factory farming (factory-farmed food is consumed by people in cities and suburbs). In 1986, however, a local, small-town issue moved to center stage and stayed there for the next decade, in one of the most sustained—and most successful—campaigns ever mounted by animal advocates.

The occasion was the Fred W. Coleman Memorial Pigeon Shoot, held every Labor Day in the village of Hegins (pronounced with a hard "g"), tucked away in the mountains of Schuylkill County in east central Pennsylvania. Held in the Hegins municipal park and attended by hundreds of paying spectators, the Shoot was an enormous block party, a place where families from miles around went to spend the day, eating hot dogs, burgers, and fried chicken, drinking beer, and chatting with neighbors they hadn't seen since last Labor Day.

But the illusion of wholesome family fun was punctured by the constant CRASH! of shotguns as shooters on seven killing fields competed to see who was the best at gunning down harmless, defenseless birds. The pigeons were stuffed into small, white boxes called "traps"—one pigeon per trap—by local children between eight and twelve years old, called "trapper boys," although a few were girls. A shooter stood twenty yards back from a line of traps with his shotgun at the ready. When he yelled, "Pull!" someone in a booth behind him would pull a string connected to the trigger of a trap. The trap was spring loaded, and would throw the pigeon three feet into the air. Sometimes the birds—who were dehydrated, weak, and disoriented from being kept in crowded crates for several days without food or water—would fly; sometimes they would simply fall to the ground and begin walking aimlessly around. Either way, the shooter would blast away at them.

Only about twenty percent were killed instantly. Another ten percent flew away uninjured. The remaining seventy percent were wounded and either died some minutes after falling back to the ground, flew away to die later of infection, exsanguination, and dehydration, or were eventually picked up by trapper boys who killed them by wringing their necks, pulling their heads off, or slamming their bodies against the sides of the oil drums into which they threw the dead bodies. Not counting the wounded birds who flew away, more than five thousand pigeons were killed every year at Hegins.[34]

As it happened, a member of Trans-Species Unlimited lived in nearby Pottsville, and alerted George Cave to the pigeon shoot. In 1984 and 1985, TSU conducted small protests at the Hegins Municipal Park. In 1986, Cave publicized the event throughout the animal rights community and called for a large-scale protest. Other groups—including PETA and the Fund for Animals—supported the call, and from then on several hundred animal rights activists spent their Labor Days in Hegins.

When TSU withdrew in 1990, the Fund for Animals took up leadership of the coalition conducting the demonstrations. The mass protests turned the pigeon shoot into a near war zone, as outraged protesters and drunken locals (the booths selling beer opened at eight o'clock in the morning, and by noon young toughs carrying plastic cups of Yuengling draft, the local favorite, were roaming the grounds looking for trouble) traded insults, obscenities, and threats. One middle-aged female activist had her face stuffed into a toilet by two female shoot supporters. Bernard Unti, one of the protest organizers, was addressing the demonstrators with a bullhorn when the Hegins police threw him to the ground, dislocating his shoulder.

In addition to typical protest tactics—signs, banners, chants, and the like—the demonstrators tried to save pigeons by dashing onto the killing field and releasing as many birds from the traps as they could before they were apprehended by shoot security or the police. Every year, dozens of activists were arrested in this way. Most received a citation, like a traffic ticket, which they paid, and were released by the end of the day. In 1991, however, a group of ten female activists, led by the Fund's national director Heidi Prescott and PETA's Ingrid Newkirk, refused to pay their fines and spent a week in the Schuylkill

County jail. The following year, a group of forty-two women, again including Prescott and Newkirk, went to jail rather than pay their fines.

The hostility, taunting, and violence reached a peak in 1992, when the Ku Klux Klan announced that they were coming to Hegins in a show of support for freedom and the right to bear arms, both of which they claimed were under attack from animal rights groups. The Fund for Animals put out a call for the largest protest ever, and more than fifteen hundred animal activists turned out, many arriving in chartered buses.

Chicago activist Steve Hindi—a martial arts student—responded to the Klan announcement by issuing a press release touting the formation of the "Black Berets." Since the police had shown their unwillingness to protect the demonstrators, Hindi explained, the protesters were going to provide their own security in the form of a cadre of martial arts experts identifiable by their black berets.

By the time Labor Day arrived, the authorities warned that they were expecting over a hundred Black Berets and would be out in force to deal with any attempts at intimidation or violence by self-appointed "security" types. What actually showed up were a dozen folks wearing black berets that Hindi had bought at an Army Surplus store. As Steve Hindi told me:

> It was a wonderful scam. It was never anything more than a joke on the shoot supporters and a zinger at the police for not protecting the demonstrators. We decided to have a little bit of fun with these guys. We had no idea it would amount to anything. I just brought the berets on a lark, and we had to scramble around to find people to wear them. Then we went around all day doing goofy martial arts stunts just to get a rise out of the shoot supporters.[35]

The shoot always opened with a "prayer breakfast" that included an invocation by a local minister and the playing of the national anthem over the public address system. This year, the Black Berets brought their own vegan breakfast food and sat down in the picnic area just before the breakfast was scheduled to start. When the locals arrived and found the Black Berets praying for "the deliverance of the pigeons from the evil clutches of those whose hearts are hardened against them," they left without pausing for either breakfast or prayer. And that was the point. In Hindi's view, "They were there to take the lives of the pigeons, and we were there to take the fun out of killing."[36] Steve Hindi's Black Berets were Sixties-style street theater at its best.

The Klan presence turned out to be two recruiters from nearby Ephrata who wandered around the park wearing white sheets and hoods looking for TV cameras so they could see themselves on television that night. Since it was a hot day and it's hard to drink beer wearing a hood, the hoods soon came off.

Apart from the staged drama of the Klan and the Black Berets, the confrontation between shoot supporters and protesters was the nastiest and most threatening ever. Protesters formed a line twenty yards long and two or three people deep on both sides of the walkway between the parking lots and the entrance to the park, so that anyone going in had to walk a gauntlet of shouted jeers, insults, and obscenities. Inside the park, bands of beer-drinking young locals looked for wounded pigeons to torment and kill and activists to intimidate.

The massive 1992 protest failed to make a dent in the pigeon shoot's support, either in Schuylkill County or in the state legislature, where The Fund for Animals had begun lobbying for a law to ban live pigeon shoots. In fact, the Hegins Labor Day Committee happily announced that since the protests had begun, the event had drawn more spectators and made more money than ever before, a claim that appeared to be true.

Instead of stopping the shoot, the protests seemed to be breathing new life into it. The leaders of several national organizations took their groups out of the coalition, telling the Fund privately that the protests had become counterproductive and carrying on with them would be a waste of scarce resources in pursuit of an unwinnable goal. They advised the Fund to cancel next year's demonstration, chalk Hegins up to experience, and move on to other issues.

Cleveland Amory and Marian Probst left the decision to Heidi Prescott, who had made the pigeon shoot a personal crusade. The problem, as Prescott saw it, was that the focus of the publicity had shifted away from the pigeons and onto the conflict between the human antagonists. And so, the solution was not to give up and go away, but to put the spotlight back where it belonged—on the suffering of the birds—while the activists worked on legislation and litigation to ban the shoots.

Prescott announced that there would be no more Labor Day protests at Hegins. Instead, the Fund for Animals was going to organize a large-scale documentation and rescue effort aimed at saving the lives of pigeons and compiling evidence that could be used in the legislature and the courts. The documentation effort had two facets. One, led by Steve Hindi, involved shooting video footage showing wounded birds left unaided, trapper boys killing birds with their bare hands, and the drunken bloodlust of the crowd. The other, led by Fund wildlife biologist D. J. Schubert, sent two-person teams to each of the seven killing fields to record the number of birds who were killed cleanly, the number wounded and retrieved, the number wounded and not retrieved, and the number of birds who escaped unharmed.

The rescue effort, led by Fund staff member Christine Wolf, Pennsylvania veterinarian Gordon Stull, and Jodi Louth, a wildlife rehabilitator and animal rights activist from Michigan, sent teams of rescuers roaming the park to collect wounded birds who had come to ground in the public areas and take them to a veterinary van parked on the main parking lot. The other aspect of rescue involved activists running onto the killing ground to release birds from the traps.

This seemed to work well for several years, and then in 1997, things got out of hand. Among those who came to Hegins that day were two dozen or more activists in their late teens or early twenties who had no patience for the Fund's nonconfrontational strategy and did not consider themselves under Fund discipline. All day long there were nasty face-offs between these "black bloc" activists, as they called themselves,[37] and local toughs, and two or three actual fights. Then, in mid-afternoon, the side window of a shooter's pickup truck was shattered and a firecracker thrown inside which set the upholstery on fire, sending billows of black smoke streaming up from the cab. Toward the end of the day, windows were smashed at the office of local insurance agent Robert Tobash, who was chairman of the Hegins Labor Day Committee and the chief organizer of the shoot. As it happened, Tobash shared office space with Bob Allen, a ranking member of the Pennsylvania state legislature. Professing outrage at the vandalism, Allen used all of his considerable influence to assure that legislation banning pigeon shoots did not pass. In the meantime, the vandalism and the enraged reaction of the local people were the lead story that night on television news all over Pennsylvania.

By now the Fund was aggressively pursuing a ban on the shoot in the courts. A registered Pennsylvania humane agent, Clayton Hulsheiser—with financial and legal support provided by the Fund for Animals, and using the documentation gathered by the Fund since 1993—had filed a complaint in the district court for Schuylkill County alleging that the shoot violated Pennsylvania's animal cruelty laws. Worried that the atmosphere of confrontation, the threat of violence, and the vandalism would damage the best chance the pigeons had, Prescott and Fund vice president Michael Markarian called off the following year's documentation and rescue. Instead, activists spent Labor Day 1998 at tourist sites all across Pennsylvania— Gettysburg, Independence Hall, the State Capitol—and distributed flyers calling for a tourist boycott of Pennsylvania as long as pigeon shoots continued.

The trial court ruled that pigeons were not animals within the meaning of the Pennsylvania cruelty statute. On appeal, the state Supreme Court overturned that decision and sent the case back for reconsideration. Seeing the handwriting on the wall, and seeing legal expenses draining away their funds, the Hegins Labor Day Committee threw in the towel. In August 1999, just days before Labor Day, they agreed to cancel the pigeon shoot in perpetuity, and in return the Fund for Animals agreed to waive $3,000 in legal expenses that the court had ruled the Committee owed the Fund.

1998 was the last Hegins pigeon shoot. After sixty-five years, no more pigeons would die on Labor Day. As of Labor Day 2006, this equates to 40,000 lives saved, with the count going up by 5,000 every year.

Beginning as a quintessential Sixties-style protest organized around massive and raucous demonstrations, civil disobedience, street theater, and media stunts, the Hegins campaign transformed itself in the 1990s as the leadership grew disillusioned with these tactics and developed new, less flamboyant and less confrontational approaches. It was this ability to adapt that ultimately led to success. In Chapters 19 and 20, we will see the animal protection movement as a whole struggle to reinvent itself in very much the same way that Heidi Prescott and Michael Markarian reinvented the Hegins campaign. Hegins is a paradigmatic case study of the process of frustration followed by adaptation and growth that has characterized the mainstream of the American animal rights movement from the mid-1990s to the present.

The March on Washington

Through the 1980s, any demonstration was sure to receive local media coverage, and protests that included civil disobedience—such as a sit-in or the unfurling of a banner from a building or bridge—had a good chance to make the national news. Congressional staff aides were reporting that animal protection elicited more constituent mail than any other single issue. New groups were springing up all the time, and soon no locality of any size was without an animal rights advocacy. The movement was bubbling with an enthusiasm that expressed itself in demonstrations, hunt sabotages, and street theater in cities all across the country.

The culmination of this exuberant childhood of the animal rights movement was the March on Washington. In the early 1980s, a small, D.C.-based lobbying group, the National Alliance for Animal Legislation (later renamed the National Alliance for Animals), led by activist Peter Linck,[38] had begun sponsoring national animal rights conferences that soon became the successors to Alex Hershaft's Action for Life gatherings. By the late 1980s, the conferences were drawing nearly a thousand attendees and were the premier annual event on the animal rights calendar.

As an adjunct to the 1990 conference, the Alliance solicited the support of other groups for an Animal Rights March on Washington in support of animal friendly legislation. Sponsored by PETA, the Fund for Animals, and literally dozens of other groups (John Hoyt's HSUS was the most notable absentee), and organized by an ecumenical steering committee chaired by Peter Linck, the March took place on June 10, 1990, when twenty-four thousand animal activists gathered on the Ellipse, just south of the White House, and marched down Pennsylvania Avenue to the east end of the National Mall facing the Capitol, where they listened to inspirational talks by leaders of the movement and sympathetic celebrities. The biggest celebrity speaking that day was actor Christopher Reeve—"Superman"—who was still five years away from the riding accident that would paralyze him. When Reeve told the marchers that animal activists should be more moderate in their demands so as not to alienate the public, he was loudly booed. When he went on to say that some animal experimentation was necessary to find a cure for diseases like AIDS, he was booed so loudly and so long that he gave up trying to finish his remarks and left the stage.

The incident encapsulated the spirit of the March, which was the spirit of the past fifteen years. As we marched along Pennsylvania Avenue, we set up an antiphonal chant. "What do we want?" a chant leader with a bullhorn would ask. "Animal Rights!" the marchers would shout back. "When do we want it?" "NOW!" Reeve was telling us to turn the animal rights movement back into an animal welfare movement, and we were telling him, "No!"

The presence of twenty-four thousand animal rights activists on the National Mall made us feel like the presence of fifteen hundred vegetarians at the Orono Conference had made Alex Hershaft feel fifteen years earlier. We were not alone, and we were not just a bunch of kooks out there on the fringes of society. We were a legitimate national movement, we were a force, we were growing, and with truth and justice on our side, we were going to win.

Had we been less caught up in the moment and a little more perspicacious, we would have seen a dark cloud filling our silver lining. When the civil rights movement was only nine years old, Martin Luther King had been able to rally two hundred and fifty thousand people to the Lincoln Memorial. When our movement was fifteen years old, we could muster almost a tenth of that number. Meanwhile, out of sight, in corporate headquarters and government offices, the animal abusers were planning a counterattack that would dramatically alter the course of the struggle. And perhaps even more damaging, there were antagonisms developing within the movement that would soon threaten to tear it apart. We saw the 1990 March on Washington as the beginning of a glorious era for animal rights. In fact, it was the end of one.

18

Direct Action: Striking Back on Land and Sea

Since its origins in the 1960s, the environmental movement has shown little interest in animal rights. In fact, with their focus on preserving species and ecosystems, environmentalists are often openly hostile to efforts to treat individual animals as having an inherent value as sentient beings. They regularly, for example, advocate killing off members of non-native species in the name of "restoring the ecosystem." Edward Abbey and Dave Foreman—two icons of radical American environmentalism—were meat eaters and hunters.

For a brief period in its history, however—from its founding in 1972 until the expulsion of Paul Watson from its board of directors in 1977—the quintessential environmental organization, Greenpeace, did take an interest in animals that seemed to go beyond concerns about populations to embrace compassion for the suffering that humans inflict on wildlife. But with Watson gone, Greenpeace quickly reverted to traditional environmental thinking.

In its earliest incarnation, Greenpeace was an uneasy alliance of Canadian environmentalists and expatriate American anti-war activists—this was the Vietnam era—located in Vancouver. They got together in 1969 to protest a series of American underground nuclear tests on Amchitka Island in the Aleutian chain that extends south from Alaska. Afraid that the blasts would literally destroy the island, and that its breakup might trigger a tidal wave that would inundate the West Coast, the activists called themselves the Don't Make a Wave Committee.

When a test was announced for September 1971, the Committee met and decided to sail a boat to Amchitka to "confront the bomb." As the meeting was breaking up, one of the Americans said good-night—as the Americans, most of whom were Quakers, often did—by making the two-fingered V sign and saying, "Peace." To which one of the Canadians replied, "Make it a green peace."[1] The term resonated with everyone in the room, although for different reasons. The Americans saw it as a symbol of unity between the peace activists and the environmentalists. The Canadians saw it as a statement that we must make peace with the earth. In any event, they decided to call their protest vessel *Greenpeace I*.[2]

By 1972, there was serious dissension in the ranks. The underlying cause seems to have been friction between the peace activists and the environmentalists, whose priorities were often out of sync with one another. The immediate cause of the breakup of Don't Make a Wave was Irving Stowe, the chairman, an American peace activist who followed the Quaker practice of reaching all decisions by consensus. Perhaps he hoped that this could hold the group together, but in fact, it led to seemingly endless rounds of lengthy meetings that went nowhere. Impatient members—primarily the Canadians, who were in the majority—voted Stowe out, re-formed the group with a more focused environmental agenda, and renamed it the Greenpeace Foundation. One of the founding directors was Paul Watson, a Canadian who had been active with Don't Make a Wave.

Watson convinced his fellow directors of the newly minted Greenpeace Foundation that defending the environment also meant defending the animals who lived in it. And in 1975, he prodded Greenpeace into doing something that no group had ever done. They outfitted a ship, which they christened *Greenpeace V*, to confront Soviet whalers that—along with fleets from Japan and Iceland—were rapidly hunting the world's largest living beings into extinction. With Canadian environmentalist John Cormack as captain, and Watson—an experienced merchant mariner—as first officer, *Greenpeace V* sailed on June 18, 1975 to conduct the world's first hunt sabotage on the high seas. On June 27, they sighted the Soviet factory ship *Dalniy Vostok* accompanied by several killer ships.[3] Watson and several other crewmembers steered small inflatable zodiacs between the whalers and their prey, making it impossible for the Russians to launch harpoons without risking the lives of the Greenpeace activists. But the Russians fired their harpoons anyway, and the world's first effort at hunt sabotage on the high seas failed.[4]

Blood on the Ice

Every winter, harp seals gather in great herds on the ice floes of the Gulf of St. Lawrence, just off the Magdalen Islands, to give birth. The babies are born on the ice—all within a few days of each other—with a soft, downy coat that is not water-repellent or buoyant, leaving them unable to swim. Yellowish at birth, after two days this baby fur turns a beautiful, pure white. When the newborn seals are about eighteen days old, they begin to molt their white fur and fill in behind it with the adults' silvery gray coat bearing the dark harp-shaped pattern on the back that gives harp seals their name. The molting is complete by the time the young seals are twenty-five days old, at which point they leave the ice and join the herd in the water.

Every February or March, the baby "whitecoat seals" are slaughtered for their fur. The sealers—usually working from fishing vessels—go onto the ice floes where the babies are nursing. Strong, lithe, and agile in the water, seals are all but helpless on ice, and the babies are completely helpless. They cannot defend themselves, and they cannot flee.

To avoid damaging the pelts, the sealers cave in the babies' skulls with clubs called hakapiks that carry a large metal spike near one end similar to the blade of a pick. Then they skin the corpses. According to too many reports to discount, in the mad rush to get as many pelts as possible as quickly as possible, it is not uncommon for baby seals to be skinned alive.

The campaign against the seal hunt began in 1964 when a camera crew from Artek Films in Montreal, who were in the vicinity to shoot footage for a television series on sport hunting and fishing, stumbled onto the commercial seal hunt by accident. Angered by what they saw, the crew filmed the hunt and circulated the film in Montreal, where a reporter named Peter Lust saw it and wrote a story about the hunt. Lust's article was picked up by wire services and newspapers around the world, creating a firestorm of international protest.

Brian Davies, president of the New Brunswick SPCA—New Brunswick faces the Gulf of St. Lawrence—went out the following year to see for himself. Having confirmed what he saw on Artek's film, Davies launched his own campaign against the hunt, and testified before a committee of Parliament, where he had to listen to the Minister of Fisheries tell the House of Commons that the Artek footage was fraudulent.

Frustrated at Ottawa's refusal to protect the seals, Davies founded the International Fund for Animal Welfare, a group that still campaigns for the protection of wildlife. Animal protection groups around the world, led by The Fund for Animals and Friends of Animals,[5] picked up the campaign, and devoted considerable money and effort to keeping the cruelty before the eyes of the public. Cleveland Amory and his counterpart at FoA, Alice Herrington, went out on the ice themselves so they could testify to the slaughter from personal knowledge. For the next two decades, the Fund for Animals and Friends of Animals remained in the forefront of groups pressing the campaign to save the baby seals.

Having failed to make a dent in commercial whaling and unable to persuade Greenpeace to take more aggressive measures against it, Paul Watson turned his attention to the baby seal hunt. He proposed that Greenpeace activists go onto the ice floes and spraypaint the whitecoat seals with harmless red dye—not all over, just enough to make the pelts worthless on the fur market. Begun in 1976, the dyeing expeditions have become an annual ritual, with multiple groups participating and the international press drawn by the possibility of violence and the presence of media celebrities like former Beatle Sir Paul McCartney, American movie and TV star Martin Sheen, and

French film star Brigitte Bardot (most of the sealers speak French as their first language, and look to France, rather than England, as their cultural home).[6]

All too frequently, the violence became real, as in 1977 when Watson was nearly murdered by sealers when he became entangled in a hoist chain hanging from the deck of a sealing ship and the crew dunked him several times in the icy water before hauling him aboard. On another occasion, a decade later, the activists were held all night in a bar and terrorized by drunken sealers. Two were dragged out onto the parking lot and spraypainted while representatives of the Canadian government, incognito, stood by and did nothing. In the morning, Watson and the activists were arrested for causing a disturbance and held for five days until Cleveland Amory and Marian Probst in New York could arrange their bail and a charter flight off the island. In 1996, a mob of angry sealers broke into Watson's hotel room in the Magdalen Islands and nearly killed him, Martin Sheen, and several crewmembers before Canadian authorities extricated them.[7]

In 1977, several Greenpeace directors demanded that Watson resign from the board and publicly apologize for "assault and destruction of property." (He had wrested a hakapik from a sealer who was about to kill a baby seal and thrown the weapon into the water.) Watson refused to apologize for saving a life and refused to step down. When his fellow directors voted to expel him from the board, Watson resigned from Greenpeace.[8] From that point on, the world's largest and best-known environmental organization has shown little interest in animals except as species and components of ecosystems.

The Sea Shepherd
Watson's plan was to form his own organization that would pursue the more aggressive tactics that Greenpeace had disavowed. And so, he went to Cleveland Amory with a proposal for buying a ship that he and a group of likeminded spraypainters could sail into the Gulf of

St. Lawrence during the seal hunt and use at other times to confront whalers. The Fund for Animals put up the purchase price, the Royal Society for the Prevention of Cruelty to Animals provided a smaller grant for operating expenses, and Watson's new group, Earthforce, soon to be renamed the Sea Shepherd Conservation Society, was born.[9]

Watson's first ship, *Sea Shepherd*, had a short but dramatic life. In March 1979, Watson—with Cleveland Amory on board—sailed to the Magdalen Islands for another confrontation with sealers. Then in late spring, *Sea Shepherd* sailed into the Atlantic in search of pirate whaling ships—ships that were killing whales in violation of international treaties regulating whaling—and one especially notorious ship in particular, *Sierra*, which Watson found operating in the Atlantic just off the coast of Portugal. When he told his crew that he planned to ram *Sierra*, all but two, Peter Woof and Jerry Doran, resigned. Watson put them ashore at Leixoes, the port for the city of Porto (also known as Oporto), and on July 16, 1979, chased down *Sierra* about a quarter-mile offshore and rammed it twice, leaving a large gash in the hull. *Sierra* returned to Leixoes, and *Sea Shepherd* was intercepted by a Portuguese destroyer.

Watson and his two crew members were not arrested, but their ship was confiscated and was about to be turned over to the whaling company that owned *Sierra* as compensation for damages when Watson and several associates slipped on board on the night of New Year's Eve, 1979 and scuttled it in the Leixoes harbor.

In the early morning hours of February 5, 1980, while *Sierra* sat in the Lisbon harbor with no one aboard, an explosion tore a hole in the hull below the waterline. Within minutes, *Sierra* capsized and sank, its murderous career over. No one has ever been publicly identified as being responsible, although a woman telephoned the Associated Press office in Lisbon a few hours after the sinking and said the bombing was dedicated to *Sea Shepherd* and was done to assure that *Sierra* would kill no more whales. At the time, Paul Watson was five thousand miles away in Quebec, preparing to go to trial the next day on charges relating to the seal hunt.[10]

A second exploit that brought Sea Shepherd to international attention occurred in the early morning hours of November 9, 1986. Two Sea Shepherd activists, Rodney Coronado, an American, and David Howitt, a Briton, slipped onto two Icelandic whaling ships berthed in Reykjavik harbor when no one was on board and scuttled them. They left Iceland undetected and were never charged.[11]

Since then, Paul Watson and the Sea Shepherd Conservation Society have continued to campaign for the protection of marine mammals, especially whales and seals, and to harass whalers and sealers. There have been several more rammings of pirate whalers, but no one, human or otherwise, has ever been killed or injured in a Sea Shepherd operation.

Retreating Toward the Brink

In 1982, the International Whaling Commission (IWC), established by international treaty in 1946 to protect whale populations, enacted a moratorium on commercial whaling to go into effect four years later. Japan, however, has continued to hunt whales, justifying it under a loophole in the moratorium that allows the killing of whales for purposes of scientific research. The intent was to allow research that would be of help in restoring whale populations, but Japan uses the research exception as a pretext to kill whales for their meat, which is a top delicacy in Japanese restaurants.

Norway resumed commercial whaling in 1993. Iceland, which had been surreptitiously engaging in whaling on a reduced scale, left the IWC in 1992. Ten years later, it rejoined, although it continued whaling using the same research exception that Japan employed. In October 2006, Iceland resumed full-scale commercial whaling. These three, Japan, Iceland, and Norway—the only nations engaging in large-scale commercial whaling—kill approximately fifteen hundred whales every year.[12]

In recent years, Japan has been encouraging small, impoverished countries in the eastern Caribbean and Africa to hunt whales and dolphins for their meat, arguing that they can turn these sea mammals into a cheap source of food that will enable the islands to reduce their dependency on expensive beef and pork imported from the developed world. The Japanese have been backing up their arguments with foreign aid and technical assistance directed to the fishing industries of these countries, which have shown their gratitude by joining the IWC and voting with Japan to end the moratorium on commercial whaling.[13]

Japan also throws into the mix an appeal to racial and colonial sensitivities. During the 2006 IWC meeting in St. Kitts, a Japanese whaling advocate told the BBC, "Environmentalists have a biased view of whales and dolphins, and I think there is an element of ethnic discrimination against us."[14]

This argument—self-serving and cynical though it may be— strikes a responsive chord in people who have suffered oppression and racial discrimination at the hands of the United States and the countries of Western Europe, which are the same countries leading the campaign to protect the whales. At the 2006 IWC meeting, Horace Waters, a member of the Eastern Caribbean Cetacean Commission, an inter-governmental body that promotes whaling and dolphin hunting, claimed that the moratorium on whaling is a form of economic colonialism:

> We have islands that may want to start whaling again. It's expensive to import food from the developed world, and we believe there's a deliberate attempt to keep us away from our resources so we continue to develop those countries' economies by importing from them.[15]

This is nonsense, of course, but the wounds and resentments that give rise to it are real and will have to be dealt with if whales and dolphins are to be protected. Humans misuse other humans, and in the backlash animals pay the price. Since it was European and American colonialism that planted the seeds for the attitude toward whaling that now prevails in much of the Third World, it seems clear that the developed countries have an obligation to the whales and dolphins to provide economic incentives to poor, maritime countries not to hunt cetaceans.

The handwriting is already on the wall. Although it will take a three-quarters majority to overturn the moratorium, Japan is making slow but steady progress. At the 2006 meeting of the IWC, held on St. Kitts from June 16 to 20, St. Kitts and Nevis introduced a resolution declaring that the moratorium "is no longer necessary." The so-called "St. Kitts Declaration" passed by one vote, 33 to 32, the first time since 1986 that a majority of IWC members has voted against the moratorium.[16]

As for the seal slaughter, in 1983 the European Parliament banned the sale of seal pelts in the European Union, leading Canada to end the commercial hunt the following year, although small local hunts, primarily by indigenous peoples, were allowed. In 1995, Ottawa, looking for ways to revive the economically depressed coastal provinces, reopened the commercial seal hunt and announced that the Canadian government would aggressively explore ways to open new markets for seal products. The following year, Paul Watson was joined on the Magdalen Islands by movie and television star Martin Sheen and the two were nearly murdered in the incident I described above, generating an international outcry against the hunt. The seal hunt continues unabated, however. In 2006, 330,000 baby harp seals were slaughtered in the commercial hunt, exceeding the quota of 325,000.[17]

In 2005, a large international coalition of animal protection groups, led by the Humane Society of the United States, the Animal Protection Institute, the Animal Alliance of Canada, the World Society for the Protection of Animals, Sea Shepherd, and others called for an international boycott of Canadian seafood to last until the Canadian government ends the seal hunt. While in theory the campaign is problematic, in that it implies that killing fish is acceptable so long as seals are protected, in practice, anything that protects seals by giving fish even a partial, temporary respite benefits both seals and fish. In 2006, the boycott is continuing and additional groups continue to sign on. And on September 6, 2006, 368 members of the

European Parliament issued a statement condemning the Canadian seal hunt and demanding that the European Union again ban the sale of seal products within the EU.[18]

The Band of Mercy

As a Hunt Saboteur in England in the early 1970s, Ronnie Lee grew frustrated with the lack of progress being made against animal abuse and decided to ratchet the campaign up a notch by destroying property used in the murder of animals. The idea was to take the weapons out of the hands of the killers by disabling them—whether the weapon was a gun, an automobile used in a hunt, or a building housing a vivisection lab. Obviously, the destroyed property could be replaced, but the hope was that the financial loss would make the animal abuse less attractive.

In 1972, Lee and a friend, Clifford Goodman, struck out on their own by forming a clandestine group they called the Band of Mercy. The name came from a children's auxiliary to the RSPCA in the Victorian era, some of whose young members are reputed to have exceeded their charter by disabling the firearms of hunters.[19] (These acts of juvenile sabotage are not reliably attested and are probably legend.)

The Band of Mercy, which never boasted more than a half-dozen members, began by slashing tires, pouring sugar into gas tanks, and otherwise taking vehicles used in hunts out of commission, which could be viewed as a natural progression from Hunt Saboteur actions. But the following year, they upped the ante and created a new category of direct action: the large-scale destruction of property by fire.

In 1973, a German company, Hoechst Pharmaceuticals, began construction on a vivisection laboratory near Milton Keynes, a "new town" created in the 1960s to be a science and technology center strategically located between Oxford and Cambridge. Reasoning that if vivisection laboratories were subject to being burned to the ground, the cost of insurance might become prohibitive, two Band of Mercy activists (presumably Lee and Goodman) set the partially completed building ablaze on November 10, causing extensive damage. Two nights later, they came back and finished the job.[20] So far as is known, this was the first instance of arson, or any form of major property destruction, in defense of animals. Despite the setback, Hoechst rebuilt, and their Milton Keynes Pharmaceutical Research Centre (now operated by a multinational conglomerate, Intervet International) is still in operation.

In June 1974, the Band of Mercy struck in a different direction by setting fire to two privately-owned boats used for killing seals along the coast of Wales. The annual Welsh seal killing spree—called a "cull" in the euphemism of the British government—was licensed by the Home Office (functioning here as a rough counterpart to the U.S. Department of the Interior) and conducted by a private company paid by the fishing industry, which regarded seals as competition for depleted stocks of fish. In the wake of the arson, the seal kill was canceled, the company went out of business, and the cull was never resumed.[21]

Violence always has unintended consequences. The Hoechst Pharmaceuticals and seal boat actions opened a raw wound in the animal rights movement that remains to this day, unhealed and apparently unhealable, in the form of hostility between those who believe that the destruction of property by arson and bombing is a legitimate tactic in the campaign to defend animals and those who believe it is not. A member of the Hunt Saboteurs, not wanting the group associated in the public mind with arson, announced the rift by offering a reward of 250 pounds sterling (about four hundred dollars at 1974 exchange rates) for information that would help the police identify the persons responsible.[22]

Through the summer of 1974, the Band of Mercy carried out a series of raids against companies that supplied animals to vivisectors, in the course of one of which they liberated six guinea pigs from a farm in Wiltshire in south England near Salisbury, making this the first known liberation of imprisoned animals in the modern history of animal rights. In August, Lee and Goodman struck the Oxford Laboratory Animals Colony in Bicester, near Oxford. Two nights later they went back, just as they had at Hoechst Pharmaceuticals—only this time, the police were waiting for them. They were arrested and sentenced to serve three years in prison. When they were released on parole after a year, Goodman left the movement—amid rumors that he had turned police informer—and Lee re-formed the Band of Mercy as the Animal Liberation Front.[23]

The Animal Liberation Front

Kim Stallwood points out that with their trademark balaclavas (ski masks, to those of us who speak only American) and their daring raids to rescue doomed animals, the ALF (usually pronounced A-L-F rather than alf) in their early years were glamorized by the media and viewed as modern-day Robin Hoods by the public.[24] As an early supporter of Ronnie Lee—although he never took part in ALF actions—Stallwood was in a unique position to observe the career of the ALF during its English honeymoon, as well as its fall from grace.

Kim Stallwood was converted to animal rights by an experience much like Alex Pacheco's. In 1973, during summer break before his final year of college, Stallwood worked on the floor of a chicken processing plant, where he was disgusted by the things he had to do. By the end of the year, he was a vegetarian. In 1976, Stallwood became a vegan and went to work for Compassion in World Farming (CIWF), a farmed-animal welfare organization founded in 1967 by English dairy farmers Peter and Anna Roberts to combat factory farming.[25]

Two years later, Stallwood left CIWF to join Frances Power Cobbe's British Union for the Abolition of Vivisection. In the 70-odd years since Cobbe's death, BUAV had become timid, hidebound, and ineffective, but it had a democratic constitution that allowed the membership to elect the board of directors. Determined to energize the old organization and bring it up to date, Stallwood and a group of likeminded activists worked to bring in younger, more progressive members, who in turn elected more dynamic, forward-looking directors. Driven by their energy, BUAV once again became a force against vivisection.[26]

One of the things that Stallwood and his allies did, beginning in 1981, was allow the ALF Press Office—the above-ground wing of the

ALF—to use BUAV office space and equipment free of charge. But as time went on, the ALF became more and more committed to violence, and Ronnie Lee began talking about the acceptability of violence against humans.

When Stallwood and other BUAV leaders resisted this movement toward violence, the ALF responded by encouraging its supporters to join BUAV so that they could take over the organization by voting ALF sympathizers onto the board. Stallwood recognized this tactic immediately because he had used it himself—successfully—in the late seventies. The breaking point came in October 1984, when Lee argued in the ALF newsletter that ALF policies should not "preclude the use of violence against animal abusers."[27] BUAV promptly expelled the ALF from their office space, the takeover attempt fizzled, and the ALF lost interest in BUAV.[28]

As time went on and ALF actions focused more on property destruction and less on liberating animals, the British media and public became increasingly disenchanted, and the ALF, dominated now by political radicals who opposed all forms of working within the system, grew more isolated from the mainstream animal rights movement, which had settled down to work on putting Lord Houghton's advice into practice by prodding the Labour party to make animal protection a high priority in their program.

At about the same time, under pressure from law enforcement, the ALF ceased entirely to be a coherent, structured organization with a leadership and a chain of command—a process of dissolution that had actually begun in the late 1970s. By the mid-'80s, the Animal Liberation Front had devolved into a name and a strategy. The strategy was to liberate animals, to inflict economic damage on animal abusers by destroying the property they used in the abuse, and in the process to take "all reasonable precautions" to avoid harm to living beings, human and nonhuman. (The ALF never took up Ronnie Lee's call for deliberate violence against humans.) Anyone who implemented the strategy could use the name; and independent cells, none of which was aware of the existence or the membership of the others, sprang up around Britain and the United

States. The only unifying points were the ALF Press Offices—one in the U.K., one in the U.S.—to which ALF cells could send press releases and videotapes of raids.

The ALF in America

There is some disagreement as to when the first ALF action in the U.S. took place, not least because the North American ALF never had any kind of centralized leadership or coherent organizational structure. From the beginning, it was made up of scattered independent cells that brought themselves into existence to undertake a specific action, and often dissolved when the action was completed, only to re-form for the next action. Initially, there wasn't even an ALF Press Office in North America, and for several years People for the Ethical Treatment of Animals played that role. An ALF cell would send a press statement describing an action—often accompanied by videotape—to PETA, which would distribute it to the media.

The first illegal direct action on behalf of animals in the United States took place in Hawaii. On May 29, 1977, two caretakers on the night shift at the University of Hawaii's Kewalo Basin Marine Mammal Laboratory, Ken LaVasseur and Steve Sipman, released two captive bottlenose dolphins named Puka and Kea into the open ocean. Calling the police after the rescue was complete, they told them the liberation had been the work of the "Undersea Railroad," a reference to the Underground Railroad that had guided slaves to freedom before the Civil War. Quickly arrested and indicted for grand theft, LaVasseur and Sipman admitted the action, but argued that it was justified because the dolphins were "slaves" who were "undergoing remorseless experiments." They were convicted of a class C felony and sentenced to community service.[29]

On March 14, 1979, four activists dressed as lab technicians—three women and a man—walked into the New York University Medical Center laboratories empty-handed and walked out with a dog, two cats, and two guinea pigs.[30] The North American ALF Press Office claims this as the first ALF action in the United States, but it is not clear whether the activists thought of themselves at the time as ALF.[31]

On December 9, 1980, unknown activists in Venice, Florida, the winter home of Ringling Brothers Barnum and Bailey Circus, spray-painted animal rights slogans on trailers belonging to the circus, the first known instance of property damage on behalf of animals in the United States.[32]

According to Ingrid Newkirk, the first ALF action in the United States was the liberation of thirty-four cats from a vivisection laboratory at the Howard University Medical School in Washington, D.C., at three o'clock in the morning on Christmas Day, 1982. The cats' back legs had been deliberately paralyzed by surgery on their spinal cords, and one died of his surgically-induced injuries before he could be spirited out of the building. The rescuers took him anyway and gave him a respectful burial.[33]

Newkirk's version of the creation of the American ALF—as told in her book *Free the Animals!*—has the first cell organized in 1982 in the Washington, D.C. area by a former police officer (whom she calls "Valerie") who resigned from the Montgomery County, Maryland police department after taking part in the Silver Spring monkeys raid. It was "Valerie" who organized the cell and led the raid on Howard University. Much of the story that Newkirk tells is undoubtedly accurate, but she goes to great lengths to disguise the identities of the ALF activists she writes about—for obvious reasons—and it is often impossible to separate fact from fiction. I would be astounded, for example, to learn that "Valerie" really was a Montgomery County police officer who had participated in the raid on IBR. That information would make her too easy to identify.

However that may be, in the 1980s ALF cells sprang up around the country, and rescues and arsons multiplied through the '80s and '90s. One of the most dramatic occurred on December 9, 1984, when ALF activists broke into the City of Hope National Medical Research Center, a well-known children's cancer facility near Los Angeles, and liberated one hundred and fifteen animals—including thirteen cats and twenty-one dogs—who were being housed in truly disgusting conditions, many severely injured, and without food, water, or medical treatment. The rescuers made videotape of conditions in the laboratory, which led to City of Hope being fined $11,000 by the U.S. Department of Agriculture, and required to build a new facility at a cost of $380,000 and hire a veterinarian.[34]

On April 21, 1985, in what may be the largest laboratory liberation ever effected, ALF activists rescued more than a thousand animals, most of whom were mice, during a break-in at the University of California at Riverside. The rescuers also destroyed equipment and files used in vivisection and spraypainted slogans on the walls. One of the rescued animals was Britches, an infant stump-tailed macaque who had been separated from his mother in the finest tradition of Harry Harlow and whose eyelids had been sewn shut with clumsy stitches of thick, rough thread. Like their colleagues at the University of Pennsylvania, the UC Riverside researchers had videotaped themselves violating the most basic standards of animal care, and the ALF rescuers took the videotape and sent it to PETA. Once again PETA made a video, called *Britches*, and they distributed far and wide a heart-rending still picture of the delicate little monkey with the brutal stitches through his eyelids.[35]

As raids grew more common, the vivisection industry began to treat them seriously and tightened their security until—by the early '90s—laboratories were all but impossible to penetrate. And so, the ALF turned to a softer target—fur farms, which are typically in isolated rural areas and have little or no security. Fur farms had the added advantage that minks and foxes could be released directly into the wild—there was no need to find homes for them—and contrary to the claims of the fur industry, captive-reared fur bearers are still wild animals, capable of fending for themselves. Also, because they are territorial, they quickly fan out and do not establish a population density that upsets the ecological balance.

Around the same time, the North American Animal Liberation Front realized that public sympathy was not translating into meaningful relief for the tortured animals, and so they began turning to more direct means to save them: burning buildings and destroying equipment. These two trends—toward fur farms and property destruction—reached their peak in the ALF's Operation Bite Back, a series of fifty raids on mink and fox farms and other fur industry facilities in the Northwest and upper Midwest during the 1990s, a number of which involved burning the facilities to the ground after the inmates had been set free.

Former Sea Shepherd activist Rod Coronado—who was widely believed, but never proven, to have been the prime instigator of Operation Bite Back—has said that twelve suppliers of pelts to the fur industry went out of business as a result of these raids.[36] Even so, the fur industry as a whole was not affected, and throughout this period fur sales actually increased. Liberation raids are of inestimable benefit to the sentient beings who are liberated, and they are justified on that basis alone. But as a tactic to reform an industry, be it fashion or medical science, neither liberation nor arson (which in my view cannot be justified) appears to have a positive impact.

In 1994, Rod Coronado was indicted for an Operation Bite Back action, the 1992 burning of a laboratory building at the University of Michigan that was doing research for the fur industry. After two years as a fugitive, Coronado, who is a Native American, was arrested living under an alias on a Yaqui Indian reservation in Arizona. On July 3, 1995, he pleaded guilty and was sentenced to fifty-seven months in a federal prison to be followed by three years of probation. He was released after serving forty-four months.

On March 24, 2004, Coronado was arrested again, this time on a felony charge of "impeding or endangering a federal officer." In the company of an *Esquire* magazine writer, Coronado was allegedly attempting to thwart a planned slaughter of "nuisance" cougars in Sabino Canyon in the Coronado National Forest near Tucson by spreading false scents and removing traps and electronic sensors. The federal authorities confiscated the journalist's notes and used them to make their case against Coronado, who was convicted on December 13, 2005, and sentenced on August 10, 2006 to eight months in prison and three years of supervised probation.[37]

Earlier in 2006, Coronado had been arrested yet again by the FBI, this time in connection with a speech he gave at a conference in San Diego when he responded to a question from the audience by describing how he had made the incendiary device that he had used to burn the University of Michigan laboratory. A press release issued by the Department of Justice described the government's theory of Coronado's crime:

> ... on August 1, 2003, at a public gathering in the Hillcrest neighborhood of San Diego, Coronado taught and demonstrated the making and use of a destructive device, with the intent that the device be used to commit arson. Hours earlier, a fire had destroyed a large apartment complex under construction in the University Towne Center area of San Diego.
>
> ... Daniel R. Dzwilewski, Special Agent in Charge, San Diego Division of the Federal Bureau of Investigation, commented, "America will not tolerate terrorists. Whether you were born here or abroad, we will not stand back and allow you to terrorize our communities under the guise of free speech."[38]

The FBI have said that they do not suspect Coronado of actual involvement in the fire, but they have not explained how Coronado's demonstration could have influenced an arson that had occurred on the previous day. Apparently simply talking about fire-starting techniques to animal rights activists in the wake of the University Towne Center arson was sufficient to merit prosecution.

The public does not like bombings or arson. They consider them—correctly, in my opinion—reckless, dangerous, and all too likely to get out of control with deadly unforeseen consequences. Thus, as news reports of arson began to overshadow news reports of rescues, the ALF quickly lost public sympathy in America—just as it had in Britain—dragging the rest of the animal rights movement along with it. As had been the case at Hegins, the specter of violence among humans turned the spotlight of public attention away from the suffering of the animals and shone it on the actions of activists. This made the animal rights movement the issue and made it easy for the exploitation industries to label not just the ALF, but the entire animal rights movement "terrorists," a label that to an unfortunate degree has stuck in the public mind.

The most important and lasting accomplishment of the ALF's arson campaign has been to convince the public that torturers and murderers are victims and animal rights advocates are criminals and terrorists. And as long as the arson continues, it can only get worse. Sooner or later, a firefighter will be killed combating an ALF blaze, and when that happens, the public demonization of the animal rights movement will be complete.

SHAC

In November 1999, a group of young activists in the U.K. concluded that the traditional tactics of the ALF—liberation and property destruction—were simply not working. And so they decided to shift the focus of their actions away from property used in vivisection and onto people employed by vivisectors. Their idea was simple, they would harass and intimidate the stockholders and employees of a vivisection company—and the stockholders and employees of companies that did business with it—until the vivisector closed up shop and went out of business. Their target was a British based firm called Huntingdon Life Sciences, and so they named their group Stop Huntingdon Animal Cruelty, SHAC (pronounced shack) for short.

Founded in the U.K. in 1952, Huntingdon Life Sciences describes itself as a "Contract Research Organization," an innocuous term for a business with some very nasty aspects. HLS does *in vitro*, animal, and clinical testing for the makers of foodstuffs, cosmetics, household products, agricultural products, and pharmaceuticals. The client defines the requirement—most often it is product safety testing— and HLS designs and performs the experiments, providing the laboratories, the research staff, and most importantly, the test subjects, both human volunteers and animal slaves. The company's website gives the impression that their primary business is clinical testing, and vivisection a mere sideline. But this is misleading. HLS is one of the world's largest vivisectors, a multi-national killer operating in the U.K., the U.S., and Japan.

The distinction between SHAC and the ALF is not always clear, and some observers believe that SHAC is not so much an organization as a campaign run by the ALF, while others see SHAC as simply an above-ground component of the ALF. Kevin Jonas,[39] former spokesperson for the ALF in America and a "campaign coordinator" for SHAC in the U.S., points out that since the creation of SHAC in 1999, "nearly 80 percent of the ALF attacks that have taken place in the US and the UK have been aimed at closing down HLS."[40] At the very least, there appears to be close coordination and an overlap in membership between the two groups.

However that may be, SHAC immediately set about making life as miserable as possible for everyone who worked for HLS or for companies that did business with it, especially its accounting and brokerage firms. They started with loud, raucous demonstrations at the main gate of the company's headquarters in Huntingdon. Employees leaving the facility were followed home, and demonstrations were set up in front of their houses, signs were posted around the neighborhood informing the neighbors that they worked for a company that killed animals, bricks were hurled through windows, some employees' cars were set on fire, ear-piercing aerosol sirens, like those used for protection against rape, were set to stay on at full volume until their charge was exhausted and thrown onto the roofs of employees' homes in the middle of the night, and employees received phone calls at home at all hours of the day and night threatening them, their spouses, and children.[41] Names, addresses, and telephone numbers of company employees were posted on SHAC's website, which the subjects regarded as a public invitation for harassment and violence. In 2001, Brian Cass, managing director of HLS, sustained serious head injuries when he was waylaid by three men wearing ski masks, beaten with ax handles, and sprayed with CS gas, a form of tear gas used in riot control.[42]

In 2000, SHAC obtained a list of HLS shareholders which included anonymous corporate and institutional investors called "nominees," which they also published on their website, subjecting the officials and stockholders of these organizations to the same treatment as HLS employees. This initiated a huge sell-off of HLS stock, which in a matter of months dropped in value to just pennies a share, threatening the company with bankruptcy. Harassment of brokerage firms representing HLS in England and the U.S. led to the company being dropped by its stockbrokers, and that combined with the loss of value of its stock led the New York Stock Exchange to delist it on December 27, 2000, and the London Stock Exchange to remove it from the main trading floor on March 29, 2001. Hoping to insulate its stockholders from SHAC, the company incorporated in the United States, where laws regarding the disclosure of investors' names are stricter than in the U.K.

SHAC USA

SHAC appeared in the U.S. sometime in 2000 or 2001 and began applying the same tactics against HLS's New Jersey facility and companies that did business with it as had been used in England. The client company that came in for the most attention was Chiron, a biotech firm based in Emeryville, California. After nearly two years of harassment aimed at employees and their families, on August 28, 2003, two pipe bombs exploded at Chiron—there were no injuries— and an anonymous claim of responsibility posted on the SHAC website, although SHAC denied any involvement in the bombing, included this threat:

> This is the endgame for the animal killers and if you choose to stand with them you will be dealt with accordingly. There will be no quarter given, no half measures taken. You might be able to protect your buildings, but can you protect the homes of every employee?[43]

Less than a week after the Chiron bombings, on September 3,

2003, a homemade bomb with the explosive packed in nails—do-it-yourself shrapnel, probably intended as a demonstration of what the bombers were capable of—detonated at the Bay Area headquarters of another HLS client, the Shaklee Corporation. Again, no one was injured, apparently by design. Responsibility for this attack was claimed by "The Revolutionary Cells of the Animal Liberation Brigade," a group no one had ever heard of and that has not been heard from since. Presumably, the Revolutionary Cells were nothing more than a name on a press release, and the work was done by people with either no organizational affiliation or an affiliation they wished to hide. The Shaklee statement contained a threat that was even more menacing than the Chiron statement.

> All customers and their families are considered legitimate targets.... You never know when your house, your car even, might go boom.... Or maybe it will be a shot in the dark.... No more will all the killing be done by the oppressors, now the oppressed will strike back.[44]

On October 5, 2003, a federal arrest warrant was issued for Daniel Andreas San Diego—whom the FBI described as an animal activist with ties to SHAC—in connection with the Chiron and Shaklee bombings, and subsequently offered a $250,000 reward for information leading directly to his arrest. The FBI has hinted that they believe other persons, including Kevin Jonas, were involved in the Chiron and Shaklee bombings, but Jonas has denied any involvement and has also denied that San Diego was affiliated with SHAC. As I write this in the fall of 2006, San Diego is still at large, and no charges have been filed against anyone else.

On May 26, 2004, seven SHAC activists, including spokespersons Josh Harper and Kevin Jonas, were arrested under an indictment issued by a federal grand jury in New Jersey, on a variety of charges stemming from the harassment and intimidation campaign.[45] The principal charges were filed under the Animal Enterprise Protection Act of 1992, which makes it a federal offense to physically disrupt or

274 THE LONGEST STRUGGLE

conspire to physically disrupt the functioning of any laboratory, farm, zoo, circus, or other business that exploits animals. Other charges included using the Internet to harass and intimidate.

Six of those charged were eventually brought to trial in New Jersey, and on March 3, 2006, they were convicted on all counts. In September, they were sentenced to prison terms ranging from one year to six years. And on October 3, 2006, one of the SHAC 7 (as they are still called), Andy Stepanian, began serving his three-year sentence, making him the first person to be imprisoned following conviction under the Animal Enterprise Protection Act.

As reprehensible as SHAC's tactics are, the trial and conviction of the SHAC activists is chilling for anyone concerned about freedom of speech. The government never alleged nor introduced evidence to show that the defendants had personally committed any of the acts of harassment and intimidation on which the charges were based. They were arrested, tried, and convicted solely on the basis of "speeches and Web postings from 2000 to 2004 that celebrated the violence and repeatedly used the word 'we' to claim credit for it."[46]

The Wedge

Every summer, FARM organizes a national animal rights conference—alternating between the Washington, D.C. area and Los Angeles—which features speakers from every faction of the movement and typically attracts over eight hundred attendees. For nearly a decade, since 1997, the FARM conference was *the* major annual event of the animal rights movement, and the only large forum at which rival factions came together and discussed their areas of agreement and difference, both publicly and privately.

In 2004, several mainstream animal protection groups, including HSUS and the Fund for Animals, withdrew their support from Animal Rights 2004, as the FARM conference was called that year, and instructed their employees not to participate on the grounds that the conference was providing a forum to advocates of violence. They seemed to be referring primarily to Kevin Jonas; Jerry Vlasak, a physician who is an outspoken supporter of the ALF; and Steven Best, a professor of philosophy at the University of Texas, El Paso, who has written and spoken in defense of the ALF and its tactics. All three had been frequent speakers at FARM's conferences.

The organizations that pulled out of Animal Rights 2004 have organized their own annual conference focused on providing training to grassroots activists in peaceful, legal tactics for advancing the animals' cause. This new conference, called "Taking Action for Animals," seems to have taken hold, and in 2006, it attracted over seven hundred participants, with Peter Singer as the keynote speaker.

Although there is certainly an element of principle involved in the decision of these groups to withdraw from the FARM conference, there may also be an element of concern for the future of the animal rights movement. The prosecution of the SHAC leaders and the imprisonment of Rod Coronado make clear several frightening realities: First, the federal government intends to pursue animal rights groups with the same fervor that it pursues Al-Qaeda. The pharmaceutical, agriculture, food service, and firearms industries have made it their goal to eradicate the animal rights movement, and the administration that their campaign contributions did so much to put in office is more than willing to lead the charge for them.

Second, actual involvement in acts of violence is no longer a prerequisite for prosecution and imprisonment. Speech that the government considers inflammatory is sufficient. And third, in the post 9/11 atmosphere, juries may be willing to convict people of "terrorism" on the basis of their beliefs or sympathies, without regard for whether they have actually committed a violent or intimidating act.

As America edges toward an era of neo-McCarthyism, with "terrorists" playing the role of "Communists," there is a campaign underway to label the entire animal rights movement "terrorists" in the same way that conservatives of an earlier generation were able to successfully slander democratic socialists and other progressives and thereby neutralize the American left. Kept in a state of fear, the public seems unwilling to take chances. With "terrorism" as with

"Communism," guilt by association is becoming an acceptable level of proof. Under these circumstances, withdrawing from the conference may have appeared to be the better part of valor to highly visible groups that depend on mainstream public support and want to live to fight another day. The ALF, SHAC, and their supporters—who have never been more than a tiny, if very noisy, minority of animal activists—are giving the animals' enemies a weapon with which to destroy the entire animal rights movement.

Already, a wedge has been driven into the movement. FARM's Alex Hershaft does not support violence and intimidation in any way, shape, or form, but he has devoted a large portion of his adult life to promoting unity within the animal protection movement, and he believes it is important to keep a dialogue open among animal advocates of all persuasions. But in today's superheated, panic-driven political atmosphere, that may no longer be possible. If it is not, something of inestimable value has been lost, and, as always, the biggest losers are the animals.

If the present climate of repression continues to worsen and the ALF and SHAC continue their mischief-making, any sort of effective animal advocacy may eventually become impossible. In 2002, just months after 9/11, the Winter Olympics in Salt Lake City, Utah featured a rodeo staged to "celebrate the heritage of the American West." In the weeks before the games, Steve Hindi—the martial arts prankster and videographer from Hegins—shadowed the Olympic torch procession in a video equipped truck (see Chapter 20) as it snaked across the country, showing undercover footage of rodeo cruelty to the crowds who lined the route. In Albuquerque, New Mexico, Hindi was stopped by police and detained in the truck for over an hour. He later learned that the FBI had told the Albuquerque police that they had received a bomb threat associated with the truck and believed that Hindi should be regarded as a possible terrorist. The FBI was never able to produce evidence of any such threat.[47] From his earliest days as an activist, Steve Hindi has spoken out loudly and consistently against violence in the movement for both philosophical and strategic reasons. As he summed up his position to me:

Everything we do is absolutely nonviolent. We take a very hard stand against any type of violence unless it is to save yourself if you're under attack. Everything we do is for the sake of saving lives, not endangering them.[48]

But that record did not stop him from being labeled a terrorist suspect.

In August 2005, Eddie Lama, who uses a van to show video footage of animal cruelty to pedestrians in New York City (see Chapter 20), told *Satya* magazine that:

Unfortunately, because of the atmosphere after 9/11, it [has become] almost impossible to show on the street without getting hassled and questioned—the van looks like a small nuclear device.[49]

If a van with TV screens on the sides looks like an atomic bomb to the people protecting New York, we are held more tightly in the grip of unreasoning fear than has generally been recognized. The charge of terrorism—given surface plausibility by the ALF and SHAC—has already begun to neutralize one of the most effective— and nonviolent—tools in the animal rights toolbox.

Apparently, Rod Coronado has also come to believe that violence is a dead end for the environmental and animal rights movements. On September 1, 2006, Coronado—serving his eight-month sentence in a privately owned and operated federal correctional center in Florence, Arizona—wrote a letter to his friends and supporters in which he said:

... [T]o preserve what I wanted to protect, I chose to engage sometimes in the destruction of property used to destroy life. I still see the rationale for what I've done, only no longer do I personally choose to represent the cause of peace and compassion in that way....

In my years past I have argued that economic sabotage was an appropriate tactic for our time.... [But] times have changed and it is now my belief that the movements to protect earth and animals have achieved enough with this strategy to now consider an approach that does not compromise objectives, but increases the likelihood of real social change....

What is won through violence must be protected with violence and I don't want to teach my children that. As long as governments and corporations sanction physical violence any who attempt to stop them with violence will be labeled terrorists.[50]

19

Things Fall Apart

P arallels are often drawn between animal slavery and African slavery before the Civil War. The comparison is apt, but usually not taken far enough. The two slaveries are alike not only in the treatment of the victims, but also in the extent to which they have permeated the institutions and customs of their societies. Slavery—animal or human—is so horrific a practice that it cannot survive unless the government, the press, the schools and universities, the entertainment media, the churches, families, and businesses all unite in its support. The primary business of any slaveholding culture is the preservation of slavery, because wherever slavery does not maintain a stranglehold on society, it dies.

In America before the Civil War, the laws of the federal government and the slave states enforced African slavery with an iron hand. In the South, dissent against slavery was punishable by prison or death; the press supported the "peculiar institution" and railed against abolitionists; public and private schools and universities taught the rightness of slavery, and churches taught that it was ordained by God. Slavery was so strongly etched into the society that it seemed self-evident to those within it that to question slavery was to question everything that was good, true, and holy. In this atmosphere, it took an invasion by an army from outside, followed by a brutal and bloody war, to end African slavery. It simply could not be ended by agitation or insurrection from within or through the political and judicial processes.

The optimism of the animal rights movement in the 1980s and at the March on Washington—our confidence that we could end animal exploitation within a generation—was based on our naïve failure to recognize this fundamental truth. Animal slavery has a grip on our society that is entirely like the stranglehold that African slavery had on the antebellum South, and it is proving far more difficult to dislodge than we had ever imagined.

Counterattack

When the animal rights movement began, there were no mechanisms in place specifically to defend animal slavery and slaughter, because it had never crossed anyone's mind that they could ever come under serious attack. The rightness of animal exploitation seemed so self-evident that for the first fifteen years of the animal rights movement, everyone assumed that animal activists could never be anything more than a few isolated loony tunes. Ignore them and they'll go away. And in that atmosphere of benign neglect, the movement prospered.

But as time went on, the animal rights movement began to appear, if not as a threat to the institutions of animal slavery and slaughter themselves, then at least a threat to the profits and peace of mind of the exploiters. Faced with this possibility, they fought back on three fronts. First, the vivisection industry hardened security at their facilities, making them all but impenetrable to would-be liberators, a tactic that—as we have seen—led the ALF to turn to arson and fur farms and SHAC to take up intimidation.

Second, the animal abuse industries began pressing at both the federal and state levels for harsh new laws and for the application of existing laws in ways that were never intended, all with a view to putting animal activists in prison for long periods of time. In 1984, all charges against Wayne Pacelle and his band of Yale hunt saboteurs were dismissed. In 1989, Heidi Prescott received a five-hundred-dollar fine for hunter harassment, and when she refused to pay it, she was sentenced to fifteen days in jail. In 2006, Rod Coronado is serving an eight-month prison sentence for a similar offense.

In 1992, Congress passed the Animal Enterprise Protection Act, which makes any "physical disruption" causing an economic loss of more than $10,000 to a business that uses animals a federal offense punishable by a year in prison. If anyone is injured as a result of the disruption, the prison time increases to ten years.[1] The act was amended in 2002, in the wake of 9/11, to identify animal activists who engage in property destruction as "terrorists," rather than vandals, thereby bringing animal activists within the ambit of the Patriot Act and other anti-terrorism laws.

In the fall of 2006, Congress enacted the Animal Enterprise Terrorism Act (AETA), which broadened the scope and stiffened the penalties of the earlier Animal Enterprise Protection Act. Among its most chilling provisions is a section that defines as "terrorists" persons who engage in Gandhi- and King-style civil disobedience against businesses that exploit animals, making them subject to federal prosecution and lengthy imprisonment. With broad bipartisan support, the AETA was passed by unrecorded voice votes in both Houses, indicating that there was no significant opposition. Only Congressman Dennis Kucinich (D-Ohio) spoke out against it. On November 27, 2006, President George W. Bush signed it into law.

The third prong of the animal abusers' counterattack against the animal rights movement was a well-funded and highly sophisticated public relations campaign. On the one hand, the abusers defended not their practices—they have been very careful to keep those well hidden—but the benefits of their products. Groups sprang up like Americans for Medical Progress, financed by the animal experimentation industry—primarily large universities that run vivisection labs funded by NIH—to convince the public that human health is dependent on animal research. Although it courts the public directly, AMP devotes most of its resources to keeping the media on their side, including conducting "background and context" briefings for reporters and sponsoring "media forums"—read, "junkets"—such as a recent cancer forum which had "a focus on the vital role laboratory animals played in the development of many successful therapies."[2]

Under pressure from animal rights campaigns, fur sales declined sharply during the 1980s and early '90s. Many of us were convinced—and not without reason—that the industry was on its last legs, and fur would be the first form of animal abuse ended by an animal rights campaign. Fur industry trade groups fought back, however, first by aggressively recruiting young fashion designers—offering them free trips to seminars in Scandinavia, sponsoring classes in the use of fur, and offering awards and prizes for the "creative and artistic" use of fur in fashion design. Then, they promoted fur in the soul and hip-hop communities until fur became a status symbol, not of wealth, but of hipness among young, trend-conscious consumers, male as well as female, white as well as black. "This isn't your mother's fur coat," became a mantra of the fur industry.

Finally, the industry put a new emphasis on fur trim, and the use of fur to decorate cloth and synthetic garments skyrocketed. Beginning in the mid '90s, fur sales began to recover, and they have been increasing ever since at a rate of about seven percent per year.[3] The superior resources of the fur industry, an excellent strategic plan, and an undisguised appeal to self-indulgence snatched victory from the hands of the animal rights movement. It is only within the past year or two—as a result of redoubled efforts by animal rights groups—that the campaign against fur has begun to gain traction and public notice again, although sales continue to rise.

* * *

The most dangerous and effective part of this counterattack has been a concerted campaign by the animal abuse industries to label animal activists as "domestic terrorists." Despite the best efforts of the ALF and SHAC to make their point for them, they were not making much headway until September 11, 2001. Since then, officials in all three branches of government, abetted by a pliable mainstream press and supported by private groups that monitor "terrorism," such as the Southern Poverty Law Center and the Anti-Defamation League, have been working overtime to convince the public that animal rights activists are terrorists and must be dealt with as such.

On May 18, 2004, John Lewis, a deputy assistant director of the FBI told the Senate Committee on Environment and Public Works:

> One of today's most serious domestic terrorism threats comes from special interest extremist movements such as the Animal Liberation Front (ALF), the Earth Liberation Front (ELF), and Stop Huntingdon Animal Cruelty (SHAC) campaign.[4]

Lewis went on to ask the Committee for new laws targeted specifically at animal and environmental terrorism "to give law enforcement more effective means to bring criminals to justice."

In its Fall 2002 newsletter, the Southern Poverty Law Center published a lengthy, inflammatory article suggesting that animal rights and environmental terrorism are significant and growing threats to the safety and economy of the country.[5] The Anti-Defamation League published a similar report in 2006.[6]

Just as all the institutions of Southern society closed ranks around African slavery, the institutions of American society are closing ranks around animal slavery now that they perceive it to be under attack, a circumstance that has profound strategic implications for the animal rights movement. Activist violence is no more able to weaken animal slavery than activist violence was able to weaken African slavery. The most important effects it is having are to alienate the public and provide an excuse for ever-more draconian measures that restrict the range of activities open to nonviolent activists and impinge on their ability to get their message across to the public. I can, for example, foresee a day in the not-too-distant future when activists who perform open rescues (see Chapter 20) or conduct undercover investigations in factory farms and vivisection labs will face long federal prison sentences as "terrorists."

Thunder without Rain

Even as the institutions of society began to rally to the defense of animal slavery and slaughter, the animal rights movement began show-

284 THE LONGEST STRUGGLE

ing cracks that threatened to split it apart. In addition to the fissure between those who promoted violence—at least against property—and those who condemned it, a second and equally divisive conflict arose in the mid-1990s centered on Gary Francione, the attorney who had negotiated on behalf of the Gennarelli monkeys. A law professor at Rutgers University, Francione pioneered the pursuit of legal rights for animals. In 1995, his groundbreaking book *Animals, Property, and the Law* advanced the proposition that the enslavement and slaughter of animals depend on their legal status as property. His proposed solution was a strategy for gaining animals legal status as persons, from which it would inevitably flow that they had certain rights which the courts would be bound to uphold—including life, the integrity of their bodies, and a reasonable opportunity to live according to their inner natures. After all, Francione reasoned, corporations had been legal persons since the 1890s, and ships are recognized as persons in maritime law, so how can anyone argue that legal personhood is limited to human beings?

In 1990, Francione and his wife Anna Charlton, also an attorney and law professor, had founded the Rutgers Animal Rights Law Clinic, which incorporated animal rights into the regular law school curriculum—the first time this had been done in an American law school—and projected the idea of legal rights for animals onto a national screen. The Clinic was cancelled in 2000, but not before it had played a pioneering role in calling into existence the new field of animal rights law. Law schools around the country now routinely offer courses in animal law (although not necessarily animal *rights* law), state bar associations have animal law sections, and there are academic journals devoted to promoting legal rights for animals.

By the mid-1990s, it was widely recognized that animal rights was not making measurable progress. Despite the best efforts of the animal rights movement for the past twenty years, the number of animals killed by human beings in the United States was going up by nearly a billion animals a year. The only area in which animal killing was actually declining was sport hunting.

Activists began looking for reasons. Henry Spira believed it was because the movement had lost its discipline and its focus. In the interests of maintaining their independent identity, their freedom to pursue their own pet projects, and their separate donor bases and fundraising campaigns, most groups had gone back to peddling outrage and abandoned the strategy of coordinated actions tightly focused on limited, incremental objectives. But while Spira remained a figure of mythic proportions, he was by now regarded almost as an historical artifact from some lost civilization, to be admired and treated with respect, but having no relevance to the present.

Like Henry Spira, Gary Francione took it as axiomatic that if the animal rights movement was failing to advance at the same rate that the civil rights and women's movements had advanced in the '60s, the fault must lie with the movement's strategy. But his critique of animal rights strategy—laid out in his 1996 book, *Rain without Thunder,* in which he accused animal activists of wanting "results without agitation," hence "rain without thunder"—was diametrically opposed to Spira's. The problem, he said, was that most groups, while they used the rhetoric of animal rights, were actually pursuing animal welfare. That is to say, they were talking about an end to all animal slavery and slaughter, but they were actually campaigning for things like better care for animals in laboratories and larger battery cages for chickens in factory farms.

Campaigns to reduce the suffering of enslaved animals, said Francione, actually retard the movement and make rights harder to achieve because they send a subtle but powerful message that animal exploitation is acceptable. This undercuts the animal rights message, and as long as the movement sends mixed messages, the public will always listen to the one that endorses their continued exploitation of animals. There is an old saying that "the perfect is the enemy of the good." Gary Francione looked at things in just the opposite way. He believed that the good is the enemy of the perfect.

Faced with the criticism that it was not possible to go directly from our present situation to perfection, Francione replied that incremental steps were acceptable, provided they were *abolitionist* steps and not *welfarist* steps. That is to say, it is acceptable to advocate the abolition of a particular form of abuse suffered by animals as a milestone on the way to abolishing all abuse suffered by those animals, but it is not acceptable to improve the living conditions of animals and reduce their suffering while they continue to endure that particular form of abuse. It is acceptable, according to Francione, to campaign for the abolition of battery cages while chickens continue to be raised for their eggs, but it is not acceptable to campaign for larger battery cages that would reduce the suffering of the chickens who are confined in them. Hence, Francione's trademark slogan, "Empty cages, not bigger cages."

At first glance, these are powerful arguments, but they seem to me to have serious flaws. First, as we have seen, the animal rights movement's lack of measurable progress is due less to the movement's strategy than to the stubbornness of the problem. Animal slavery and slaughter are so woven into the fabric of our society that it was naïve of us to think they could be undone in a single generation.

Second, since we cannot liberate all animals in the immediate—or even the foreseeable—future, I believe that we have a moral obligation to relieve their suffering to whatever extent we can, in whatever way we can. We cannot deliberately allow real animals to suffer in the present for the sake of a future utopia that they will never live to see.

And finally, I am convinced that rather than undercut the animal rights message, "welfarist" reforms can reinforce it by forcing people to think of animals as sentient, sensitive individuals whose wellbeing matters. This paves the way for more far-reaching reforms in the future, and ultimately for abolition. Welfarist reforms become a problem only when they are presented as the ultimate goal. When they are pursued as milestones on the way to that goal, they are a vital part of the solution.

Gary Francione's other argument was aimed at the large, national animal protection groups, which he claimed were bloated bureaucracies with overpaid leaders that were starving small grassroots organizations of desperately needed resources by using their sophisticated fundraising apparatus to suck in donations that the grassroots could put to better use.

Francione's criticism of the national animal rights movement, expressed in a take-no-prisoners style of rhetoric, soon made him a polarizing figure. It alienated movement leaders and rank-and-file supporters of national groups, while striking a chord with many grassroots activists who wondered exactly what the nationals were doing with their six- and seven-figure budgets while local groups were struggling to make a difference on a shoestring.

In 1994, Peter Gerard and the National Alliance for Animals began preparing for a second March on Washington, to take place in 1995. Because of scheduling and logistical difficulties, it was eventually postponed until the following year, but in the meantime, it had stirred up unexpected controversy. Gary Francione condemned the March as an enormous waste of money. It was, he argued, a frivolous diversion of scarce resources from the really important work that was being done at the grassroots level. He called for the March to be cancelled, and failing that, he urged local activists and grassroots groups to stay home. Others took up the call, and for several months the March was a hot-button issue throughout the movement.

When the March was finally held on June 23, 1996, only three thousand people attended. If the walk down Pennsylvania Avenue in 1990 had been a joyous celebration, this retracing of the route had all the energy and exuberance of a funeral procession. Just eight months earlier, Minister Louis Farrakhan had rallied an estimated seven hundred thousand people to the National Mall for his Million Man March. Both sides in the abortion controversy were able to bring tens of thousands of demonstrators to the Mall on a moment's notice. And the best we could do for animals was three thousand.

Even though there was a shortage of marchers, there was no shortage of speakers, and the program ran overlong, as such programs tend to do. By the time philosopher Tom Regan mounted the podium to deliver the concluding address, it was late in the afternoon. Tom Regan is a native of Pittsburgh who has lived his entire adult life in the South, where he has acquired the drawl and distinctive oratorical style of a Southern preacher, recognizable by anyone who has heard the speeches of Dr. Martin Luther King, Jr. To a Tidewater Virginia

boy like me, who grew up on Southern preaching, Regan is a mesmer-
izing speaker, and I thought his call for faith in our cause and unity
in pursuit of our goals was one of the best animal rights speeches I
had ever heard. Unfortunately, not many others got to hear it.
Between people from out of town whose chartered buses had to leave
an event that was running over schedule, and people who had simply
grown dispirited and drifted away, only two hundred and seventy-
four marchers were there to hear Regan's talk. I know. I counted the
house.[7]

Judging by the number of animal groups and the size of their
membership, the movement was still growing. There were more animal activists in 1996 than there had been in 1990. But in 1990, they
had enthusiastically turned out for the March, and six years later they
stayed home in droves. Gary Francione's calls for a boycott were certainly a factor, but I think it would be easy to overstate their importance. In the years between the marches, animal activists had come to
realize that activism based on demonstrations, civil disobedience, and
marches was no longer working; it no longer suited the temper of the
times. Unless you brought out enormous numbers of people or committed some utterly outrageous act, the media didn't even bother to
cover these events any more, which effectively rendered them futile. It
was time to move on to other strategies, and because they were closer
to the action, so to speak, grassroots activists recognized this before
the national leadership did.

Although we did not realize it as we stood watching Tom Regan
address an audience that included almost as many curious or
bemused tourists as activists, the disappointing turnout for the
March did not signal the decline of animal rights. It was a sign that
activists were regrouping to continue the struggle, by means better
suited to the current political climate and the level of maturity that
the movement had attained. The grassroots were not rejecting the
national leadership—or the national organizations—they were just
way out in front of them.

20

But the Center Takes Hold

Sixties-style activism had successfully kick-started a new movement, but when it failed to achieve the quick successes that it
had gained for the anti-war, civil rights, and women's movements, it gradually burned itself out. By the mid-1990s, animal
activists had begun setting quietly about the business of developing a
new set of strategies, as they settled in for the long haul in a political
and social atmosphere that was growing increasingly hostile to animal rights, even as more and more young people were taking up the
cause. Ten years in, that project remains very much a work-in-
progress, but some major themes have emerged around which the
contemporary animal rights movement is working to organize itself.

The Quest for Unity and Political Clout
In 1987, the leaders of the largest and most active American animal
protection groups created the Summit for the Animals, a forum
where they could meet to discuss the state of the movement and
informally coordinate campaigns and strategy. The dialogue at the
Summit is private, and the group works so quietly that many in the
movement have never even heard of it. But it is practically the only
forum in existence for promoting unity in the animal protection
movement and providing the various groups with at least a minimal
level of coordination. In 2006, the Summit renamed itself the
National Council for Animal Protection and began to focus on shar-

ing resources and expertise and developing a long-range program of public opinion polling that will allow the movement to package and target its message more professionally and effectively.

For the past decade, one of the prime advocates of the Summit as an instrument for unifying the animal rights movement and moving it forward has been Kim Stallwood, who as a young activist in England had revitalized the British Union for the Abolition of Vivisection (see Chapter 18). Recruited by Ingrid Newkirk and Alex Pacheco, Stallwood relocated to the United States in 1987 to become executive director of PETA, a post he held for five years. In 1993, he was named Editor in Chief of *The Animals' Agenda* magazine, replacing former editor Kim Bartlett, who had left in a disagreement with the Board of Directors over editorial policy and gone on to co-found (with Merritt Clifton) *Animal People*, a highly regarded newspaper-format periodical that reports on animal rights activities around the world.

In 2002, the *Agenda* went out of business, the victim of a confluence of circumstances that included the emergence of the worldwide web as a quick and convenient source of specialized news and information; the refocusing of the nation's priorities following 9/11, which led to a downturn in charitable giving not related to the disaster; and a lack of support from within the movement the *Agenda* had served for more than two decades. Most national groups, although they were generous in providing the magazine with financial support, did not promote it to their membership, apparently because they wanted their members to get their animal rights news from their own in-house publications and websites, which promote their own efforts and support their own fundraising.

As an insider at the highest levels of the American animal rights movement for the past twenty years, with a background in the British movement (which has been consistently out in front of the rest of the world), Kim Stallwood is in a unique position to assess the state of the movement. And he has concluded that if we hope to begin making measurable progress for animals in the foreseeable future, the leadership must radically readjust their thinking.

The movement has a weak history of being able to partner and build coalitions. We need to engage in movement-wide long-term strategic thinking instead of jumping from one crisis to the next without stopping to think about where our individual campaigns fit into the big picture. An orchestra in which every member insists on being a soloist will make nothing but noise. The same is true of a movement in which every group pursues its own agenda.[1]

Stallwood's second insight, which ties into the first, focuses on the way that most animal activists—both leadership and rank and file—conceptualize animal rights.

We have framed the animal issue as a matter of persuading people to adopt a cruelty free lifestyle. That is not wrong, but it is incomplete and grossly inadequate. Animal rights is also a matter of public policy. Most people are not going to become vegan until we have a public policy in America that embraces the moral and legal status of animals. And to achieve that, we need to establish an overarching campaign—not disjointed pieces of a campaign, each run independently by a different group—to put animal protection on the national political agenda. This is what was done in the United Kingdom and then in the European Union, and it is why the UK and the EU are so far ahead of us today.[2]

When the *Agenda* closed its doors, Kim Stallwood founded the Animals and Society Institute, which describes itself as an "animal rights public policy institute," *i.e.*, a think tank for the animals' cause, focused on developing a public policy agenda that can be supported by a wide spectrum of animal rights groups. To that end, he is working with activists from across the movement to develop the Animals' Platform, a statement of principles that he hopes can be used to inject animal protection into our national political dialogue and give the animals the kind of clout in America's legislatures that they have gained in the U.K. and Europe.

A somewhat different approach to empowering the animal rights movement in the public policy arena is represented by the Humane Society of the United States. In January 2005, HSUS merged with the Fund for Animals and, as part of the merger, created the Humane Society Legislative Fund to lobby at the state and federal level on behalf of animals. In September 2006, HSUS and the Doris Day Animal League—founded by the legendary singer and actress in 1987 specifically to promote federal legislation to protect animals—announced their merger. Today, the Humane Society Legislative Fund is the largest and best-funded animal lobbying group in the United States.

Show and Tell

One school of thought within the post-1996 animal rights movement is that the priority for animal activism should be sensitizing the public to the horror of animal enslavement and slaughter. Chickens rescued from factory farms cannot go on Larry King and describe their suffering. They have to depend on activists to tell their stories for them. But it is all too easy for a public that enjoys the benefits of animal abuse to ignore animal activists or dismiss their horror stories as hyperbole. What is needed (some activists reason) is a way for abused animals to speak for themselves. And the only way that can happen is for activists to show the abuse and its results to the public, allowing the bodies of the victims to say what their voices cannot.

With *Unnecessary Fuss* and *Britches*, PETA had proven the power of video to get the attention of people who might otherwise be inclined to discount or resist the message of animal activists. But video activism presents two challenges: how to get the footage and how to get it in front of the people who need to see it.

Steve Hindi has been a pioneer in undercover video. In 1992, Hindi founded the CHicago Animal Rights Coalition (CHARC, pronounced "shark"), a grassroots group that campaigned against animal exploitation in the greater Chicago area, which he renamed

SHowing Animals Respect and Kindness (SHARK) when the group went international a few years later.

In one of CHARC's first initiatives, Hindi went to the Illinois State Department of Agriculture with complaints about egregious cruelty at a northern Illinois cattle auction. No one would believe him. A reformed deep-sea fisher and shark hunter, who had taken to video-taping his adventures when friends back in Illinois had trouble believing his stories of challenging sharks alone in a 17-foot aluminum boat, Hindi naturally turned to his video camera for support. A few weeks later, he went back to the Ag Department with undeniable evidence, forcing the state to step in and curb the auction's worst abuses.[3] It was a small victory, but a real one in an arena where victories of any kind are few and far between. Steve Hindi was sold on the value of video in animal rights campaigns.

In the 1990s, SHARK turned its attention to rodeos and bullfighting, and remains in the forefront of the campaign against them. When he realized that Pepsi-Cola was a major advertiser at bullrings in Spain and Mexico, Hindi launched a national campaign to force PepsiCo to withdraw their support, using video taken at actual bullfights. "I always thought we could knock Pepsi out of the bull ring with the video," Steve Hindi told me. "We had video of every kind of abuse you could imagine. We even had footage of a bull bleeding to death in the ring leaning against a Pepsi ad for support. He collapsed and died right in front of the ad."[4]

In addition to footage taken at bullfights and rodeos, Hindi and his undercover videographers have also pioneered the use of ultralight aircraft with a camera attached to the pilot's helmet, a technique he believes the movement should adopt for documenting canned hunts, contest kills, dog fights, deer culls, and other forms of outdoor cruelty where it is impossible to get within camera range on the ground.[5]

Steve Hindi's approach to animal activism is based on his belief that most people are naturally compassionate and tolerate cruelty only because they are able to look the other way and tell themselves that it's not really as bad as the activists say it is. He believes that to succeed, the animal rights movement must show people the cruelty. We must arouse people's compassion by making it impossible for them to turn their heads away and pretend that it's not really happening. When a large-enough segment of the public has been forced to confront the vicious reality of animal abuse in this way, then and only then will it be possible to pass the laws and get the court decisions that will establish the rights of animals. As Hindi described his approach to me:

> SHARK supports sign carrying protests, but that's not enough by itself. Protests alone get you very little. You have to go in with video cameras and get the goods.[6]

A new technique for "going in and getting the goods" was born when an employee of Alpine Poultry in New South Wales, Australia, telephoned Patty Mark, president of Animal Liberation Victoria, one of Australia's leading animal rights groups, to tell her of cruelty and abuse in the company's intensive confinement chicken sheds. After an extensive investigation that included having an ALV member take a job briefly at Alpine, ALV conducted the first known "open rescue" on March 5, 1992. Mark and a small group of ALV volunteers went into an Alpine confinement building at night, removed several of the most seriously ill chickens, took extensive videotape footage of conditions inside the building, and then called both the police and the press to tell them who they were, what they had done, and why, and that they were waiting for police and reporters to come and see for themselves.

A front-page story ran nationally in the Australian press, headlined "The Dungeons of Alpine Poultry," that condemned the cruelty of industrial egg production, not the activists who conducted the rescue. By being nonviolent and not hiding their identities, Patty Mark and her open rescue team projected to the public an image of animal activists as compassionate rescuers rather than furtive, destructive criminals; they had kept the primary focus of the media coverage off themselves and on the suffering of the chickens. In the ensuing years, ALV and other groups in Australia have conducted dozens of open rescues, most in industrial chicken farms, and no one has yet spent more than short periods in jail.[7]

The concept of open rescues came to America in 1999 when Patty Mark addressed a conference organized by United Poultry Concerns' Karen Davis (see below). Held at UPC's headquarters and sanctuary in Machipongo, Virginia on June 26–27, the "Forum on Direct Action" brought together "key activists" to discuss the future of direct action in the wake of the breakdown of traditional animal activism. Mark's story and the accompanying video footage became the centerpiece of the conference, which also featured presentations by ALF spokesperson Katie Fedor and Freeman Wicklund, a former editor of *No Compromise*—a magazine dedicated to support for the ALF— who had broken with the underground group in the spring of 1998 by publishing an essay rejecting violence in favor of Gandhi-style *satyagraha* campaigns.[8]

It was Wicklund's group, Compassionate Action for Animals (CAA), based in Minneapolis-St. Paul, that carried out the first known open rescue in America. On June 24, 2000, Wicklund and other CAA activists entered a battery cage egg farm in LeSueur, Minnesota run by Michael Foods—a major Midwestern supplier— and rescued three hens. Regarding this as a reconnaissance, CAA did not publicize the rescue. Then, on January 14, 2001, they re-entered the facility, rescued eleven hens, videotaped the rescue, and announced their action to the press.[9] Perhaps because they were in the agricultural heartland, the media took little notice. But five months later, a D.C.-based group, Compassion Over Killing (COK), made headlines nationwide with videotaped footage from an open rescue at a Maryland egg farm.

Compassion Over Killing was founded in 1995 as a school club by Paul Shapiro, a fifteen-year-old high school student at Georgetown Day School, a socially progressive private school in the exclusive Tenleytown neighborhood of Washington, D.C. Although the D.C. area was home to several national animal rights groups, it had no grassroots organization that worked on issues locally. To fill this gap, Shapiro, animal rights activist Miyun Park, and several friends took

COK beyond the walls of Georgetown Day School in 1996 and transformed it into the region's local animal rights group.[10]

From the beginning, COK focused most of its attention on animal agriculture and the promotion of a vegan lifestyle. As Shapiro told me:

> Of the roughly 10,200,000,000 animals killed every year in the United States, 10,000,000,000 are farmed animals. Animal agriculture is where the movement needs to expend the vast majority of its energy and resources.[11]

Shapiro and Park both participated in Karen Davis' Direct Action Conference, where they heard Patty Mark's presentation on open rescues. In March, April, and May 2001, accompanied by two other COK activists, they made a series of surreptitious, nighttime visits to the intensive confinement buildings of Ise (pronounced ee-say) America—one of the country's largest egg producers—in Cecilton, Maryland on the Eastern Shore of the Chesapeake Bay, where they took "dozens of hours" of video footage. The last visit was on May 23, 2001, when they also rescued eight hens.[12]

On June 6, 2001, reacting to COK's video footage, *The Washington Post* ran a lengthy story that focused on the inhumane conditions at Ise America. When newspapers and television stations across the country picked up the story, millions of people learned that eggs are the product of unspeakable cruelty. The same day, COK released a documentary made from the Ise footage entitled *Hope for the Hopeless*. Unwilling to admit to the horrific conditions revealed in the video, Ise America declined to prosecute the COK activists, claiming that they were "not certain" that the video had been taken at their facility.[13]

Since then, CAA, COK, and other groups across the country have undertaken dozens of videotaped open rescues, which have become an important means of raising the consciousness of the public about the cruelty of animal agriculture. In the words of Paul Shapiro,

"Videotaped open rescues allow the animals to communicate with people in a way that they really can't through any other medium."[14]

* * *

Once videotape of animal cruelty has been obtained, the challenge becomes one of getting people to look at something they really do not want to see. Working independently, SHARK's Steve Hindi and a Brooklyn construction contractor turned animal rights activist, Eddie Lama, came up with similar solutions: customized vehicles that have been transformed into traveling DVD players.

As part of his campaign to persuade Pepsi-Cola to stop advertising in bullrings, Steve Hindi bought five thousand dollars' worth of PepsiCo stock and notified the company that he intended to speak at the next stockholders meeting (1998), which is the right of any stockholder. When PepsiCo refused to allow him to show his bullfight video to the stockholders, he put two small television sets in a van that he parked in front of Pepsi headquarters and drew crowds of employees, stockholders, and press. The following year, after an eighteen-month campaign, Pepsi withdrew its advertising support for bullfights.[15]

Realizing the value of the video van, in 2000 Hindi had a box truck customized to include a giant television screen built into each side that could show video constantly, whether the truck was parked or moving. Calling it the "Tiger Truck," SHARK has taken it around the country exposing the hidden cruelty of bullfights and rodeos.

Like Henry Spira, Eddie Lama was converted by a cat. When it fully struck him that the kitten who had come into his life was a sentient, sensitive, loving being, he began asking himself why we love some animals and imprison and slaughter others. Before long, he had started leafleting for local AR groups and wondering what he could do to make people see the horror of animal exploitation. He soon realized that images hit people harder than words, and that video has more impact than still pictures.

And so in the late '90s, he began putting a VCR and a TV set in a van, which he would park on a street with heavy pedestrian traffic, open the side door, revealing a television screen facing the sidewalk, run a video of fur farming or trapping, and stand nearby passing out leaflets and talking with anyone and everyone who was interested. The van was so successful, not just in attracting attention, but in getting people to stop, watch for a while, and begin thinking seriously about what they were seeing, that Lama was inspired to take the next logical step. He customized a van—which he called the FaunaVision van—with large TV screens built into the sides.

In 2000, Tribe of Heart, an organization created in 1997 by Jenny Stein and James LaVeck to produce compassion-based documentaries, released *The Witness*, which used the story of Eddie Lama and the FaunaVision van to deliver a powerful anti-fur message. Screened at film festivals around the world, *The Witness* has collected prestigious awards and critical praise.

In 2000, PETA produced the first edition of *Meet Your Meat*, a twelve-minute video that shows the cruel realities of factory farming. Two years later, an updated version was released, featuring a narration by actor Alec Baldwin that concludes with an appeal for everyone to go vegetarian. PETA updates *Meet Your Meat* continuously and distributes it free of charge over the Internet and via DVD.[16]

Activism in the Age of the Internet

With radio, television, newspapers, and magazines, a small number of (mostly) wealthy service providers have near absolute control over the information, analysis, and opinions available to the public. But with the arrival of cheap and easy access to the Internet in the late 1990s, that situation changed dramatically. The most important development for animal rights since the publication of *Animal Liberation* may be the explosive growth of activism via the worldwide web and email.

Large, established groups like PETA and HSUS are able to put thousands of pages of material—including pictures and video—on multiple websites at minimal cost, reaching audiences they could only dream about before. *Meet Your Meat,* for example, gets an average of 100,000 hits per month, and PETA's GoVcg.Com website typically hosts 350,000 visitors in the same period.[17] At the same time, small groups, and even individual activists, are able to create websites and get their message out to the public quickly, easily, and economically. Already, the worldwide web is spreading the animal rights message, including pictures and video, farther and faster than had ever been possible.

The drawback, of course, is that people have to deliberately access the material. Unlike the Tiger Truck and the FaunaVision van, websites reach primarily people who want to view the material on them. Even so, I believe that the massive animal rights presence on the worldwide web is a fundamental reason for what I regard as the most hopeful sign for the future of the movement: the rapidly growing number of young people—from middle school to college age—who are going vegan and identifying with animal rights.

A second effect of the electronic revolution is that, instead of being the sole province of two or three periodicals and the newsletters that the larger groups send out to their members, animal rights news and views are now being published by hundreds of organizations and thousands of activists. Information about atrocities and campaigns can be made available to hundreds of thousands of people in real time at almost no cost. At the same time, activists spread out across the country are no longer dependent on the national groups to decide what goals will be pursued, what campaigns will be launched, and how campaigns will be conducted. The worldwide web has brought a kind of grassroots democracy to animal activism that could not have been achieved a decade ago.

Just as important, the appearance of both local and national user groups, chat rooms, and electronic mailing lists has made it possible for activists anywhere and everywhere to have the kinds of discussions that used to be possible only within a very restricted locality or only once or twice a year by the small fraction of activists who are able to attend national conferences. In my observation, this is already having a strong positive effect, in preventing activists from feeling isolated and overwhelmed, and in keeping up their morale and their determination to stay active in the movement.

Sanctuaries as Advocacy

There have always been sanctuaries, but it was the Fund for Animals that—in 1979—first integrated refuge and advocacy by opening the Black Beauty Ranch and tying it into their campaigns in defense of wild horses and burros and circus animals.

The first national organization created specifically for the purpose of building advocacy campaigns around a refuge for the abused and abandoned was Farm Sanctuary. Founded by the husband-and-wife team of Gene and Lorri Bauston, Farm Sanctuary opened in 1986 in a rowhouse in Wilmington, Delaware with a shed in the backyard that served as a shelter. Rescued farmed animals were brought in, rehabilitated, and adopted out as quickly as possible to make room for new arrivals. The following year, the sanctuary moved to two acres of farmland near the town of Avondale, just over the Delaware line in southeastern Pennsylvania. With every available penny going to the care of the animals for whom they were providing a home of last resort, the Baustons lived in a converted school bus, sweltering in the summer and freezing in the winter.[18]

In their downed animals campaign, Farm Sanctuary rescued "downers"—animals who arrive at the slaughterhouse too sick, weak, or injured to walk—and gave them a home at the sanctuary. At the same time, the Baustons took undercover video footage of downers and used the contrast between the cruelty of the slaughterhouse and the nurturing of the sanctuary to promote legislation banning the sale of downed animals.

In the summer of 1990, Farm Sanctuary moved to a 175-acre farm in Watkins Glen, New York, near Ithaca, that had been purchased the previous fall, and in 1993 they opened a second sanctuary on a 300-acre farm north of Sacramento, California.[19] Using the sanctuaries as a foundation and placing a strong emphasis on humane education—

built around guided tours of the farms—Farm Sanctuary campaigns aggressively against factory farming and in support of a vegan diet.

Other sanctuary/advocacy groups soon sprang up around the country, such as Animal Place, founded in 1989 by humane educator Kim Sturla and veterinarian Nedim Buyukmihci on sixty acres in Vacaville, in northern California. Although Animal Place campaigns are aimed mostly at children and young people—through children's books and humane education materials authored by Sturla, as well as tours of the sanctuary—in 2005 Animal Place made a rare breakthrough in the movement's often frustrating efforts to reach the general public via the mainstream media, when twenty-seven public television stations in twenty-two cities aired the Animal Place–produced documentary *The Emotional World of Farmed Animals*. Featuring best-selling author Jeffrey Moussaieff Masson (*When Elephants Weep*, *The Pig Who Sang to the Moon*), *The Emotional World of Farmed Animals* spread the message that pigs, cows, and chickens are sensitive beings with rich interior lives and that activists who rescue them from factory farms and give them loving care are compassionately working to redress a grave injustice.

Along with Farm Sanctuary, the sanctuary-based advocacy organization that has had the most impact on the shape and direction of the animal rights movement is a group with the unlikely name of United Poultry Concerns.

UPC was founded in 1990 by University of Maryland English professor Karen Davis in her backyard in suburban Darnestown, Maryland. The conventional wisdom in the animal rights movement was that the way to connect with the public was to concentrate on "cute and cuddly" or "charismatic" animals. When Davis began consulting with movement leaders about her plans to create an organization devoted to poultry, she was advised to focus on pigs instead, because "you'll never get people to care about chickens."[20] But chickens account for ninety percent of the animals enslaved and slaughtered for food and fiber, and Davis was determined to make people pay attention.

Operating since 1998 from a sanctuary that is home to a hundred rescued fowl, mostly chickens, located in Machipongo, in the heart of industrial chicken country on the Eastern Shore of Virginia, Davis has—sometimes by knowledge (she has become an internationally recognized expert on poultry and the poultry industry; her books *Prisoned Chickens, Poisoned Eggs* and *More Than a Meal: The Turkey in History, Myth, Ritual, and Reality* are the definitive animal rights works on poultry), sometimes by eloquence, sometimes by sheer willpower and perseverance—redirected the animal rights movement to the point that nearly every group that works on farmed animal issues devotes significant resources to poultry. Thanks to Karen Davis, chickens and turkeys are now front-and-center on the animal rights agenda.

Negotiating with the Enemy

Realizing that twenty-five years of campaigning for the abolition of all forms of animal enslavement and slaughter had brought about no overall improvements in the treatment of animals and no reduction in the killing, activists began looking for ways to make small, but con- crete, changes that would make a difference in the lives of the animals who are suffering in the here and now. As it developed in the open- ing years of the twenty-first century, this strategy involved two facets, one aimed at the producers and the other at the consumers of animal products. Both represent a turning-away from simply "generating outrage" and the adoption of Henry Spira's strategy of making small, concrete gains that bring victory closer one step at a time.

On the production side, groups like PETA, the Humane Society of the United States, and United Poultry Concerns negotiate directly with animal abuse industries for incremental improvements in the quality of life of the animals they exploit and for the increased avail- ability—and visibility—of vegetarian and vegan meals.

In 1996, Ingrid Newkirk recruited Bruce Friedrich—a Catholic peace activist who had devoted the previous six years to managing Washington, D.C.'s largest charitable kitchen—to be PETA's vegetar- ian coordinator. A vegan since 1986 out of concern for world hunger,

Friedrich was converted to animal rights in 1993, when he read Andrew Linzey's *Christianity and the Rights of Animals* (see Chapter 16). Unabashedly, he declares that, "Without my Catholic faith, I wouldn't be an activist. Jesus' simple-minded dedication to making the world a better place is the motivation for my activism."[21]

Promoted in 2002 to Director of Vegan and Farmed Animal Campaigns, and named Vice President for International Grass Roots Campaigns in 2006, Bruce Friedrich has been a driving force behind PETA's vegetarian and vegan campaigns for the past decade. In October 2003, *Details*, an upscale magazine aimed at a young, male audience, ranked him number five on their list of "the 50 most influential men under 38." The following year, at Alex Hershaft's AR 2004 conference, he was voted into the Animal Rights Hall of Fame, an honor normally reserved for older activists with longer service in the movement.

One of the most successful of Bruce Friedrich's campaigns was an initiative supported by an array of other groups to persuade McDonald's, the largest retailer of animal products in the world, to require its suppliers to provide their hens at least seventy-two square inches of space per bird and end the egregious practice of "forced molting," in which birds are starved and deprived of sleep to stimulate egg production. After an eleven-month campaign that included demonstrations, boycotts, and extensive publicity and advertising, McDonald's conceded in September 2000. Subsequent campaigns have persuaded Wendy's, Burger King, Safeway, and other retailers to follow suit. As a result, death rates in the intensive chicken operations used by these companies have fallen from eighteen percent to two percent.[22] While it is true that a hundred percent of the chickens are slaughtered, the dramatically lower death rate prior to slaughter is a strong indicator that birds with more space who do not have to endure forced molting experience less stress and suffering during their brief lives. And when your life is as bleak as the lives of battery chickens, anything that makes it less miserable is a blessing.

In recent years, Compassion Over Killing has been working with restaurants in the D.C. area to encourage them to offer vegetarian and vegan menu choices. At last count, more than 125 restaurants were displaying a COK decal in their window that reads, "Proud to serve vegetarian and vegan meals."[23] Other groups in other cities are conducting similar campaigns.

HSUS' No Battery Eggs campaign encourages distributors and retailers—including university dining halls—to sell only eggs laid by hens who were not confined in battery cages. To date, several large retail chains, including Whole Foods Market and Wild Oats Natural Marketplace have gone cage-free, while over a hundred universities have ended or steeply reduced their use of battery eggs.[24]

Meeting People Where They Are

On the consumer side of the movement toward incremental but concrete changes are campaigns being undertaken to encourage people who are unwilling to go vegan right away to move gradually in that direction. HSUS' farmed animals campaigns, for example, stress "The Three Rs: Refinement, Reduction, and Replacement," a slogan borrowed from earlier anti-vivisection campaigns. "Refinement" means purchasing cage-free animal products; "reduction" means eating fewer animal products; and "replacement" means moving toward a vegetarian or vegan diet.[25] For people who are open to adopting a cruelty-free lifestyle here and now, HSUS publishes an all-vegan "Guide to Vegetarian Living."

This campaign reflects the philosophy of Wayne Pacelle—the former national director of the Fund for Animals who had led the Yale field protest against hunting—who became President and CEO of HSUS in 2004, and who has been vegan since his undergraduate days. The bulk of HSUS' public support comes from mainstream Middle Americans who are concerned about animal suffering, but who are well outside the animal rights and vegetarian communities. Recognizing that this renders HSUS ill-suited to be on the cutting edge of animal rights, Pacelle's strategy seems to be to take advantage of his organization's size and its unrivaled credibility with the general public to move animal rights into the American mainstream. Pacelle's "new" HSUS is trying to position itself to make a cruelty-free lifestyle normal, acceptable, and even desirable to everyday Middle America.

Carving out theoretically pure positions on animal rights does the animals little good if the public refuses to adopt them. Once the parameters of a cruelty-free lifestyle have been defined, the great American meat-eating, leather-wearing, vivisection-supporting, circus-attending public must be persuaded to change their lives in ways that most are loath even to consider. The hard truth is that there is simply no way to cut this Gordian knot. It will break the sword of anyone who tries. It must be unraveled slowly, patiently, one strand at a time. And this is the task that Wayne Pacelle has set for HSUS—to meet people where they are and nudge them gently but persistently in the right direction. In the 1970s and '80s, the need was for a new paradigm defining our relationship to animals. In the first decade of the twenty-first century, that paradigm has been defined. Today's most pressing need is for the public to begin living it.

Francione-style "abolitionists" lump groups that try to move people gradually towards vegetarianism in with groups like American Humane, that oppose the worst abuses of factory farming without promoting vegetarianism. This, I think, is misguided. The former are adopting a strategy to accomplish over time what they cannot achieve overnight, an end to animal agriculture. The latter are attempting to preserve animal agriculture by mitigating its worst horrors and assuring people that when these reforms are made, meat eating will be morally acceptable. COK founder and HSUS director of farmed animal campaigns Paul Shapiro puts it this way:

> When a company stops buying or selling battery eggs, it reduces animal suffering. Unlike battery hens, cage-free hens are able to walk, spread their wings, and lay their eggs in nests—all behaviors that are important to the birds. We're reducing the number of birds confined in battery cages by hundreds of thousands, and that's the first real progress that

has been made against what is perhaps factory farming's cruelest practice.

Cage free isn't cruelty free. But it is a lot better. And if better is the best that we can get for the animals right now, I'll take it and then start working for something better yet. My goal is to reduce as much animal suffering as possible, and I'm not willing to abandon these animals to the most horrible abusive suffering for a utopia that won't arrive for many years. Veganism is about reducing the suffering of animals; it is not about the personal purity of activists.[26]

CONCLUSION

The Dream and the Work

G iven the challenge facing the animal rights movement, it is unrealistic to expect that we should have made by now the kind of measurable progress that my fellow marchers and I expected back in 1990. What we do have a right to expect, however, is that we should have begun to tear away the cloak of invisibility that protects animal slavery and slaughter and gained public recognition that animal rights is a serious moral and social issue. And at that we have succeeded remarkably well.

In 1975, the very idea of animals being liberated or having rights had occurred only to a handful of philosophers and activists, mostly in England. To the public, including the intelligentsia, the notion would have seemed laughable, just as it did to Irwin Silber. Now everyone is aware of animal rights, and no one is laughing. This, in itself, is progress. But there is a lot more.

In 1975, very few outside the AR/vegetarian community had ever heard the word "vegan." Now "vegan" is regularly used in mainstream newspapers and magazines without explanation, and—the most hopeful sign of all—it is understood by practically everyone under thirty, and not just in the cities on the coasts. My wife Patti Rogers and I live just outside a city of less than forty thousand in western Maryland's Cumberland Valley. We can walk into any restaurant in town and ask if an item on the menu is vegan, and the high school and college students who make up the bulk of the service staff will know exactly what we mean. Even better, they will often say something like, "You're vegan? That's so cool." Or "My boyfriend's sister is vegan." Or best of all, "I'm vegan, too."

There are at least three slick national vegetarian magazines, two of which cater to a mainstream rather than an activist audience, and three periodicals specifically for animal activists. (See Recommended Resources.) Thirty years ago, none of these, and nothing like them, existed. When *Animal Liberation* appeared, practically the only books on animal rights dated from the Victorian era. Today, there are hundreds.

Twenty-plus years ago, when Patti and I first became vegan, there were only a very few vegetarian or vegan meat analogues available, and those had to be purchased at Seventh-Day Adventist stores, or ordered by mail from tiny companies struggling to stay in business. Many of these products were not particularly appetizing. Now there is a wide array of vegan turkey, bacon, hot dogs, cold cuts, burgers, barbeque ribs, barbeque chicken, soy milk, meltable cheese wrapped as individual slices, ice cream in all flavors, you name it. These products are delicious, and many of them are available in mainstream supermarkets. Purists may look down on these analogs, but they are the key to vegan outreach. And if no animal suffers or dies in their production, why should we care if they are marketed as imitation meat? Online companies like Pangea, MooShoes, Heartland Products, Vegan Essentials, Sticky Fingers Bakery, and a host of others are making vegan food, shoes, clothing, and personal care and household products easy to get, no matter where you live. We are beginning to make our presence felt in the marketplace, and where the marketplace goes, the society will follow.

But the greatest cause for optimism is that young people, especially on high school and college campuses, cannot conceive that animal rights and vegetarianism would not be serious personal and social issues, like environmentalism, human rights, women's rights, gay rights, and so on. This "normalization" of animal rights and veganism among the young is perhaps the most important achievement of the animal rights movement thus far, for this is the unmeasurable progress that lays the foundation for the measurable progress that will be achieved by coming generations of activists.

For the past year or two, there has been an enthusiasm and optimism spreading through the animal rights movement like nothing I have seen since the 1990 march. In the course of writing this book, I have talked with activists all over the country, and in their voices I could hear the kind of excitement about the state of the movement that I have not heard for fifteen years. But today's is a more realistic optimism than we felt in the '80s. Today's activists do not expect us to win overnight, and perhaps not even in their lifetimes. But they do expect us to win. And they are prepared to settle in for the long haul with confidence and determination.

There are, I think, two reasons for this new spirit that has got the animal rights movement feeling good about itself again. First, a generation of activists has come of age that did not experience the disillusionment that their elders lived through. When they came into the movement—for the most part, within the past dozen years—it had become obvious that animal rights was a marathon, not a sprint, and so they took up activism with no illusions about how hard or how long the struggle would be. Because of this, they measure success by a different yardstick than activists in the '80s. Instead of disappointment because they cannot get everything they want, they feel a sense of accomplishment at every gain that is made for animals. And that brings us to the other reason that I see for the new spirit of animal rights.

Insisting on all or nothing—and, naturally enough, getting nothing—generates a feeling of frustration and failure. It is isolating and alienating, and creates a siege mentality in which we begin to see our own fecklessness as a sign of intellectual and moral superiority. This, in turn, leads to a kind of fundamentalism, a holier-than-thou mindset that pursues strategies that are designed to preserve our own moral purity and intellectual rigor rather than relieve the suffering of animals. And that is a formula for stagnation and self-indulgent pessimism.

By contrast, a steady string of small advances brings with it a feeling of progress. It generates optimism and a sense of community with all of those who are moving forward with us one step at a time. The strategy of working for limited but concrete victories that make a real difference in the lives of animals is not only good for the animals, it is essential to the morale of the activist community. It is, in fact, revitalizing a movement that just a few years ago had been in danger of sliding into a permanent doldrums.

*   *   *

For more than 2,500 years—since the days of Lord Mahavira, the Buddha, the Later Prophets, and Pythagoras—men and women of compassion and goodwill have sustained the struggle for a world in which no sensitive being is imprisoned, enslaved, tortured, or killed simply because it suited humankind to do so. And the end of that struggle is not yet in sight. Today, we still face the same twofold challenge that has faced the defenders of the most helpless of the helpless since the Axial Age: first and foremost, to bring closer the day when all sentient beings will live securely in a world without cruelty; and in the meantime, to relieve as much suffering as we are able.

Our strategy, therefore, must be to accomplish the possible while inspiring those who will come after us to achieve the impossible. We must dream the impossible dream and broadcast that dream so that every year, every decade, every generation, there are more and more of us who share it. All the while, we must never retreat from doing what we can. To abandon either the dream or the work is to abandon the animals, because it is this union of the impossible dream with the possible work that will bring success. Nothing else will. At some time that we cannot yet see, the dream and the work will merge, brought into reality by generations of dedicated dreamers and workers, and the animals will be freed forever from what George Orwell's philosopher pig called by its true name: "the tyranny of human beings."

Recommended Resources

Note that the recommendations here are, of necessity, only a small fraction of the excellent materials that are available. They are intended merely as entry points for readers who want to learn about animal rights.

Books

DeGrazia, David. *Animal Rights: A Very Short Introduction.* Part of the "Very Short Introductions" series, this is a concise but thorough run-through of the major issues.

Francione, Gary. *Introduction to Animal Rights: Your Child or the Dog?* An accessible, comprehensive introduction to the theory and the practical implications of animal rights, by an attorney and law professor who is a leading proponent of legal rights for animals. The Appendix alone, "Twenty Questions (and Answers)," is worth the purchase price.

Linzey, Andrew. *Animal Gospel.* An accessible introduction to animal rights as Christian practice.

Regan, Tom. *Empty Cages.* Especially recommended for people who see the fundamental justice of the animal rights position but are reluctant for a variety of reasons to identify with it.

Ryder, Richard D. *Painism: A Modern Morality.* No jargon, no abstruse theories, no utilitarian arithmetic, and no rights whose origins nobody can quite figure out. A solid, commonsense, compassion-based ethics that includes all sentient beings.

Schwartz, Richard. *Judaism and Vegetarianism.* The definitive work on animal rights and vegetarianism from the perspective of Judaism.

Singer, Peter. *Animal Liberation.* Thirty years later, Singer's book is still a "must read."

Tuttle, Will. *The World Peace Diet: Eating for Spiritual Health and Social Harmony.* A compassionate, comprehensive, and readable meditation on the implications of our diet for our physical, moral, spiritual, and social wellbeing.

Periodicals

Animal People. Newspaper-format periodical that reports on trends and events of interest to animal activists around the world. An invaluable source of information for and about activists. www.animalpeoplenews.org.

Animals' Voice. An important source of news and opinion for animal activists—newly reborn after a hiatus of several years. www.animalsvoice.com/PAGES/home.html.

Satya. An always-engaging and informative magazine that views environmentalism, social justice, animal advocacy, and vegetarianism as facets of the same truth. Many of the most important debates within the animal rights community are carried on in the pages of *Satya.* www.satyamag.com.

VegNews. Informative and entertaining general-interest slick paper magazine for vegetarians and animal activists. www.vegnews.com.

Web Sites

Animal Place. www.animalplace.org.

Association Humanitaire d'Information et de Mobilisation pour la Survie des Animaux (AHIMSA). Excellent French-language site based in Canada. www.ass-ahimsa.net.

Compassion Over Killing (COK). www.cok.net.

FARM. www.farmusa.org.

Farm Sanctuary. www.farmsanctuary.org.

GoVeg. A PETA website focused on vegan and vegetarian lifestyles. An excellent resource for both new and long-time ethical eaters. www.goveg.com.

The Humane Society of the United States (HSUS). The gateway to multiple websites covering every aspect of animal exploitation. www.hsus.org.

In Defense of Animals. www.idausa.org.

JesusVeg. A PETA website featuring resources on vegetarianism and animal rights from Christian and Jewish perspectives. www.jesusveg.com.

People for the Ethical Treatment of Animals (PETA). www.peta.org.

PETA2. PETA's website for kids and teenagers. www.peta2.com.

Rincon Animal. New Spanish-language site based in the United States. www.rinconanimal.com

The Sea Shepherd Conservation Society. www.seashepherd.org.

Showing Animals Respect and Kindness (SHARK). www.sharkonline.org/about.mv.

The Society of Ethical and Religious Vegetarians (SERV). An ecumenical site with information and resources on vegetarianism and animal rights from the perspective of the world's religions. www.serv-online.org.

SuperVegan. An outstanding new website of news, links, and an informative blog, everything for the vegan and animal activist. www.supervegan.com.

United Poultry Concerns (UPC). www.upc-online.org.

VegCooking.com. An extensive and informative PETA website for the vegetarian and vegan cook. www.vegcooking.com.

The Vegetarian Resource Group. Excellent website with a focus on vegetarian and vegan cooking and nutrition. www.vrg.org.

VegSource. Vegetarian central! An impressive array of expert columnists, fact sheets, and discussion groups covering every aspect of a vegan or vegetarian lifestyle. www.vegsource.com.

World Animal Net. A searchable database of more than 17,000 animal protection organizations around the world, including links to more than 10,000 websites. worldanimalnet.org/new.asp.

Notes

Introduction
1. Ellison, p. 3.
2. "Vivisection." On the *Encyclopaedia Britannica* website at concise.britannica.com/ebc/article-9382118. Viewed on February 12, 2006.

1: The Roots of Evil
1. Goodall, p. 9.
2. Cartmill, p. *xi*.
3. Ibid., pp. 225–226.
4. There were no dairy products before the domestication of animals like cows and goats; and before the domestication of chickens, eggs were limited to those that could be stolen from nests.
5. "Arms and Armour," p. 1.
6. Keddie.
7. Diamond, pp. 42–47.
8. Orwell, p. 5.
9. Census Bureau.
10. I Samuel 14:32–35.
11. Zoroaster's traditional date is around 1000 BCE, but scholars generally agree that this is too early, and place him in the Axial Age. The earliest of the Later Prophets may date to as early as 780 BCE. The earliest of the Vedas, the *Rig Veda*, is traditionally dated to 1500 BCE, but, while the *Rig Veda* contains material from this earlier time, in its present form it is a product of the Axial Age. The earlier books of the Hebrew Scriptures underwent their final major editing sometime between 621 BCE (the date of Deuteronomy) and *c.*400 BCE.

2: The Challenge of *Ahimsa*
1. "Horses in World War I."
2. *Akaranga Sutra*, I:5:5:3. I have modernized the translation slightly.

Parenthetical phrases were inserted by the translator for clarity in English.

3.   *Akaranga Sutra*, I:4:2:4.

4.   *The Dhammapada*, verse 129.

5.   Claims that the Buddha ate meat and permitted his followers to do so are specious. For a thorough discussion of this question, see Phelps, *The Great Compassion*, pp. 55–84.

6.   Interview with His Holiness the Dalai Lama, November 10, 1998. See Phelps, *The Great Compassion*, pp. 154–157.

7.   On the website of the Wildlife Trust of India at www.wildlifetrustofindia.org/html/news/2005/050406_dalai_lama.htm. Viewed on June 16, 2005.

8.   Phelps, *The Great Compassion*, pp. 51–54.

9.   *Mahabharata*, XIII:113.8 and XIII:114.11. Quoted in Chapple, p. 16.

10. Walters and Portness, p. 41.

11. *Tirukural.*

12. York.

13. The view of ancient Indian history and the development of Hinduism that I describe here has been generally accepted by historians for nearly a century. However, it has recently been challenged by proponents of the Hindu Nationalist movement, who insist that modern Hinduism be understood as an entirely Aryan creation that owes nothing to non-Aryan and non-Vedic influences. They have been joined by a few Western scholars, who seem equally unwilling to ascribe the spiritual attainments of the Renouncer movement to non-Indo-European sources. According to this view, the Aryans migrated peacefully into the Indian subcontinent over a period of several centuries where they found a dying civilization that had been all but destroyed by natural disasters, primarily floods. The indigenous people were gradually absorbed into Aryan society, upon which they had little or no influence. The principal evidence for this theory is archeological discoveries suggesting that floods had severely damaged several Indus Valley cities prior to the arrival of the Aryans. However, the ancient Indian epics allude to an invasion and conquest, and their testimony cannot be lightly dismissed. A society weakened by natural disaster is vulnerable to conquest, and so the conventional view is by no means inconsistent with the archeology. The revisionist theories appear to owe more to contemporary politics and cultural pride than to unbiased scholarship.

3: The Challenge Comes West

1.   The quotation is one of a number of short maxims attributed to

Pythagoras that circulated widely in the ancient world but had no specific literary source. Some of these maxims are nonsensical in their plain meaning and require interpretation, such as "Avoid the weasel," which was taken to mean, "Stay away from gossips." But given the widespread attestation by ancient writers that Pythagoras practiced and taught vegetarianism, there is no reason to place "Abstain from eating animals" in that category. One somewhat confusing Pythagorean maxim was "Keep your hands off the beans." The ancients were divided on whether this was advice on avoiding flatulence, an injunction not to participate in politics (some Greek cities conducted elections by having the voters drop beans in jars labeled with the candidates' names), or was based on an esoteric belief that beans, like animals, possessed souls. Guthrie and Fideler, p. 160.

2. Ovid, p. 337 (Book XV).
3. Guthrie and Fideler, p. 160.
4. Ovid, pp. 337–338 (Book XV).
5. In some parts of the Empire, depending on climate and custom, elephants and camels were also used for labor and transportation.
6. The frequency of religious holidays (Rome, for example, had nearly fifty) came close to creating a six-day workweek. But, of course, not all working animals got all the religious holidays off. The Greco-Roman world had nothing like the Jewish Sabbath, which required all humans and animals to rest one day a week. (The word "week" is an anachronism that I am using for convenience; the Greek and Roman calendars were not divided into weeks, although the Jewish calendar was.)
7. Ryder, *Animal Revolution*, p. 18.
8. Sorabji, pp. 124–125. Ryder, *Animal Revolution*, p. 19.
9. Plato, p. 185 (*Phaedo*, 118a). Asclepius was the god of healing. Why Socrates owed him a sacrifice is unclear and much debated, but unless he had recently been cured of an illness that we are unaware of, it seems likely that he wanted to thank Asclepius for curing him of the disease of life.
10. Xenophon, p. 68 (*Memoirs of Socrates*, I.1).
11. Aristotle, p. 23 (I:8).
12. Sorabji, p. 132.
13. Ibid., pp. 122–125.
14. Plutarch, p. 547 ("On the Eating of Flesh I," *Moralia*, 994). As I have already noted, bread was the staple of the Greek and Roman diet. It was served at every meal, at which it was at least theoretically the main course. For the poor and for slaves, who made up the vast majority of the population, bread was usually the only course. Vegetables, fruit, cheese, and meat were considered delicacies, and the Greek words for

them were *opsa* and *opsaria* (singular *opson, opsarion*), which literally refer to something supplemental, not really necessary, an indulgence, perhaps even a bonus. The translator here has employed the word "appetizer," to convey this idea, but the *opsa* were eaten along with the bread, not ahead of it. In fact, to eat an *opson* without eating bread in the same course was considered gluttonous and rude.

15. Ibid. The ellipsis indicates a break in the manuscript. Only fragments of both essays have survived.
16. Plutarch, p. 569 ("On the Eating of Flesh II," *Moralia*, 997).
17. Plutarch, p. 549 ("On the Eating of Flesh I," *Moralia*, 994).
18. Plutarch, p. 563 ("On the Eating of Flesh II," *Moralia*, 996).
19. Walters and Portness, pp. 42, 44.

4: Judaism Crafts a Compromise

1. For example, Genesis 1:21, 1:24, and 2:19, where *nephesh chayah* refers to animals, and 2:7, where it refers to a human being. In Genesis 9:10, 9:12, 9:15, and 9:16, it refers to humans and animals collectively. For a discussion of *nephesh chayah*, see Phelps, *Dominion of Love*, pp. 57–61, and Regenstein, pp. 47–48.
2. Genesis 1:28 (*New American Standard Bible*).
3. Phelps, *Dominion of Love*, pp. 49–56.
4. Hesiod, pp. 40–42 (*Works and Days*, 100–170).
5. Walters and Portness, p. 45.
6. Genesis 1:29–30 (*NASB*).
7. Genesis 9:2–3 (*NASB*).
8. For Abel, see Genesis 4:4; for Abraham, see Genesis 15:9–10; for Moses, see Leviticus 8:22–28.
9. I Kings 8:63.
10. Leviticus 19:18 (*NASB*). The date of Leviticus is much debated, but it seems likely to have been edited into final form during or shortly following the Babylonian exile (586–458 BCE).
11. Isaiah, Jeremiah, Ezekiel, and the twelve "Minor Prophets" (so called because the books bearing their names are very short). The Later Prophets whose extant writings include condemnations of sacrifice are Isaiah, Jeremiah, Hosea, Micah, and Amos. (See Phelps, *The Dominion of Love*, pp. 77–82.)
12. I Samuel 14:31–35.
13. "The Dietary Laws as an Atonement for Flesh Eating" by Louis A. Berman, in Kalechofsky, p. 151.
14. Exodus 20:10; Deuteronomy 5:14.
15. Berman, *op. cit.* in Kalechofsky, pp. 150–164.

16. The only exception is wine, which is a later addition to the original system. There is no Biblical basis for making wine subject to rules of *kashrut*, and there are no rules in the Bible that could reasonably be applied to wine.

5: Jesus vs. Aristotle

1. Matthew 9:13 and 12:7 (*NASB*). In the original Greek, the phrase "the innocent" is plural.
2. Matthew 21:12–13 (*NASB*).
3. The earlier citation was Jeremiah 7:21–23. Jesus was quoting Jeremiah 7:11.
4. See, for example, Hebrews, Chapter 10.
5. This case is examined in detail in Phelps, *Dominion of Love*, pp. 108–139.
6. Luke 24:36–43. See Phelps, *Dominion of Love*, pp. 116–119.
7. Galatians 1:11–17 (*NASB*).
8. I Corinthians 9:9–14 (*NASB*).
9. I Corinthians 10:25–31 (*NASB*).
10. Romans 14:2–4.
11. For a discussion of Paul, animals, and vegetarianism, see Phelps, *Dominion of Love*, pp. 155–175.
12. Augustine, *On Christian Teaching*, p. 16 (I:39).
13. Augustine, *The City of God*, pp. 31–32 (I:20).
14. Ryder, *Animal Revolution*, p. 30.
15. Judaism was more or less tolerated, but Jews were subject to frequent, widespread, and murderous outbreaks of anti-Semitism that were at least condoned and often encouraged by the Church.
16. Aquinas, *Summa Theologica*, II, 64, 1. The quotation is from Augustine's *The City of God*, I, 20.
17. Aquinas, *ST,* II, 25, 3. By "the love of charity," Aquinas means something like "lovingkindness."
18. Aquinas, *ST,* quoted in Regenstein, p. 72.
19. Ibid. Emphasis added.
20. Rome became part of the newly united Italy in 1870. Prior to that, it was ruled by the Pope.
21. E. S. Turner, pp. 162–163.
22. Quoted in Gaffney, pp. 160–161.
23. Philip Neri (1515–1595) was a vegetarian who sometimes purchased birds in the market and set them free.
24. For an insightful, informative discussion of vegetarianism, the Catholic Church, and the Franciscan Order, see Berry, pp. 191–240.

25. Bonaventure, p. 222 (*Life*, 5.6).
26. *Luther's Works*, ed. Jaroslav Pelikan. St. Louis: Concordia, 1955, 9:220, quoted in Regenstein, p. 78.
27. Quoted in Huff, pp. 69, 70.
28. Particularly Isaiah 11:6–9 and Romans 8:19–21. See Phelps, *Dominion of Love*, pp. 57–66.
29. Wesley.
30. Ibid. Emphasis added.

6: Secular Offerings to a Savage God
1. Ryder, *Animal Revolution*, p. 42. Spencer, pp. 190–191.
2. Quoted in Spencer, p. 192.
3. Ray Greek, M. D., in Miserandino.
4. Guerrini, pp. 6–8. Although Aristotle practiced dissection extensively, there is no evidence that he ever engaged in vivisection. Claims that the philosopher Alcmaeon of Croton (*c.*450 BCE) had engaged in vivisection a hundred years earlier are now discounted by scholars (Huffman).
5. Although they were few, there were other ancient vivisectors, such as the Roman encyclopedist Aulus Cornelius Celsus (25 BCE–50 CE).
6. Since the capillaries that connect the arteries to the veins are too small to see with the naked eye, early researchers believed that arteries and veins constituted two separate systems.
7. Guerrini, pp. 20–21, 28–33.
8. The circulation of blood was first described by Ibn-Al-Nafis (1213–1288), a prominent Syrian physician and jurist, and subsequently accepted by Muslim medical science ("Al-Nafis" in *Wikipedia*). Whether Harvey was aware of the Muslim view is disputed.
9. Letter to Henry More, dated February 5, 1649. Quoted in Singer, *Animal Liberation*, p. 201, and Hoch.

7: A Few Rays of Enlightenment
1. The veins that run between the folds of tissue ("mesenteries") that anchor the intestines to the abdominal wall.
2. Those who believed, like Descartes, that animals were insentient machines were known as "mechanists." Those who believed that animals were conscious were called "vitalists." Vitalists used the term "mechanist" as an insult, and *vice versa*.
3. Voltaire.
4. Rousseau, *Emile*, pp. 28–29, 140-141.
5. Saunders.

6. Setting dogs and cats to fight one another was a popular children's pastime, widely viewed by adults as harmless fun of the "boys-will-be-boys" variety until the animal welfare movement of the nineteenth century changed public attitudes.

7. Rousseau, *Emile,* p. 255.

8. Ibid., pp. 340–341.

9. Montaigne, p. 482 ("On Cruelty").

10. Scruton.

11. Rousseau, *The Social Contract and Discourses*, p. 47.

12. Rawls, pp. 448–449.

13. Singer, *Animal Liberation*, p. 202.

14. Pushpin was a simple children's game. We might say, "Tic-tac-toe is as good as poetry."

15. I.e., whether it is covered with fur.

16. Bentham, p. 311 (17:1:4, note 1). Italics in original.

17. Quoted in Sebo.

18. Kant, pp. 239–241.

19. Sebo.

20. Ibid.

8: "Pain Is Pain"

1. *The Massachusetts Body of Liberties.* I have modernized the spelling and capitalization.

2. Ryder, *Animal Revolution*, p. 48.

3. Spencer, p. 206.

4. Quoted in Ryder, *Animal Revolution*, p. 48. I have modernized the spelling and capitalization.

5. Franklin.

6. Franklin. Saunders.

7. An antecedent to Primatt's book was a sermon delivered in 1772 by Rev. James Granger, "An Apology for the Brute Creation, or Abuse of Animals Censured." (In the eighteenth century, "apology" meant "defense.") Granger later reported that his sermon aroused "disgust" in both congregations to whom he delivered it. Nevertheless, it survived and was published by the RSPCA not long after its founding in 1824. E. S. Turner, pp. 72–73.

8. Primatt, p. 35.

9. Primatt argues elsewhere that nonhuman animals have no memory of the past and no anticipation of the future. His point here is that these disabilities do not lessen their experience of pain or disqualify them from being entitled to our compassion.

10. Primatt, pp. 20–21. Italics in original.
11. See Richard D. Ryder, in Primatt, p. 11.
12. Primatt, pp. 126–127. Italics in original. By "believe it to be the ground of your hope," Primatt means that Christians should regard mercy, including mercy to animals, as a requirement for salvation.
13. "They are incapable of hope, because they can neither reflect nor foresee. The present moment is as eternity to them." (Primatt, p. 40). And, "[T]hey do not seem to us to have any idea or fear of death....the brute, having no idea of an hereafter, cannot suffer any terror on account of death....death to a brute is nothing terrible" (pp. 35–36).
14. Clarke and Linzey, p. 188.
15. Quoted in Clarke and Linzey, pp. 130–131.
16. Ryder, *Animal·Revolution*, p. 49.

9: "Harassing the Lower Orders"

1. The Georgian era (1714–1837) included the reigns of Kings George I through IV and William IV. The Victorian era began with the coronation of Queen Victoria in 1837 and ended with her death in 1901.
2. Gompertz, pp. 63–64. Italics in original.
3. Quoted in E. S. Turner, p. 112.
4. E. S. Turner, pp. 110–113.
5. Quoted in Ryder, *Animal Revolution*, p. 80.
6. E. S. Turner, p. 123.
7. E. S. Turner, p. 123. Ryder, *Animal Revolution*, pp. 79-82.
8. Ryder, *Animal Revolution*, pp. 82–83.
9. Reproduced in *The History of the RSPCA*.
10. There had been earlier efforts to create an animal welfare society in England, dating back at least to 1809, but none seems to have survived longer than a few weeks (*The History of the RSPCA*).
11. E. S. Turner, pp. 125, 131, 141.
12. "About the RSPCA—History."
13. *The History of the RSPCA*.
14. Ibid.
15. Ryder, *Animal Revolution*, p. 87.

10: The Great Meddler

1. "Great Humanitarian." A droshky was an open carriage, with either two wheels or four, often used as a taxicab.
2. Collins.

3. Dracker.
4. Ryder, *Animal Revolution*, p. 196.
5. Dracker.
6. Ibid.
7. Pennsylvania Society for the Prevention of Cruelty to Animals (PSPCA) website, "History." Ryder, *Animal Revolution*, pp. 196–197.
8. Amory, *Ranch of Dreams*, pp. 22–23. MSPCA, "History of the MSPCA." Beers, p. 48.
9. Amory, *Ranch of Dreams*, p. 25.
10. PSPCA website, "History."
11. Beers, p. 64.
12. Dracker.
13. "HSUS Pet Overpopulation Estimates."
14. "HSUS Pet Ownership Statistics."
15. "HSUS Pet Overpopulation Estimates." "Gains against Shelter Killing ... " p. 18.
16. National Council on Pet Population Study and Policy. The survey was discontinued in 1997 because so few shelters responded.
17. Glen, pp. 15ff.
18. San Francisco Animal Care and Control.
19. Levine-Gronningsater.
20. Ibid.
21. Mountain.
22. PETA website at www.helpinganimals.com/Factsheet/files/FactsheetDisplay.asp?ID=38. Viewed on January 11, 2006.

11: The Pit of Despair
1. Guerrini, pp. 67–69.
2. Ibid., pp. 71–72. Bichat's full name was Marie François Xavier Bichat, but he preferred to be known as Xavier Bichat.
3. Lemaire.
4. Ryder, *Victims of Science*, p. 122.
5. Paul Elliott, "Vivisection and the Emergence of Experimental Physiology in Nineteenth-century France," in *Vivisection in Historical Perspective*, edited by Nicholas A. Rupke, London, Routledge, 1990.
6. Quoted in E. S. Turner, pp. 213–214.
7. *Introduction to the Study of Experimental Medicine* (1926 edition), vol. 1, p. 35. Quoted in Ryder, *Animal Revolution*, p. 102.
8. Quoted in Ryder, *Victims of Science*, pp. 123–124.

9. Ryder, *Victims of Science*, p. 122.
10. Removing the eyes and amputating the hooves of living horses was a regular part of the training of veterinary students at Alfort.
11. E. S. Turner, pp. 203–204.
12. Quoted in Ryder, *Victims of Science*, p. 124.
13. Guerrini, p. 74. Ryder, *Victims of Science*, p. 123.
14. Guerrini, p. 86.
15. Quoted in Ryder, *Victims of Science*, p. 122.
16. Guerrini, pp. 96–97.
17. Silk is the cocoon of the silkworm larva. To keep them from severing the threads when they mature and gnaw their way out, silkworms are boiled alive in their cocoons.
18. Guerrini, p. 96.
19. Ibid., pp. 98–99.
20. Ibid., p. 114.
21. Ibid., p. 115.
22. Ibid., p. 120.
23. Astoundingly, David Oshinsky, in his Pulitzer Prize–winning *Polio: An American Story,* puts the number at 100,000. When invisibility is impossible, defenders of animal abuse turn to Plan B: minimization.
24. Quoted in Slater.
25. Slater.
26. Harlow. Guerrini, pp. 129–133. Slater. "Harry Harlow" in *Wikipedia*. Tavris.

12: Requiem for a Little Brown Dog

1. Guerrini, p. 74.
2. Throughout this chapter, my description of the life and activities of Frances Power Cobbe is drawn primarily from *Power and Protest*, the authoritative and highly readable biography by Lori Williamson.
3. Among other things, Schiff was removing the thyroid gland from dogs in an effort to learn its function. The dogs, of course, died. Schiff (1823–1896) is credited with creating a technique for using thyroid extract to treat people with thyroid disease.
4. Williamson, pp. 106–107. Guarnieri, p. 109. Florence is the capital of the Italian province of Tuscany.
5. Guarnieri, pp. 109, 116.
6. Quoted in Williamson, p. 116. Williamson points out that the phrase "demons let loose from hell" does not appear in Cobbe's petition.
7. Quoted in "Vivisection and Experimentation Debate" in *Wikipedia*.
8. The first was Elizabeth Garrett Anderson, who initially qualified to prac-

tice medicine in 1866 through a loophole that the Royal College of Physicians promptly closed when they realized what had happened.

9. Quoted in Wallechinsky and Wallace.

10. Ibid.

11. My account of Anna Kingsford's psychic attacks on Bernard, Bert, and Pasteur, reflects the commonly accepted view among historians. It derives from Edward Maitland, who edited and published Kingsford's papers, including her diaries, following her death, and wrote the biography that is the primary source of information about her. Recently, some Kingsford disciples have suggested that the story is fiction, pointing out, accurately enough, that writing fiction was Maitland's primary occupation (he was a novelist), and that he sometimes showed an overblown sense of the dramatic. Maitland's aim, however, was to portray Kingsford as a saint and enshrine her memory for the ages, so it hardly seems likely that he would turn her into a psychic murderer for the sake of drama, or even to show her spiritual power.

12. Finsen and Finsen, pp. 47–48.

13. Ibid., pp. 48, 51.

14. The principal exception to this was the pound seizure laws, which were often opposed by humane organizations.

15. American Humane, "How American Humane Began."

16. Finsen and Finsen, p. 50.

17. Quoted in Finsen and Finsen, p. 51.

18. Finsen and Finsen, p. 51.

19. Kean.

20. "Brown Dog Affair" in *Wikipedia.*

21. Quoted in E. S. Turner, p. 215.

22. Kean. "Brown Dog Affair" in *Wikipedia.* Website of Dr. Joe Cain, Senior Lecturer in the history and philosophy of biology at University College, London. Dr. Cain's website includes photographs of both the original monument and the modern replacement. www.ucl.ac.uk/sts/cain/projects/brown_dog/index.htm. Viewed on March 29, 2006.

13: *Ahimsa* Returns to the West

1. Spencer, pp. 253–254. James Turner, pp. 17–18. Iacobbo and Iacobbo, p. 10. Akers, *A Vegetarian Sourcebook,* p. 198. Different sources date the founding of the Bible Christian Church to 1807, 1808, or 1809, reflecting the fact that Cowherd's split with the New Church proceeded in stages by fits and starts, and there is no single break point that everyone can agree on. By 1809, however, the BCC was clearly established as an

independent church with its own building and no further ties to any branch of the Swedenborgian New Church.

2. Spencer, p. 261.
3. Several excellent histories of the wider vegetarian movement are available, and to readers who are interested, I recommend *The Heretic's Feast* by Colin Spencer and *Vegetarian America* by Karen and Michael Iacobbo.
4. Percy Shelley.
5. Ibid.
6. Carol Adam's classic *The Sexual Politics of Meat* includes an insightful analysis of *Frankenstein* (Chapter 6).
7. Schopenhauer, pp. 108–109.
8. Ibid., p. 111.
9. Ibid., p. 113.
10. Ibid., pp. 114, 115.
11. Ibid., p. 116.
12. Quoted in Iacobbo and Iacobbo, p. 57.
13. Iacobbo and Iacobbo, p. 58.
14. Iacobbo and Iacobbo, pp. 60–61. Fruitlands Museum.
15. Spencer, pp. 263–264. John Davis. "Joseph Brotherton" on *Spartacus Educational* at www.spartacus.schoolnet.co.uk/PRbrotherton.htm. Viewed on April 10, 2006.
16. John Davis.
17. Ibid. Italics in original.
18. Iacobbo and Iacobbo, pp. 71–73.
19. Ibid., p. 73.
20. Thoreau, *Walden*, p. 277 ("Higher Laws"). Emphasis added.
21. Thoreau, *Walden*, pp. 246 ("The Ponds"), 267 ("Baker Farm"), and 274 ("Higher Laws").
22. Thoreau, *Walden*, p. 274 ("Higher Laws").
23. Quoted in William Stroup, "Henry Salt on Shelley: Literary Criticism and Ecological Identity." On the website of the Romantic Circles Praxis Series published by the University of Maryland. Undated. www.rc.umd.edu/praxis/ecology/stroup/stroup. Viewed on January 23, 2007.
24. Salt, p. 106.
25. Quoted in International Vegetarian Union, "Henry S. Salt: Extracts from Books and Articles." The quotation is from *The Story of My Cousins* (1922).
26. Quoted in International Vegetarian Union, "Henry S. Salt: Extracts from Books and Articles." The quotation is from *Seventy Years among Savages* (1921).
27. Salt, p. 64.

28. Quoted in Carloff.
29. Gandhi, *Autobiography*, p. 43.
30. Gandhi, "The Moral Basis of Vegetarianism."
31. Merton, p. 68.
32. Akers, "Truth Force and Vegetarianism."
33. Henry Salt had actually used the phrase nearly two decades earlier, when he wrote, in *The Humanities of Diet: Some Reasonings and Rhymings* (1897), "The logic of the larder is the very negation of a true reverence for life, for it implies that the real lover of animals is he whose larder is fullest of them.... It is the philosophy of the wolf, the shark, the cannibal." (Quoted in International Vegetarian Union, "Henry S. Salt: Extracts from Books and Articles.") Schweitzer, however, was unaware of this.
34. Schweitzer, *The Philosophy of Civilization*, p. 309.
35. Quoted in Free, *Animals, Nature, and Albert Schweitzer*, p. 25. (The quotation is from *Out of My Childhood and Youth*.)
36. Free, *Animals, Nature, and Albert Schweitzer*, p. 41.
37. Klinkenborg.

14: One Step Forward, Twenty Steps Back
1. This is a traditional cattle song that dates to the 1860s.
2. Giehl, p. 186.
3. Rifkin, *Beyond Beef*, p. 71.
4. The railroads' standard was forty hours, the point after which so many animals died in the cattle cars that profits were affected.
5. American Humane, "Beginning of a Movement."
6. Unti, p. 3.
7. American Humane, "Farm Animals."
8. Patterson, p. 58.
9. James R. Barnett, "Introduction to *The Jungle*," in Sinclair, p. *xi*.
10. In October 2006, the USDA amended its regulations to include trucks within the definition of "common carrier," thereby covering them under the Twenty-Eight Hour Law.
11. Charles.
12. Masson, p. 138.
13. Scully, pp. 265, 267. Masson, pp. 38–40.
14. Davis, p. 100.
15. Mason and Singer, p. 55. Email from Paul Shapiro dated September 11, 2006.
16. Park, pp. 174–177. Graphic video footage of more recent COK investigations can be seen at www.cok.net/investigations. Viewed on May 5, 2006.
17. Interview with Paul Shapiro, May 30, 2006.

15: Heralds of Change

1. Quoted in "Donald Watson Obituary," on the website of the Vegan Society at www.vegansociety.com/phpws/index.php?module=announce&ANN_user_o p=view&ANN_id=68. Viewed on May 7, 2006. This brief sketch of Watson's life is largely drawn from the obituary.
2. But it is not always properly pronounced. Lexicographers seem to have an inexplicable fondness for VEJ-un. In more than twenty years, I have never heard an actual vegan, British, North American, or Australian, pronounce it any way but VEE-gun.
3. Hagenmayer. Interview with Freya Dinshah, May 11, 2006. Jay Dinshah was born Hom Dinshah Ghadiali. But since her husband was commonly known as Dinshah, and Ghadiali can be difficult for most Americans to pronounce properly, Mrs. Dinshah and her children took Dinshah for their family name (Freya Dinshah, p. 1). Parsees (also spelled Parsi and Farsi) are followers of the ancient Persian religion of Zoroastrianism whose ancestors fled to India in the wake of the Muslim conquest of Persia.
4. International Vegetarian Union, "H. Jay Dinshah." Interview with Freya Dinshah, May 11, 2006. Email from Freya Dinshah to the author dated August 16, 2006.
5. Interview with Freya Dinshah, May 11, 2006.
6. Ibid.
7. Interview with Freya Dinshah, May 11, 2006. Email from Freya Dinshah to the author dated August 16, 2006. "22nd World Vegetarian Congress, Ronneby Brunn, Sweden," on the website of the International Vegetarian Union at www.ivu.org/congress/wvc73/briefs.html. Viewed on May 14, 2006.
8. Iacobbo and Iacobbo, p. 184. Interview with Freya Dinshah, May 11, 2006. Email from Freya Dinshah to the author dated August 16, 2006.
9. Interview with Alex Hershaft, May 5, 2006.
10. Finsen and Finsen, p. 61. Animal Welfare Institute.
11. Quoted on ThinkExist.Com at en.thinkexist.com/quotes/christine_stevens. Viewed on May 14, 2006.
12. Animal Welfare Institute website at www.awionline.org/aims.htm. Viewed on May 15, 2006.
13. Unti, pp. 2–3. The other three founders from AHA were Helen Jones, Larry Andrews, and Marcia Glaser (Unti, p. 3).
14. Unti, p. 105.
15. The most important exceptions to this rule were The Fund for Animals and Friends of Animals, both of which produced several leaders of the AR movement, including Wayne Pacelle, Michael Markarian, Heidi Prescott, Priscilla Feral, and Lee Hall. But these two groups transitioned

themselves into AR organizations that practiced and promoted vegetarianism, thereby providing a congenial home for AR activists.

16. Quoted in Guither, p. 42.
17. In describing the Grand Canyon burro rescue and the creation of Black Beauty Ranch, I have primarily drawn on Marshall, on conversations with Cleveland Amory, and on an email from Michael Markarian dated September 15, 2006.
18. The figure of 115,000,000 land animals and birds is based on statistics for the 2002–2003 hunting season provided to the Fund for Animals by state wildlife agencies and the U.S. Fish and Wildlife Service. No one keeps statistics on the number of fish caught by anglers, but the USFWS reports that in 2001, there were 37,000,000 anglers in the U.S. The 185,000,000 figure is based on a conservative estimate of five fish per angler per year. The actual number may be significantly higher. Most AR groups, including the Fund for Animals, have not campaigned against angling because they believe it would soak up scarce resources to little effect. PETA has campaigned against angling since the mid-'90s.
19. Figures published by the U.S. Fish and Wildlife Service in their *National Survey of Hunting, Fishing and Wildlife Related Reaction* indicate that hunted venison costs the hunter approximately twenty-one dollars a pound.
20. Email from Wayne Pacelle to the author dated August 11, 2006. Hunt sabotages had begun in England in the 1950s (see Chapter 16).
21. Interview with Heidi Prescott, May 4, 2006.

16: The Age of the Pioneers
1. Poole.
2. Ibid.
3. Interview with Kim Stallwood, May 18, 2006. Hollands, p. 169.
4. Interview with Kim Stallwood, May 18, 2006. Hollands, pp. 172–173.
5. Because it went into effect the following year, it is sometimes cited as The Hunting Act of 2005.
6. "Huntsman Guilty of Breaking Ban," posted August 4, 2006 on the BBC News website at news.bbc.co.uk/2/hi/uk_news/england/devon/5245458.stm. Viewed on August 18, 2006.
7. Free, "Ruth Harrison."
8. Quoted in Ryder, *Animal Revolution*, p. 5.
9. Ryder, *Animal Revolution*, p. 6.
10. Ryder, "All Beings That Feel Pain ... "
11. Apparently, its first inclusion in a formal publication was in Ryder's contribution to *Animals, Men and Morals* in 1971. Godlovitch et al., p. 81.

12. Ryder, *Animal Revolution*, p. 6. Jones.
13. Godlovitch et al., p. 7.
14. Ibid., p. 238. Italics in original.
15. Ryder, Singer, Clark, and Linzey went on to become leading figures in the animal rights movement. John Harris is reported to have abandoned philosophy to become a social worker. Stanley Godlovitch became a professor of philosophy but, as best I have been able to determine, did no further work on animal rights. Roslind and Stanley Godlovitch are said to have divorced. She dropped out of sight, and I have been unable to learn where she went or what she has done in later life.
16. An American edition did, in fact, appear, but it fared no better than the British prototype.
17. Singer, "Animal Liberation."
18. This description of the events leading to the publication of *Animal Liberation* is taken primarily from Singer, *Ethics into Action*.
19. Linzey, p. 57.
20. The description of Henry Spira's activities that follows is drawn primarily from Spira, "Fighting to Win"; Singer, *Ethics into Action*, pp. 54–74; and Markus, "Henry Spira."
21. Singer, *Ethics into Action*, pp. 45–47.
22. Spira, p. 196.
23. Ibid., pp. 195–196.
24. Markus
25. Amory, *The Compleat Cat*, pp. 60–61 (*The Cat Who Came for Christmas*).
26. Finsen and Finsen, p. 61. Italics in original.
27. Singer, *Ethics into Action*, p. 80.
28. Ibid., pp. 93–94.

17: The Sixties' Last Hurrah

1. Interview with Alex Hershaft, May 5, 2006.
2. Interview with Alex Hershaft, May 5, 2006. Email from Alex Hershaft to the author dated August 29, 2006.
3. Interview with Alex Hershaft, May 5, 2006.
4. Interview with Alex Hershaft, May 5, 2006. Email from Alex Hershaft to the author dated August 29, 2006.
5. Interview with George Cave, June 7, 2006.
6. Ibid.
7. Interview with George Cave, June 7, 2006. Interview with John Goodwin, June 9, 2006. Barker has donated large amounts of money to animal causes, and in 1988, just weeks before his appearance in the Fur Free Friday march, he quit as host of the Miss USA and Miss Universe

beauty pageants—which he had hosted for twenty-one years—because the sponsors insisted on including furs in the winners' prize packages. (Biographical sketch of Bob Barker on the website of CBS Television at www.cbs.com/daytime/price/about/bios/cast_bios_bbarker.shtml. Viewed on June 9, 2006.)

8.   Interview with George Cave, June 7, 2006.

9.   Finsen and Finsen, pp. 82–83.

10. Interview with Alex Hershaft, May 5, 2006. Patterson, pp. 144–145.

11. Address to the plenary session of the Animal Rights 2001 conference, Tyson's Corner, Virginia, July 1, 2001.

12. Interview with Alex Hershaft, May 5, 2006.

13. Ibid.

14. Ibid.

15. Interview with Alex Hershaft, May 5, 2006. FARM website at www.farmusa.org. Viewed on May 30, 2006.

16. *Arkangel*.

17. Information provided to the author by Ingrid Newkirk, August 25, 2006.

18. *Arkangel*. Capitals in original.

19. This biographical sketch of Ingrid Newkirk is drawn largely from Guillermo, pp. 34–36.

20. Pacheco with Francione, p. 135.

21. Watson, *Sea Shepherd*, pp. 220, 228–229.

22. This description of the Silver Spring monkeys case is largely drawn from Pacheco with Francione, Guillermo, and information provided to the author by Ingrid Newkirk, Kathy Snow Guillermo, and Rick Swain.

23. Pacheco with Francione, pp. 136–137.

24. Barnes, pp. 157–167.

25. Swain retired from the Montgomery County Police in 1996, and is now director of investigations for HSUS.

26. Newkirk, pp. 22–26.

27. Not long thereafter, Roger Galvin left the state's attorney's office to go into private practice in Montgomery County, where his practice included defending animal activists arrested in connection with demonstrations and hunt sabotages. He has also been active in the Animal Legal Defense Fund, an organization of attorneys working for animal protection founded in 1979 by Joyce Tischler.

28. This description of the Gennarelli campaign is based primarily on information provided by Ingrid Newkirk and Sharon Lawson, and on Finsen and Finsen, pp. 70–71.

29. Gennarelli eventually developed his scale. Known as the "Abbreviated Injury Scale," it is a widely accepted standard for categorizing the severity of traumatic bodily injury.

30. Quoted in Finsen and Finsen, p. 68.
31. The "hundredth monkey syndrome" was enjoying a fad then, and Newkirk hoped the image of 101 protestors would graphically symbolize the need for a new paradigm for our thinking about animals. Finsen and Finsen say "100" and then, a few lines down, "101" (p. 70), and contemporary press reports give varying estimates approximating 100, but in her comments to me on an early draft of this passage, Newkirk was quite clear that it was 101.
32. The NIH headquarters resembles a large university campus, criss-crossed with streets and sidewalks, with over three dozen buildings, including offices, laboratories, a hospital, libraries, open spaces with grass and trees, multiple parking lots, and a Metro station. Before 9/11, access was not restricted, there were several entrances to the campus, no passes were required except to enter certain buildings, primarily laboratories, and the entire campus was heavily trafficked, with people and cars coming and going at all hours of the day and night.
33. PETA website at www.peta.org/feat/annualreview05/numbers.asp. Viewed on July 14, 2006.
34. I attended the Hegins pigeon shoot with the Fund for Animals every year from 1989 on. This description of the Hegins pigeon shoot and the protests is based primarily on my own observations and interviews with Heidi Prescott (May 4, 2006), George Cave (June 7, 2006), and Steve Hindi (May 17 and August 17, 2006).
35. Interview with Steve Hindi, May 17, 2006.
36. Interview with Steve Hindi, August 17, 2006.
37. "Black bloc" usually refers to a march in which the participants dress in black and wear black ski masks or tie black bandanas over their faces for anonymity. The "black bloc" activists at Hegins dressed in black but did not cover their faces.
38. Peter Linck subsequently changed his name to Peter Gerard. (As a sign of their commitment to gender equality, he and his fiancée both changed their names to Gerard when they married.)

18: Direct Action: Striking Back on Land and Sea

1. Weyler, p. 1.
2. *Greenpeace I* was seized by the U.S. Coast Guard (and soon released, along with the crew, who paid a fine), but the test was delayed until November. Don't Make a Wave quickly chartered a second boat, which they called *Greenpeace Too*. But the Americans were expecting them, and conducted the test ahead of schedule, before *Greenpeace Too* could reach the site.

3.   In the mid-twentieth century, commercial whaling had gone industrial.
     To allow their ships to stay out longer and be more productive, the
     Soviets sent them in fleets consisting of several small killer ships, which
     did the actual hunting, and a much larger factory ship, which butchered
     the dead whales, extracted and stored the oil, and processed and froze
     the meat.
4.   Watson, "An Open Letter to the Norwegians," *Sea Shepherd* (p. 34), and
     Seal Wars (p. 61). In the "Letter," Watson dates this event to 1973.
     However, in both *Sea Shepherd* and *Seal Wars*, he dates it to 1975. 1975 is
     the correct date, as Weyler and other sources confirm.
5.   Friends of Animals, founded by Alice Herrington in 1957, was among
     the most active of the "transitional groups" that I have described above.
     Now headed by Priscilla Feral, it has itself transitioned into the leader of
     the "fundamentalist" school of animal rights that I describe in Chapters
     19 and 20.
6.   Brigitte Bardot is probably the francophone world's best-known animal
     advocate, both personally and through the Brigitte Bardot Foundation
     (*Fondation Brigitte Bardot* at www.fondationbrigittebardot.fr). She has
     done incalculable good work for animals. Unfortunately, she has closely
     identified herself with the xenophobic, quasi-fascist National Front
     party of Jean-Marie LePen, in which her husband, Bernard d'Ormale, is
     a leading figure.
7.   These incidents and others are described in Watson, *Seal Wars* and *Sea
     Shepherd*. The nearly fatal dunking and the hotel room assault were cap-
     tured on videotape and seen around the world.
8.   Watson, *Seal Wars*, pp. 104–106.
9.   This transaction has been described by both Amory and Watson.
     Amory, *Compleat Cat*, pp. 137–141 (*The Cat Who Came for Christmas*,
     Chapter 7). Watson, *Seal Wars*, pp. 111–112.
10. The description of the *Sierra* campaign is based on Watson, *Sea
     Shepherd*, pp. 207–251.
11. Manes, pp. 187–200.
12. Since the collapse of the Soviet Union, Russia has generally abided by
     the moratorium, although it engages in some whaling under an excep-
     tion for indigenous peoples.
13. "Japan Hits Out at 'Polarised' Whaling Council," *The Guardian*, June 16,
     2006.
14. "Whaling Views," BBC News website at news.bbc.co.uk. Viewed on June
     19, 2006.
15. Ibid.
16. "Japan Gains a Key Whaling Victory," BBC News website at

news.bbc.co.uk/2/hi/science/nature/5093350.stm. Viewed on June 19, 2006.

17. The Sea Shepherd Conservation Society website at www.seashepherd.org/seals. Viewed on October 19, 2006.

18. "EU Legislators Want Ban over Canada's Seal Hunt," Associated Press, September 6, 2006. See the CTV website at www.ctv.ca/servlet/ArticleNews/story/CTVNews/20060906/seal_hunt_europe_060906/20060906?hub=Canada. Viewed on September 16, 2006.

19. Molland, pp. 68–69. Stallwood, p. 82.

20. Molland, p. 69.

21. Ibid., p. 70.

22. Ibid., pp. 70–71.

23. Ibid., pp. 71–74.

24. Stallwood, pp. 83–84.

25. Interview with Kim Stallwood, May 18, 2006.

26. Ibid.

27. Quoted in Stallwood, p. 84.

28. Stallwood, pp. 84–85. Interview with Kim Stallwood, May 18, 2006.

29. "Escape of the Dolphins." Baer. Hoover.

30. Best and Nocella, p. 26. Finsen and Finsen, pp. 100–101.

31. Animal Liberation Front.

32. Guither, p. 221.

33. Newkirk, pp. 82–104.

34. Finsen and Finsen, pp. 103–104. "Blast from the Past."

35. Finsen and Finsen, p. 104. "Blast from the Past."

36. Coronado, "Direct Actions," p. 178.

37. "Notorious SAB." "Rod Coronado and Mott Crozier Found Guilty."

38. Department of Justice.

39. The original, and apparently still the legal, spelling of "Jonas" is "Kjonaas," pronounced "Jonas."

40. Jonas, p. 267.

41. Alleyne.

42. "Brian Cass" in *Wikipedia*. Viewed on July 5, 2006.

43. Quoted in Lewis 2004.

44. Ibid.

45. Hanley et al.

46. Kocieniewski and Schweber.

47. Interview with Steve Hindi, May 17, 2006.

48. Ibid.

49. "Hitting the Streets."

50. Coronado, "Message."

19: Things Fall Apart
1. "Animal Enterprise Protection Act of 1992."
2. Americans for Medical Progress.
3. Fur Information Council of America.
4. Lewis 2004.
5. "From Push to Shove."
6. Anti-Defamation League. Both the SPLC and the ADL began by performing an important function, the former tracking the Ku Klux Klan and other violent racist groups, and the latter tracking anti-Semitic activities. As those threats declined, however, both have striven to maintain their own importance by magnifying the threat represented by various groups at both ends of the political spectrum. Since 9/11, they have jumped on the "terrorism" bandwagon.
7. In the wake of the March's failure to attract large-scale participation, and the finger-pointing that followed, Peter Gerard left the animal rights movement. He has not been active since.

20: But the Center Takes Hold
1. Interview with Kim Stallwood, May 18, 2006.
2. Ibid.
3. Interview with Steve Hindi, May 17, 2006.
4. Ibid.
5. Ibid. A "contest kill" is a competition in which the entrant who kills the most animals in a specified period of time wins a prize. Prairie dogs, coyotes, crows, and pigeons are popular victims in contest kills.
6. Interview with Steve Hindi, May 17, 2006.
7. "COK Talks with ... Patty Mark." On one occasion, Mark spent 10 days in jail, and on another, 5 days.
8. I was a participant in the conference, and this description is based primarily on my recollections. See also the website of United Poultry Concerns at upc-online.org/fall99/upc_daa_forum_pics.html and upc-online.org/99daa_review.html. Viewed on August 3, 2006.
9. Interview with Freeman Wicklund, August 3, 2006.
10. Interview with Paul Shapiro, May 30, 2006.
11. Ibid.
12. Park, pp. 174–179. Interview with Paul Shapiro, May 30, 2006.
13. Park, pp. 179–180.
14. Interview with Paul Shapiro, May 30, 2006.
15. Interview with Steve Hindi, May 17, 2006.
16. Interview with Bruce Friedrich, May 7, 2006. *Meet Your Meat* can be viewed on the PETA website at www.meat.com. Viewed on July 26, 2006.

17. Email from Bruce Friedrich, August 24, 2006.
18. Interview with Gene Baur, August 3, 2006. When they married, Gene and Lorri combined their last names to form "Bauston." Since they separated in 2005, Gene has resumed the use of his birth name, Baur. Lorri continues to use Bauston. Farm Sanctuary is now run by Gene Baur. In October 2005, Lorri Bauston founded Animal Acres, a sanctuary/advocacy group located north of Los Angeles, near Palmdale, California.
19. Interview with Gene Baur, August 3, 2006. Farm Sanctuary website at www.farmsanctuary.org/about/index.htm. Viewed on August 3, 2006.
20. Interview with Karen Davis, May 13, 2006.
21. Interview with Bruce Friedrich, May 7, 2006.
22. Ibid.
23. "Restaurant Outreach Program" on the Compassion Over Killing website at www.cok.net/camp/rest. Viewed on July 29, 2006.
24. Humane Society of the United States (HSUS) website at www.hsus.org/farm_animals/factory_farms/the_hen_factory_farm/no_battery_eggs.html. Viewed on July 30, 2006. Email from Paul Shapiro dated September 9, 2006.
25. HSUS website at www.hsus.org/farm/humaneeating/rrr.html. Viewed on July 30, 2006.
26. Interview with Paul Shapiro, May 30, 2006.

Selected Bibliography

Adams, Carol J. *The Sexual Politics of Meat: A Feminist-Vegetarian Critical Theory*. New York: Continuum, 2000.

Akaranga Sutra [Acharanga Sutra]. On The Internet Sacred Text Archive website at www.sacred-texts.com/jai/akaranga.htm. Viewed on October 15, 2005.

Akers, Keith. "Truth Force and Vegetarianism." At www.compassionatespirit.com/gandhi.htm. Viewed on April 17, 2006.

———. *The Lost Religion of Jesus: Simple Living and Nonviolence in Early Christianity*. New York: Lantern Books, 2000.

———. *A Vegetarian Sourcebook: The Nutrition, Ecology, and Ethics of a Natural Foods Diet*. Denver: The Vegetarian Press, 1983.

Alleyne, Richard. "Terror Tactics That Brought a Company to Its Knees." *The Daily Telegraph*, January 19, 2001. See www.telegraph.co.uk/news/main.jhtml?xml=/news/2001/01/19/ncam119.xml. Viewed on July 1, 2006.

American Humane. "Beginning of a Movement." At www.americanhumane.org/site/PageServer?pagename=wh_mission_farm_animals. Viewed on April 1, 2006.

———. "How American Humane Began." At www.americanhumane.org/site/PageServer?pagename=wh_mission_history. Viewed on April 1, 2006.

———. "Farm Animals." At www.americanhumane.org/site/PageServer?pagename=pa_farm_animals. Viewed on April 30, 2006.

American Vegan Society. "History." At www.americanvegan.org/history.htm. Viewed on May 10, 2006.

Americans for Medical Progress website. At www.amprogress.org/site/c.jrLUK0PDLoF/b.933817/k.D675/OVERVIEW.htm. Viewed on July 10, 2006.

Amory, Cleveland. *Ranch of Dreams: The Heartwarming Story of America's Most Unusual Animal Sanctuary*. New York: Viking, 1997.

———. *Cleveland Amory's Compleat Cat*. New York: Black Dog and Leventhal, 1987, 1990, 1993. (Amory's three most popular books: *The Cat Who*

Came for Christmas, The Cat and the Curmudgeon, and *The Best Cat Ever,* in a single volume.)

———. *Mankind? Our Incredible War on Wildlife.* New York: Harper and Row, 1974.

"The Animal Enterprise Protection Act of 1992—Public Law 102-346, August 26, 1992." On the website of the U.S. Dept. of Agriculture at www.nal.usda.gov/awic/legislat/pl102346.htm. Viewed on July 10, 2006.

Animal Liberation Front. "History of the Animal Liberation Front." At http://animalliberationfront.com/ALFront/Premise_History/ALF_ History.htm. Viewed on June 29, 2006.

Animal Welfare Institute. "Animals Worldwide Lose Their Strongest Advocate." At www.awionline.org/cs/release.htm. Viewed on May 14, 2006.

Anti-Defamation League, Law Enforcement Agency Resource Network. "Ecoterrorism: Extremism in the Animal Rights and Environmentalist Movements." At www.adl.org/learn/ext_us/Ecoterrorism.asp?LEARN_Cat=Extremism& LEARN_SubCat=Extremism_in_America&xpicked=4&item=eco. Viewed on July 10, 2006.

Aquinas, Thomas. *Summa Theologica.* On the New Advent website at www.newadvent.org/summa. Viewed on August 6, 2005.

Aristotle. *Politics.* Translated by Ernest Barker. Oxford: Oxford University Press, 1998.

Arkangel for Animal Liberation. "Voice of the Voiceless" (interview with Ingrid Newkirk). At www.arkangelweb.org/interviews/ingridnewkirk.php. Viewed on May 31, 2006.

"Arms and Armour, History of." On the HistoryWorld website at www.historyworld.net/wrldhis/PlainTextHistories.asp?historyid=aa89.

Augustine. *The City of God.* Translated by Henry Bettenson. London: Penguin Books, 2003.

———. *On Christian Teaching.* Translated by R. P. H. Green. Oxford: Oxford University Press, 1999.

Baer, Andrea. "Born Free: Maui Confronts the Thorny Issue of Dolphins in Captivity." *The Honolulu Weekly,* November 14, 2001. See www.honoluluweekly.com/archives/coverstory%202001/11-14-01%20Dolphin/11-14-01%20Dolphin.html. Viewed on June 29, 2006.

Barnes, Donald J. "A Matter of Change." In *In Defense of Animals,* edited by Peter Singer. New York: Harper and Row, 1985.

Beers, Diane L. *For the Prevention of Cruelty: The History and Legacy of Animal Rights Activism in the United States.* Athens, Ohio: Swallow Press/Ohio University Press, 2006.

Bentham, Jeremy. *The Principles of Morals and Legislation.* New York: Hafner Press, 1948. (Originally printed in 1780 and first published in 1789.)

Berry, Rynn. *Food for the Gods: Vegetarianism in the World's Religions.* New York: Pythagorean Publishers, 1998.

Best, Steven, and Anthony J. Nocella II, editors. *Terrorists or Freedom Fighters? Reflections on the Liberation of Animals.* New York: Lantern Books, 2004.

"Blast from the Past—'80s Lab Raids." *No Compromise,* Issue 15. See www.nocompromise.org/issues/15blast_past.html. Viewed on June 30, 2006.

Bonaventure. *The Soul's Journey into God; The Tree of Life; The Life of St. Francis.* Mahwah, New Jersey: Paulist Press, 1978.

Bulliet, Richard W. *Hunters, Herders, and Hamburgers: The Past and Future of Human-Animal Relationships.* New York: Columbia University Press, 2005.

Carloff, Andy. "Henry Stephens Salt." At www.punkerslut.com/articles/henrystephenssalt.html. Viewed on April 17, 2006.

Cartmill, Matt. *A View to a Death in the Morning: Hunting and Nature through History.* Cambridge, Massachusetts: Harvard University Press, 1993.

Catechism of the Catholic Church with Modifications from the Editio Typica. New York: Doubleday, 1995.

The Catholic Encyclopedia (1914 edition). On the New Advent website at www.newadvent.org/cathen. Viewed on August 7, 2005.

U. S. Census Bureau. "Historical Estimates of World Population." At www.census.gov/ipc/www/worldhis.html. Viewed on November 24, 2005.

Chapple, Christopher Key. *Nonviolence to Animals, Earth, and Self in Asian Traditions.* Albany, New York: State University of New York Press, 1993.

Charles, Dan. "The Tragedy of Fritz Haber." Broadcast over National Public Radio on July 11, 2002. See www.npr.org/programs/morning/features/2002/jul/fritzhaber/. Viewed on May 1, 2006.

Clarke, Paul A. B., and Andrew Linzey, editors. *Political Theory and Animal Rights.* London: Pluto Press, 1990.

"Closing in on Polio." *Time* magazine, March 29, 1954.

"COK Talks with Open Rescue Pioneer Patty Mark." *The Abolitionist,* Issue 14, Winter-Spring 2003.

Collins, Lauren. "The Talk of the Town—Municipal Velvet." *The New Yorker,* January 16, 2006. See www.newyorker.com/talk/content/articles/060116ta_talk_collins. Viewed on January 9, 2006.

Coronado, Rod. "Direct Actions Speak Louder Than Words." In *Terrorists or Freedom Fighters? Reflections on the Liberation of Animals,* Steven Best and Anthony J. Nocella II, editors. New York: Lantern Books, 2004.

——. "Message from Rod Coronado in Prison." At http://supportrod.org/update.php?u=20060901. Viewed on September 16, 2006.

Darwin, Charles. *The Expression of the Emotions in Man and in Animals* (1872). Reprinted in *From So Simple a Beginning: The Four Great Books of Charles Darwin*, edited and with an introduction by Edward O. Wilson. New York and London: W. W. Norton and Co., 2006.

Davis, John. "The Origins of the 'Vegetarians.' On the website of the International Vegetarian Union at www.ivu.org/history/societies/vegsoc-origins.html. Viewed on April 10, 2006.

Davis, Karen. *Prisoned Chickens, Poisoned Eggs: An Inside Look at the Modern Poultry Industry.* Summertown, Tennessee: Book Publishing Company, 1997.

Department of Justice. "Self-Proclaimed Member of the Earth Liberation Front Charged with Demonstrating the Use of a Destructive Device." Press release dated February 22, 2006. On the website of the San Diego Office of the Federal Bureau of Investigation, at http://sandiego.fbi.gov/dojpressrel/press-rel06/sd022206.htm. Viewed on July 5, 2006.

Descartes, René. *Discourse on the Method of Rightly Conducting the Reason, and Seeking Truth in the Sciences.* On the website of Literature.Org, the Online Literature Library, at www.literature.org/authors/descartes-rene/reason-discourse. Viewed on September 16, 2005.

The Dhammapada: The Path of Perfection. Translated from the Pali with an Introduction by Juan Mascaro. London: Penguin Books, 1973.

Diamond, Jared. *Guns, Germs, and Steel: The Fates of Human Societies.* New York: W. W. Norton and Company, 1999.

Dinshah, Freya. "Compassion and Community," unpublished notes on the life and work of H. Jay Dinshah.

Dinshah, H. Jay. *Out of the Jungle: The Way of Dynamic Harmlessness.* Malaga, New Jersey: The American Vegan Society, 1995. (Originally published 1967.)

——, editor. *Here's Harmlessness: An Anthology of Ahimsa.* Malaga, New Jersey: The American Vegan Society, 1993. (First edition published 1964.)

Dracker, Prune. "ASPCA History: Regarding Henry." *Animal Watch* (the journal of the ASPCA), Spring 1996. Updated version on the ASPCA website at www.aspca.org/site/PageServer?pagename=about_history. Viewed on December 10, 2005.

Ellison, Ralph. *Invisible Man.* New York: Vintage Books, 1995. (Originally published 1952.)

"Escape of the Dolphins." In *Time* magazine, June 18, 1977. See http://jcgi.pathfinder.com/time/archive/preview/0,10987,915120,00.html. Viewed on June 29, 2006.

Finsen, Lawrence, and Susan Finsen. *The Animal Rights Movement in America: From Compassion to Respect.* New York: Twayne Publishers, 1994.

Francione, Gary L. *Rain without Thunder: The Ideology of the Animal Rights Movement.* Philadelphia: Temple University Press, 1996.

——. *Introduction to Animal Rights: Your Child or the Dog?* Philadelphia: Temple University Press, 2000.

Franklin, Benjamin. *The Autobiography of Benjamin Franklin.* At www.totse.com/en/ego/literary_genius/bfaut10.html. Viewed on October 29, 2005.

Free, Ann Cottrell, editor. *Animals, Nature, and Albert Schweitzer.* Washington, D.C.: The Flying Fox Press, 1988.

——. "Ruth Harrison: A Tribute." *Animal Welfare Institute Quarterly*, Fall 2000, Volume 49, No. 4. See www.awionline.org/pubs/Quarterly/fall00/f00harrison.htm. Viewed on May 5, 2006.

"From Push to Shove: Radical Environmental and Animal Rights Groups Have Always Drawn the Line at Targeting Humans. Not Anymore." On the website of the Southern Poverty Law Center at www.splcenter.org/intel/intelreport/article.jsp?aid=42. Viewed on July 10, 2006.

Fruitlands Museum website. At www.fruitlands.org/overview.php. Viewed on April 12, 2006.

Fur Information Council of America website. At www.fur.org/poen_faqs.cfm. Viewed on July 10, 2006.

Gaffney, James. "The Relevance of Animal Experimentation to Roman Catholic Ethical Methodology." In *Animal Sacrifices: Religious Perspectives on the Use of Animals in Science,*" edited by Tom Regan. Philadelphia: Temple University Press, 1986.

"Gains against Shelter Killing Come Hard in the Gulf States, West, and Midwest." *Animal People*, Vol. XVI, No. 6, July/August 2006.

Gandhi, Mohandas K. *Autobiography: The Story of My Experiments with Truth.* Mineola, New York: Dover Publications, 1983.

——. "The Moral Basis of Vegetarianism." On the website of the International Vegetarian Union at www.ivu.org/news/evu/other/gandhi2.html. Viewed on April 18, 2006.

Germonotta, Tony. "PETA President Condemns Dumping, Defends Euthanizing Animals." *The Virginian-Pilot* (Hampton Roads, VA), June 18, 2005. See http://home.hamptonroads.com/stories/story.cfm?story=87978&ran=1191 83&tref=po. Viewed on December 24, 2005.

Giehl, Dudley. *Vegetarianism: A Way of Life.* New York: Barnes and Noble, 1979.

Glen, Samantha. *Best Friends: The True Story of the World's Most Beloved Animal Sanctuary.* New York: Kensington Books, 2001.

Godlovitch, Stanley, Roslind Godlovitch, and John Harris, editors. *Animals, Men and Morals: An Inquiry into the Maltreatment of Non-humans.* New York: Grove Press, undated. (Originally published 1971.)

Goldsworthy, Adrian. *Roman Warfare.* London: Smithsonian Books, HarperCollins, 2000.

Gompertz, Lewis. *Moral Inquiries on the Situation of Man and of Brutes.* Fontwell, Sussex: Centaur Press, 1992. (Originally published 1824.)

Goodall, Jane. *Harvest for Hope: A Guide to Mindful Eating.* New York: Time Warner Book Group, 2005.

"Great Humanitarian." Unattributed review of *Angel in Top Hat* by Zulma Steele. In *Time* magazine, November 30, 1942. See http://time-proxy.yaga.com/time/archive/preview/0,10987,766720,00.html. Viewed on December 10, 2005.

Guarnieri, Patrizia. "Moritz Schiff (1823–96): Experimental Physiology and Noble Sentiment in Florence." In *Vivisection in Historical Perspective,* Nicolaas A. Rupke, editor. London and New York: Routledge, 1987.

Guerrini, Anita. *Experimenting with Humans and Animals: From Galen to Animal Rights.* Baltimore: The Johns Hopkins University Press, 2003.

Guillermo, Kathy Snow. *Monkey Business: The Disturbing Case That Launched the Animal Rights Movement.* Washington, D.C.: National Press Books, 1993.

Guither, Harold D. *Animal Rights: History and Scope of a Radical Social Movement.* Carbondale and Edwardsville, Illinois: Southern Illinois University Press, 1998.

Guthrie, Kenneth Sylvan, and David Fideler. *The Pythagorean Sourcebook and Library: An Anthology of Ancient Writings Which Relate to Pythagoras and Pythagorean Philosophy.* Grand Rapids, Michigan: Phanes Press, 1988.

Hagenmayer, S. Joseph. "Jay Dinshah, 66, American Vegan Society Leader." *The Philadelphia Inquirer,* June 15, 2000. On the website of the International Vegetarian Union at www.ivu.org/news/oct2000/dinshah.html. Viewed on May 10, 2006.

Hanley, Robert, Janon Fisher, and Stacy Albin. "Seven Animal Rights Activists Arrested." *The New York Times,* May 27, 2004. See http://select.nytimes.com/search/restricted/article?res=FA0C14FE385A0 C748EDDAC0894DC404482. Viewed on July 5, 2006.

Harlow, Harry F. "The Nature of Love." *American Psychologist,* 13: 573–685. See http://psychclassics.yorku.ca/Harlow/love.htm. Viewed on February 5, 2006.

Hart, Donna, and Robert W. Sussman. *Man the Hunted: Primates, Predators, and Human Evolution.* Cambridge, Massachusetts: Westview Press, 2005.

Hesiod. *Theogony, Works and Days.* Translated by M. L. West. Oxford: Oxford University Press, 1999.

"Hitting the Streets: The *Satya* Interview with Eddie Lama." *Satya* magazine, August 2005. See www.satyamag.com/aug05/lama.html. Viewed on July 26, 2006.

Hoch, David. "Animal Rights and the Law: Readings 6." At http://bear.cba.ufl.edu/hoch/animallaw/readings_6.htm. Viewed on September 17, 2005.

Hollands, Clive. "Animal Rights in the Political Arena." In *In Defense of Animals*, Peter Singer, editor. New York: Harper and Row, 1986.

Hoover, Will. "Activists Protest UH Dolphin Lab." *The Honolulu Advertiser*, June 2, 2002. See http://the.honoluluadvertiser.com/article/2002/Jun/02/ln/ln18a.html. Viewed on June 29, 2006.

"Horses in World War I." Unattributed. At www.historylearningsite.co.uk/horses_in_world_war_one.htm.

"HSUS Pet Overpopulation Estimates." On the website of the Humane Society of the United States at www.hsus.org/pets/issues_affecting_our_pets/pet_overpopulation_and_ownership_statistics/hsus_pet_overpopulation_estimates.html. Viewed on December 24, 2005.

"HSUS Pet Ownership Statistics." On HSUS website at www.hsus.org/pets/issues_affecting_our_pets/pet_overpopulation_and_ownership_statistics/us_pet_ownership_statistics.html. Viewed on December 24, 2005.

Huff, Peter A. "Calvin and the Beasts: Animals in John Calvin's Theological Discourse." *Journal of the Evangelical Theological Society*, Vol. 42, No. 1, March 1999. See www.etsjets.org/jets/42/42-1pp067-075_JETS.pdf. Viewed on August 9, 2005.

Huffman, Carl. "Alcmaeon." In *The Stanford Encyclopedia of Philosophy (Summer 2004 Edition)*, Edward N. Zalta, editor. See http://plato.stanford.edu/archives/sum2004/entries/alcmaeon. Viewed on January 21, 2006.

Huntingdon Life Sciences website. At www.huntingdon.com/index.php?currentNumber=0&currentIsExpanded=0. Viewed on July 1, 2006.

Hyland, J. R. *God's Covenant with Animals: A Biblical Case for the Humane Treatment of All Creatures*. New York: Lantern Books, 2000.

Iacobbo, Karen, and Michael Iacobbo. *Vegetarian America: A History*. Westport, Connecticut: Praeger Publishers, 2004.

"Intake and Outcome Report." On the website of Animal Care and Control of New York City at www.nycacc.org/site/c.ikLTJ9MUKtH/b.574805/k.B099/Our_Statistics.htm. Viewed on December 11, 2005.

International Vegetarian Union. "The Vegetarian Society of the UK: 150 Years in the Forefront of Vegetarian Campaigning." At www.ivu.org/news/3-98/vegsocuk.html. Viewed on April 15, 2006.

———. "Henry S. Salt: Extracts from Books and Articles." At www.ivu.org/history/salt/texts.html. Viewed on April 17, 2006.

344   THE LONGEST STRUGGLE

Jasper, James M., and Dorothy Nelkin. *The Animal Rights Crusade: The Growth of a Moral Protest*. New York: The Free Press, 1992.

Jonas, Kevin. "Bricks and Bullhorns." In *Terrorists or Freedom Fighters? Reflections on the Liberation of Animals,* Steven Best and Anthony J. Nocella, II, editors. New York: Lantern Books, 2004.

Jones, Margery. "History of Oxford Vegetarians." On the website of the International Vegetarian Union at www.ivu.org/oxveg/AboutOV/history.html. Viewed on May 17, 2006.

Kalechofsky, Roberta, editor. *Judaism and Animal Rights: Classical and Contemporary Responses*. Marblehead, Massachusetts: Micah Publications, 1992.

Kant, Immanuel. *Lectures on Ethics*. Translated by Louis Infield. Indianapolis, Indiana: Hackett Publishing Company, 1963.

Kean, Hilda. "An Exploration of the Sculptures of Greyfriars Bobby, Edinburgh, Scotland, and the Brown Dog, Battersea, London." *Society and Animals*, Volume 11, Number 4, 2003. On the website of the Society and Animals Forum at www.psyeta.org/sa/sa11.4/kean.shtml. Viewed on March 29, 2006.

Keddie, Grant. "The Atlatl Weapon." On the website of the Royal British Columbia Museum, www.royalbcmuseum.bc.ca/hhistory/atlatl/atlatl.html.

Klinkenborg, Verlyn. "Appreciations: Adwaitya." *The New York Times,* March 28, 2006. See http://select.nytimes.com/search/restricted/article?res=F20A10F93F540C7B8EDDAA0894DE404482. Viewed on April 10, 2006.

Kocieniewski, David, and Nate Schweber. "Six Animal Rights Advocates Are Convicted of Terrorism." *The New York Times,* March 3, 2006. See http://select.nytimes.com/search/restricted/article?res=FA0B13F73C550C708CDDAA0894DE404482. Viewed on July 5, 2006.

Lemaire, Jean-François. "François Magendie." On the website of the French Ministry of Culture at www.culture.gouv.fr/culture/actualites/celebrations2005/magendie.htm. Viewed on January 14, 2006.

Levine-Gronningsater, Anna. "Case of Cruelty or Compassion?" *The Christian Science Monitor,* July 25, 2005. See www.csmonitor.com/2005/0725/p11s02-lire.html. Viewed on December 24, 2005.

Lewis, John E. "Statement of John E. Lewis, Deputy Assistant Director, Counterterrorism Division, Federal Bureau of Investigation, Before the Senate Judiciary Committee, May 18, 2004." On the website of the Federal Bureau of Investigation at www.fbi.gov/congress/congress04/lewis051804.htm.Viewed on July 5, 2006.

Li, Chien-hui. "A Union of Christianity, Humanity, and Philanthropy: The

Christian Tradition and the Prevention of Cruelty to Animals in Nineteenth Century England." *Society and Animals: Journal of Human-Animal Studies,* Volume 8, Number 3, 2000. On the website of the Society and Animals Forum at www.psyeta.org/sa/sa8.3/chien.shtml. Viewed on November 11, 2005.

Linzey, Andrew. *Animal Theology.* Urbana, Illinois: University of Illinois Press, 1995.

Manes, Christopher. *Green Rage: Radical Environmentalism and the Unmaking of Civilization.* Boston: Little, Brown and Company, 1990.

Markus, Erik. "Henry Spira: The Veg.com Interview." At www.vegan.com/issues/1998/sep98/spira.htm. Viewed on May 21, 2006.

Marshall, Julie Hoffman. *Making Burros Fly: Cleveland Amory, Animal Rescue Pioneer.* Boulder: Johnson Books, 2006.

Mason, Jim, and Peter Singer. *Animal Factories* (revised and updated). New York: Harmony Books, 1990.

The Massachusetts Body of Liberties. On the website of Bartleby.Com, Great Books Online, at www.bartleby.com/43/8.html. Viewed on October 4, 2005.

Massachusetts Society for the Prevention of Cruelty to Animals. "History of the MSPCA-Angell: MSPCA Historical Timeline." On the MSPCA website at www.mspca.org/site/pp.asp?c=gtIUK4OSG&b=126831. Viewed on May 13, 2006.

Masson, Jeffrey Moussaieff. *The Pig Who Sang to the Moon: The Emotional World of Farm Animals.* New York: Ballantine Books, 2003.

Merton, Thomas, editor. *Gandhi on Non-Violence: A Selection of the Writings of Mahatma Gandhi.* New York: New Directions Publishing, 1965.

Miserandino, Dominick A. "Greek, Dr. Ray—Author of *Sacred Cows and Golden Geese.*" On the Celebrity Café website at www.thecelebritycafe.com/interviews/dr_ray_greek.html. Viewed on September 14, 2005.

Molland, Noel. "Thirty Years of Direct Action." In *Terrorists or Freedom Fighters? Reflections on the Liberation of Animals,* Steven Best and Anthony J. Nocella, II, editors. New York: Lantern Books, 2004.

Montaigne, Michel de. *The Complete Essays.* Translated by M. A. Screech. London: Penguin Books, 1991.

Moran, Victoria. *Compassion, the Ultimate Ethic: An Exploration of Veganism.* Wellington, Northhamptonshire, UK, 1985.

Mountain, Michael. "To Kill or Not to Kill." On the Best Friends Animal Sanctuary website at www.bestfriends.org/nomorehomelesspets/resourcelibrary/tokillnot.cfm. Viewed on December 16, 2005.

National Council on Pet Population Study and Policy. "The Shelter Statistics Survey: 1994–1997." At www.petpopulation.org/statsurvey.html. Viewed on December 17, 2005.

The New American Standard Bible, Updated Edition. La Habra, California: The Lockman Foundation; Eugene, Oregon: Precept Ministries International and Harvest House Publishers, 2000.

Newkirk, Ingrid. *Free the Animals! The Untold Story of the U.S. Animal Liberation Front and Its Founder, "Valerie."* Chicago: The Noble Press, 1992.

"Notorious SAB." *EarthFirst! Journal,* Volume 24, No. 5, Lughnasadh [August] 2004. See www.earthfirstjournal.org/articles.php?a=830. Viewed on July 5, 2006.

Orwell, George. *Animal Farm.* New York: Alfred A. Knopf, 1993.

Oshinsky, David M. *Polio: An American Story.* New York: Oxford University Press, 2005.

Ovid. *Metamorphoses.* Translated by Mary M. Innes. London: Penguin Books, 1955.

Pacheco, Alex, with Anna Francione. "The Silver Spring Monkeys." In *In Defense of Animals,* edited by Peter Singer. New York: Harper and Row, 1985.

Park, Miyun. "Opening Cages, Opening Eyes: An Investigation and Open Rescue at an Egg Factory Farm." In *In Defense of Animals: The Second Wave,* edited by Peter Singer. Oxford: Blackwell Publishing, Ltd., 2006.

Patterson, Charles. *Eternal Treblinka: Our Treatment of Animals and the Holocaust.* New York: Lantern Books, 2002.

Pennsylvania Society for the Prevention of Cruelty to Animals (PSPCA) website. At www.pspca.org/engine.asp?deva=AboutUs.History. Viewed on December 10, 2005.

Phelps, Norm. *The Great Compassion: Buddhism and Animal Rights.* New York: Lantern Books, 2004.

———. *The Dominion of Love: Animal Rights According to the Bible.* New York: Lantern Books, 2002.

Plato. *The Last Days of Socrates: Euthyphro, Apology, Crito, Phaedo.* Translated by Hugh Tredennik and Harold Tarrant. London: Penguin Books, 1993.

Plutarch. *Moralia: Volume XII.* Translated by Harold Cherniss and William C. Helmbold. Cambridge, Massachusetts: Harvard University Press, 1957.

Poole, Steve. "The History of the Hunt Saboteurs Association: Part I." On the website of the Hunt Saboteurs Association at http://hsa.enviroweb.org/features/hist1.html. Viewed on May 29, 2006.

Porphyry. *On Abstinence from Animal Food.* On the ThriceHoly.Net website at http://thriceholy.net/Texts/Porphyry.html. Viewed on October 15, 2005.

Primatt, Humphrey. *The Duty of Mercy and the Sin of Cruelty to Brute Animals.* Edited by Richard D. Ryder. Fontwell, Sussex: Centaur Press, 1992. (Originally published 1776.)

Pulford, Cedric. "Debate Continues on Incorporating Animal Sacrifices in Worship." *Christianity Today,* Week of October 23, 2000. See www.christianitytoday.com/ct/2000/143/34.0.html. Viewed on January 17, 2006.

Rawls, John. *A Theory of Justice, revised edition.* Cambridge, Massachusetts: The Belknap Press of Harvard University Press, 1999.

Regan, Tom. *The Case for Animal Rights, updated with a new preface.* Berkeley and Los Angeles: University of California Press, 2004.

——. *Empty Cages: Facing the Challenge of Animal Rights.* Lanham, Maryland: Rowman and Littlefield Publishers, Inc., 2004.

——, editor. *Animal Sacrifices: Religious Perspectives on the Use of Animals in Science.* Philadelphia: Temple University Press, 1986.

Regenstein, Lewis G. *Replenish the Earth: A History of Organized Religion's Treatment of Animals and Nature.* New York: The Crossroad Publishing Company, 1991.

Rifkin, Jeremy. *Beyond Beef: The Rise and Fall of the Cattle Culture.* New York: Dutton, 1992.

——. *The European Dream: How Europe's Vision of the Future Is Quietly Eclipsing the American Dream.* New York: Tarcher/Penguin, 2004.

The Rig Veda: an Anthology. Translated by Wendy Doniger. London: Penguin Books, 1981.

"Rod Coronado and Mott Crozier Found Guilty." On the Guerrilla News Network website at http://harmony.gnn.tv/blogs/11367/rod_coronado_and_mott_crozier_found_guilty. Posted December 13, 2005.

Rousseau, Jean-Jacques. *Emile.* Translated by Barbara Foxley. London: Everyman, 1993.

——. *The Social Contract and Discourses.* Translated by G. D. H. Cole. London: Everyman, 1993.

Royal Society for the Prevention of Cruelty to Animals. "About the RSPCA—History." At www.rspca.org.uk/servlet/Satellite?pagename=RSPCA/RSPCARedirect&pg=about_the_rspca&marker=1&articleId=996827934749. Viewed on November 9, 2005.

——. *The History of the RSPCA.* On the website of the Animal Legal and Historical Center of the Michigan State University College of Law, at www.animallaw.info/historical/articles/arukrspcahist.htm. Viewed on November 7, 2005.

Ryder, Richard D. *Animal Revolution: Changing Attitudes toward Speciesism.* Oxford: Berg, 2000.

———. *Victims of Science: The Use of Animals in Research,* revised edition. London: National Anti-Vivisection Society Limited, 1983.

———. *Painism: A Modern Morality.* London: Centaur Press, 2001.

———. "All Beings That Feel Pain Deserve Human Rights." *The Guardian,* August 6, 2005. See www.guardian.co.uk/animalrights/story/0,11917,1543799,00.html. Viewed on May 16, 2006.

Salt, Henry S. *Animals' Rights Considered in Relation to Social Progress.* Clarks Summit, Pennsylvania: Society for Animal Rights, Inc., 1980. (Originally published 1892.)

"San Francisco Animal Care and Control." On the website of the San Francisco city government at www.sfgov.org/site/acc_page.asp?id=6656. Viewed on December 23, 2005.

Sanderson, Robert. "History of the Longbow." At www.o-r-g.org/~azaroth/university/longbow.html.

Sannuti, Arun M. "Vegetarianism: The Road to Satyagraha." On the website of the International Vegetarian Union at www.ivu.org/history/gandhi/road.html. Viewed on April 18, 2006.

Saunders, Angela. *"O Unnatural Murderer!" Vegetarian Trends in 18th-Century Europe and America.* Paper presented October 14, 2001 to the Culinary Historians of Washington, D.C. See www.chowdc.org/Papers/Saunders%202001.html. Viewed on September 22, 2005.

Schopenhauer, Arthur. *The Basis of Morality.* Mineola, New York: Dover Publications, 2005.

Schultheis, Erin. "Harry F. Harlow." On the website of Muskingum College at www.muskingum.edu/~psych/psycweb/history/harlow.htm. Viewed on February 6, 2006.

Schweitzer, Albert. *The Philosophy of Civilization.* Translated by C. T. Campion. Amherst, New York: Prometheus Books, 1987.

———. *Out of My Life and Thought.* Translated by C. T. Campion. New York: Holt, Rinehart, and Winston, 1949.

Scruton, Roger. "Animal Rights." *City Journal,* Summer 2000. See www.city-journal.org/html/10_3_urbanities-animal.html. Viewed on October 2, 2005.

Scully, Matthew. *Dominion: The Power of Man, the Suffering of Animals, and the Call to Mercy.* New York: St. Martin's Press, 2002.

Sebo, Jeff. "A Critique of Kantian Theory of Indirect Moral Duties to Animals." *Animal Liberation Philosophy and Policy Journal,* Center on Animal Liberation Affairs, Dr. Steve Best, Chief Editor; Volume II, Issue 2. See www.cala-online.org/Journal/Issue3/A%20Critique%20of%20the%20Kantian%20Theory.htm#author. Viewed on October 7, 2005.

Shah, Previn K. "Jain Ethics: The Twelve Vows of the Layperson." At
    www.sacred-texts.com/jai/12vows.txt. Viewed on October 16, 2005.
Shelley, Mary. *Frankenstein, or the Modern Prometheus.* New York: Pocket
    Books (Simon and Schuster), 2004.
Shelley, Percy. "A Vindication of Natural Diet." On the VegInfo website at
    www.veginfo.dk/eng/texts/shelley1.html. Viewed on October 30, 2005.
Sinclair, Upton. *The Jungle.* Urbana and Chicago: University of Illinois Press,
    1988. (Originally published 1906.)
Singer, Peter. *Animal Liberation,* Second Edition. New York: The New York
    Review of Books, 1990. (First edition published 1975.)
———. *Ethics into Action: Henry Spira and the Animal Rights Movement.*
    Lanham, Maryland: Rowman and Littlefield Publishers, Inc., 1998.
———. "Animal Liberation." *The New York Review of Books,* Volume 20,
    Number 5, April 5, 1973.
———. *Practical Ethics,* Second Edition. Cambridge, UK: Cambridge University
    Press, 1993.
Slater, Lauren. "Monkey Love." *The Boston Globe,* March 21, 2004. See
    www.boston.com/news/globe/ideas/articles/2004/03/21/monkey_love/.
    Viewed on February 5, 2006.
Société Protectrice des Animaux website. www.spa.asso.fr/association/his-
    toirc.asp. Viewed on December 10, 2005.
Sorabji, Richard. *Animal Minds and Human Morals: The Origins of the
    Western Debate.* Ithaca, New York: Cornell University Press, 1993.
Spencer, Colin. *The Heretic's Feast: A History of Vegetarianism.* Hanover, New
    Hampshire: University Press of New England, 1995.
Spira, Henry. "Fighting to Win." In *In Defense of Animals,* edited by Peter
    Singer. New York: Harper and Row, 1985.
Stallwood, Kim. "A Personal Overview of Direct Action in the United
    Kingdom and the United States." In *Terrorists or Freedom Fighters?
    Reflections on the Liberation of Animals,* Steven Best and Anthony J.
    Nocella, II, editors. New York: Lantern Books, 2004.
Tavris, Carol. "Deconstructing Harry." In American Scientist Online: the
    Magazine of Sigma Xi, the Scientific Research Society, at www.american-
    scientist.org/template/BookReviewTypeDetail/assetid/17181;jsessionid–a
    aa5EzkSfQcnrr. Viewed on February 6, 2006.
Tirukural. With English translation by Kavi Yogi Shuddhananda Bharatiar. At
    www.tamilnation.org/literature/kural/kuralE1.htm. Viewed on
    September 24, 2005.
Thoreau, Henry David. *Walden and Other Writings.* Edited and with an
    Introduction by Joseph Wood Krutch. New York: Bantam Dell, 2004.
Tolstoy, Leo. "The First Step." On the website of the Siberian Center for Vedic

Culture at www.geocities.com/Tokyo/Courtyard/8761/f33.htm. Viewed on April 21, 2006.

Turner, E. S. *All Heaven in a Rage.* New York: St. Martin's Press, 1965.

Turner, James. *Reckoning with the Beast: Animals, Pain, and Morality in the Victorian Mind.* Baltimore: The Johns Hopkins University Press, 1980.

Tuttle, Will, Ph.D. *The World Peace Diet: Eating for Spiritual Health and Social Harmony.* New York: Lantern Books, 2005.

Unti, Bernard. *Protecting All Animals: A Fifty-Year History of the Humane Society of the United States.* Washington, D.C.: The Humane Society Press, 2004.

Voltaire (François-Marie Arouet). "*Bêtes*" from *Dictionnaire Philosophique.* At www.voltaire-integral.com/Html/17/betes.htm. Viewed on September 18, 2005.

Wallechinsky, David, and Irving Wallace. "Anna Kingsford: Psychic Killer." Excerpted from *The People's Almanac, No. 3.* See www.thebirdman.org/Index/Fight/Fight-AnnaKingsford—PsychicKiller.html. Viewed on March 11, 2006.

Walters, Kerry S., and Lisa Portness, editors. *Religious Vegetarianism from Hesiod to the Dalai Lama.* Albany, New York: State University of New York Press, 2001.

Watson, Paul. *Sea Shepherd: My Fight for Whales and Seals.* As told to Warren Rogers. New York: W. W. Norton and Co., 1982.

——. *Seal Wars: Twenty-five Years on the Front Lines with the Harp Seals.* Buffalo, New York: Firefly Books, 2003.

——. "An Open Letter to the Norwegians." Published in the newspaper *Nordlys* on January 8, 1993. See www.highnorth.no/Library/Movements/Sea_Shepherd/le-to-th.htm. Viewed on June 11, 2006.

Wesley, John. "The General Deliverance," Sermon No. 60, text from the 1872 edition. In *Sermons of John Wesley,* on the website of the General Board of Global Ministries of the United Methodist Church at http://gbgm-umc.org/umhistory/wesley/sermons/serm-060.stm. Viewed on August 8, 2005.

Weyler, Rex. "Waves of Compassion: The Founding of Greenpeace. Where Are They Now?" *Utne.* See www.utne.com/web_special/web_specials_archives/articles/2246-1.html. Viewed on June 12, 2006.

Wicklund, Freeman. "Direct Action: Progress, Peril, or Both?" in *Terrorists or Freedom Fighters? Reflections on the Liberation of Animals,* Steven Best, and Anthony J. Nocella, II, editors. New York: Lantern Books, 2004.

Wikipedia: The Free Encyclopedia. At http://en.wikipedia.org/wiki/Main_Page.

Wild, Simon. "Henry Salt." At www.henrysalt.co.uk/index_old.html. Viewed
    on April 14, 2006.
Williamson, Lori. *Power and Protest: Frances Power Cobbe and Victorian
    Society.* London: Rivers Oram Press, 2005.
Winograd, Nathan J. "No Kill Solutions: Our Philosophy." On the website of
    No Kill Solutions at www.nokillsolutions.com/philosophy.htm. Viewed
    on December 21, 2005.
Xenophon. *Conversations of Socrates.* Translated by Hugh Tredennik and
    Robin Waterfield. London: Penguin Books, 1990.
York, Lavina Melwaninew. "Beloved Sindhi Religious Leader is Honored as
    Hindu of the Year." *Hinduism Today*, January, February, March, 2003. See
    www.hinduismtoday.com/archives/2003/1-3/50-53_vaswani.shtml.
    Viewed on October 3, 2005.
Zimmer, Heinrich. *Philosophies of India.* Published posthumously and edited
    by Joseph Campbell. Princeton, New Jersey: Princeton University Press,
    1969.

INDEX

Of Related Interest from Lantern Books:

Free the Animals
The Amazing True Story of the Animal Liberation Front
INGRID NEWKIRK

"A moving story about extreme cruelty and extreme courage and an inspirational and practical guide for anyone bent on challenging the system."—Oliver Stone

Terrorists or Freedom Fighters?
Reflections on the Liberation of Animals
EDITED BY STEVEN BEST, PHD AND ANTHONY J. NOCELLA II,
FOREWORD BY WARD CHURCHILL

"An unapologetic, impassioned, articulate and above all, rational defense of the militant tactics and philosophy of those on the front lines to save the earth and all its creatures. This authoritative work ought to be mandatory reading for everyone concerned with the future of creative dissent, radical change, and putting ethics into action."
—Ramsey Kannan, AK Press

101 Reasons Why I'm a Vegetarian
PAMELA RICE

"If you've ever been curious about vegetarians and why they eat the way they do, Pam Rice is the woman to tell you. Without sentimentality or preaching, she provides a clear and thoughtful understanding of one of the most important choices a person can make. You don't have to be a vegetarian to benefit from this book. You only need to care about your health and the health of our planet."—John Robbins

To order, visit www.lanternbooks.com.